THE STATES OF ITALY

General Editors: EDWARD ARMSTRONG and
R. LANGTON DOUGLAS

A HISTORY OF PERUGIA

" Reverere gloriam veterem et hanc ipsam senectutem, quæ in homine venerabilis, in urbibus sacra. Sit apud te honor antiquitati, sit ingentibus factis, sit fabulis quoque."—C. PLINII CÆCILII SECUNDI, *Epistolæ et Panegyricus*, viii. 24.   *Ad Maximum.*

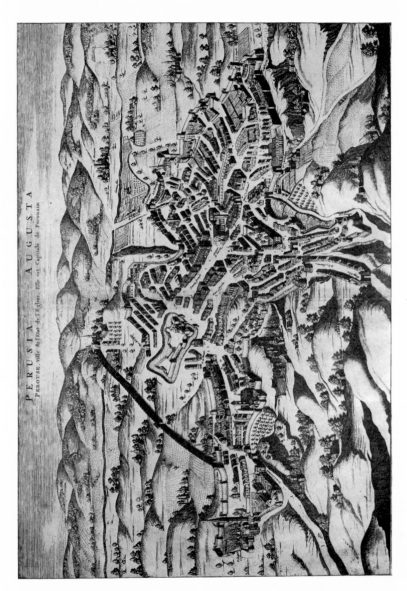

PERUSIA AUGUSTA
PEROUSE, ville & Etat de l'Eglise, Elle ou Capitale de Perousin

BIRD'S-EYE VIEW OF THE CITY OF PERUGIA

GREATLY REDUCED FROM AN ENGRAVING OF THE XVIITH CENTURY

A HISTORY OF PERUGIA

BY

WILLIAM HEYWOOD

EDITED BY

R. LANGTON DOUGLAS

WITH TWENTY-ONE ILLUSTRATIONS

METHUEN & CO.
36 ESSEX STREET W.C.
LONDON

First Published in 1910

PREFACE

viii   A HISTORY OF PERUGIA

FOR many people Perugia is simply the town of Perugino and of the Baglioni ; yet the Umbrian school of painting is a product of the Age of the Despots, and, except in name, the free Commune was a thing of the past before the Baglioni rose to power in the fifteenth century. The Perugia over which they lorded it had long since fallen from the position of an independent city-state to that of a mere provincial town whose history is quite without significance.

The years of Perugia's greatest prosperity belong to the thirteenth and fourteenth centuries. During the first half of the Trecento her story comprehends not only that of the neighbouring communes she absorbed, but also that of the Ecclesiastical State ; and it is probable that, but for her unswerving loyalty to the Guelf cause, the temporal power of the Papacy would hardly have survived the removal of the Apostolic See to Avignon. Upon this Perugia's claim to a definite place in the history of Italy principally rests, since it is obvious that, if the history of the Papal States is important, that of the Commune which saved them to the Church must be important also.

Unfortunately, however, her sons were too busy doing great deeds to have leisure to record them ; and, if we except the *Eulistea* of Bonifazio da Verona (compiled about the year 1293), we possess no contemporary Perugian chronicles until towards the close of the following century, while the frequent gaps which

occur in the precious series of the *Annali Decemvirali*
often render it quite impossible to obtain any adequate
knowledge of Perugian history from Perugian sources.
No Perugian chronicle is to be found in the *Rerum
Italicarum Scriptores*; Sismondi treats the Commune
which so long held the hegemony of Umbria as a wellnigh negligible quantity, and, almost up to the opening
of the present century, the published materials available for a history of Perugia, and especially for a
history of the period which witnessed her greatest
triumphs, were still extraordinarily meagre. Only
since the Vatican documents were made accessible
has it become possible to reconstruct the past, and
much remains to be done in the way of original
research before the story of the Commune can be
written with any approach to finality. Yet much has
already been accomplished. The foundation of the
Società Umbra di Storia Patria, in 1895, inaugurated
a new era, and the indefatigable labours of such ripe
scholars as Comm. Luigi Fumi, Count Vincenzo
Ansidei, and Marchese Giustiniano Degli Azzi Vitelleschi have cast a flood of light upon a number of
important questions which were previously involved
in almost hopeless obscurity.

It thus becomes necessary to readjust our precon-
ceived ideas with regard to Perugian history; and it
is the aim of the following pages to enable the English
reader to make that readjustment with the least possible expenditure of time and labour. They represent,
in short, a synopsis of the latest Italian researches;
and, save for the occasional verification of facts with
regard to which the printed authorities are at variance,
I have had, with one exception to be noted later, but
little recourse to any unpublished sources of informa-

tion. Indeed, had I adopted any other methods, my
labours must have been protracted over far more than
the four and a half years which I have already devoted
to the book.

Even so, the task which I have sought to perform
has been by no means an easy one, and has entailed
the study of many histories and chronicles besides
those of Perugia ; among others of Spoleto, Assisi,
Todi, Orvieto, Gubbio, Città di Castello, Viterbo,
Arezzo, Cortona, Siena, Bologna, Urbino, Rimini,
and, of course, Florence and Rome. That I have
been unable to avoid occasional digressions is largely
due to the fact that so little has hitherto been published in English with regard to the majority of these
communes ; for albeit, during all the fourteenth century until the coming of Albornoz, in 1353, Perugia
was the pivot round which the papal policy in Umbria
revolved, the strongest and most enduring force in all
the Ecclesiastical State, she was never strong enough
to guide the whirlwind and direct the storm, nor great
enough to give unity to circumstances of extraordinary
complexity. Thus, if she sometimes seems, for the
moment, to occupy a secondary position in my narrative, that could hardly have been avoided unless I was
prepared to credit my readers with a somewhat ideal
knowledge of Italian history in all its local details.

Moreover, I am inclined to believe that, so long as
a city possesses a history in the true sense of the term,
the reaction of that city's life upon its environment is
the really important thing ; whereas, on the contrary,
when history has fallen to the level of biography, the
environment no longer interests us except with a view
to its effect upon the city. Thus, this book naturally
divides itself into two parts : the *history* of Perugia

up to the war with Siena, and the *biography* of Perugia after that disastrous event. And this leads me to another consideration. Historical events of any magnitude can, of course, be adequately treated of in any language ; but a biography is a far more intimate thing; and it may well be doubted whether even approximate correctness of local colouring can be achieved in a foreign tongue. For this reason, in the latter part of this work, and especially in the last two chapters, I have not hesitated to increase considerably the number of *verbatim* quotations inserted in the footnotes. To this the serious student of things Italian will hardly be likely to take exception, while the general reader, being forewarned, can very easily avoid annoyance by confining his attention to the text.

For the rest, the principal sources, both contemporary and modern, which I have consulted in the preparation of this volume, have been scrupulously cited at every step ; and I hope that all writers hereinafter mentioned, who are still alive, will accept once and for all the expression of my sincere acknowledgments for the assistance I have derived from them. I also owe personal thanks to Dott. Francesco Briganti, Vice Bibliotecario della Comunale di Perugia, to Cav. Dott. Narciso Mengozzi of Siena, to Cav. Dott. Eugenio Casanova of the R. Archivio di Stato in Naples, to Messrs Edmund G. Gardner, Edward Hutton, Robert W. Carden, and to the Rev. J. K. Wilson ; while a special debt of gratitude is due to Count Vincenzo Ansidei for the elucidation of many difficulties, and to Marchese Giustiniano Degli Azzi for his rare generosity in lending me a manuscript copy of the Statute of 1342 which he has prepared for publication, and which, it is to be hoped, may shortly see the light. Finally, I have to tender my warmest thanks to my friend Professor Francesco Guardabassi, who not only placed his library at my disposal and continually aided me with encouragement and advice, but also most kindly consented to read through my completed manuscript, thus enabling me to lay before the public a work which has survived the test of critical examination by a distinguished Perugian *erudito*.

W. H.

PREPO
June, 1909

TABLE OF CONTENTS

LIST OF ILLUSTRATIONS

A HISTORY OF PERUGIA

CHAPTER I

OF THE LEGENDARY ORIGIN OF PERUGIA

THE origin of Perugia, like that of many other Italian cities, is lost in a mist of legend; and he who would penetrate the black obscurity of those remote ages must be content to follow paths which are illuminated by no more certain light than the fitful and fantastic gleams of fable and tradition. Seek as he may, he will find nothing certain and little which is even probably true : yet not for that will his labour be in vain. The legends at which we smile to-day were believed by the men who made Perugia great among the city-states of Italy ; they influenced their actions and, doubtless, helped to create their ideals ; and it is, I think, arguable that, for the student of the mediæval Communes, the legends of those Communes are almost more important than the records of their Roman or Etruscan past. The former scintillate with life and motion ; from them we can hope to learn something of the men with whose doings we are concerned and whose thoughts and motives we would fain understand. The latter are all too often nothing more than an arid catalogue of names and dates. " History to be true, must condescend to speak the language of legend ; the belief of the times is part of the record of the times." [1]

Justin tells us that Perugia (*Perusia*) was founded by

---

[1] MILMAN, *History of Latin Christianity*, ii. 82.

the Achæans ;[1] and Servius speaks of her as having been settled by the Umbrian tribe of the Sarsinates, who inhabited the Apennines.[2]   At the rise of the Roman Republic, she was one of the twelve cities of the Etruscan confederation, and her massive walls enclosed a great arsenal for the manufacture and storing of military weapons.[3] Livy twice mentions her among the chief towns of Etruria —*capita Etruriæ* : once classing her with Cortona and Arretium, and once with Volsinii and Arretium. In the latter passage, he speaks of the trio as *urbes validissimæ*.[4] Now, according to Herodotus and the classical writers generally, the Etruscans came from Lydia[5]—a tradition which naturally led to the belief that Perugia itself was built by the Lydians ; and it was upon this supposition that the most ancient legends of the origin of the city were founded. Thus, we are told that, when the Lydians arrived in Umbria and yet doubted where they should take up their abode, " they beheld two doves, one whereof carried in its beak an ear of corn, and the other a branch laden with olives ; while after them followed a great wild boar, bearing between his tusks a bunch of grapes." This sight was accepted by the wanderers as one of happy augury and as a sign that here more than elsewhere was there great abundance of corn and wine and oil. " Wherefore they went no further but

---

[1] JUSTINUS, *De Historiis Philippicis et totius mundi originibus*, xx. 1— " Perusini quoque originem ab Achæis ducunt."

[2] SERVIUS, *ad Æn.*, x. 201—" Sarsinates qui Perusiæ consederant." Compare DENNIS, *The Cities and Cemeteries of Etruria* (Everyman's Library edition), Vol. II. p. 409.

[3] W. CORSSEN, *Ueber die Sprache der Etrusker* (Leipzig, 1874), i. 222.

[4] TITUS LIVIUS, ix. 37 ; x. 37.

[5] See HERODOTUS, i. 94. On the other hand, Dionysus of Halicarnassus declared that the Etruscans were a people indigenous to Italy—ἐπιχώριον τὸ ἔθνος— but his views seem to have carried little or no weight with his contemporaries ; and, indeed, it was only after the lapse of seventeen centuries and a half that he at last found a champion in Nicolas Ferret.   Later on, the great Niebuhr advanced the opinion that the Etruscans were a tribe from the Rhætian Alps, who conquered the Tyrrhene Pelasgi, the earlier possessors of the land.   It is, however, obviously incompatible with the scope and object of the present work to enter into this much-vexed question.   Suffice it to say that the Lydian origin of the Etruscans seems now to be generally accepted by the best authorities.   For an able résumé of recent literature on the subject the reader is referred to the article of B. MODESTOV, *La questione Etrusca*, in the *Rivista d'Italia* of June 1903.

remained in that place, and gave to Perugia its origin, its name and its surname."[1]   The allusion is, of course, to the title of AUGUSTA, which was adopted by the city as its "surname" when it was colonized by Octavius Cæsar.   The Perugians, however, preferred to seek a more ancient and honourable origin for this addition ; and, as late as the seventeenth century, one of their historians seriously discusses the question whether Perugia took her cognomen from Augustus or Augustus his from Perugia.[2]

During the Middle Ages, when it was devoutly believed by every people that they were directly descended from ancestors who had been present at the siege of Troy, the classical tradition of the Lydian origin of the city was forgotten, and Perugia discovered a Trojan founder (sometimes confused with Ulysses), HEVLIXSTES PERVSINE CONDITOR VRBIS, whose effigy may still be seen on the upper cistern of the Fonte Maggiore ; while the oldest chronicle of the Commune, written in Latin verse by Bonifazio of Verona, bears the title *Eulistea*.[3]   "And know ye that there were many barons with Ulysses ; there was Antemon, who set his fortress upon the mountain of Porta Sole, the which was a great baron ; and there was Landorno, who set his fortress upon the hill of Landone; and there was the Master of the Tower, who was descended from the house of Nimrod ; and he was the master who builded the many

[1] CIATTI, *Memorie annali et istoriche delle cose di Perugia*, Parte I. Lib. i. pp. 8-9.   The legend is also mentioned by POMPEO PELLINI, *Dell' Historia di Perugia* (In Venetia, MDCLXIV. appresso Gio: Giacomo Hertz.), Parte I. p. 2. Pellini has been justly entitled "the Father of Perugian history."   Remarkable for its scrupulous accuracy and largely based upon original documents, his *Historia* still holds its pride of place, not only as the earliest but also as the best and fullest history of the city.   The first two volumes, which though difficult to procure are still procurable, carry the narrative down to the year 1489.   The third volume, which was published only with the first edition, has become extremely rare.   Even the copy possessed by the *Biblioteca Comunale* of Perugia is incomplete as far as the printed text is concerned, though the lacunæ are filled up in manuscript.   In comparison with this exhaustive work the modern *Storia di Perugia* of LUIGI BONAZZI (Perugia, Santucci, 1875-9) is of very little value, and the judicious reader will accept few of its statements without verifying them.

[2] CIATTI, *op. cit.*, Parte III. Lib. i. p. 357.

[3] See the *Archivio Storico Italiano*, XVI. i. pp. 1 *et seq.*, and compare G. MAZ-ZATINTI, *Di Bonifacio da Verona, autore dell' Eulistea*, in *Bollettino della Soc. Umbra di Storia Patria*, Vol. II. (1896) pp. 557-561.

Towers ; and he set his fortress toward Porta Bornia." [1]
According to this legend, the name of the city was derived
from a bear (*orsa*) which Ulysses encountered on his arrival
in those parts—*Perorsa* (Per-Orsa), *Peroscia*, *Perugia*.

Others, however, told a different story, attributing the
origin of the name to the sixth century of our era, when,
after the destruction of Perugia by Totila, " Iustinianus
Imperator, who had in prison many barons and kings of
the Gothic, Vandal and Longobard nations, commanded
them to rebuild Perugia and Gubbio and many other towns,
at their own cost. Now, the kings which rebuilt Perugia
were two ; one was the King of Persia and the other was
the King of Russia (*Roscia*) ; and therefore was the name
of the city, which aforetime was Tyberia, changed to Perugia ;
and of the two names of those kings was made one name, to
wit Perugia, which signifieth Persia and Russia." [2] There
were " portmanteau words " before Lewis Carroll.

Meanwhile, the Florentines, painfully conscious of the
comparative modernity of their own city, were busy invent-
ing a series of fables which might reduce their neighbours
to their own level. Weak or no longer existent towns, such
as Cortona, Chiusi and Luni, were admitted to have been
" antichissime e potentissime " ; even Pisa, which, in the fourteenth century, was already decadent, received its due ; but
Siena and Perugia, being still powerful, were shamelessly
libelled. For the latter, Giovanni Villani discovers an epony-
mous founder in Perus, a Roman Consul, who, after a campaign
in Germany, was ordered not to return to Rome : wherefore,
he and his legionaries " abode in that place where is one of
the hills (*l' uno corno*) of the City of Perugia, as exiles and
enemies of the Republic. Thereupon, the Romans sent an
army against them, which encamped upon the other hill (*in
sull' altro corno*) to make war upon them as rebels of the

---

[1] G. DEGLI AZZI, *Un Romanzo del Sec. XIV, sulle origini poetiche dell'
Umbria*, in *L'Umbria, Rivista d'Arte e Letteratura*, Perugia, luglio 1901,
num. 13 *et seq.*

[2] ARMANNINO GIUDICE, *Fiorita.* Conto xxxiii. (Cod. Mediceo Palatino 119,
nella Nazionale di Firenze) ; A. GRAF, *Roma nella memoria e nelle immagina-
zioni del Medio Evo* (Torino, Loescher, 1882), Vol. I. p. 25 n.

Republic of Rome : but, when they had been there some time, the one host made peace with the other ; and, because the situation was good, they continued to dwell there. Thereafter, of the two places they made the City of Perugia and named it after the name of the first consul which stablished himself there."[1]

Fazio degli Uberti, who is said to have generally relied upon Villani for his facts, tells much the same story ; but (possibly urged thereto by the exigencies of metre) substitutes Perseus, King of Macedon, for the consul Perus :

> Carcar passammo e Rodo, e un fiumicello
> Attraversammo per veder Perugia,
> Che, com' è in monte, ha il sito allegro e bello.
> Perséo, che bandito qui s' indugia
> Per gli Romani dopo molta guerra,
> La nominò, se alcun autor non bugia.[2]

If, however, the Florentines sought to impugn the antiquity of Perugia by attributing to her a Roman origin, the Perugians themselves began to be discontented with their Greco-Trojan legend, which, during the fourteenth and fifteenth centuries, appears to have been gradually supplanted by what we may call the Biblical legend. According to this latter, the city owed its origin to the patriarch Noah, transformed into Janus, the two-faced, looking backward for six hundred years before the Flood, and forward for the three hundred years which he was still to live, and during which he was destined to see the World repeopled by his descendants.[3] The metamorphosis of the patriarch into the god seems to have been connected in some mysterious manner with the discovery of wine. *A vino invento Ianus fortassis sit dictus nam Iain hebreis vinum est.*[4] Be this as it may, he built the twelve cities of Etruria in the twenty-second year of the reign of Ninus, 1927 years after the Creation of the World, 270 after the Flood, and 1278

---

[1] G. VILLANI, *Cronica* (edizione Dragomanni), i. 46.   As to his libels on Siena compare LANGTON DOUGLAS, *A History of Siena* (London, Murray, 1902), pp. 4-5.

[2] *Il Dittamondo*, iii. 10.

[3] ". . . nam utrumque mundum, veterem et novum, spectavit; quasi vultus geminos habuisset."

[4] CIATTI, *op. cit.*, i. 11.   Compare also A. GRAF, *op. cit.*, i. 80-89.

before the foundation of Rome.[1]   In the Colle Landone (*Iani domus*) we have an obvious record of his sojourn in Perugia ; as also in the termination " giano " (*Janus*), which occurs so frequently in the names of the surrounding villages —*e.g.* Margiano, Torgiano, Migiano, Chiugiano, Corgiano, Val di Giano, etc. etc.—while the region of Umbria itself was so called " because the first inhabitants were those who, in the Universal Deluge, happily escaped from the rains (*imbres*, ὄμβροι)." [2]

In the seventeenth century, the Franciscan Felice Ciatti, in a work which is a marvel of misdirected erudition, laboured diligently to reconcile these legends and others, on the theory of successive invasions, and he quotes with approval the words of Sixtus V., who, while preaching in Perugia, in Lent, 1553, thus addressed his hearers : " No marvel is it if, to-day, ye Perugians possess the justice of the Armenians, the wisdom of the Greeks, the prosperity of Augustus and the sanctity of Noah, for ye are descended from them all." [3]

Such and such like are the legends of the foundation of the city.   Let us now turn to those which treat of the origin of the mediæval Commune.

In a *Romanzo*, written in the Umbrian dialect, which seems to belong to the latter half of the fourteenth century, but which is evidently based upon earlier traditions,[4] we read that, what time Charlemagne descended into Italy and while yet he was warring in Lombardy, the Count of

[1] CIATTI, *ubi cit.*, pp. 22-23 ; PELLINI, i. 6 ; BARTOLI, *Storia della Città di Perugia* (Perugia, Santucci, 1843), i. 6.   The historians are not in complete accord with regard to these dates.

[2] CIATTI, *ubi cit.*, p. 22.   Compare also MUZI, *Memorie ecclesiastiche e civili di Città di Castello* (Città di Castello, F. Donati, 1842), i. 8, where the following passage is quoted from Pliny : *Umbrorum gens antiquissima Italiæ existimatur, ut quos Ombrios a Grecis putant dictos, quod inundatione terrarum imbribus superfuissent.*

[3] "Non è maraviglia se hoggi godete Perugini la giustitia degli Armeni, la sapientia de' Greci, la felicità di Augusto, e la santità di Noè, essendo voi loro figlioli."

[4] G. DEGLI AZZI, *op. cit.*   In translating this legend, I have endeavoured to follow the *ipsissima verba* of the original as closely as is consistent with the space at my disposal.   I have reduced the narrative to about a third of its actual length.

Perugia, a descendant of the ancient Greek founders of the city, died, leaving a daughter named Prossimana, the fairest and wisest lady in all the land. Such was the fame of her beauty that a certain prince called Orgoglioso, lord of Amelia and of the Ducato, became enamoured of her and was minded to take her to wife. Wherefore, he gathered much folk, on foot and on horseback, and went up against the City of Perugia. And, when he came to Ponte S. Giovanni, he encamped there and sent ambassadors to demand the demoiselle Prossimana for his lawful spouse and lady, and therewithal the signory of the city, threatening that, if she were not delivered unto him peaceably, he would take her by force to be his slave and concubine and would lay waste Perugia with fire and sword.

Thereupon, the elders of the city spake one to another, saying, "How can we, who have no seignior, resist him?" For the brother of Prossimana was but a boy. And they said, "Nevertheless, rather will we all die than that he should take her by force and for other than his lawful wife and lady." Then spake the demoiselle unto her brother Golía and said, "My brother, what can I do that the city be not imperilled and that I fall not into the hand of Orgoglioso? Meseemeth that, for our salvation, it were well that I promise to do that which he demandeth, if so be he will first bring unto me as prisoners two of the Paladins of Charlemagne; and thus, peradventure, he may be slain by the Paladins of Charlemagne." And Golía said, "My sister, thou hast resolved wisely." Wherefore, even so was it answered Orgoglioso. And Orgoglioso was passing glad and said that willingly would he do the bidding of the demoiselle; but first he demanded to have the signory of Perugia and to be called Orgoglioso of Persia[1]; and on no other condition would he undertake that adventure. Now, when this was told unto the demoiselle and unto them that governed the city, they were minded to do even as Orgoglioso

---

[1] ". . . ma prima vòle el titolo de la cità de Peroscia e vuole essere chiamato l' Aregolglioso de Persia." This strange title of "Orgoglioso di Persia," of course, carries our thoughts back to the legend of the origin of the city which connects it with the Kings of Persia and of Russia. (See page 4 *supra*.)

demanded.   Wherefore, Orgoglioso came into the city with two companions only ; and they led him unto the temple which, to-day, is called S. Lorenzo, and there they took a golden staff (*bacchetta*) from the altar and set it in his hand in token of the signory of the city ; and hard by stood Golía, the brother of Prossimana.   And because Orgoglioso earnestly besought that he might look upon the demoiselle, her brother and divers other citizens went to fetch her ; and they brought her into the temple, all clothed on with goodly raiment, as beseemed so fair and great a lady.   And when Orgoglioso had looked upon her, if aforetime he had desired her, thereafter so greatly was he enamoured of her that nevermore, whether by day or night, could he think of aught else than how he might possess her.

Now Charlemagne was in Lombardy, besieging a city of heretics which was called Cuma [1] ; and Orgoglioso straightway departed with all his following and went thither and encamped upon a hill over against the host of Charlemagne and challenged him to send forth two of his barons to do battle.   And there came a son of Charlemagne, and Orgoglioso jousted with him and overthrew him and bare him to his pavilion and gave commandment that he should be well guarded ; and, anon, he returned to the lists and blew upon his horn that Charlemagne might send another to joust with him.   Thereupon, Oliver, the Paladin, armed himself and mounted his horse and came forth against Orgoglioso ; and Orgoglioso overthrew him and led him to his pavilion and gave commandment that he should be well guarded ; and he returned no more to joust but gat him up and departed by night with all his host, and, riding day and night over plains and mountains, came to the City of Perugia with his two prisoners,[2] and demanded possession of the demoiselle.

---

[1] Marchese Degli Azzi suggests that this "città de ereticie ch' avea nome Chuma," and which was destroyed by Charlemagne, may have originated in some confused recollection either of the fate of Como, in 1127, or of that ancient Cuma in Campania which, in the twelfth century, became a nest of outlaws and bandits, and was consequently razed to the ground.

[2] In Perugia, at the end of the fifteenth century, there was a building, "Il a la Porta della Penna," which still bore the name of "la prigione di Orliviere

Then were Prossimana and her brother exceeding sorrowful and wept sore ; but Orgoglioso delivered his prisoners unto the demoiselle ; and, when she saw Oliver, she was enamoured of him and told him all her case and besought him to counsel her if on any wise she might escape out of the hand of Orgoglioso. Then said Oliver unto the demoiselle, "Within five days, that Falcon of Christendom, the Count Roland,[1] will certainly come hither, and Orgoglioso must needs do battle with him unless he be willing to make himself a Christian ; neither will all the gold in the world suffice to save him ; for it is not the usance of a valiant warrior to depart by stealth when he hath overthrown a knight."[2]   Now, when the demoiselle had heard these words, she sent her brother Golía to Orgoglioso to know his will.   And Orgoglioso said, "I desire to have the demoiselle in my possession."   Whereupon, Golía made answer, "We are not kitchen knaves or serfs that we should be dealt with after this sort.   First do thou prepare a feast and proclaim thy marriage throughout thy dominion, as is seemly ; for otherwise, rather will she die than become thy bride."   And that saying seemed good unto Orgoglioso, and he caused proclamation to be made through all his realm that, at the end of fifteen days, he would take the lady Prossimana to wife ; and he ordained a great hunting, to the end that he might have store of venison and all things meet for the marriage festival.   And ever the demoiselle sought the company of Oliver and held converse with him.

Now, when the Count Roland heard that Oliver had been overthrown and carried away prisoner, he was sore grieved

paladino."   See A. FABRETTI, *Cronache della Città di Perugia* (Torino, Coi Tipi privati dell' Editore), Vol. II. p. 116.

[1] "lo chonte Orlando, falcone de Cresstenta."   Cf. *Paradiso*, xviii. 43-45. Elsewhere Charlemagne is compared to an Eagle beneath whose wings the Church found shelter (Canto vi. ll. 94-96).   If Charlemagne was the Eagle, Roland was the Falcon of Christendom.

[2] It seems that, in modern parlance, the conduct of Orgoglioso had been unsportsmanlike.   According to the rules of chivalry, instead of departing with his prisoners, he should have returned to the lists on the following day in order to afford the other Paladins an opportunity of avenging the discomfiture of their companions.

and sware by God that he would never rest until he had delivered him. Wherefore, he set forth alone and followed hard after Orgoglioso ; but he overtook him not, because he had travelled very swiftly for the love which he bare to Prossimana, and also because the Count Roland was constrained to make many jousts and battles on the way. Nathless, at the last, he drew nigh unto Perugia and came unto a castle hard by the city, which is called Corciano, wherein there dwelt a young and lusty noble, hight Cornaletto. And, when Cornaletto saw the Count Roland, he mounted his horse and went forth to meet him, and asked him who he was and whither he fared. Thereto the Count made answer that he was a French knight,[1] who rode seeking adventures. Then said Cornaletto unto him, " In good sooth, if thou goest to Perugia, thou mayest look to be either slain or made prisoner, for in that city there is a lord hight Orgoglioso, who, a few days agone, took from Charles of France two of his Paladins ; and I myself, if only I were armed, would so deal with thee that thou shouldst go no further to trouble Orgoglioso with this matter." The Count replied, " If thou desirest to joust with me, get thee hence and arm thyself. I will await thee gladly." So Cornaletto departed and armed himself and returned unto

[1] " e lo Chonte dicie chomo esso era vno chaualiere francesscho." In my *Palio and Ponte* (London, Methuen & Co., 1904) I translated *i nobili Franzesi* "the French nobles" ; and thereby called down upon my head the thunders of the *Athenæum* (see the issue of Dec. 31, 1904). The reviewer, presumably, would have had me use the word "Frankish" instead of "French." I am, however, still impenitent and would pose him with the following question : Which is less pardonable, a merely apparent historical inaccuracy, or a very real linguistic anachronism? That it would be an anachronism to translate *franzesi* or *francesscho*, in this connection, by any other word than "French" appears to me indisputable. Possibly, however, my critics have never read the *Morte Darthur*. If so, I beg to refer them to that work. They will find it enlightening. It would also be interesting to learn how they would translate (say) into Italian the following passage from Marlowe (*The First Book of Lucan*) :

When Cæsar saw his army prone to war,
And fates so bent, lest sloth and long delay
Might cross him, he withdrew his troops from *France*,
And in all quarters musters men for Rome.

Another equally apposite passage, from Holland's *Livy*, is quoted by TRENCH, *A Select Glossary of English words used formerly in senses different from their present* (London, Parker & Son, 1859), p. 83.

the Count Roland and said, "Sir, mount thy horse and take thy lance, for I have long wished to do battle with one of these Frenchmen, who are said to be such valiant warriors." Roland mounted his horse and set his lance in rest and they jousted together ; but, first, he humbly besought Cornaletto to become a Christian, and Cornaletto promised to do so if he were worsted in that jousting ; wherefore, all the thought of the Count was not to slay him.   Nevertheless, Cornaletto was overthrown and lay as one dead.   Thereupon Roland lighted down from his horse and gat him to the fountain of a Convent which was near at hand, and brought water in his helmet and bathed the face of Cornaletto until he came to himself.   And, when he could speak, Cornaletto besought the Count to tell him his name, and he led him to his castle and entertained him honourably.   And Roland baptised him, and promised that, thereafter, the rite should be more solemnly administered by Turpin, the Archbishop ; and that night they slept together.   On the morrow, the Count revealed his name to Cornaletto and made him a knight and gave him his arms.   Therefore doth the Commune of Corciano bear the arms of Roland the Paladin until this day.[1]   Thereafter, they gat them to Perugia.

Now, the demoiselle was looking out of her window, and she beheld Roland come unto the meadow [2] which is without the city ; and he set his lance upright in the ground, with its pennon fluttering in the wind, whereby it might be seen from afar.   And, when Prossimana saw the same, she was exceeding glad ; and she sent a messenger out of the gate to demand who this might be ; and the messenger returned and said unto her in the presence of Oliver, "This is a very great and noble knight with a goodly horse and his arms are argent and gules."   Then said Oliver, "Madam, it is the most puissant man in all the World, the Falcon of Christendom."   Thereupon, the demoiselle sent to Orgoglioso,

[1] Quarterly argent and gules, with a coronet above the shield.   See R. COLLESI, *Memorie storiche e amministrative del C. di Corciano* (Città di Castello, Tip. Lapi, 1902), p. xi.

[2] "lo prato."   Compare my *Palio and Ponte, op. cit.*, p. 104 n. 2.   According to a chronicle published by FABRETTI (*ubi cit.*, p. 117) Roland pitched his pavilion where the Church of S. Angelo now stands.

saying, " I thought not to be besieged in mine own city. Verily, I am more unfortunate than any other woman." Then Orgoglioso hastened and put on his armour and went forth from the gate toward the Count Roland. . . . And they jousted together and break each of them his lance ; wherefore they set their hands to their swords, and Orgoglioso smote the Count right fiercely, and the Count smote him not again but ever abided his time. Therefore the son of Charlemagne, who was looking on, said unto Oliver, " Roland loseth the battle " ; but Oliver, who knew his manner of fighting, made great festival in his heart. Thereafter, when the Count perceived that Orgoglioso was labouring for breath and began to be aweary, he spake unto him and said, " Wilt thou be baptized ? " But he would not, neither would he surrender, because he greatly hated all Christians, and because the demoiselle Prossimana was looking on. So the Count, seeing that Orgoglioso would not surrender, took Durendal with both hands, and smote him upon the helm and clave his head downward even to the teeth. Now, when the demoiselle saw that Orgoglioso was dead, she set her love upon the Count Roland who had slain him, and she said unto Oliver, " I beseech thee, if so be that I have used thee well, give me that knight for my husband." But Oliver laughed and said, " Never hath he known woman, for he is a pure virgin. It were waste of words to ask him." Then said the demoiselle, " Therefore will I be thy bride, and I pray thee to make me a Christian." And, afterward, Count Roland entered into the city and caused the demoiselle and the citizens to be baptized : and Oliver wedded the demoiselle.

Meanwhile, Charlemagne, who greatly feared for Roland, in that he had ridden forth alone, departed out of Lombardy with all his host ; and never did he draw bridle, by day or by night, till he came to the City of Perugia ; and when he came thither, Orgoglioso was dead, and the demoiselle Prossimana was wedded, and much folk had been made Christians. And, after Charlemagne was come, many more were baptised ; and therefore Perugia took for its arms the Griffin, which was the device of Oliver. And Charlemagne

passed into the Ducato ; and, ever as he went, he caused all
men to be baptized, even unto Rome ; and the Pope blessed
him and all his folk ; and he abode much time in Rome,
and afterward returned to Lombardy and gave battle to the
City of Cuma ; and, in that war, Cornaletto was slain ; and
Oliver returned to France.   And, after he had departed, the
demoiselle lived but a little while ; wherefore the city was
left in the governance of the people.   Moreover, by Oliver
and by the demoiselle, was it freed from every tribute for
all time to come, save only from the tithes which were paid
to the Church ; for Charlemagne commanded that these
should be paid.   Then were the parishes made and the
Bishop of the City, as beseemeth Christian men.

Such is the Carlovingian legend of the origin of popular
government in Perugia, as it was told by the *favolatori* of
the Trecento.   Of the origin of the arms of the city there
are, however, several other accounts which have no connection with the Paladin Oliver.   Thus, some writers would
have us believe that the heraldic Griffin of Perugia is a
perpetual memorial of the occupation of Etruria by the
Armenian *Griffoni*, the extent of whose dominions is proved
(says Ciatti) by the large number of towns which have
adopted the Griffin as their device ;   among the rest,
Volterra, Grosseto, Montepulciano, Lucignano, Narni and
San Miniato.[1]   According to the most picturesque tradition,
however, the Perugian arms are commemorative of a mighty
hunting to which the people of Perugia challenged the
people of Narni.   On that occasion, the Perugians encountered and slew a griffin in the mountain which has ever
since been called Monte Griffone, and, after taking the
hide and talons as a trophy, left the flayed and gory carcass
to the Narniesi—a division of the spoils which is said to
account for the fact that the device of Perugia is a White
Griffin (white being the natural colour of the beast) on a
red field ; while that of Narni is a Red Griffin on a white

---

[1] CIATTI, *op. cit.*, Parte I. Lib. ii. p. 50.   See, however, L. PASSERINI, *Le
Armi dei Municipj Toscani* (Firenze, 1864), p. 158, where the arms of S. Miniato
are said to have been, first, a Lioness with a sword in her paw, and afterwards a
Lion.

field.[1]   Neither should we regard this narrative as open to suspicion merely because certain sceptical persons have treated the griffin as a fabulous monster.   On the contrary, to deny its actual existence would (according to Ciatti) be equivalent to denying the Word of God, " since in Leviticus and Deuteronomy, in the Bibles translated by St Jerome and Procopius, the griffin is mentioned among the unclean animals." [2]

In this connection it is interesting to note that, in 1540, two griffin's claws, mounted with silver, were still to be found among the *argentaria* of the Magnificent Priors ; [3] but whether these had belonged to the griffin which was slain in the aforesaid hunting I know not.   One of them may, perhaps, have been the same claw which, in the preceding century, was presented by Charles VII. of France to the Perugian General of the Order of St Francis,[4] and which was preserved for at least two hundred years, as a priceless treasure, in the Palazzo Pubblico.   The second claw, however, would thus remain unaccounted for.   According to Ciatti, the foot from which the claw given by Charles VII. had been taken was still to be seen, in the seventeenth century, hanging in the Chapel Royal at Paris ; and, says he, " so big is it and so enormous are the talons, that, if we may venture to reconstruct the whole animal from this foot, we are constrained to believe that that which hath been written about the griffin is true, and that he can snatch up and fly away with a great bull or the largest of horses." [5]

It has been well said that the two forces which, in the Middle Ages, most powerfully swayed the minds of men were the spirit of faction and the sentiment of religion.   The former set a cross-bow or a sword in the hand of every true citizen and impressed the whole country-side with the appearance of a vast military encampment ; while the latter mani-

---

[1] CIATTI, *ubi cit.*, p. 110.   [2] *Ibid.*, p. 48.

[3] " Doi onghi di grifone, di grandezza d' un corno di vitello legati con finimento d' argento." FROLLIERE, *La Guerra del Sale*, cap. xi., in the *Arch. Stor. It.*, XVI. ii. 448.

[4] *See Arch. Stor. It.*, XVI. i. 628-629 ; FABRETTI, *Cronache*, etc., *op. cit.*, ii. 32.

[5] CIATTI, *op. cit.*, Parte I. Lib. ii. p. 49.

THE PERUGIAN GRIFFIN

fested itself in the numerous and splendid temples and in the yet more numerous monasteries with which the cities of Italy were studded.[1] Neither, in this respect, did Perugia fall behind her neighbours ; and, therefore, we feel no surprise when we find that, side by side with the fables of Noah, of Ulysses and of Charlemagne, invented to render splendid and glorious the origin of the temporal and material city, there also exist legends of Saints and Martyrs who, by their good works, miracles and prayers, gave to that same city a splendid and ancient spiritual life.

If Ciatti is to be believed, the conversion of Perugia to the faith of Christ occurred in Apostolic times, a certain Ercolano, a convert of St Peter, being the first Bishop (A.D. 56).[2] We have, however, no very satisfactory proof that he ever existed ; and, in spite of all the pomp with which, in 1378, his relics were brought from Antignolla to Perugia, it is quite possible that he is nothing better than a myth.[3] Be this as it may, he must by no means be confounded with his celebrated namesake, Ercolano II., of whom I shall have occasion to speak more fully hereafter, and who, like S. Costanzo, was reverenced by the Perugians as one of the Advocates and Protectors of their city.

[1] Every honest student of the Middle Ages must, of course, admit the terrible contrast between Catholic theory and Catholic life, and can feel nothing but gratitude for Mr Coulton's fearless exposure of the gross absurdities which have too long obtained currency concerning the so-called " Ages of Faith " (see G. G. COULTON, *From St Francis to Dante*, London, David Nutt, 1907). Yet it is none the less indisputable that, during the centuries which preceded the Renaissance, the sentiment of religion was wellnigh universal ; and "the life of the Middle Ages dissevered from its superstitions would be as incomprehensible as the *Iliad* without its contending deities, *Paradise Lost* without its Satan, or the twentieth century without its railways, its Röntgen rays and its wireless telegraphy. . . . The existence of the celestial powers and their intervention in human affairs were facts to be calculated upon and allowed for ; and thus the religion of the thirteenth and fourteenth centuries was, in one way, extremely sincere. It may not have led to virtuous living—if a man was not a miscreant, a misbeliever, that was of quite secondary importance—but it did lead to a very constant and vivid realization of the superhuman, while, in some sort, men followed the maxim of the Apostle, and, whatsoever they did in word or deed, did all in the name of the Lord . . ." (Compare my *A Pictorial Chronicle of Siena*, Siena, E. Torrini, 1902, pp. 40-41.)   [2] CIATTI, i. 423.

[3] BARTOLI, i. 83-84 ; CRISPOLTI, *Perusia Augusta discritta* (Perugia, 1648), Lib. I. cap. xiii. p. 70.

S. Costanzo, who succeeded Ercolano I., is said to have suffered martyrdom during the reign of Marcus Aurelius ; [1] and since, from the year 56 to the persecution under that Emperor, a period of well nigh a century and a quarter had elapsed, the early Perugian Bishops would appear to have reached a good old age in spite of the troublous times in which they lived.   Others, however, assert that S. Costanzo obtained the crown of martyrdom under Antoninus Pius, "before the promulgation of the edict in favour of the Christians" ; [2] while Crispolti is of opinion that Ercolano I. was a successor instead of a predecessor of S. Costanzo.[3] We are still in the realm of pure legend.

The miracles attributed to S. Costanzo are of the usual character.   Like S. Ansano, the Baptist of Siena, he was immersed in boiling water without suffering the least inconvenience.   Trial was then made of red-hot coals, over which he walked unscathed, and he was afterwards stripped stark naked and covered with burning cinders, while he sang psalms and spiritual songs.   Finding that neither fire nor water could injure him and that nothing could induce him to stop preaching, the pagan magistrates finally ordered him to be put to death, and he was accordingly beheaded on the 29th of January, a day which has ever since been observed by the Perugians in his honour.   During the Middle Ages, the ceremonial seems to have been one of great magnificence, and, on the vigil of the festival, the magistrates of the Commune, the citizens, the clergy and the religious orders were wont to go in procession to the Church of the Saint, bearing in their hands innumerable torches, the size and weight of which were determined by law.[4]   In modern times, the good Bishop has become the patron of Perugian lovers, and his image is believed to have acquired the somewhat undignified habit of winking at those young people whose matrimonial projects he approves.   This image, which is, in fact, nothing but a big wooden doll, is generally kept in a cupboard in the sacristy, in company with a frivolous-looking, golden-

---

[1] PELLINI, i. 95.   [2] CIATTI, i. 473.   [3] CRISPOLTI, *op. cit.*, pp. 255 *seq.*
[4] PELLINI, i. 370.   See also the *Primum volumen statutorum Auguste Perusie*, etc.   Rubric 380 : "De faculis et candelis dandis," etc.

haired Madonna ; but, on the day of the festival, it is enthroned in state behind the high altar.   The piazza before the church is crowded with lads and lasses and country folk, and the proceedings do not tend to edifying. As an old woman remarked to the present writer, "Je par, signore, che'n santo abbia da fa' 'l ruffiano ! "

A far more important saint than S. Costanzo—the most important, indeed, in all the Perugian calendar—is Ercolano II., who suffered martyrdom for the part which he played in the defence of the city against the armies of Totila. According to Gregory the Great, Perugia was beleaguered for seven years ;[1] the besiegers in vain attempted to corrupt the Greek general, Cyprian ; and, after his treacherous murder, the garrison and the citizens still resisted valiantly, inspired to great deeds by the exhortations of their heroic bishop, who laboured unceasingly to communicate to his flock some portion of his own self-sacrificing zeal.   Minister- ing to the sick, shriving the dying, encouraging the waverers and preaching trust in God, from whom alone cometh deliverance, he roused the people to superhuman exertions ; and when, at last, after long months of famine and disease, the survivors were minded either to surrender or to sally forth and perish sword in hand, he prevailed upon them to make one last effort to deceive the enemy, hoping that, even at the eleventh hour, the Lord might vouchsafe to show forth His power on their behalf.

The story is thus told by Felice Ciatti : " The holy Bishop . . . counselled that all the grain which was left should be brought forth ; and so much did his sanctity and authority avail that search was everywhere made through- out the city ; and, at the last, one small measure of wheat was brought unto him, which had been gathered together by diligent sweeping of all the granaries.   Then, to the wonder and silent indignation of the people, he caused the only lamb which was found in all the afflicted city to be led thither, and gave it to eat of that grain ; and, after that

---

[1] Compare herein BARTOLI, i. 120, and BONAZZI, *Storia di Perugia dalle Origini al* 1860 (Perugia, Tip. Santucci, 1875), Vol. I. p. 144.

it had well fed and was stuffed marvellously full, he gat him up to the highest part of the walls and, by main force, cast it down to the ground ; whereupon, by reason of its extreme repletion and also because of the height of its fall, it burst asunder and so died.   Thereafter, when the Bishop had departed, certain Goths came to the place where the dead lamb lay and carried it away to their camp.   Now, when the captains of the Goths, who had hoped that the Perugians were already reduced to such straits that they must shortly surrender for lack of victuals, beheld that animal all stuffed with grain, they were angered and said, ' Verily, in vain do we seek to take Perugia while the citizens have so much wheat that they give it to their beasts and such excess of meat that they fling it over their walls.'   Wherefore they were minded to abandon the siege.   But it befel that a young clerk, who came by chance upon the walls, spake to certain Goths, and of his simplicity revealed unto them the extreme necessity of the citizens and the great mortality which was consuming them by reason of their lack of food.   The which thing being made known in the camp and likewise the artifice of the holy Bishop, those savage Goths were roused to fury, and, with great clamour, flew to arms and attacked the deserted walls with marvellous vehemence.   The Greeks and Perugians hastened to the defence of the city ; but what could that miserable and famine-stricken remnant do to avert so great ruin ? "

In the celebrated affresco of Bonfigli, a different version of the story appears to have been followed.   There, instead of a lamb, we see an ox, while Ciatti's " young clerk— *fanciullo chierico* "—is depicted as a deliberate traitor, who has betaken himself to the camp of the besiegers to disclose to them the critical condition of the city.   Moreover, we may, perhaps, infer that this latter variant of the legend was the one which was generally current in the Middle Ages, since, among the statues of the upper cistern of the Fonte Maggiore, we find, next to that of S. Ercolano, the figure of a priest with the inscription, CLERICVS PRODITOR SANCTI ERCVLANI.

THE SIEGE OF PERUGIA BY TOTILA
FROM THE AFFRESCO OF BONFIGLI

Thus, whether by treachery or by folly, the stratagem of the Bishop failed of its purpose, and Perugia fell into the hands of the Barbarians.   The general of the Goths sent to Totila to ask what should be done with the people and the Bishop, and received this answer : " Let a strip of flesh be flayed off the Bishop from his head even unto his heel,[1] and afterward behead him.   Smite all the people who are found in the city with the edge of the sword." The atrocious order was duly carried out, though some writers tell us that the decapitation preceded the flaying ; the body was cast down from the walls, and lay (where the little octagonal church of S. Ercolano now stands) exposed to the insults of the Barbarians, until " certain folk, moved by human compassion, took up the head and the trunk and buried them hard by the wall, and with them the body of a little child "—the same, according to some versions of the legend, being that of the *fanciullo chierico*.   Forty days later, Totila issued a proclamation permitting such of the citizens as had sought safety in flight to return to their homes ; and " they forgat not the life which their Bishop had led among them, but sought diligently for his body to give it Christian burial.   And the body of the child which had been buried with him they found all stinking and full of worms, but the body of the Bishop was whole and sound as upon the day when it was buried.   Moreover, the venerable head was united to the trunk, even as though it had never been severed therefrom ; neither was there any wound to be seen in all that holy body ; and, when they had turned it over, there was no scar where the flesh had been flayed off, nor any sign that ever had knife come nigh it.   Then, the citizens, rejoicing in so great a miracle, buried the venerable body of the Bishop and Martyr Ercolano, with hymns and lauds, in the Church of S. Pietro ; and there that child which was full of worms, and had been buried for forty days, was raised from the dead and lived thereafter seven years ; and, when he died, he

---

[1] In this connection Ciatti tells us that, in his day, the same penalty was still commonly inflicted " in certain parts of Germany ; and (says he) when I was in Prague, in 1622, I beheld divers examples thereof in the persons of heinous criminals."

was buried in the same church.   Afterward, because it was fitting that the holy body of the Blessed Ercolano should rest in the city which he had governed and wherein he had received the crown of martyrdom, it seemed good unto Ruggiero, the venerable bishop of the said city, and to all the people that that body should be translated to the Church of S. Lorenzo ; and with great reverence and devotion it was borne thither ; and the aforesaid Bishop erected the altar and consecrated it in honour of the blessed Martyr Ercolano, and there is he venerated even unto this day.   And the day of his translation is celebrated on the first day of March, honourably, by all the people." [1]

Like similar festivals in other cities, the day of S. Ercolano was quite as much a holiday as a holy day, and many of the ceremonies had a greater political than religious significance.

On the 28th of February, the vigil of the feast, the image of the Saint, *honoranda et relevata bene honorabilis et pulcra*, was borne in solemn procession through the city, enthroned upon a richly draped car, drawn by horses covered with housings of red cloth embroidered with white griffins, and accompanied by the Magistrates of the Commune, the *Arti*, the clergy and the religious orders, bearing votive candles in their hands.[2]   On the following morning, two prisoners were released " for the love of God," [3] and the syndics of the subject towns, in the names of their respective communities and according to the terms of their submissions to the Republic, brought offerings of candles, of money and of *palii*.   Thus, in 1216, the Consuls of Montone undertook to send annually a *palio* or a candle *valentem c solidos denariorum*, or its equivalent in money, at the option of the

[1] *Leggenda e Miracoli di Sant' Ercolano, da un codice perugino del secolo XV.*, pubblicata per cura de A. SCARAMUCCI (Perugia, Santucci, 1880), pp. 7-8.   See also CIATTI, *op. cit.*, Vol. III. (*Perugia Pontificia*), pp. 65-68 ; PELLINI, i. 108-109.   As to the removal of the body to S. Lorenzo, compare BARTOLI, i. 122.   In 1609, Bishop Napoleone Comitoli translated a part of the sacred relics to the Church of S. Ercolano.   A full account of the ceremony will be found in the *Memorie di Cesare Rossi*, published by FABRETTI, *Cronache*, v. 220.

[2] *Primum volumen statutorum*, etc., Rubrics 93 and 381-385.

[3] *Ibid.*, Rubric 187.

Potestà or Consuls of Perugia;[1] in 1214, the Count Tancredi "de Sartiano" promised to pay yearly four marks of good silver;[2] in 1259, the Commune of Cagli agreed to send a *palio* which was to be carried upon a lance "*a porta infra civitatem Perusii usque ad Ecclesiam Sancti Herculani*," where it was to be consigned to the magistrates of the city;[3] in 1323, Spoleto covenanted to present "a *palio* of silk upon a horse covered with scarlet,"[4] and, in 1355, Montepulciano "a palio of red velvet silk of the value of at least 25 florins of gold, *equester et publice distensum in quadam aste in signum subiectionis.*"[5] In the middle of the fourteenth century, nearly all the neighbouring cities acknowledged the suzerainty of Perugia and did her homage, on the 1st of March, "at the foot of the Campanile of S. Lorenzo."[6]

Another feature of the holiday programme was a horse race, the prize for which was provided by the Commune and generally consisted of one of the *palii* offered by the vassal towns;[7] while the majority of able-bodied males flocked to the Campo di Battaglia to take part in their great national game—a species of *Mazzascudo*, but so intimately connected with stone-throwing that it took therefrom its title of *La Battaglia de' Sassi*. The opening match of the season was always played on the day of S. Ercolano and in his honour; and, in spite of the homicidal character of the sport, it maintained its popularity until well into the fifteenth century, when, after much opposition, it was at last abolished by the efforts of Fra Bernardino of Siena.[8]

[1] V. ANSIDEI e L. GIANNANTONI, *I codici delle sommissioni al C. di Perugia* in *Bollettino della Soc. Umbra di St. Patria*, Vol. I. (1895) p. 151.

[2] *Bollettino* cited, Vol. VIII. (1902) p. 149.   [3] *Ibid.*, Vol. III. (1897) p. 199.

[4] FABRETTI, *Cronache*, i. 11.   [5] *Archivio Storico Italiano*, XVI. i. 181 n.

[6] See PELLINI, i. 906; BONAZZI, i. 436.

[7] *Primum volumen statutorum*, etc.   Rubric 93.

[8] As to the "Battaglia de' Sassi" see my *Palio and Ponte* (London, Methuen & Co., 1904), Book II. chap. ii., where the game is fully described.   Compare also the Statute of 1342, Lib. iii. Rubric 117 : "*De la bataglia da non fare en piazza,*" the principal part of which is printed by Dott. RANIERO GIGLIARELLI, in his *Venere. Racconto Storico della metà del Sec. XIV.* (Perugia, Donnini, 1903), pp. 383-385.   Some account of the game will also be found in *The Story of Perugia*, by M. SYMONDS and L. DUFF GORDON (London, Dent & Co., 1904), pp. 45 *et seq.*

Thus, of all the festivals of the Perugian year, that of S. Ercolano was by far the most imposing, and it is possible that Franco Sacchetti was not wholly wrong when he declared that "the Perugians believe more in S. Ercolano than they do in Christ, and hold that he is above the greatest saint in Paradise."[1]

[1] SACCHETTI, *Nov.* 169: "I Perugini credono più in santo Ercolano che in Cristo; e tengono sia innanzi al maggiore santo in Paradiso."

CHAPTER II

THE BIRTH OF THE COMMUNE

THE earliest documentary evidence of the existence of the Commune of Perugia belongs to the year 1130, when the inhabitants of Isola Polvese made submission to the Republic, "in the presence of the whole Perugian people, in the Piazza of S. Lorenzo and in the hand of the consuls."[1] Thus, in a moment, the Commune rises up before us, full armed and free, like Pallas Athene from the head of Zeus. What was the manner of its birth we do not know; but the most natural supposition is that, like so many of her neighbours, Perugia gradually succeeded in emancipating herself from the rule of a Bishop-Count.[2] This theory, I admit, does not find favour with most of the modern historians of the city;[3] but, none the less for that, it may be worth examining, since, if we fail to accept it, we shall at least be nearer to the truth by the exclusion of an untenable hypothesis.

Not only in Lombardy,[4] but in Central Italy also, the majority of the cities were ruled by Bishops, who exercised temporal as well as spiritual authority. Thus, up to the middle of the twelfth century, the name of the Archbishop of Pisa appears in conjunction with those of the consuls

---

[1] "in presentia de toto populo perusino in platea sancti Laurentii et in manu consules." The document is printed by BARTOLI, *op. cit.*, i. 216.

[2] Such is the opinion of BONAINI, *Prefazione alle Cronache Perugine*, in *Arch. Stor. It.*, XVI. i. p. xxviii.

[3] See, for example, BARTOLI, i. 233; SCALVANTI, *Considerazioni sul primo libro degli statuti perugini* (Perugia, Tip. Boncompagni, 1895), pp. 16-19; BRIGANTI, *Città Dominanti e Comuni Minori nel Medio Evo, con speciale riguardo alla Repubblica Perugina* (Perugia, Unione Tip. Cooperativa, 1906).

[4] See LANZANI, *Storia dei Comuni Italiani dalle Origini al* 1313 (Milano, Vallardi, 1882), pp. 96-105; W. F. BUTLER, *The Lombard Communes* (Charles Scribner's Sons, 1906), chap. ii. and pp. 54 *seq.*

in grants made to the Republic ;[1] while, at a yet earlier
period, the Bishops of Lucca laid claim to a jurisdiction
which extended as far as the confines of the Patrimony,
including, on the one hand, Sovana, Roselle, Populonia,
and, on the other, the valleys of the Elsa, of the Evola
and of the Era.[2]   Moreover, even to-day, the division of
Sorbano, in the Pisan mountains, into *Sorbano del Vescovo*
and *Sorbano del Giudice*, preserves an obvious record of
the rivalry which existed between those prelates and the
Counts or other imperial magistrates.[3]   In Florence, the
first blind gropings after freedom were manifested by
popular uprisings against the Bishop Mezzabarba;[4] and
we have ample documentary evidence that, between 1137
and 1170, Siena emancipated herself from episcopal rule,
finally driving forth to exile and death a prelate who
had dared to fulminate excommunications against her
consuls.[5]   Under her Bishops Arezzo rose to power;[6] in
Volterra, by a diploma of Henry VI., the election of
consuls was not valid without the consent of the Prince-
bishop of the city ;[7] while the neighbouring Massa was
governed by Bishop-Counts as late as the beginning of the
thirteenth century.[8]

In Umbria, in like manner, we find the Bishops still

[1] G. VOLPE, *Studi sulle istituzioni comunali a Pisa, Sec. XII.-XIII.* (Pisa, Tip.
successori Fratelli Nistri, 1902), pp. 8 *et seq.* ; SCALVANTI, *La tradizione romana
nelle consuetudini medioevali* (Perugia, Tip. Cooperativa, 1897), pp. 25-29.

[2] E. CASANOVA in the *Bullettino Senese di St. Patria*, Vol. XII. (1905) p. 118.
See also G. VOLPE, *ubi cit.*, pp. 9 *et seq.*

[3] RONDONI, *Sena Vetus* (Torino, Bocca, 1892), p. 11.

[4] P. VILLARI, *I primi due secoli della storia di Firenze* (2a edizione, 1898),
i. 77.   Compare also SANTINI, *Studî sull' antica costituzione del C. di Firenze*,
in *Arch. Stor. It.*, Serie V. Tom. xvi.

[5] RONDONI, *op. cit.*, pp. 12-13 ; DAVIDSOHN, *Siena interdetta sotto un papa
senese* in *Bullettino Senese*, etc., *op. cit.*, Vol. V. (1898), pp. 63 *seq.* ; LANGTON
DOUGLAS, *A History of Siena, op. cit.*, chap. ii. pp. 19-24.

[6] REPETTI, *Dizionario geografico-fisico-storico della Toscana*, Vol. I. p. 113.

[7] GIACHI, *Saggio di Ricerche Storiche sopra lo Stato Antico e Moderno di
Volterra* (Firenze, Tip. Sborgi, 1887), P. II. c. iv. pp. 254 *seq.*   S. Gimignano
was, at one time, included in the diocese of Volterra, whose Bishops exercised
temporal as well as spiritual jurisdiction over it.   See PECORI, *Storia della
Terra di S. Gimignano* (Firenze, Tip. Galileiana, 1853), pp. 36 *seq.*

[8] L. PETROCCHI, *Massa Marittima* (Firenze, Venturi, 1900), P. II. c. iii.
pp. 225 *et seq.*

clothed with temporal power, although, here as elsewhere, their authority was waning fast and was already shared by the consuls.   Thus when, in 1180, Città di Castello submitted to Perugia, the consuls who made the submission expressly declared that they did so " with the consent of the Bishop, of the clergy and of all the people." [1]   Three years later, the submission of Gubbio was made *consensu et volun-tate episcopi*.[2]   In 1202, the Bishop Ugolino was present and consented to the submission of Nocera ; [3] while, as late as 1219, it was stipulated in the submission of Cagli that the covenants entered into should be ratified by the Bishop of that city.[4]   It would be easy to multiply examples, but enough has probably been said to show that the hypothesis that, anterior to the rise of the free Commune, the Bishops of Perugia possessed temporal as well as spiritual juris-diction, is at least one which is strongly supported by analogy.

Moreover, in the twelfth century, the Bishop of Perugia seems to have occupied precisely the position which we should expect a Bishop to occupy who, having lost his temporal power, had cheerfully acquiesced in the new order of things.[5]   Not only was he supreme in eccle-siastical affairs, but, in civil matters also, the citizens, no doubt, often submitted themselves to the decisions of his tribunal ;   while his spiritual jurisdiction extended far

---

[1] *Bollettino della R. Deputazione di Storia Patria per l' Umbria*, i. 139 (Doc. i.—" Civitatis Castelli submissio ").

[2] *Ibid.*, i. 141 (Doc. ii.—" Submissio civitatis Eugubij ").

[3] *Ibid.*, i. 145 (Doc. vi. —" Civitatis Nucerij submissio ").

[4] *Ibid.*, ii. 133 ; BARTOLI, i. 327.

[5] It was not the policy of the Communes which had emancipated themselves from the episcopal suzerainty to degrade their former rules.   On the contrary, they were often allowed to preserve many of the outward forms and symbols of their old authority, and were treated with the utmost respect.   Thus, in Siena for example, under the government of the *Ventiquattro*, the Bishops still possessed what almost amounted to an indirect power of legislation, since not only was it their province to interpret the law when it was contradictory or doubtful, but they were also permitted to be present at the sessions of the *Tredici Emendatori*—a privilege which they continued to exercise even under the jealous and exclusive oligarchy of the *Nove*.   See *Il Constituto del C. di Siena dell' anno* 1262 (edition ZDEKAUER), Dist. I. Rubrics 128, 141, 192, and pp. xix-xx of the *Dissertazione* which precedes the text.   Compare also *Il Costituto del C. di Siena volgarizzato nel* 1309-1310, Dist. I. Rubric 145.

beyond the narrow territories which owned the authority of the new-born Commune, and was exercised in all the towns and villages of the diocese, through the agency of the *pievani*, parish priests and other clergy, who, as having cure of souls, were subject to his Ordinary.[1] Thus, little by little, the way was prepared for the extension of the communal dominion, until, in the thirteenth and fourteenth centuries, the boundaries of the *contado* were once more identical with those of the diocese.[2] Originally elected by popular suffrage, the Bishop was long regarded by the people as their natural protector and safeguard against feudal oppression, and, in the twelfth century, he seems to have still been occasionally clothed with a delegated authority which made him, for the time being, the chief magistrate of the Commune. In the submission of Castel della Pieve, in 1188, it was provided that, if the consulship of Perugia should be in abeyance (*si non esset consulatus*) the authority of the Republic should, for certain purposes, be vested in the Bishop.[3]

Those, on the other hand, who discard the hypothesis of a Bishop-Count, are inclined to believe that the birth of the Commune took place at least as early as the tenth century. In Perugia, they argue, the traces left by the Barbarian invasions were less profound than elsewhere ; the old Latin traditions never died, and, even during the Longobard domination, the city was in intimate relationship with the Empire and with Rome. Maurice, the first Duke of Perugia of whom we have record, was executed by Agilulf because he opened his gates to a Greek garrison ;[4] and during the widespread insurrection provoked by the edicts of Leo the Isaurian, the city was governed by a Greek, "Agatho Perusinorum dux," who is spoken of as Captain of the Roman army.[5] To the intervention of Pope Zacharias

---

[1] For the extent of the Episcopal jurisdiction in the twelfth century compare BARTOLI, i. 229-231 and 238-240.   [2] See BRIGANTI, *op. cit.*, pp. 13-14.

[3] BARTOLI, i. 259 ; *Bollettino* cited, i. 142-143.

[4] MURATORI, *Annali*, ad annum 592.

[5] MURATORI, *Annali*, ad annum 741 ; BONAZZI, i. 169 ; BARTOLI, i. 150 ; MARIOTTI, *Saggio di memorie istoriche, civili ed ecclesiastiche della Città di Perugia* (Presso Carlo Baduel Stamp. Cam. e Vesc., Perugia, 1806), i. 52.

Perugia owed her deliverance from the arms of Rachis;[1] and both Stephen III. and Adrian I. summoned men from the Duchy of Perugia to garrison Rome against Desiderius.[2] The friendly relations with the Papacy were yet further cemented by the Donation of Charlemagne,[3] followed, in 817, by the celebrated diploma of Louis the Pius, whereby he granted and confirmed to Pope Paschal and his successors *Perusiam cum tribus insulis suis.*[4]

Under the Carlovingian Emperors, the increased power and dignity of the Church unquestionably tended to secure a large measure of prosperity for those cities which enjoyed her protection ; while the subsequent degradation of the Papacy, during the first half of the tenth century, left them free to work out their own salvation. Thereafter, with the invasion of Otho the Great, the Italian Kingdom, founded by the Longobards, recognized by the Franks and recently claimed by powerful Italian feudatories, virtually ceased to exist. All shadow of union disappeared and the Peninsula was abandoned to those slowly working influences which were destined to divide it into as many separate states as there were populous cities. It is to this period that the historians of Perugia, both ancient and modern, attribute the origin of consular government.[5] Proof they have none. The century which gave birth to the consulate was the eleventh. Even in Pisa, we have no trustworthy record of such a magistracy anterior to 1033 ; and, if Perugia was, in fact, governed by consuls in the tenth century, no other Commune can boast a liberty more ancient.[6]

Nevertheless, while it is extremely difficult to accept the

---

[1] MURATORI, *Annali*, ad annum 749.

[2] BONAINI, *Prefazione* cited, pp. xxvii-xxviii.

[3] MURATORI, *Annali*, ad annum 774 ; MILMAN, *History of Latin Christianity* (4th edition), iii. 45.

[4] See herein SCALVANTI, *Un' opinione del Bartolo sulla Libertà Perugina*, in *Bollettino* cited, Vol. II. pp. 83 *seq.*, where the question of the authenticity of the document is discussed at length. In any case, the donation, whether spurious or not, was confirmed by subsequent Emperors. See MARIOTTI, *Saggio*, etc., *op. cit.*, i. 55.

[5] PELLINI, i. 149 ; BARTOLI, i. 187, 215 ; BONAINI, *loc. cit.*, p. xxviii.

[6] Compare L. FUMI, *Codice dipl. della Città d' Orvieto*, in the *Documenti di Storia Italiana* (Firenze, Vieusseux, 1884), Tom. VIII. p. iii.

position that Perugia so far outran her neighbours, there is, perhaps, no insuperable objection to the view that her government, even in the tenth century, may have been largely democratic, and that her *boni homines* were already able to make their influence felt in the conduct of public affairs. Certain it is that the names of the ten consuls, recorded in the submission of Isola Polvese, are, as Bonazzi points out, emphatically plebeian [1]—a fact which would seem to indicate either that the people had already obtained a complete victory over the aristocracy, or that Perugia had never been ruled by feudal seigniors. The latter is the theory adopted by Dott. Briganti, who unhesitatingly declares that the city "never had feudal seigniors, and that its Bishop was never invested with comital power." [2]

The earliest documentary evidence which we possess of the existence of a privileged class in Perugia is, I believe, to be found in the Diploma of Henry VI. [3] In that instrument, in addition to the great feudatories of the *contado*, both ecclesiastical and lay, whose fiefs were excepted from the jurisdiction of the Commune, mention is made of "Perugian knights—*milites perusini*," who were given a specified share in certain regalia. Thus, the whole of Lake Thrasymene having been declared imperial property, an exception was made with regard to three hundred tench, which were granted in feud to the Perugian knights— *exceptis trecentis tencis quas militibus perusinis in feudo concessimus*—while, in like manner, the right of levying *vida sive pedagium* was reserved to the Crown, with the exception of *quinque solidi de soma* granted *militibus perusinis in feudo*. In this connection it may be observed that a grant of three hundred tench would have been little less than derisory if

[1] BONAZZI, i. 228-229.

[2] " Retta sempre da un governo democratico non ebbe signori feudali, nè mai il vescovo fu insignito del potere comitale." BRIGANTI, *op. cit.*, p. 17. For other examples of Communes which, at a very early period, were wholly democratic, consult R. CAGGESE, *Un Comune libero alle porte di Firenze nel secolo XIII*. (Firenze, Seeber, 1905) pp. 53 *et seq.*

[3] *Datum in campo Eugubii VII. idus Augusti MCLXXXVI.* It is printed by BARTOLI, i. 253-256. A copy will also be found in the Communal Library of Perugia. *Libro delle Sommissioni*, segnato "A," c. 35r. Compare *Bollettino* cited, Vol. V. (1899), pp. 431-435.

the grantees had been at all numerous. This, however, throws no light upon their rank or origin, which is as much wrapped in obscurity as that of the "*nobili veniticci*" of Siena.[1] Some few of them may have come in the train of that Lodovico Baglioni, *Dux Sveviae*, whom Frederick Barbarossa appointed Imperial Vicar, in 1162 ;[2] but the majority were probably men of Frank or Longobard race, descended, perhaps, from the officials of the Perugian Dukes, or from the *Valvassores* of the Bishops ; and their limited numbers may account for the early development of the government of Perugia on democratic lines. Indeed the struggle between the classes seems not to have begun until after the numbers of the civic nobility had been increased by the concession of citizenship to the feudal seigniors of the *contado*, and of such concessions we have no very satisfactory evidence before the end of the twelfth century.[3]

The number of the consuls, in whose hands the inhabitants of Isola Polvese made submission, was, as I have said, ten ; and as we know that, from very early times, Perugia was divided for administrative and military purposes, into five wards or *rioni*, which were known as "*Porte*" and corresponded with the five principal gates of the city,[4] it seems only reasonable to suppose that the

[1] See C. PAOLI, *I "Monti" o fazioni nella Rep. di Siena*, in the *Nuova Antologia*, Serie III. Vol. XXXIV., fasc. 15, p. 403.

[2] The diploma is printed by BARTOLI, *op. cit.*, pp. 235-236 ; and, although its authenticity has been disputed (see BONAZZI, i. 240), we are informed by PELLINI (i. 193) that he himself saw the original document "in forma di Bulla Imperiale, co' suoi sigilli et anni." On the whole subject see L. DE BAGLION DE LA DUFFERIE, *Histoire de la Maison de Baglion. Les Baglioni de Pérouse. D'après les Croniqueurs, les Historiens, les Archives* (Poitiers, Société Française d'imprimerie e de librairie, 1907), pp. 366-367, and compare V. ANSIDEI, *Alcuni appunti per la Storia delle famiglie perugine. Baglioni e Degli Oddi* (Perugia, Unione Tip. Cooperativa, 1901), p. 9, where the theory that the Baglioni came to Italy with Frederick Barbarossa is apparently accepted.

[3] Compare MURATORI, *Annali*, ad annum 1205.

[4] MARIOTTI, *Saggio*, etc., *op. cit.*, i. 14-15. These gates were P. S. Petri, P. Solis, P. S. Angeli, P. S. Subxanne, P. Heburnea ; and it is observable that, just as the *contado* of Siena was divided into three districts corresponding with the division of that city into *Terzi* (L. ZDEKAUER, *Il Constituto del C. di Siena, op. cit.*, p. lxviii. § 60), so was the Perugian *contado* divided into five districts corresponding with the division of Perugia into *Porte* (BRIGANTI, *op. cit.*, p. 112,

number of consuls was due to this division, there being two consuls for each Porta. Later on, at the time of the submission of Castel della Pieve (1188), we find that the consuls had been increased to sixteen, the first mentioned of these being a certain "Rainerius de Capelle, consul et camerarius."[1] Now, the *Camerarius*, or, as he is sometimes called, the *Massarius* of the Commune, was the magistrate to whom was entrusted the care of the public monies,[2] and, according to Bartoli, he was *ex officio* president of the Consular College, which would thus contain only fifteen ordinary members, namely, three for each Porta.[3] In this connection it is noticeable that, in after years, when the rule of the consuls had been superseded by that of the Potestà, we still find the *Camerarius* mentioned in the submissions, as, for example, in 1216, when the consuls of Castello di Montone made their submission to Giovanni Giudice, Consul of the Romans and Potestà of Perugia, and to Gualfredo, *Camerarius* of the Commune of Perugia.[4]

By the elder writers, the origin of the office of Potestà in Perugia is generally attributed to the year 1191;[5] but, as early as 1177, we have record of a certain "Rainerius Potestas Perusiæ," who was present in Venice at the reconciliation of Pope Alexander and the Emperor;[6] and,

---

§ 37. See also *Bollettino* cited, ii. 132, Doc. xiv., which treats of the appointment of a Commission or *balìa* "ad inveniendum et dividendum per Portas et consequenter per Parrochias totum terrenum laboraticum Comunis Perusij ubicumque esset"). That these extramural districts were not only dependent on, but actually included in the *Porte*, seems clear from the words of Matarazzo (*Arch. Stor. It.*, XVI. ii. 31), where he tells us how "per la Porta di Sant' Agnolo vennero correndo dal ponte del Pattolo li inimici, e cursero e appredaro per insino a li molina de lo Rio." Thus, in the Perugian chronicles, the word *Porta* has three distinct meanings, namely, (1) a Gate, (2) a Ward of the City called from a Gate, and (3) a Ward of the City *plus* the extramural territory dependent thereon.

[1] *Bollettino* cited, i. 142 (Doc. iii.—"Submissio Castri Plebis").

[2] BONAINI, *Prefazione* cited, pp. xlix *et seq*. As to the office of *Massarius* see the Statute of 1279, Rubric "Qualiter Massarius et ejus notarii eligantur et de eorum salario," and compare the Statute of 1342, Lib. i. Rubric 48.

[3] BARTOLI, i. 259.

[4] *Bollettino* cited, i. 150 (Doc. x.—"Montonis submissio").

[5] BARTOLI, i. 266; MARIOTTI, *Saggio*, etc., *op. cit.*, ii. 187.

[6] See *La Cronaca Veneta detta Altinate*, Lib. v., in the *Arch. Stor. It.*, viii. 183.

even if it should be thought that this was one of the new German Potestà or *Teutonici*, through whose agency Frederick was now trying to govern Italy,[1] another Potestà, "D. Pandulfus de Sigura Romanorum Consul et Perusinorum Potestas," who was evidently a civic magistrate, appears in a document of 1183.[2] It is, however, to be observed that, in Perugia as elsewhere, the institution of this office was, at first, purely experimental. In the early days of communal freedom, there were few available administrative precedents, and each separate transaction was wont to be carried through by a *balìa* or commission of *boni homines*, expressly chosen for the purpose. The appointment even of the highest magistrates often partook of the nature of a tentative arrangement, which might be annulled or modified according to the exigencies of the moment;[3] and we are, therefore, not surprised to find that, in Perugia, as in Pisa,[4] in Siena,[5] and in the neighbouring Communes of Città di Castello,[6] Spoleto,[7] Todi,[8] and Orvieto,[9] the introduction of the *potestaria* was not immediately destructive of consular Government.[10] For some years the Potestà and the consuls either ruled together or the two magistrates alternated—a state of things which is clearly mirrored in the Bull of Innocent III., given from Todi, in 1198, whereby he grants certain privileges to the

---

[1] VILLARI, *I primi due secoli della Storia di Firenze* (edition cited), i. 122.

[2] *Bollettino* cited, i. 141 (Doc. ii.—"Submissio civitatis Eugubij").

[3] See L. ZDEKAUER, *La Vita pubblica nel Dugento* (Siena, Tip. Lazzeri, 1897), pp. 12-13 ; G. VOLPE, *op. cit.*, p. 305.

[4] G. VOLPE, *op. cit.*, p. 305.

[5] See my *Historical Introduction* to Miss L. OLCOTT's *Guide to Siena* (Siena, Torrini, 1903), pp. 24-25.

[6] MUZI, *Memorie civili della Città di Castello* (Città di Castello, Donati, 1844), i. 11.

[7] A. SANSI, *Storia del C. di Spoleto dal Secolo XII. al XVII.* (Foligno, Sgariglia, 1879), Parte I. pp. 133-134.

[8] CECI, *Todi nel Medio Evo* (Todi, Trombetti, 1897), Vol. I. pp. 82-83.

[9] FUMI, *Codice diplomatico*, etc., *op. cit.*, p. 49, Doc. lxxi. : "Nos consules vel potestas."

[10] Compare also R. CAGGESE, *Un Comune libero alle porte di Firenze nel Secolo XIII.*, *op. cit.*, pp. 31-34.

Perugians and certain authority and jurisdiction "ad potestatem vel consules qui pro tempore fuerint."[1]

Originally, the affairs of the mediæval Communes were, no doubt, regulated by customary law—those *bonæ consuetudines* which the citizens proclaimed so courageously and fought for so heroically ; and these, on taking office, the magistrates were sworn to observe and to enforce.[2] At a very early period, the oath (*breve*) of each official was committed to writing, and such *brevia* in the aggregate formed the first *lex scripta*, the *Constitutum*.[3] This *Constitutum* seems to have been revised every year,[4] and in it were inserted, for greater solemnity, all the more important treaty obligations of the State, to the end that they might be annually guaranteed by oath. Indeed, the earliest record which we have of the *Constitutum* of Perugia is referable to this practice. In the alliance entered into with Foligno, in 1201, it was provided that *consules vero qui utraque civitate pro tempore fuerint IN CONSTITUTO CIVITATIS JURABUNT hanc societatem servare inlesam* ;[5] while, according to the "*sacramenta*" which were exchanged

---

[1] This document is printed in its integrity both by PELLINI (i. 222) and BARTOLI (i. 279). See also *Bollettino* cited, vi. 322 (Doc. lxx.—"De jurisdictione data comuni P. per Apostolicam Sedem cum receptione ipsius Civitatis sub protectione apostolica ").

[2] See, for example, the "Formola del Giuramento degli Uffiziali del C. d' Orvieto," published by FUMI, *Codice Diplomatico*, etc., *op. cit.*, pp. 49-51, Doc. lxxi.

[3] See *Il Constituto del C. di Siena* (edition ZDEKAUER), p. xiv and Index s.v. 'Breve.' Compare BONAINI, *Prefazione* cited, p. xxxiv. According to the *Statuto di Todi* (1275), published by G. CECI and G. PENSI (Todi, Trombetti, 1897), Parte I. Rubric 2 : "*De juramento civium et comitatensium,*" each *civis* swore : "Si (exsisterit) aliquod capitulum Constituti Comunis Tuderti quod pertineat ad meam artem istud observabo."

[4] At the submission of Gualdo (1208), the Perugian consuls promised that all the stipulations therein contained should be inserted in the *Constitutum* when it should be renewed, and that their successors "ita observabunt ET ANNUALITER IN COSTITUTO APPONENT." *Bollettino* cited, i. 147. Compare SANSI, *op. cit.*, i. 138 ; G. MANCINI, *Cortona nel Medio Evo* (Firenze, Tip. Carnesecchi, 1897), p. 128. In the fourteenth century the annual revision was generally abandoned. Thus, in 1327, the *Statutari* of Arezzo wrote : "Aretinorum mos in condendo quolibet anno Statuta, et quod ea sint valitura per annum, laboriosus et prorsus inutilis potest a rerum experientia iudicari."

[5] *Bollettino* cited, vi. 327 (Doc. lxxiv.—"Conventiones inter Perusinos et Fulginates "). See also BONAINI, *Prefazione* cited, p. xxxiii., and BARTOLI, i. 287-288.

between the consuls of Perugia and of Siena, in the following March, the former undertook to cause to be inserted "*in Constituto et Brevi ad quod Consules Perusini jurant,*" and the latter "*in Constituto et Brevi ad quod Consules Senenses jurant,*" a rubric which should oblige the future consuls or Potestà of either Commune to swear the *societas* now concluded between them.[1] In the submission of Castello di Montone, fourteen years later, the stipulation is even more explicit.[2] So too, in 1238, when Oddone "Petri Gregorij," Senator of Rome and Potestà of Perugia, was obliged to absent himself from the city, he appointed, as his vicar, his son Pietro, "to the end that he might swear the *Constitutum* of the Perugian Commune and keep and perform each and every section therein contained."[3]

Like other cities, Perugia had her General and Special Councils,[4] and, later on, her Captain of the People, who was assisted by ten *Anziani*, two for each Porta.[5] Under the protection of this magistracy, the *Arti* gradually concentrated all the authority of the State in their own hands, and the *Consuls of the Arts* became the principal magistrates of the Republic. In the last quarter of the century, the Potestà no longer swore, on taking office, to observe the *Constitutum*; the *Popolo*, the wealthy middle class, was now predominant, and his oath ran: "Statuta Comunis et Populi et reformationes Artium servabo."[6] Finally, about

---

[1] R. Arch. di Stato in Siena, *Caleffo Vecchio*, a c. 31. Compare *Il Constituto del C. di Siena* (edition Zdekauer), p. xxxi. See also Dist. iii. Rubr. 385: "*De concordia observanda inter Senenses et Perusinos.*"

[2] *Bollettino* cited, i. 150 (Doc. x.—"Montonis submissio"). The document is printed in full by Muzi, *Memorie civili*, etc., *op. cit.*, i. 34-37.

[3] "ad portandum et exercendum regimen et guidamentum perusinorum . . . et ad jurandum constitutum ipsius Civitatis perusinorum . . . et ad servandum et faciendum omnia et singula capitula que in ipso constituto continentur."— *Bollettino* cited, ix. 131 (Doc. cxviii.).

[4] Bonaini, *Prefazione* cited, pp. xliv-xlv.

[5] *Ibid.*, pp. xliii-xliv. As to note 1 on page xliv, the reader should, however, compare the *Correzioni ed aggiunte* in Arch. Stor. It., Vol. XVI. P. ii. pp. 687-689.

[6] See *Il giuramento del Podestà secondo lo Statuto Perugino del 1279*, edito da A. Fabretti, Torino, 1886, con i tipi privati dell' Editore. As to the *Statutum Populi*, compare G. Degli Azzi Vitelleschi, *La Rappresaglie negli Statuti Perugini* (Perugia, Tip. Boncampagni, 1895), pp. 57 *et seq.*

the year 1303, a further change was made in the title and composition of the supreme magistracy, the five Consuls of the Arts being superseded by ten Priors—DOMINI PRIORES ARTIUM ET POPULI.[1]

Naturally, the triumph of the *Arti* was not achieved without a struggle : and, in Perugia as elsewhere, the Nobles and the proletariat made common cause against the People.

Originally, as we have seen, the *milites* formed a privileged class which was favoured and protected by the Empire. They were probably governed by no special statute except with regard to their military duties ; and, in their relations with one another, they doubtless observed the *consuetudines feudorum.* Moreover, it is presumable that, as in other cities, the *Societas Militum* possessed its own property, and that its intercourse with the *Societas Populi* was regulated by special agreements which enabled them to live side by side without too much friction.[2] As long as their rights and privileges were not interfered with, the Nobles seem to have troubled themselves but little about the tradesmen and artisans whose humble dwellings clustered beneath the walls of their towered palaces ; and, by holding aloof in haughty contempt of the great body of the citizens, they must have early taught the People to regard themselves as the true representatives of the Commune.

During the feudal period, the Nobles, of course, enjoyed immunity from taxation ;[3] and, apparently, it was not until the thirteenth century that the People began to protest

---

[1] PELLINI, i. 333 ; BONAZZI, i. 378 : *Brevi Annali* ad ann. 1303, in *Arch. Stor. It.*, XVI. i. 60.

[2] See BONAINI, *Prefazione* cited, pp. xxxv-xxxvi, and *Bollettino* cited, xii. 281 (Doc. clxxiv.), where we read of a loan "pro comunitate militum perusinorum." Compare also *Il Constituto del C. di Siena* (edition ZDEKAUER), p. xxxii.

[3] HALLAM, *Middle Ages* (11th edition), i. 189. Both Italy and England may be said to have early developed a feudalism of their own ; but in France this exemption of the nobility from taxation continued until quite modern times. Compare, for example, VETTORI, *Sommario della Storia d' Italia dal* 1511 *al* 1527 (*Arch. Stor. It.*, App. VI. p. 293), where, speaking of the *regno di Francia*, he says : "Non resta però che non sia una grande tirannide che li gentiluomini . . . non paghino gravezza alcuna ; e sopra li poveri villani si posino tutte le spese."

against this privilege.[1] To understand the indignation
which that protest aroused we must recall the fact that
it was no mere question of a payment of money. Regarded
from a feudal standpoint, the payment of taxes would con-
stitute an admission of the suzerainty of the Commune,
and, consequently, a descent in the feudal scale. It would
partake of the nature of an attornment; and, instead of
continuing to hold directly from the Emperor by the high
and honourable tenure of knight-service, the feudatory,
who submitted to pay taxes, might be deemed to have
accepted a mesne lord, from whom he held by base tenure.
The fact that the Communes had obtained diplomas from
Emperor or Pope had, probably, been regarded by the
milites with contemptuous indifference until they perceived
that the men whom they still looked upon as scarcely
higher than *aldiones* or *coloni*, had, by means of those
same diplomas, attained, in their corporate capacity, to a
position of equality with themselves, and now desired to
treat them as vassals, or, at the best, to transform them
from gentlemen and feudatories of the Empire into private
members of a body politic consisting of plebeians, whom, as
yet, they had only not learned to hate, because to have
hated anything so low would have been beneath their
dignity.

Of the first outbreak of hostilities between the Nobles and
the People we have no certain knowledge; but we learn
from a bull of Innocent III., given at Viterbo in September
1214,[2] that, in that year, he had sent a Cardinal Legate to
make peace between them. The conditions agreed to prove
that the Nobles had been shorn of many of their privileges,
and that the general principle of their liability to taxation
was already admitted. They were, in fact, no longer *milites*
in any but the military sense of the term; from feudal
seigniors they had become citizens. It was provided that
from henceforward neither Potestà nor consuls should levy

---

[1] See SALVEMINI, *Magnati e Popolani in Firenze dal* 1280 *al* 1295 (Firenze,
Tip. Carnesecchi, 1899), p. 53, and authorities there cited.
[2] This Bull is printed by BARTOLI, i. 310-312. See also PELLINI, i. 234, and
Bollettino cited, viii. 152-153, Doc. xcv.

collecta vel muttita save for three causes, namely : 1, for the service of the Church ; 2, for the service of the Roman People ; 3, for the service of the Emperor or his Nuntius, and 4, when the People of Perugia should wage war by common consent.[1]   Such *collecta* was to be made " fideliter per parochiam vel capellam," two persons being thereto elected from each parish, who should swear to carry out their duties impartially and diligently, excusing no man for friendship, kinship or other unjust reason : while it was further stipulated that no such tax should be levied as long as money remained in the public treasury "ad salvam equorum . . . secundum constitutum civitatis."

And here it may be remarked that the clause which provided that the tax-gatherers should swear to make their levy faithfully, " nec excusent aliquem amicitia vel consanguinei- tate vel alio dolo," was no empty formula. In the mediæval communes, the dominant faction invariably sought to assess the property of their opponents unjustly, and to burden them with the major part of the public expenses ;[2] and we are, therefore, by no means surprised to learn that "the enduring harmony of peace," which was established and confirmed by Innocent, lasted but a little while. No sooner did war with Gubbio make it necessary to " facere collecta " than new dissensions arose, and Honorius III. was called upon to interpret the bull of his predecessor. The papal decision, given in February 1218, was in the nature of a compromise,[3] and, like most compromises, probably satisfied no one. From henceforward we find the nobles straining every nerve to establish an aristocratic government in Perugia. If they had been forced to become citizens, they were determined to share the emoluments as well as the

[1] On the "Stone of Justice," which was set up by the Potestà Ramberto "de Ghisileriis," in 1234, and which may still be seen in the outer wall of the Cathedral, this principle of taxation was confirmed: "scilicet quod nec colta nec data nec mistum fiat, ponatur nec detur in civitate perusina nec in ejus suburbiis, nisi quatuor de causis tantum, scilicet PRO FACTO DOMINI PAPE ET IMPERATORIS ET ROMANORVM VEL PRO GENERALI GVERRA QVAM HABERET COMVNIS PERVSII PROPTER SE." Compare PELLINI, i. 250.

[2] For numerous instances see SALVEMINI, *Magnati e popolani in Firenze*, *op. cit.*, pp. 55-57, and authorities there cited.

[3] *Bollettino* cited, viii. 156-157, Doc. xcix.

burdens of citizenship, to oppress rather than to suffer
oppression ; and it is said that they found a powerful ally
in Andrea de' Montemellini, who was Potestà in that year.
The People, however, took up arms, and, having deposed
Andrea, elected Ugone di Grotto in his stead.[1]   A little
later we find the Nobles intriguing with the Pope, who,
according to Bonazzi, showed himself quite willing to espouse
their cause, if he could thereby obtain an actual instead of a
nominal suzerainty.[2]   There is a total lack of details, but
we may presume that the People successfully defended the
liberties of the Commune and inflicted a severe defeat upon
the conspirators, since, in the following year (1223), we find
the Nobles and their adherents in exile.

The war which followed lasted for several years, and it
was only through the efforts of Gregory IX. that peace was
finally restored, in 1228.[3]   The *fuorusciti* turned for assistance to Città di Castello and Gubbio, both of which had
recently suffered from Perugian aggressions, and were only
too ready to seize any opportunity of humbling the pride of
their powerful neighbour.   On the 4th of May, 1223, the
Castellani entered into alliance with the exiles, and, on the
11th of June, at Fratta, "filiorum Uberti," Gubbio joined
the confederation.   In return for assistance in men and
money, the Nobles agreed to a rectification of the Perugian
frontier, which they swore to carry into effect as soon as
they should have obtained the victory over their enemies.[4]
The allies seem to have met with considerable success.
Montone was reduced in 1227 ;[5] and, in the same year, the
Nobles succeeded in returning to Perugia, where (says
Pellini) "they used passing great cruelty toward them of
the opposite faction."[6]   The details of the struggle are,
however, of very little importance compared with the information which is afforded us by the phraseology of the con-

---

[1] The authority is CIATTI, *op. cit.*, Parte III. (*Perugia Pontificia*), p. 299.
According to MARIOTTI (*Saggio*, etc., ii. 197-8), Andrea de' Montemellini was
Potestà in 1218, "Ugo Grotto" in 1221.   [2] BONAZZI, i. 273.

[3] BONAZZI, i. 279 ; MARIOTTI, *Saggio*, etc., iii. 429-430 ; BARTOLI, i. 346.

[4] MUZI, *Memorie Civili, op. cit.*, i. 43-44. See also the convention of the
23rd June, published in *Arch. Stor. It.*, XVI. ii. 479-482.

[5] MUZI, *ubi cit.*, pp. 37-38.   [6] PELLINI, i. 241.

ventions of May 4th and June 11th, 1223 (above referred to), for from them we learn that the three classes which, from the fourteenth century onward, were known in Perugia as the Nobles or *Gentiluomini*, the *Raspanti* and the *Beccarini* were already existent, in fact if not in name.[1]

From the days of Gregory IX. to the beginning of the fourteenth century we hear absolutely nothing of the struggle between the Nobles and the People. It may be that the question of taxation was amicably settled, and that, for a time, the honours and emoluments of office were more or less equally divided between the two classes, as seems to have been the case in Siena under the government of the Ventiquattro.[2] Certain it is that, in the opening years of the Trecento, we find men of noble birth among the leaders (*caporali*) of the Raspanti.[3] That the influence of the Papacy was exercised rather in favour of the aristocracy than against it we can well believe. Innocent III. has been called the founder of the States of the Church; he was certainly the first Pope who claimed the rights of an Italian prince, and, as Italian princes, his successors gradually lost all sympathy with the cause of the People. When the Empire had been reduced to feebleness, the Popes had no further need of their republican allies and became intolerant of civic liberties.[4] Bonazzi's account of the intrigues of Honorius III. with the Nobles of Perugia may or may not be true, but there is nothing improbable about it; and it is noticeable that the "Ordinances of Justice" had no counterpart in Perugia until long after the Papal See had been removed to Avignon, the first important example of class legislation which remains to us being the *Libro Rosso*, of 1333.[5] Moreover, it can hardly be doubted that, after 1266, the aristocracy found a powerful ally in Charles of Anjou, whose whole education and training had made him

---

[1] See Note at the end of the chapter, pp. 42-46.

[2] LANGTON DOUGLAS, *op. cit.*, p. 113.

[3] PELLINI, i. 329; *Brevi annali*, ad ann. 1303.

[4] CREIGHTON, *A History of the Papacy*, i. 24-27.

[5] FABRETTI, *Documenti di Storia Perugina* (Torino, Coi Tipi privati dell' Editore, 1887), Vol. I. pp. 98-122.

utterly contemptuous of democratic pretensions,[1] and who certainly showed himself only too ready to favour the Guelf nobility of Florence.[2]

Neither should we forget the fact that the Nobles formed the cavalry branch of the communal armies, and that, until the general introduction of mercenary troops, the People had need of their services. In street-fighting the Nobles often found themselves at a disadvantage, but, in the open country, the value of the burghers as soldiers was almost negligible. The battles of Santa Petronilla, of Montaperto and of Campaldino prove it. Nor was this the result of cowardice ; it was due simply to the fact that, while the Nobles fought on horseback, the People fought on foot. The merchant and artisan had no time to waste in acquiring the difficult art of war, and their undisciplined ranks were easily broken by a cavalry charge. The *milites* won the day and the *pedites* slaughtered behind them.[3] Moreover, we may, perhaps, infer that the military organisation of the *Popolo* was even less efficient in Perugia than elsewhere. Certain it is that in all her annals we find no mention of the *Carroccio*.[4]

[1] As to the broad line drawn between the high-born and ignoble classes in France, compare HALLAM, *op. cit.*, i. 191-194, and Note xii. pp. 321 *et seq.*

[2] P. VILLARI, *I primi due secoli*, etc., *op. cit.*, Vol. I. p. 263 ; SALVEMINI, *op. cit.*, cap. i. §. 5.

[3] P. VILLARI, *Niccolò Machiavelli e i suoi tempi* (Milano, Hoepli, 1895), Vol. I. pp. 16-17. Compare my *Palio and Ponte*, *op. cit.*, p. 36 n. 1.

[4] The *Carroccio* was, of course, introduced by the great Archbishop Heribert of Milan, to enable the civic levies, the *pedites*, to take the field against the feudal chivalry (LANZANI, *op. cit.*, p. 101. *Cf.* BUTLER, *The Lombard Communes*, *op. cit.*, p. 62); and it was early adopted by nearly all the Communes of Italy. In Siena, the People took the military oath before the *Carroccio*, while the Nobles swore upon their standards. (See my *Palio and Ponte*, *op. cit.*, p. 36 n., and compare p. 57 n.). If the *Carroccio* of any city was taken in battle the citizens held themselves "sore shamed" (see COULTON, *op. cit.*, p. 136) ; and every student of Italian history must remember the last memorable stand of the Florentines round their *Carroccio* on the disastrous field of Montaperto (L. ARETINO, *Ist. Fior.*, Lib. ii.). Thus, judging from analogy, I confess that, personally, I find it extremely difficult to imagine an adequate military organization of the *pedites* without it.

Purely as a matter of curiosity, it may be interesting to note, in this connection, that the *Carroccio* was once used in English warfare ; for what else was the great carriage whereon the standard was erected which gave to the Battle of North-allerton its alternative name of the " Battle of the Standard "?

There is a notable passage in the chronicle of Dino Compagni, where he tells us how, after the Battle of Campaldino, two of the Priors of the Commune of Florence went to the camp before Arezzo, and "much were they blamed therefor, because it was not their business, but that of gentlemen habituated to war."[1] To the democracy belonged the arts of peace and of government. "'Let us leave,' they cried, 'the trade of war to those bear's cubs, those lion's whelps, whom our fathers drove from their lairs and constrained to live within our walls and to bear the chains of citizenship. Let us leave war to them as their ancestral heritage, as a vent for their fierce passions, as a new kind of unconscious homage which they, the feudatories, shall pay to the Commune they serve. Little reck we that their pride may be thereby increased. Enough for us that our supremacy be unimpaired ; and for that we will not neglect to provide.' Thus did those old merchants speak and act. The *Grandi* chafed, but fought and conquered, and conquered for the People, their master, for the men who, by the pens of their smug chroniclers, afterwards cast in their teeth the barbarity of those very wars which they had themselves directed and by which they themselves had profited. Yet the *Grandi*, also, had their historians ; and the Poet, who was destined to sing the incursions of the Florentines into Aretine territory, and the surrender of the foot soldiers at Caprona, was himself one of those 'gentlemen habituated to war,' who, albeit he had become a *popolano*, preserved, among the cherished memories of his youth, those episodes of a military career which Compagni, the vendor of silk, and Villani, the merchant, would have blushed to lay to the charge of their partners in the shop or their colleagues in the government."[2]

Thus did the People regard the Nobles, as fierce hounds to be held in leash, or as falcons, only to be unhooded when the quarry was in sight. Yet it was long before they forgot

---

[1] DINO COMPAGNI, *Cronica Fiorentina* (Firenze, Barbèra, Bianchi e Comp., 1858), Lib. i. pp. 24-25.

[2] I. DEL LUNGO, *Da Bonifazio VIII. ad Arrigo VII. Pagine di Storia Fiorentina per la Vita di Dante* (Milano, Hoepli, 1899), p. 33.

their own social inferiority. Lowell's "backwood's Charlemagne of Empires new," who

> meeting Cæsar's self would slap his back,
> Call him 'Old Horse' and challenge to a drink,

had no prototype in the Italian Republics : and the Nobles
continued to be treated with every outward mark of defer-
ence and respect. They served as Potestà in allied or vassal
communes ; they were sent on honourable embassies to
Kings and Princes, and, even when it was necessary to put
one of them to death, that which was due to his rank was
not forgotten, but he was beheaded "assai onorevolmente
siccome si apparteneva a gentiluomo e cavaliere."[1] At
home, however, they were gradually excluded from all share
in the government ; and, later on, were crushed to earth by
unequal laws which practically left them at the mercy of the
proletariat.[2]

Thus, we perceive that, in its general features, the government and internal history of Perugia, in the twelfth and
thirteenth centuries, differed but little from that of the other
communes of Central Italy. There are, however, many
details on which we do not, as yet, possess sufficient data to
enable us to speak with certainty. No critical edition of the
Perugian statutes has been published, nor any edition at all
of the earlier and more important ones, and we are therefore
compelled to base our opinions on uncertain inferences drawn
from such isolated notices as are to be found in the *Codici
delle Sommissioni* and other kindred documents. It is true
that, under the auspices of the *Società Umbra di Storia
Patria*, the work of research is steadily progressing ; but
much yet remains to be done before that complicated system
of checks and counter-checks which regulated the powers of
the mediæval magistrates can be thoroughly understood.

[1] Fabretti, *Cronache*, i. 142, 168.
[2] See Chapter XII., *infra*.

NOTE

(See page 38 *supra*)

The treaty between Città di Castello and the Perugian *fuorusciti* (which is printed by MUZI in his *Memorie Civili*, Vol. I. p. 43) begins as follows :

Ugo Ugolini Latini Potestas Civitatis Castelli, cum camerario et Alberto de Promano Judice jurant CAPITANEIS MILITUM DE PERUSIIS ET PEDITUM DE PARTE MILITUM SEU MAGNATUM, *quod juvabunt et consulent expensis et reditibus Civitatis Castelli* MILITES ET PEDITES *et eorum heredes Perusinos, qui sint* EX PARTE MILITUM SEU MAGNATUM *et de lite habita et existenti vel futura cum* POPULARIBUS PERUSII *facere guerram, etc.*

Here we have three distinct classes amongst the Perugians : the *Pars militum*, with whom the Castellani were allied ; the *Populares*, against whom they agreed to take up arms, and, finally, the *Pedites de Parte militum*. The *Milites seu Magnates* were, of course, the Nobles, men who had a definite rank as members of the feudal aristocracy, and who were distinguished from the rest of the citizens by the dignity of knighthood.[1] The *Populares*, on the other hand, were the People, the *Popolo*, who had long been predominant in the state, and who were determined to keep the government in their own hands. The question remains to be answered : Who were the *Pedites de parte militum*? Were they *Populares* who had betrayed their order and sided with the Nobles, or were they men of an entirely different social class? The words themselves tell us nothing ; for just as the word *miles* was used indifferently to mean a horse-soldier or a Noble, because the Nobles invariably fought on horseback, so the word *pedes* might mean either a foot-soldier or one of the class from which the foot-soldiers were drawn. *Populares*, *pedites* and *populi* are, in fact, interchangeable terms, any one of which might, with perfect propriety, be translated by the English word "people," and used in contradistinction to *milites* or *magnates*. In the documents of the period, however, the word People (*populus*, *popolo*) has numerous meanings,[2] two of which we may, I apprehend, profitably examine in this connection.

In its first and most comprehensive sense, the term *popolo* included every individual outside the ranks of the *magnati* (*magnates*) living within the communal jurisdiction, whether citizen or *contadino* ; and, generally speaking, it is in this wide sense that the word *popolare* is used in the penal statutes which deal with crimes or torts committed by the Nobles against the People. In addition to this social meaning, there is, however, a much narrower political one, which is certainly of far greater

[1] SALVEMINI, *La dignità cavalleresca nel C. di Firenze* (Firenze, 1896), pp. 14-28.

[2] See REZASCO, *Dizionario del linguaggio storico-amministrativo italiano*, s.v. "Popolo."

importance to the student of the struggle between the classes. Regarded from a political standpoint, the *popolo* was composed exclusively of persons belonging to certain definite associations, which, in the aggregate, constituted a political organization, opposed to the *magnati* and contending with them for the absolute control of the Commune. These associations comprised a relatively small proportion of the *popolo* in its wider sense: and the entire population outside the contending parties was absolutely excluded from any participation in the government of the state. Whether the Commune were aristocratic or democratic, it was always oligarchal: the great mass of the citizens had no political rights, but only duties.[1]

Thus Varchi, writing after the Communal Era was over and looking back across the centuries, tells us that "the inhabitants of Florence are of two sorts: some are subject to taxation, that is to say, they pay the *decime* on their property, and are inscribed in the books of the Commune; certain others are not taxed; and these, in that they live, for the most part, by manual labour and very base crafts, we will call *plebeians*; the which, albeit they have lorded it at divers times in Florence, ought not ordinarily to think of, and much less to aspire to, public affairs in well-ordered governments."[2]   In like manner, the Sienese historian, Giugurta Tommasi, speaking of an embassy which was sent to the Guelf rebels, in 1262, says that "it included every grade of citizens, commencing with the *Grandi* and descending to the *artifici minuti*, who did not form part of the People—*che non erano di Popolo.*"

We may therefore take it that, in the thirteenth century, the *Popolo* included only the upper middle class, the "fat burghers," men of intelligence and wealth; and these were unquestionably the *Populares* against whom the Castellani were allied with the *Pars militum*[4]: while the *Pedites de parte militum* were, I conceive, the plebeians, the *popolo minuto*, who had espoused the cause of the Nobles. It was the old story over again. Just as, two centuries earlier, the Bishops of Lombardy turned to the *populares* for assistance against the *valvassores*,[5] so did the Nobles now seek the help of the proletariat against the People.

In Perugia, as we have seen, the *populares*, who were opposed to the *magnates*, were called "Raspanti": and this title, if we may believe Ciatti, was allusive to the arms of the city, which they adopted as their own—a Griffin, with claws raised as if to strike or clutch (*raspare*, to claw).[6]   Others, however, with more probability, attribute the origin

---

[1] See, on the whole subject, SALVEMINI, *Magnati e Popolani*, etc., *op. cit.*, pp. 30-36.

[2] VARCHI, *Storia fiorentina*, iii. 22.

[3] TOMMASI, *Historie di Siena* (Venezia, 1626), Parte II. Lib. vi. p. 24.

[4] Compare PELLINI, i. 242, where the principal families which appertained to the *Popolari* are enumerated.

[5] See LANZANI, *op. cit.*, pp. 100-101.

[6] CIATTI, *op. cit.*, iii. (*Perugia Pontificia*), viii. 307.

of the name to the Cat which the People adopted as its emblem.[1]   The
adherents of the Nobles, on the other hand, the *Pedites de parte militum*,
were the prototype of the class which was afterwards known as the
Beccarini—the word *beccarino* being a diminutive of *beccaro*, the old form
of *beccaio*, a butcher—and it is worthy of note (although it may, perhaps,
not be advisable to push the inference too far) that, in the mediæval
communes, the butchers, who, in times of civic tumult, showed no
reticence in using as weapons the instruments of their trade, often
proved extremely valuable allies to the faction which they favoured ;[2]
while, in the chronicles of the period, we have more than one example
of the assistance which they rendered to the Nobles in their struggle
with the People.   Thus, in 1254, Ghiberto da Gente made himself
seignior of Parma "cum adiutorio beccariorum" ;[3] in Siena, the Tolomei
were frequently joined by the butchers in their insurrections against the
merchant oligarchy of the Nove,[4] while Machiavelli tells us that, in 1343,
"i beccaj ed altri dell' infima plebe" took up arms in favour of the Duke
of Athens.[5]

In later times, the *Beccarini* were violent and dissolute men, who,
relying upon the protection of the great families they served, became
a terror to all peaceable citizens.   In the last quarter of the fourteenth
century, the Maggior Sindaco was compelled to increase the number of
his attendants and constables by reason of "the many evil and lawless
deeds which the *Beccarini* perpetrated by day and also by night" ;[6] the
keepers of the public brothels were allowed to go armed that they might
be able to protect the inmates from their violence ;[7] and, in the chronicles

[1] BARTOLI, i. 341.   Compare PELLINI, i. 1122, and my *Palio and Ponte,
op. cit.*, p. 145.   In his *Les Baglioni de Pérouse (op. cit.*, p. 4), Count L. DE
BAGLION DE LA DUFFERIE speaks of "la faction bourgeoise, dite des *Raspanti*
(de '*raspare*,' *voler*), surnom que lui vaut le chat qu'elle a choisi pour emblème" ;
and that the word *raspare* does mean "to steal" as well as "to clutch" or
"claw" is, of course, indisputable.   There were *Raspanti* in Pisa, as well as in
Perugia, and their title was said to be due to the fact that there were among them
"quelli che erano arraffatori de' denari e delli bene del Comune di Pisa" (*Cronica
di Pisa* in MURATORI, *R.I.S.*, xv. 1018) ; while, in the middle of the fourteenth
century, the *Raspanti* of Perugia were, perhaps, equally dishonest.   See page
241, and note 2 on page 242, *infra*.

[2] See SALVEMINI, *Magnati e Popolani*, etc., *op. cit.*, pp. 70-71.

[3] Compare the chronicle of Fra Salimbene of Parma.   In the Italian translation of CANTARELLI, the passage in question will be found in Vol. I. p. 328.
See also COULTON, *From St Francis to Dante, op. cit.*, p. 255.

[4] *Cronaca Sanese* in MURATORI, *R.I.S.*, xv. 60, 65.   Compare also *Frammento di una cronachetta senese*, published by N. MENGOZZI and A. LISINI in
1893, per le nozze Sarrocchi-Partini (Siena, Tip. Lazzeri), p. 26.

[5] *Istorie fiorentine*, Lib. ii.

[6] *Arch. Stor. It.*, XVI. i. 234-235 n. ; MARIOTTI, *Saggio*, etc., *op. cit.*,
iii. 511.

[7] "Ancho per obviare aie forestiere e aie forebunde e aie *becharine* e aie vaga-
bunde, acciò che le dicte meretrice o fante staiente ello dicto luoco non sieno

of the fifteenth century, the word *beccarino* is generally equivalent to "bravo." [1] This, however, was far from being the case with the *Pedites de parte militum*, in 1223, a large proportion of whom were probably craftsmen of the lesser Arts, who, being themselves excluded from all participation in the government, preferred to follow the fortunes of the feudal Nobility rather than that of the parvenu Raspanti. Their choice, so far from being a betrayal of their class, was the result of loyalty to their old masters and employers; and not only the *homines* of the Nobles, but also the *spadari*, the *fabbri*, the *sellari* and the rest, quite naturally threw in their lot with the *magnati*. Even in modern England there is surely a greater *camaraderie* between the country gentleman and his groom than there is between the same gentleman and his tailor, or, for that matter, between the tailor and the groom. I take it that our own civil war, in the seventeenth century, could furnish many a parallel with the *Pedites de parte militum* of old Perugia.

Thus was the city divided into two hostile camps; and since the men of the same political views naturally drew together, the three wards of Porta S. Susanna, Porta S. Angelo and Porta Sole were inhabited almost exclusively by the adherents of the Nobility and took the name of *Parte di Sopra*; while the Raspanti and their followers, who, for the most part, lived in Porta S. Pietro and Porta Borgne, were known as the *Parte di Sotto*. In the chronicles of Perugia, the names *Parte di Sopra* and *Parte di Sotto* possess both a political and topographical signification, being referable alike to the factions of the Nobles and of the Raspanti and to the districts in which they dwelt.[2]

The earliest mention of the Raspanti is, I believe, to be found in the *Brevi Annali*, under the year 1302; but it is, as Bonaini remarks, quite possible that, in the passage referred to, the chronicler adopted the phraseology of his own day to indicate a pre-existing faction.[3] The word *beccarino* is certainly of later origin, and it is worthy of note that Theodoric of Niemes confounds the Beccarini with the Nobles[4]—a mistake which may have arisen from the fact that both they and their masters had, no doubt, acquired a thoroughly well-merited reputation for butcherliness. The aristocracy had many wrongs to avenge, and, whenever they succeeded in temporarily wresting the government from

---

esforzati," etc. FABRETTI, *Documenti*, etc., *op. cit.*, i. 64. See also *La prostituzione in Perugia nei Secoli XIV., XV. e XVI.* (Torino, 1890) by the same author.

[1] FABRETTI, *Cronache*, ii. 33; *Arch. Stor. It.*, XVI. i. 630; *Cronaca di Pietro Angelo di Giovanni* in *Bollettino* cited, iv. 347, 376; ix. 35, 68, etc.

[2] See my *Palio and Ponte*, *op. cit.*, pp. 144-145, and authorities there cited.

[3] *Arch. Stor. It.*, XVI. i. lxii n.

[4] "In eadem civitate Perusina sunt tres ordines seu status civium, nam quidam sunt nobiles, qui dicuntur *Beccarini*, et post eos maiores de populo, qui Raspantes nuncupantur, et minutus populus." Compare BARTOLI, i. 341.

the hands of the People, they washed out old injuries in blood. During the *Reggimento de' Gentiluomini*, from 1384 to 1393, the cry of " Death to the Raspanti ! " hardly ever ceased ; "nel qual tempo (says the chronicler) regnarono in questa povera città inganni, rapine, omicidi, assassinamenti, latrocinii, adulterii, violenze, sacrilegi e licenza d' ogni male." [1]

---

[1] *Arch. Stor. It.*, XVI. i. 259.

CHAPTER III

THE CONQUEST OF THE CONTADO

WHEN the cities first began to extend their jurisdiction beyond the circuit of their own walls, the whole countryside was in the hands of feudal lords, who, if weakened by the events of the preceding centuries, still continued to be formidable enemies; and the struggle which followed was, in fact, a struggle between the Italian people and the remnants of their Longobard, Frank and German conquerors. It is often spoken of as a war against feudalism, and is said to have resulted in the destruction of the last vestige of feudality.[1] Such statements, however, are open to serious question, and would probably never have been made had adequate attention been paid to the history of the rural districts and of the conquered towns and territories. Within the walls of the cities feudalism perished early, and the relations of the citizens with one another were often regulated by laws which were rather Latin than Teutonic; but the relations of those cities with their dependencies remained feudal to the last.

With feudalism, as a system, the communes had no quarrel. They accepted it frankly, fully realizing that, in order to impose their authority upon the feudal barons of their *contadi*, it was necessary that they themselves should enter the feudal fold. After their liberties had been guaranteed by imperial diplomas, they became the great feudatories of the Italian Kingdom, and, in the eye of the law, their relations with the Emperor were the same as those of the Dukes and Margraves of Germany; while the Nobles of the *contado*, whom they forced to do them homage,

---

[1] See, for example, J. A. SYMONDS, *History of Italy*, in the *Encyclopædia Britannica* (ninth edition), Vol. XIII. p. 474.

were thereby relegated to the position of arrière vassals. The feudal chain was not broken : a new link was welded into it.[1]

Feudal was the dedication of Siena to the Queen of Heaven,[2] feudal the offerings of *palii* and *ceri* exacted by Pisa, by Siena, by Perugia and by countless other cities at the hands of the subject towns and seigniors of their dominions,[3] and feudal also the serfdom which continued to exist, albeit in a modified form, among the labourers of the Perugian *comunanze* up to the fall of the Republic in the sixteenth century.[4]

When, in 1107, the Florentines began the conquest of their *contado*, "they made war upon every walled place and upon every fortress which obeyed them not," enlarging their borders "by violence rather than by right."[5] Perugia, on

[1] RONDONI, *op. cit.*, pp. 2, 24-25 ; LANZANI, *op. cit.*, Lib. ii., cap. ii., and especially pp. 110-111 ; VILLARI, *I primi due Secoli*, etc., *op. cit.*, Vol. I. p. 32 ; SANSI, *op. cit.*, i. 8. Every difficulty in accepting this view will, I think, vanish away when once we have realized the cardinal fact that the communes only entered the feudal hierarchy in their corporate capacities, and that the aggregate of natural persons, who went to make up the legal person, corporation or *universitas*, were thus freed, as individuals, from all feudal obligations. It is true that, as time went on, the old feudal baronage tended to disappear, either elbowed out of existence or absorbed into the new corporate feudatories ; but the feudal chain was no whit less firmly linked together because its successive rings consisted of legal instead of natural persons. The creation of corporate feudatories struck no blow at the feudal system as such, and did nothing to break in upon the feudal compact. On the contrary, it reinforced and strengthened it, with the result that, as a modern writer has well said, "Italy is the country where feudalism in its essence most flourished and longest survived."—W. BOULTING, *History of the Italian Republics* (London: Routledge & Sons, 1906), p. 25. Compare E. HUTTON, *In Unknown Tuscany* (London : Methuen, 1909), pp. 15-19.

[2] See my *Palio and Ponte*, *op. cit.*, Chap. ii.

[3] *Ibid.*, pp. 14-15, 59-60. Compare also PELLINI, i. 906-907 ; C. GUASTI, *Le Feste di S. Giovanni Batista in Firenze* (Firenze, 1884), pp. 17 *seq.* ; SANSI, *op. cit.*, i. 152, and pp. 20-21 *supra*.

[4] "Ad hoc (laborare et colere) etiam teneantur eorum filii et nepotes et eorum discendentes," etc., Statute of 1528, Vol. II., Rubric 50. The Commune of Perugia was itself a great rural proprietor ; and its lands (*comunanze*) were tilled by labourers who were generally paid in kind, receiving a half share of the crops which they raised (*mezzadria*), and who occupied a position midway between freemen and slaves. They were, it is true, no longer mere chattels, and they possessed certain rights ; but they were bound to the land and were unable to change their condition. See on the whole subject BRIGANTI, *op. cit.*, cap. I., "*Del contado e delle condizioni dei suoi abitanti.*"

[5] G. VILLANI, *Cronica*, iv. 25, 36.

the contrary, albeit, when occasion arose, she too could draw the sword and wield it valorously, did not adopt such lawless and forcible methods. Instead of cutting down the feudal forest and extirpating it root and branch, she chose rather to trim and cultivate it, if so be she might turn it to her advantage. The Florentine *carroccio* advanced more swiftly, but the road travelled by Perugia equally led to art, to commerce and to glory.

It was the object of Perugia to induce the feudal seigniors to accept her overlordship voluntarily, thus avoiding both open hostilities and the enduring rancours which must have followed in their train. To achieve this end it was necessary that she should be powerful and respected; and her first step was to seek allies and vassals. Nor did she seek in vain. The desire for liberty had begun to animate all classes of the Italian people, and every solitary hamlet on the green banks of the Nestore and of the Nicone, every cluster of houses, however humble, in all the wide Umbrian plain, aspired to possess its own consuls and its own statutes; and each little village, as it threw off the yoke of the feudal oppressor and constituted itself an *universitas hominum*—a community of men instead of slaves—turned for protection to the free Commune.[1] Such doubtless was the reason of the submission of Isola Polvese, in 1130,[2] and of Isola Minore, in 1174.[3] Nor is it without significance that, among the covenants entered into by the Polvesani, there was one distinctly subversive of the authority of the feudal nobles, whom they undertook not to receive upon the island without the express consent of the Perugian consuls.[4]

Moreover, not only villages, but towns and communes also, sought the friendship and protection of Perugia; and,

[1] BRIGANTI, *op. cit.*, cap. i. § ii. p. 30. Compare SALVEMINI, *op. cit.*, p. 32; ZDEKAUER, *La Vita pubblica nel Dugento* (Siena, Lazzeri, 1897), p. 90.

[2] BARTOLI, i. 216. Compare p. 23 *supra*.

[3] *Bollettino* cited, v. 429 (Doc. lxi.—"Sommissione dell' Isola Minore").

[4] "In predicta Insula non recolligemus personam de comite neque de cataneis de milite sine parabola de perusini consules." In *Bollettino* cited, v. 427 (Doc. lx.) this clause is paraphrased as follows: ". . . a non raccogliere la pesca *de comite neque de cataneis de milite*," etc. The rendering in question is, however, an obvious slip of the pen. I have examined the original document. Compare also BRIGANTI, *op. cit.*, p. 28 n.

4

one after another, many of the smaller cities of Umbria voluntarily submitted themselves to their stronger neighbour.   It was an age in which men strove for liberty, not for independence.   The whole world was feudal, and no free man might live without a lord.   Perugia herself was content to owe allegiance to the Emperor if thereby she might have freedom ; and when, in 1198, she became a vassal of the Church, her freedom suffered no eclipse ; she merely exchanged a lay for an ecclesiastical overlord.   Even Dante, lover of freedom as he was, wrote a book to prove the necessity of a supreme monarchy—"the universal religion of human nature."   How then shall we wonder that the smaller communes were ready to become dependencies of the greater ?

In 1180, Città di Castello and, in 1183, Gubbio entered into alliance with Perugia *ad faciendum pacem et guerram et hostem et parlamentum*, virtually acknowledging her overlordship and becoming her vassals or "accomandate."[1]   Then followed the submission of Castel della Pieve, in 1188,[2] and of the neighbouring village of Gioncheto, in 1189.[3]   Nocera submitted in 1202,[4] Gualdo in 1208,[5] and Cagli in 1219.[6] Of the causes of these submissions we know scarcely anything with certainty.   Some of them, like those of Città di Castello and Gubbio, may have been made more or less unwillingly ;[7] but some also were unquestionably voluntary. Of the latter class the submission of Gualdo is a typical example.[8]   Thus Perugia became the head and centre of a powerful confederation, not of conquered cities, but of allies

---

[1] *Bollettino* cited, i. 139 (Doc. i.—"Civitatis Castelli submissio"); i. 141 (Doc. ii.—"Submissio civitatis Eugubij").

[2] *Bollettino* cited, i. 142 (Doc. iii.—"Submissio Castri Plebis").

[3] The document is printed by BRIGANTI, *op. cit.*, p. 55.   See also *Bollettino* cited, v. 435 (Doc. lxiv.—"Submissio Jonketanorum").

[4] *Bollettino* cited, i. 145 (Doc. vi.—"Civitatis Nucerij submissio").

[5] *Bollettino* cited, i. 147 (Doc. vii.—"Gualdi submissio ad Comitatum et submissio Arcis Flee").

[6] *Bollettino* cited, ii. 133 (Doc. xvi. — "Calij submissio").   Compare also BARTOLI, i. 327-330, where the document is printed in its entirety.

[7] See P. CENCI, *Le Relazioni fra Gubbio e Perugia nel periodo comunale*, in *Bollettino* cited, xiii. 521 *et seq.*

[8] See R. GUERRIERI, *Storia di Gualdo Tadino* (Foligno, Campitelli, 1900), p. 42.

THE CHURCH OF S. ANGELO

and willing vassals. Her wars of conquest were singularly few, but she never hesitated to draw the sword to protect the rights which her diplomacy had won ; and woe to those towns and seigniors who, having once acknowledged her suzerainty, wearied of her yoke and endeavoured to regain their independence ![1]

One of the earliest acquisitions of Perugia was *Il Chiugi*, the fertile plain between Lake Trasimeno and the Chiana,[2] which embraced an area some thirty-three miles in circumference, and is said to have yielded annually more than 11,000 *corbe* of wheat. The chief town in this district was Castiglione del Lago (*Castilionis Clusini, Castrum Clusini*), picturesquely situated upon a rocky promontory on the western side of the Lake, over against Isola Polvese. It apparently belonged to the Abbots of Capolona, a Benedictine monastery in the *contado* of Arezzo ;[3] while the Panzoni, who were feudal seigniors of Cortona, seem also to have acquired or usurped certain rights in the place. In 1184, Ugo, Abbot of Capolona, with the consent of the monks, of the Prior, and of the Chancellor of the Monastery, gave and submitted to the City of Perugia Castiglione del Lago, *ad ostem faciendam et ad parlamentum et ad coltam et ad datam*,[4] the Panzoni assenting to the transaction. It was stipulated that the walls of the town should be destroyed and that no fortress should be built there in the future. Once every three years, as well as at every election of consuls in Perugia, the consuls of Castiglione were to swear fealty. The Abbot, together with the Panzoni mentioned in the instrument of submission (*cum prenominatis proceribus*), undertook, in case the covenants entered into were not duly observed, to pay a penalty of a hundred pounds of pure gold. More than nine hundred of the inhabitants of

---

[1] Compare the chronicle attributed to GRAZIANI in *Arch. Stor. It.*, XVI. i. 522 (at the top of the page)—a remarkable passage which clearly expresses the Perugian view of the matter.

[2] " . . . terrenum Clusij positum inter lacum et Clanes."

[3] See REPETTI, *Dizionario* cited, i. 180, *s.t.* "Badia di Capolona."

[4] This was the usual formula. It was, in fact, an undertaking to send a contingent in time of war (*ad hostem faciendam*), not to declare war or make treaties with other towns without the consent of Perugia (*ad parlamentum*), and to be subject to tribute (*ad coltam et datam*). In return Perugia gave her protection.

Castiglione swore fealty to the Commune in the Piazza of Perugia.[1]

As to the reason of this submission, we may, I think, presume that Abbot Ugo was willing to be rid of a town which he could not protect against the usurpations of the Panzoni, while the Castiglionesi themselves, probably, hoped to enjoy a greater degree of freedom under the rule of Perugia than under that of lawless feudal seigniors. They, however, seem soon to have wearied of the restrictions under which they were placed, and almost immediately began to rebuild their walls ;[2] while, in 1190, the Panzoni raised the whole of *Il Chiugi* against Perugia.[3]   During the war which followed, Castiglione is said to have been reduced to ruins, and a terrible vengeance was wreaked on the inhabitants.[4] On the 31st January, 1193, the Panzoni were compelled to come to terms with the victorious Commune ; and, together with the other nobles of Cortona (*cum omnibus proceribus cortonensibus*), they made submission of all the lands which they possessed between that town and S. Benedetto di Moiano,[5] agreeing to pay annually, on the festival of S. Ercolano, *decem libras infortiatorum,* by way of tribute. It was also stipulated that they should make war upon Cortona, if she refused to consent to those terms.[6]

The "destruction" of Castiglione can, however, have been only partial, since, in 1196, the Emperor Henry VI.

---

[1] *Bollettino* cited, v. 429-431 (Doc. lxii.—"Submissio Castiglionis Clusini") ; BRIGANTI, *op. cit.*, 84-86 ; PELLINI, i. 229 ; BARTOLI, i. 247-249. The last-mentioned author appears to think that the Castiglionesi only undertook not to fortify their town on the side towards the Lake. This, however, seems to me hardly to be borne out by the words of the document.

[2] See the Diploma of Henry VI. (1186): "Item volumus et presenti pagina sanctione precipimus ut Castrum Clusini nullus edificet eo modo quo nuper inceptum fuit edificari ab hiis qui de vicinia illuc convenerant," etc. (BARTOLI, i. 253-256).

[3] MANCINI, *Cortona nel Medio Evo, op. cit.*, p. 17.

[4] See *Bonifacii Veronensis de rebus a Perusinis gestis. Ann. MCL.- MCCXCIII. Historia metrica quæ vocatur "Eulistea,"* in *Arch. Stor. It.*, XVI. i. 7, n. 1.

[5] ". . . a Cortona inferius usque ad Sanctum Benedictum de Moiano versus Lacum et usque ad Clanas."

[6] *Bollettino* cited, v. 436-437 (Doc. lxv.) ; BRIGANTI, *op. cit.*, 69-70 ; MANCINI, *op. cit.*, pp. 17-18.

promised, in consideration of the payment by the Perugians
of six thousand libbre "lucensium," to cause the place to be
destroyed not later than the end of May in the following
year ; [1] an undertaking which we may, perhaps, infer that
he duly carried out, as we read, in an Aretine chronicle,
under the date 1197 : " Et est facta destructio Castilionis
Clusij." [2]   Be this as it may, we find that it was besieged
by the Perugians in 1198, when the Aretines occupied
Il Chiugi, and that the treaty which ended the war between
the two communes was stipulated in the pavilion of Giovanni
Buonconte, Potestà of Perugia, which was pitched before
the beleaguered town.[3]   It was agreed to divide the coveted
territory ; [4] but it is doubtful whether Arezzo actually gained
anything, inasmuch as Perugia seems to have remained in
possession.[5]   Moreover, her ascendency in the Val di Chiana
was still further increased in 1214, when Count Tancredi of
Sarteano in the Senese submitted to the Perugian consuls
all the lands which he and his brother possessed to the
eastward of the Chiana, promising to buy a house and
vineyard " in civitate perusina " and to become a citizen of
the Republic." [6]

To the northward, the submission of the Marquis Ugolino,
in 1189, extended the dominion of Perugia as far as Fratta
" filij Uberti " (the modern Umbertide) ; [7] and his submission
is the more noteworthy, if, as appears reasonably certain,
he was one of the seigniors of Castiglione Ugolino (*filij
Hogolini*), whose lands and castles had been excepted from

[1] *Bollettino* cited, vi. 320 (Doc. lxviii.)   This instrument is not dated, and
BARTOLI (p. 265) is of opinion that it was executed in 1194. See, however,
Bollettino, loc. cit., n. 2.

[2] MURATORI, *Rer. Italic. Script.,* xxiv. 858.

[3] " In obsidione Castiglionis Clusini, in tentorio Iohannis Bonicomitis Perusinorum Potestatis."

[4] *Bollettino* cited, vi. 320-321 (Doc. lxix.—" Pax et concordia inter Perusinos
et Aretinos ").

[5] MANCINI, *op. cit.,* p. 19.

[6] *Bollettino* cited, viii. 149 (Doc. xciii.—" Submissio Sartiani ").   See also
BRIGANTI, *op. cit.,* pp. 59-60, where a large part of the instrument is textually
reported.

[7] *Bollettino* cited, i. 144 (Doc. iv.—" Submissio castri filiorum Uberti ") ;
BARTOLI, i. 261 ; PELLINI, i. 208.

the jurisdiction of the Commune by the Diploma of
Henry VI., only three years before.[1]

A further accession of territory was obtained, in 1202,
by the submission of the Marquises Uguccione and Guido
"filij q. Ranerij Marchionis," whose fiefs in the Val di
Nicone included many important towns and villages, among
the rest, Monte Gualandro, Castel Nuovo, S. Maria di
Pierle, Lisciano and Reschio [2]; while, in the autumn of the
same year, Abbot Manno of the Monastery of S. Maria *de
Petrorio* "gave, conceded, submitted and subjected to the
consuls of the Commune of Perugia all the walled places,
villages, towns, vassals and serfs (*homines et familias*) which
the Church of the said monastery possessed in the Perugian
contado and diocese, and especially every right which the
said Church hath *in castro Vernançani* (Vernazzano) *et curia
sua et Abadia de Perle.*"[3] In 1208, the Count Bulgarello
and his sons submitted Castello di Fossato;[4] and, in
1212, Gualtiero and Girardino, sons of Ranuzio Malguardi,
seigniors of Castello di Val di Marcola, not only made
submission but accepted a Perugian castellan to whom they
delivered up their keep and tower,[5] their object being to
obtain protection against Gubbio. Nor are we surprised to
learn that a few years later Perugia was compelled to go to
war with her old ally for the defence of her new vassals.[6]
In like manner, the submission of Montone, which seems to
have been brought about through the influence of the
Marquis Ugolino, in 1216,[7] gave great offence to Città di

---

[1] *Bollettino* cited, v. 432 n. 3; BARTOLI, i. 262-263 n.

[2] *Bollettino* cited, i. 144-145 (Doc. v.—" Submissio Montis Gualandri, Castri
Novi," etc.).

[3] *Bollettino* cited, viii. 136 (Doc. lxxvii.—"Submissio locorum et terrarum
monasterij Sancte Marie de Petrorio"). See also BRIGANTI, *op. cit.*, p. 88.

[4] *Bollettino* cited, viii. 143-144 (Doc. lxxxvii.—"Submissio castri Fossati");
BRIGANTI, *op. cit.*, 57-58.

[5] BRIGANTI, *op. cit.*, pp. 61-63, where a large part of the instrument is
textually reported.

[6] BARTOLI, i. 322; compare P. CENCI, *Le Relazioni fra Gubbio e Perugia*, etc.,
in *Bollettino* cited, xiii. 534 *et seq.*

[7] MUZI, *Memorie civili, op. cit.*, i. 34-36, where the submission of Montone is
printed. See also *Bollettino* cited, i. 150-151 (Doc. x.—" Montonis submissio").
A misprint in the document as reported by MUZI has led BONAINI (*Prefazione*

Castello, and was, in fact, one of the principal reasons which led her to espouse the cause of the Perugian *fuorusciti,* in 1223.[1] The treaty of Perugia with Cagli, in 1219, contains special stipulations for mutual defence and assistance against the Eugubini and Castellani.[2]

Meanwhile, the events which followed the spoliation of Conrad, Duke of Spoleto, by Innocent III.[3] had involved Perugia in hostilities with Assisi. In 1198, the Assisani demolished the fortress which dominated their town, and then, flushed with victory, turned their arms against the nobles, destroying their palaces and towers in the city and their castles in the country.[4] To this lawlessness and violence, the moderation displayed by Perugia in dealing with the feudatories of her *contado,* must have formed a marked contrast ; and it was but natural that the nobles of Assisi should beseech her intervention on their behalf. On the 18th of January 1200, Girardo Gislerio, a part of whose lands lay in Perugian territory, swore allegiance to the consuls and demanded to be made a citizen of Perugia.[5] On the 23rd of the same month, his example was followed by Fortebraccio and Oddo, the sons of Leonardo,[6] whose tower and palace of Sassorosso had been razed to the ground ; while, later on, other seigniors sought refuge in Perugia together with their retainers.[7] The refusal of Assisi to make amends for the outrages committed forced on a war ; and the reparation, which negotiations had failed to secure, was exacted at the point of the sword.

cited, p. xxxiii *et passim*) into a mistake touching the date of this submission, which he attributes to the year 1210.

[1] See p. 37 *supra.*

[2] *Bollettino* cited, ii. 133 (Doc. xvi.—"Callij submissio") ; BARTOLI, i. 327-330.

[3] MURATORI, *Annali,* ad ann. 1198 ; SANSI, *op. cit.,* i. 27 ; GREGOROVIUS, *Storia della Città di Roma nel Medio Evo* (Roma, Soc. Editrice Nazionale, 1900-1901), Vol. II. Lib. ix. cap. i. p. 663.

[4] CRISTOFANI, *Storie d'Assisi* (Assisi, Tip. Sensi, 1875), Vol. I. pp. 85 *seq.*

[5] *Bollettino* cited, vi. 323 (Doc. lxxi.—"Cittadinanza concessa a Girardo *Gislerij Alberici*") ; BRIGANTI, *op. cit.,* p. 50 ; BARTOLI, i. 282.

[6] *Bollettino* cited, vi. 324 and n. 1 ; BARTOLI, i. 283.

[7] *Bollettino* cited, viii. 138 (Doc. lxxx.) ; 141 (Doc. lxxxiii.) ; CRISTOFANI, *op. cit.,* i. 89.

Peace was concluded in 1205, the Assisani being compelled to restore to the *fuorusciti* all their possessions, both in the city and the *contado*, to rebuild their towers and palaces and to make compensation for the injuries inflicted.[1] Among the material benefits which accrued to the victors was the submission of Valfabbrica [2] and the acquisition of certain rights in Colle Strada.[3] This was the war in which, if we may believe the legend,[4] St Francis, then a youth of some twenty summers, was taken prisoner by the Perugians and kept for a year in the Campo di Battaglia, "beneath the spot where the Palace of the Captain of the People now stands in the Piazza del Sopramuro." [5]

It were tedious to follow further the submissions of the various towns and seigniors of the Perugian State, for here there is no great feudal house which, towering above its peers, may form the protagonist of a thrilling narrative. Siena had her Aldobrandeschi, lords of Monte Amiata and the Maremma, justly celebrated in story and in song ; [6] Florence her Guidi, so terrible and so potent that Sanzanome does not hesitate to declare of one of them, Guido the Old, that *per se quasi civitas est et provincia* ; [7] but the feudatories who submitted to Perugia were lesser men, whose shoulders bowed themselves easily to receive the yoke, and who, for the most part, bore it patiently and without repining. Their names appear in the *Libri delle Sommissioni* ; we know what promises they made, and, sometimes, whether they kept faith or no ; but there

[1] *Bollettino* cited, viii. 140-141 (Doc. lxxxiii.). Compare also pp. 145-147 (Doc. lxxxix.-xc.).

[2] *Bollettino* cited, viii. 144 (Doc. lxxxviii.—"De castro Vallis Fabrice non redificando") ; BARTOLI, i. 298 ; PELLINI, i. 230 ; BRIGANTI, p. 89.

[3] *Bollettino* cited, viii. 137 (Doc. lxxviii.—"Concessione allodiale fatta dal C. di P. di bene' nelle pertinenze di Colle Strada ") ; BARTOLI, i. 293.

[4] D'ALENÇON, *S. Francisci Assisiensis Vita et Miracula* (Rome, Desclée, Lefebvre e Cie, 1906), P. II. c. i. In the English translation of Mr A. G. FERRERS HOWELL (*The Lives of St Francis of Assisi by Brother Thomas of Celano*, Methuen & Co., 1908) the passage in question will be found on p. 147.

[5] BONAZZI, i. 261.

[6] See E. HUTTON, *In Unknown Tuscany* (Methuen, 1909), chapter x. pp. 139-164, and note on pp. 229-231.

[7] *Gesta Florentinorum* (Florentine edition), p. 129.

is nothing personal, nothing human, that we can lay hold of to make a picture with. The chronicles speak not of them, the poets sing them not, and one sole epithet might suffice for them all :

> Their bones are dust ; their good swords rust ;
> Their souls are with the Saints, we trust.

Yet, not for that are the records of their submissions useless ; and he who would understand the history of Perugia during the twelfth and thirteenth centuries can by no means afford to neglect them, inasmuch as it is through them alone that we can gain an adequate notion of the splendid, steadfast, onward march of the Commune to its predestined position of predominance in Umbria. Neither does any excuse for refusing to study them remain, now that the discriminating and painstaking labours of Count Vincenzo Ansidei and Dr Luigi Giannantoni have made their contents accessible to all the world.[1]

[1] *I codici delle sommissioni*, etc., *op. cit.*, in *Bollettino* cited, Vol. I. *et seq.*

CHAPTER IV

THE COMMUNE AND THE EMPIRE

IT is usual to speak of Perugia as having been always Guelf;[1] but the statement is, I think, hardly borne out by the facts, since she certainly did not become whole-heartedly Guelf until the death of the Emperor Henry VI. had made the Papacy the dominant power in Italy.

On the 18th of June, 1155, Frederick Barbarossa received the imperial crown at the hands of Hadrian IV., the only English successor of St Peter, and then, passing northward through Umbria, sacked and burned Spoleto, which had refused to pay the *fodrum* demanded of her;[2] while, if we may believe the legend, Gubbio was only saved from a like fate by the intervention of her saintly bishop, Ubaldo.[3] Thus it would seem that from Spoleto the imperial line of march lay through Foligno and Nocera along the Flaminian Way, leaving Perugia to the westward; and although, according to Ciatti, the Perugians sent ambassadors to Frederick inviting him to visit their city,[4] the statement can have but little weight, since it appears to have been made on the authority of Cyprian Manente, one of the most untrustworthy of historians.[5]

[1] See, for example, the Statute of 1528, Vol. I. Rubric 473, "*De officio capitaneorum Partis Guelfe*," where Perugia is spoken of as having sided with the Church against Frederick Barbarossa. The rubric in question, which also contains a curious specimen of mediæval etymology, is reprinted in *Bollettino* cited, xiv. pp. xxxv-xxxvi.

[2] MURATORI, *Annali*, ad ann. 1155; SANSI, *op. cit.*, i. 12-13. See also F. GORI, *Sulla distruzione di Spoleto e sulle antiche vie percorse dall' esercito del Barbarossa*, etc., in *Bolletino* cited, iv. 47-56.

[3] See L. M'CRACKEN, *Gubbio Past and Present* (London, Nutt, 1905), pp. 35-37.

[4] CIATTI, *op. cit.* III. (*Perugia Pontificia*) Lib. vii. p. 228.

Compare FUMI, *Codice Diplomatico*, etc., *op. cit.*, pp. iii-v.

In 1165, according to Pellini,[1] but more probably in 1162,[2] Perugia gave herself to Frederick Barbarossa, who, in the same year, created Lodovico Baglioni Duke of Suabia, Imperial Vicar *in civitate Perusina et in omni ejus destrictu* ;[3] while, even after the star of the great Hohenstaufen had begun to wane, the Perugians still continued faithful to his cause and to that of his Antipope, Calixtus III., who seems to have consecrated the altar of S. Lorenzo, between 1170 and 1177.[4]

When, in 1174, Archbishop Christian of Mayence ravaged Umbria and the Marches, destroying Terni, sacking Narni and subduing Spoleto and Assisi,[5] the fact that we hear nothing of Perugia leads us to suppose that she was still imperial, and consequently unmolested. Nor did the rout of Legnano and the subsequent Treaty of Venice shake her loyalty. Enough to prove it the opening words of her convention with Gubbio, in 1183, which was made "ad honorem Dei et domini Imperatoris Archicancellarij Christiani et Ducis ;"[6] while, three years earlier, in her alliance with Città di Castello, the "Most Victorious Emperor" was dutifully recorded,[7] although the Castellani had long since made their peace with the Pope.[8]

In 1185, Frederick Barbarossa appeared in Tuscany, and, according to the chroniclers,[9] deprived all the cities, save Pisa and Pistoia, of their *contadi*. In September he passed into the Ducato, and, from Castello di Coccorone, which, in the previous year, he had given to Foligno, in reward for the faithful services which she, "indefessa strenuitate," had rendered to him and his,[10] he granted a

[1] PELLINI, i. 192.

[2] SCALVANTI, *Considerazioni*, etc., *op. cit.*, pp. 47-48.

[3] BARTOLI, i. 235-236.   As to the authenticity of this document, see p. 29, note 2, *supra*.

[4] L. ROTELLI, *Il Duomo di Perugia* (Perugia, Tip. Santucci, 1864), p. 11 n.

[5] MURATORI, *Annali*, ad ann. 1174; SANSI, *op. cit.*, i. 15; BONAZZI, i. 239.

[6] *Bollettino* cited, i. 141 (Doc. ii.—"Submissio civitatis Eugubij ").

[7] *Bollettino* cited, i. 139 (Doc. i.—"Civitatis Castelli submissio ").

[8] MUZI, *Memorie civili*, *op. cit.*, i. 15.

[9] G. VILLANI, v. 12 ; MURATORI, *Annali*, ad ann. 1185.   Compare VILLARI, *op. cit.*, i. 133.

[10] The original diploma is preserved among the archives of the Commune of Foligno.   It is not to be found in the *Regesta Imperii*.

diploma to Spoleto, pardoning all her offences and once more receiving her to his grace.[1]   In 1186, Orvieto seems to have been besieged by Henry, King of the Romans,[2] and certain writers inform us (among them Manente) that she obtained succours from Perugia and Spoleto as well as from numerous other towns.   The story is, however, grossly improbable, and if, in fact, Perugians and Spoletini were found within the beleaguered city, they must have been *fuorusciti*, whose only hope of returning to their homes lay in the triumph of the papal cause.[3]   Indeed, a sufficient refutation of the fable will be found in the famous privilege which was granted by Henry to his faithful Perugians (*fideles nostri cives perusini*) on the 7th of August of the same year, whereby their right to elect consuls was fully recognized and jurisdiction was given them over the whole of their *contado*, except the lands and castles of certain feudatories.   The possessions also of the Countess Matilda, whether in the city or the *contado*, were granted to the Commune in perpetual feud, and the Perugians were declared free from the extortion of the regalian rights of forage, food and lodging for the imperial troops, it being agreed that, when the King, the Emperor or any Legate of theirs should pass through the *contado* of Perugia with an army, they should do so "cum consilio Consulum Perusine Civitatis." Jurisdiction was given to the Commune in all causes arising in the city or its territories, a right of appeal to the Emperor being, however, reserved where the sum in dispute amounted to twenty-five imperial pounds.   "For this so magnificent concession of liberality," the citizens were to pay a tribute of 100 Lucchese pounds (*centum libras Lucensium*), and to swear fealty to the Emperor.[4]   Thus did Perugia become a powerful feudatory in the heart of Umbria, to be numbered,

[1] SANSI, *op. cit.*, i. 21.   See also *Documenti storici inediti*, published by the same author (Foligno, 1879), Part II. Doc. v. p. 205.

[2] MURATORI, *Annali*, ad ann. 1186.   It is, of course, possible that the *Urbs Vetus*, referred to, may be Città Vecchia instead of Orvieto.

[3] Compare SANSI, *Storia del C. di Spoleto, op. cit.*, i. 22.

[4] This diploma has been frequently printed.   See, for example, BARTOLI, i. 253-257 ; BRIGANTI, *op. cit.*, 26-27 ; SCALVANTI, *Considerazioni*, etc., *op. cit.*, 49 ; *Bollettino* cited, v. 431 (Doc. lxiii.) ; and compare pp. 28, 54 *supra*.

henceforward, among the *Grandi Vassalli*, the peer of any Duke, Marquis or Count among them all.[1]

In June, 1190, Barbarossa was drowned on his way to Palestine, and was succeeded by his son Henry VI. For the moment it seemed as if the policy of Hildebrand and his successors was doomed to failure, and that the Banner of the Church was about to be replaced by the Eagle of the Hohenstaufens. In the eight short years of his reign, Henry acquired a degree of authority to which none of his predecessors had ever attained. Lord of the Two Sicilies and King of Lombardy, he dominated the whole Peninsula, and was able to defy with impunity that power before which his greater father had been compelled to bow. The anathemas of the Vatican, which had not arrested his victories, were equally ineffectual to impede his usurpations. He treated the inheritance of the Countess Matilda as the exclusive property of the Empire, and bestowed it upon his brother, Philip of Suabia. To his Grand Seneschal, Markwald of Anweiler, he gave, as a dukedom, all that vast expanse of country which stretches along the Adriatic from the territory of Bologna to the Neapolitan confines, including the Romagna and the March of Ancona. The Contea di Molise, with many other lands forming the Patrimony of St Peter, were granted to Conrad of Hurselingen, Duke of Spoleto and Count of Assisi, while other German and Italian nobles received other feuds. Thus, beyond a precarious sovereignty within the walls of Rome, the power of the Pope was reduced to well-nigh nothing, and the Lombard Republics, hemmed in and suffocated between the German provinces and these new Imperial fiefs, felt that their independence was once more in imminent peril. Even the loyal Perugia seems to have been threatened with the destruction of her liberties ; for, if we may credit Bartoli, Philip of Suabia laid siege to the city, in 1195, maintaining that the Tiber still formed the eastern boundary of Tuscany and that Perugia was, consequently, a part of his Duchy.[2] The magistrates, however,

---

[1] Compare p. 47 *supra*.

[2] BARTOLI, i. 268-269. The statement is confirmed by the *Annales Camaldulenses*, Tom. i. p. 154, where we read that " Philippus Dux Tusciæ, alter filius

succeeded in convincing him that their freedom was guaranteed by Imperial and Royal diplomas ; whereupon he withdrew his army, and, on July 3rd, in the Church of S. Salvatore " de Poziali," confirmed to the citizens the privileges granted them by his brother and seignior, Henry, Emperor of the Romans.[1] That he claimed jurisdiction over Città di Castello appears clear from a document published by Muzi, in his *Memorie Civili* ;[2] while the imposts which he levied upon the ecclesiastics of that town were found so intolerable that they appealed for relief to the Emperor.[3] In 1197 he invaded the Roman Campagna, and it seemed as if nothing could save the few fortresses which still remained to the Church, when the news of his brother's death recalled him to the North. The Emperor was sincerely mourned by his own countrymen, and was buried at Palermo with royal pomp amid the lamentations of all his army ; but the Italians rejoiced exceedingly :

> Omnia cum Papa gaudent de morte Tyranni.
> Mors necat, et cuncti gaudent de morte sepulti,
> Apulus, ac Calaber, Siculus, Tuscusque, Ligurque.[4]

Even those communes which were stanchly imperial had begun to feel uneasy, and breathed more freely now that their too powerful suzerain was no more.

The death of Henry led first to the abandonment, and then to the total ruin of the imperial system which Frederick had initiated in Central Italy.[5] Within a few weeks, Florence had organized a league of Tuscan cities against the Empire ; and, on November 11th, at S. Genesio, the ancient *Vico Wallari*, which Repetti calls " the Roncaglia of Tuscany,"[6]

Friderici Ænobarbi imperatoris, et frater Henrici imperatoris, præsenti anno M.C.XCV. Indict. xiii., anno vero eius Ducatus primo, Kalendis Iulijs, IN OBSIDIONE PERVSII, recepit Monasterium Fontis Avellanæ sub sua protectione." On the other hand BONAZZI (i. 250) calls the whole story "a silly fable" and disputes the authenticity of the document in question. It appears, however, to be accepted as genuine by no less an authority than Count VINCENZO ANSIDEI (*Bollettino* cited, vi. 319 n. 1).

[1] *Bollettino* cited, vi. 318-319 (Doc. lxvii.).

[2] MUZI, *Memorie civili*, etc., *op. cit.*, i. 18.   [3] *Ibia.*, p. 19.

[4] MURATORI, *Annali*, ad ann. 1197.

[5] VILLARI, *I primi due secoli*, etc., *op. cit.*, 121 *et seq.*

[6] REPETTI, *Dizionario* cited, i. 352, *s.t.* " Borgo San Genesio." SANSI

the Lucchese, the Florentines, the Sienese and the Samminiatesi swore to maintain it, the solemnity of the proceedings being enhanced by the presence of two Cardinals of the Church. The main terms of the treaty were alliance for the common defence against all who should attack the League, and an undertaking not to make truce or peace "with any Emperor, King, Prince, Duke or Marquis," without the consent of the Rectors of the said League. War was to be declared against every city, town, count or bishop who, being invited to join the alliance, should refuse to do so ; for the chief object of the confederation was, as Professor Villari remarks, to take advantage of the Emperor's decease to secure to the cities the complete possession of their respective territories. To effect this it was necessary that Tuscany should be united, and, consequently, adherence to the League must, as far as possible, be made compulsory. Moreover, it is to be noted that the fact that the communes were banded together against the Empire by no means implied that their alliance was intended for the protection or benefit of the Pope. His pretensions to the inheritance of the Countess Matilda were wholly ignored ; and, while it was declared that no Emperor, King, Duke or Marquis should be recognized without the approval of the Roman Church, it was made perfectly clear that, if the Pope should wish to join the League, he must accept its terms in order to gain admittance. Should he ask assistance to reconquer his own territories, the Rectors were to consider his request ; but nothing was to be done for him except by their orders ; and in no case could any help be afforded him if the territories of which he desired to take possession were in the hands of the communes or of the allied cities. Nothing could be more explicit ; and hardly had the Rectors been sworn in than Innocent wrote to the two Cardinals who had given their countenance to the proceedings at S. Genesio, declaring that, in many points, the League *nec utilitatem contineat, nec sapiat*

(*Storia del C. di Spoleto*, *op. cit.*, i. 14) states that S. Genesio was "near Siena," whereas, as a matter of fact, it was close to Samminiato al Tedesco, in the lower Val d' Arno. This mistake of Baron Sansi's is followed by G. CECI, *Todi nei Medio Evo* (Todi, Trombetti, 1897), Vol. I. p. 61.

honestatem, at the same time expressing his intention of enforcing his rights to the Duchy of Tuscany. No notice was taken of him, however, and before long he considerably lowered his tone. In February, 1199, we find him urging the Pisans to join the League ;[1] while, about the same time, he consented that the communes over which he claimed jurisdiction "in Tuscia et Ducatu Spoleti" should do the like.[2] Nevertheless, it is certain that there was no yielding on the part of the confederated cities, and although the Pope, grown wiser by experience, became a declared and energetic champion of the League against the Empire, this only availed to increase his moral and political influence, without winning him one hand's breadth of territory or enabling him to enforce one of his pretended rights over Tuscany.[3]

That Perugia became a member of the League we know from the fact that the names of "Amadeus perusinus rector" and "Pierus de Cupa de Perusio" appear among the signatories to the instrument whereby, in 1203, Siena ceded to Florence that portion of her *contado* which had been adjudged to the latter by the iniquitous arbitrament of Ogerio ;[4] while, two years later, when the Rectors assembled at S. Quirico in Osenna to adjudicate whether Montepulciano was situated in the Sienese *contado* or not, we find, among their number, a certain "Dominus Gluttus pro civitate Perusij," together with a witness, "Pierus de Cupa Perusiæ civitatis."[5]

According to Bonazzi (though, after his wont, he gives us no authority for the statement) Perugia joined the League

---

[1] For this account of the organization of the Tuscan League I am mainly indebted to Professor VILLARI's *I primi due secoli*, etc., *op. cit.*, Vol. I. pp. 142-146.

[2] "Et obtinuerunt a Summo Pontifice, ut etiam Civitates Ecclesiæ, quæ sunt in Tuscia et Ducatu Spoleti, se illis in hoc Societate conjungerent." MURATORI, *Dissertazione*, xlviii.

[3] According to HALLAM (*Middle Ages*, edition cited, i. 382) the cities of Tuscany were "impelled by Innocent" to organize the League, an obvious error in view of the documents published by Santini and Ficker and cited by VILLARI, *ubi cit.* Compare also GREGOROVIUS, *op. cit.*, Vol. II. Lib. ix. cap. i. p. 663.

[4] SANTINI, *Documenti dell' Antica Costituzione del C. di Firenze* (Firenze, Vieusseux, 1895), p. 131 (Doc. xlviii.).

[5] MURATORI *Antiquitates It. M. Aevi*, Diss. L. Doc. vi.

in 1198 ;[1] and, if this be so, her motives may not be far to seek. One of the main objects of the contracting parties was, as we have seen, to obtain complete possession of their respective *contadi*. Florence was determined to destroy the increasing power of Semifonte ; Siena coveted Montalcino ; and it is a significant fact that hardly had Arezzo given in her adherence to the League than she invaded *Il Chiugi*.[2] Brief as was the war which followed, it no doubt sufficed to prove to Perugia that her only prudent policy was to join the Tuscan confederation ; and it is not impossible that her willingness to divide the disputed territory was due to her apprehension lest the allied cities should intervene on behalf of her adversary. Moreover, the triumphant progress of Innocent, during that same summer, when he received the homage of Spoleto, Assisi, Rieti, Foligno, Norcia, Gubbio, Todi, Città di Castello and other communes,[3] may well have created no little uneasiness in a city which, though now ready to swear fealty to the Church, had but yesterday been imperial.

In September, Innocent was in Perugia, where he re-consecrated the altar of S. Lorenzo, which, it was feared, had been *execratum*, not *consecratum*, by Calixtus III. ;[4] while, on October 2nd of the same year, he published, at Todi, the celebrated Bull whereby he received Perugia under the protection of the Church, confirming her right to elect consuls and to govern herself by her ancient customs.[5] Thus the Perugians forsook, for ever, the imperial cause and became *fideles* of the Apostolic See. There was no sudden rupture ;[6] but the Empire was vacant, and, before another Cæsar arose

---

[1] BONAZZI, *op. cit.*, i. 262.

[2] See p. 53 *supra*.

[3] GREGOROVIUS, *op. cit.*, Vol. II. Lib. ix. cap. i. p. 663. Thus did the *Ducatus Spoletanus* become an integral part of the Ecclesiastical State, distinct from the Patrimony of St Peter, the Romagna and the March of Ancona. See herein FUMI, *I Registri del Ducato di Spoleto* (Perugia, Unione Tip. Cooperativa, 1903), pp. 1-2.

[4] MARIOTTI, *Saggio*, etc., *op. cit.*, iii. 418 ; ROTELLI, *Il Duomo di Perugia, op. cit.*, p. 11 n. Compare p. 59 *supra*.

[5] PELLINI, i. 222 ; BARTOLI, i. 279-280 ; *Bollettino* cited, vi. 322 (Doc. lxx.).

[6] Compare BONAINI, *Prefazione*, etc., *ubi cit.*, p. xxxiii.

5

to claim their allegiance, they had become wholly Guelf.
Henceforward, what was said of the Bolognesi might equally
be said of them : " Honor, amor, reverentia partis Guelfæ in
cordibus [Perusinorum] sunt sculpta et coniuncta ut lux et
solis radius est in sole." [1]

[1] V. VITALE, *Il Dominio della Parte Guelfa in Bologna* (Bologna, Zanichelli,
1902), p. 78.

CHAPTER V

THE COMMUNE AND THE PAPACY

ON the 4th of October, 1209, Otho of Brunswick received the imperial crown at the hands of Innocent, and, from that moment, became his implacable enemy. As he marched northward by the great Via Francigena,[1] he stormed Montefiascone and occupied Acquapendente and Radicofani. On the 25th he was at Poggibonsi. Not only the Ghibelline cities of Siena and Pisa opened their gates to him, but also Samminiato, Florence and Lucca. From Tuscany he turned upon Umbria. In December, he was master of Terni, of Foligno, and of the territories, if not the cities of Perugia and Orvieto ; while, to the northward, the *contado* of Città di Castello blazed out into rebellion, many of the feudal seigniors declaring for the Emperor. He cut off all communication with Rome, and even ecclesiastics, proceeding on their business to the Pope, were robbed. Vain were the most earnest appeals to his gratitude, vain the most awful admonitions, excommunication itself. Innocent had raised up for himself a more bitter foe than the proudest and most ambitious of the Hohenstaufen.[2]

[1] A generic name given to those main roads which, during the period of the descent of the Franks into Italy, led through Tuscany to Rome. The *Via Francigena*, here referred to, is, of course, that which passed through Poggibonsi, Siena, Buonconvento, S. Quirico, Radicofani, Acquapendente, Bolsena, Montefiascone, Viterbo and Sutri, entering Rome by Porta Castello. REPETTI, *Dizionario* cited, v. 716.

[2] GREGOROVIUS, *op. cit.*, Vol. II. Lib. ix. c. ii. p. 699, and notes 59, 60, on pp. 708-709 ; MILMAN, *History of Latin Christianity* (London, 1867), v. 234-235 ; BOULTING, *op. cit.*, 141 ; CIATTI, *op. cit.*, iii. (*Perugia Pontificia*), Lib. viii. p. 277 ; BONAZZI, i. 264 ; SANSI, *Storia del C. di Spoleto*, *op. cit.*, i. 35 ; MUZI, *op. cit.*, i. 33. The only historian who asserts that Otho IV. actually occupied Perugia is Ciatti, and his general standard of accuracy is not such as to lead us to give much credit to so improbable a statement.

In the hour of his peril, he bethought him of the Tuscan League, the sworn enemy of the Empire, and especially of Perugia, which he had visited only two years earlier, and which, perhaps, formed his headquarters for several months.[1] Nor did she fail him at his need. On February the 28th, 1210, on the Vigil of the Festival of S. Ercolano, in the Palace of the Commune, the Perugians swore to the Apostolic Legate, who had come to receive their oath of fealty, that they would defend the Roman city of St Peter when summoned thereto by the Pope or his successors. They, however, stipulated that they should only be required to serve between Perugia and Rome, and that, if they were called upon to advance beyond the latter city, they should be free to decline to do so. In return, Innocent undertook that, in any peace made with the Emperor, Perugia should be included, and promised to maintain the citizens in all their customs and all their rights, " in electione consulum seu potestatis quam in appellationibus tam in hominitiis et ceteris aliis." [2]

Thus, the service to be rendered by the Commune was such as became free men—*servitium militis* or knight-service [3]—and, although the citizens swore fealty to the Pope, it is hardly too much to say, with Ciatti and with Bartoli, that it was "rather a fealty of confederation than of submission." [4] Moreover, it is worthy of note that the Perugians regarded the obligations they had assumed as binding them not only to the Pope, but also to Rome and to the Roman people. The greatness of the old Republic was not forgotten : *Senatus Populusque Romanus* were still

---

[1] According to BARTOLI (i. 300) the Pope's sojourn in Perugia was of the briefest ; but we have evidence that he was there in February, in August and in September, 1207. See SANTINI, *Documenti*, etc., *op. cit.*, P. iii. p. 373, Doc. ix. ; FUMI, *Codice Diplomatico*, *op. cit.*, p. 56, Doc. lxxx., and MARIOTTI, *Saggio*, etc., *op. cit.*, iii. 418.

[2] *Bollettino* cited, i. 149-150 (Doc. ix.—"Juramentum Perusinorum ad summum Pontificem," etc.).

[3] As a general rule, under the feudal system, military service was limited as to *time* ; but a limit of *place* was not uncommon. Compare HALLAM, *Middle Ages* (11th edition), i. 172 and note (h): "Dominus Sabrandus dictus Chabot dicit quod non debet servitium domino regi, nisi in comitatu Pictaviensi," etc.

[4] CIATTI, *ubi cit.*, viii. 279 ; BARTOLI, i. 303.

words to conjure with ; and in the heyday of her fierce and strenuous youth, the Commune of Perugia was proud to render loyal service to the once mighty Mistress of the World.[1] Nor is it without significance that, in 1186, when the Perugians swore fealty to Henry VI., the Roman Republic was in alliance with the Emperor.

At the submission of Gualdo, in 1208, the consuls of both communes swore to the observance of the terms of the convention " *salvo in hijs omnibus honore et præcepto DOMINI PAPÆ ET DOMINI SENATORIS ALMÆ URBIS ROMANÆ* " ;[2] an exception repeated in the submission of Montone, eight years later.[3] Many of the Potestà of Perugia came from Rome ; and, in the documents of the period, we frequently find them described as " the illustrious Senator of the Gentle City and Potestà of Perugia," " Consul of the Romans and Potestà of Perugia," and the like ; while almost all the alliances with other cities and submissions of communes, towns and villages, begin with the formula : " To the honour of God and of the Roman Church and of the Commune of the Gentle City," or with other words of a like tenor, expressive of the utmost reverence and affection for Rome.[4]

During their relentless persecution of the second Frederick, the Popes, and especially Gregory IX., were often resident in Perugia. There they were able to mature their ambitious schemes in safety ; while the city which sheltered and protected them reaped a rich reward for its loyalty in praise and privileges. Thither, in June, 1228, came Gregory, driven from Rome by a Ghibelline revolt ; and thence he directed the invasion of the Kingdom of Naples. He was still in Perugia when, in May, 1229, Frederick landed at Brindisi, and, unfurling the Banner of the Cross against the Banner of the Keys, repelled and defeated the

---

[1] BONAINI, *Prefazione* cited, p. xxxix.

[2] *Bollettino* cited, i. 147-148 (Doc. vii.—" Gualdi submissio "). The document in question is published in its integrity by R. GUERRIERI, *Storia di Gualdo Tadino, op. cit.*, pp. 44-46.

[3] *Bollettino* cited, i. 150-151 (Doc. x.—" Montonis submissio ").

[4] See V. ANSIDEI, *Alcune notizie sui rapporti fra Roma e Perugia nel Secolo XIII.*, in *Bollettino* cited, i. 591-599.

conquering armies of the Church.   Only in February, 1230, did the Pope return to Rome, and, in 1234, he was again in Perugia, where he remained until December, 1236.   On his departure, he was escorted by eight hundred horse, under the command of Marcovaldo, Potestà of Perugia, who, on the 5th of the same month, at Todi, made oath on behalf of the Commune to defend and preserve the Patrimony of Saint Peter in Tuscany and the Duchy of Spoleto "in devotion, subjection and fidelity to the Holy Roman Church and to our lord the Pope, both spiritually and temporally."[1]

Thus Perugia virtually assumed the position of Papal Vicar in Umbria ; and, in the following year, we find her organizing a confederation of Umbrian cities, which, while no mention was made of the Emperor, was practically directed against him.   On the 16th of November, in the presence of the General and Special Councils, convened " ad sonum campanorum, more solito," in the Palace of the Commune, the representatives of Spoleto, Todi, Gubbio and Foligno entered into an alliance with Perugia and with one another, for the common defence, " to the honour and praise and reverence of Almighty God, the Father, the Son and the Holy Ghost, of the most glorious Virgin Mary, of the Apostles Peter and Paul, of the Holy Roman Church, our Mother, and of the Supreme Pontiff, our lord Pope Gregory IX."   All the allies stipulated that nothing in the instrument of confederation should be construed as binding them to take up arms against the Church, while Perugia, Todi and Spoleto made a like exception in favour of the City of Rome.[2]

A few days later, Frederick defeated the Lombards with enormous loss at the Battle of Cortenuova, and the Milanese

---

[1] The document is published by V. ANSIDEI, *loc. cit.*, p. 594.   The rights, privileges, jurisdiction and liberties of the Commune of Perugia were scrupulously safeguarded by the following proviso: " Salvis comuni Perusij et universitati privilegiis, cortibus, iuribus, usibus, iurisdictionibus, libertate, tenutis, possessionibus omnibus et singulis que quos et quas comune Perusij et universitas eiusdem actenus habuit et nunc habet."

[2] BARTOLI, i. 372-377 ; *Bollettino* cited, ix. 128-130 (Doc. cxv.—"Societas inter Tudertinos Fulginates, Spoletanos et Eugubinos ") ; SANSI, *op. cit.*, p. 61 ; CECI, *Todi nel Medio Evo, op. cit.*, i. 129 ; CENCI, *op. cit.*, in *Bollettino* cited, xiii. 544.

carroccio was sent, with a pompous inscription, to the papal capital, a gift to the People of the " Gentle City."

In 1239, the Emperor, who had once more been excommunicated by Gregory, resolved to transfer the war from Lombardy to the Patrimony. He celebrated his Christmas at Pisa, and, in February, 1240, invaded the papal territories by the way of Arezzo. From the March of Ancona the gay and gallant Enzo came to meet him, " beautiful of body, with a face like an angel and long fair curls falling even to his belt." [1] It is said that he endeavoured to force his way through the *contado* of Perugia, but met with so vigorous a resistance that he abandoned the attempt, and marching by Città di Castello, Gubbio and Gualdo, reached Foligno, which had already repudiated the Guelf alliance and sent ambassadors to Frederick to do him homage.[2] Her example was followed by Spello, Bevagna and Bettona ; and, although Spoleto and Todi remained faithful to Perugia and to the Pope, Orte, Città Castellana, Corneto, Sutri, Montefiascone, Toscanella and Viterbo welcomed the Emperor with open arms.[3] For the moment it seemed that Rome itself must fall into his hands ; but the aged Pope was not dismayed ; from every pulpit Franciscan and Dominican friars preached a crusade for the defence of the Holy See, and in a single day a powerful army was assembled. Frederick revenged himself by putting to death all the prisoners he made who wore the Cross ; but his campaign had failed of its principal object, and a new danger threatened him in the form of a General Council, which Gregory summoned for the following Easter, to decide between himself and his enemy.[4]

[1] L. ALBERTI, *Libro primo della Deca seconda dell' Historia di Bologna* (Bologna, 1588), c. 17, cited by L. FRATI, *La prigionia del re Enzo a Bologna* (Bologna, Zanichelli, 1902), p. 7. Compare *La cronaca di Fra Salimbene parmigiano*, volgarizzata da C. CANTARELLI (Parma, 1883), i. 216, and COULTON, *From St Francis to Dante, op. cit.*, p. 124.

[2] BARTOLI, i. 383-384 ; CIATTI, *op. cit.*, iii. (*Perugia Pontificia*), ix. 330 ; SANSI, *Storia del C. di Spoleto, op. cit.*, i. 67-69 ; CECI, *Todi nel Medio Evo, op. cit.*, i. 132.

[3] MURATORI, *Annali*, ad ann. 1240.

[4] GREGOROVIUS, *op. cit.*, Vol. II. Lib. ix. cap. v. pp. 781-783 ; SISMONDI, *Storia delle Republiche Italiane de' Secoli di mezzo* (Milano, Pagnoni), Vol. I. cap. xvi. p. 341 ; BOULTING, *op. cit.*, p. 149.

In April, 1241, many French prelates assembled at Nice and embarked upon Genoese vessels which were sent to convey them to Rome ; but the Emperor was not idle ; Enzo came from Sicily with all the galleys he could muster, and Pisa sent her fleet to lie in wait for the enemy at Meloria. On the 3rd of May, between the islands of Giglio and Montecristo, the hostile armadas joined battle. Of the twenty-seven Genoese galleys three were sunk and nineteen taken. The captured Cardinals, Bishops, Abbots and Priors were carried prisoners to Naples and Sicily, or, as some say, to Pisa, where it is related that the Cardinals were distinguished from their fellow-captives by being furnished with silver chains.[1] On the 21st of August, Gregory died of rage and grief ; and, on the 6th of October, the aged and infirm Celestine IV., who succeeded him, followed him to the tomb, after a pontificate of only sixteen days. For nearly two years the papal throne was vacant, and the Guelf party might have been utterly ruined had not the Senator, *Matheus Rubeus*, gallantly " mounted the breach which the Cardinals had basely deserted, and, with prudence and courage, defended the City of Rome and served the cause of the Church." [2]   It was he who, on the 12th of March, 1242, " in domo Sancte Marie de Capitolio," concluded the celebrated league with Perugia, Narni and other Guelf communes, whereby the allies swore not to make peace with Frederick or desert one another so long as the war between the Empire and the Church should endure, " to the honour of Almighty God and to the honour and reverence of the Holy Roman Church and of the gentle and glorious City of Rome and of the Commune of Perugia and the Commune of Narni, and of all other towns, states and communes which shall take and keep the oath hereinafter set forth, with the consent of the Senate and the Roman People." [3]

---

[1] " . . . et cardinales predicti in Canonica nova pisani capituli cum compedibus curialibus argenteis collocati fuerunt, ubi fere per triennium permanserunt." *Istorie Pisane* in *Arch. Stor. It.*, VI. i. p. 502 n.

[2] GREGOROVIUS, *op. cit.*, Vol. II. Lib. ix. cap. v. p. 788.

[3] BARTOLI, i. 388. See also E. NARDUCCI, *La lega romana con Perugia e con Narni contro Federico II.*, Narni, Tip. Gattamelata, 1862. The document is printed on pp. 39 *et seq.*

In 1241, Frederick had made himself master of Spoleto ; [1] and, from thenceforward, the malcontents in Perugia [2] were in constant communication with the imperial agents in that city and in Foligno.[3] In 1245, according to the *Brevi Annali*, " the Perugians were discomfited in the plain of Foligno by the folk of Frederick the Emperor ; " [4] while, on the 31st of March in the following year, when Cardinal Rainerio Capozzi, at the head of the Perugian and Assisan levies, advanced against Spoleto, the Imperialists were once more completely victorious.   The battle took place beneath the walls of Spello, and, besides those who were slain and wounded, five thousand prisoners are said to have been taken.[5] A little later, the Emperor himself invaded the territory of Perugia and pitched his camp at Sansoste (S. Sisto).[6] It is, probably, to one of these reverses that the story told by Fra Salimbene of Parma is referable.   So great, says he, was the panic of the fugitives and so complete their demoralization " that one old woman of Foligno drove ten Perugians to prison, armed only with a rod of reed ; and other women did the like ; for the Perugians had no heart to resist them, such was the confusion which God had sent upon them in that battle." [7] The demolition of the walls of Foligno, in 1282, is said to have been due to the memory of this indignity, and it is unquestionable that the defection of their old ally irritated the Perugians beyond measure.   Among the contemporary documents which bear witness to this fact may be cited one of February 13th, 1251, wherein the Folignati are stigmatized as " betrayers of God, of the Church and of the Commune of Perugia—*Dei et Ecclesie et Comunis Perusij*

---

[1] SANSI, *Storia del C. di Spoleto, op. cit.*, i. 72.   See also *Documenti storici inediti, op cit.*, P. II. p. 277 (Doc. xxxix.).

[2] As to the existence of an imperial faction in Perugia, compare J. ZELLER, *Histoire d'Italie* (ad ann. 1240), cited by BOULTING, *op. cit.*, p. 149.

[3] BARTOLI, i. 390.

[4] *Arch. Stor. It.*, XVI. i. p. 55.

[5] MURATORI, *Annali*, ad ann. 1246 ; SANSI, *Storia del Comune di Spoleto, op. cit.*, i. 78.

[6] *Brevi Annali, ubi cit.*, p. 55.

[7] *Cronaca di Fra Salimbene* (edition cited), ii. 56 ; COULTON, *op. cit.*, 203.

proditores." [1]   Not even the Popes themselves could restrain the desire of the Perugians for vengeance ; and when Martin IV. excommunicated them for devastating " the whole Bishopric of Foligno even to the ditches of the city," they burned him and his Cardinals in effigy.[2]

In 1247, Orvieto appears to have become temporarily Ghibelline,[3] and, although Spoleto returned to her allegiance in the autumn of the same year,[4] the adherents of the Emperor did not lose heart.   Disaffection was rife even in the *contado* of Perugia, and Raniero, Andrea and Avultrone de' Montemelini, lords of the strong fortress of Monte Gualandro, on the frontiers of the Cortonese, openly espoused the imperial cause.   The letters of the Commune were disregarded, and its ambassadors were driven from the walls by showers of stones.   Thereupon, the Montemelini and their adherents were outlawed, and the citizens marched to take vengeance on the rebels (May, 1249).   Monte Gualandro was sacked and destroyed, and, though Raniero and his brothers made good their escape, the corpse of their father, Andrea di Giacomo, was torn from its sepulchre and, after having been subjected to every kind of insult and indignity, was dragged through the streets of Perugia by the mob.[5]   By a Bull, given from Lyons, on the 9th of February, 1251, and directed to the Potestà and Council of the Commune, Innocent IV. confirmed the sentence of outlawry against the Montemelini and approved the confiscation of their possessions, desiring " to utterly extirpate the pestilence of such great wickedness with the authors

---

[1] *Bollettino* cited, ii. 141 (Doc. xxiv.).

[2] *Cronaca di Fra Salimbene, loc. cit.* ; COULTON, *loc. cit.* ; MURATORI, *Annali*, ad ann. 1282 ; GREGOROVIUS, *op. cit.*, Vol. III. Lib. x. cap. iv. p. 84 n. 59.

[3] FUMI, *Codice Diplomatico*, etc., *op. cit.*, p. 174 (Doc. cclxv.).

[4] SANSI, *Storia del C. di Spoleto, op. cit.*, i. 79.

[5] PELLINI, i. 259 ; BARTOLI, i. 393-398 ; BONAZZI, i. 292-293.   See also the Statute of 1279, Rubric 52, the major part of which is printed by BRIGANTI, *op. cit.*, pp. 72-73 notes.   Andrea di Giacomo had been Potestà of Perugia, in 1218 (see MARIOTTI, *Saggio*, etc., ii. 197, and compare p. 37 *supra*), of Florence, in 1228 (G. VILLANI, vi. 5 ; DEGLI AZZI VITELLESCHI, *Le Relazioni tra la Rep. di Firenze e l' Umbria*, etc., *secondo i documenti del R. Arch. di Stato in Firenze*, Perugia, Tip. Cooperativa, 1904, Vol. I. p. 255), and of Todi in 1238 (CECI, *op. cit.*, i. 131.

thereof." [1] The language of the Pontiff was almost as violent as the actions of the populace.[2]

In 1250, Castel della Pieve, which had revolted from Perugia, returned to its allegiance, and other submissions followed ; [3] while, in December, Frederick passed away, worn out and broken-hearted, at his Apulian castle of Fiorentino. For the last few years of his life disaster had dogged his footsteps. The once faithful Parma had rebelled against him ; [4] his trusted friend and counsellor Pier della Vigna had betrayed him ; [5] his son Enzo was languishing in a Bolognese prison ; [6] all his schemes had failed, and all his toils and victories had profited him nothing. His great antagonist had conquered.

The news of his death was received by the Guelfs with tumultuous joy. Innocent prepared to return to Italy, and, after a triumphant progress through Lombardy, reached Perugia in November, 1251.[7] Nor did he resume his journey toward Rome till he was peremptorily summoned thither by the Senator Brancaleone, in 1253.[8] During his residence in Perugia, he did all in his power to prove his gratitude for her unwavering loyalty ; [9] and, in a Privilege of the 3rd of October, 1252, which was addressed to the Bishop of the city and which is still preserved among the municipal archives, he recalls the exceeding great affliction

---

[1] ". . . tanti criminis pestem funditus cum auctoribus extirpare." This Bull is still preserved among the Archives of Perugia. It is published by BARTOLI, i. 399. Compare *Bollettino* cited, x. 63 (Doc. cxxiii.).

[2] It remained for Pope Alexander IV. to temper justice with mercy and to compel the Commune to reinstate the children of the rebels in all their rights. BARTOLI, i. 490.

[3] PELLINI, i. 260 ; *Bollettino* cited, ix. 132 (Doc. cxx.) ; x. 61-62 (Doc. cxxi.-cxxii.).

[4] BUTLER, *The Lombard Communes, op. cit.*, pp. 301-302 ; COULTON, *op. cit.*, Chap. x. pp. 115 *et seq.*

[5] F. NOVATI, *Pier della Vigna*, in "Con Dante e per Dante." Discorsi e Conferenze tenute a cura del comitato Milanese della Società Dantesca Italiana, M.DCCC.XCVIII. (Milano, Hoepli), pp. 1-33.

[6] See the learned monograph of L. FRATI, *La prigionia del Re Enzo a Bologna*, Bologna, Zanichelli, 1902.

[7] MARIOTTI, *Saggio*, etc., *op. cit.*, iii. 435.

[8] MURATORI, *Annali*, ad ann. 1253 ; GREGOROVIUS, *op. cit.*, Vol. II. Lib. ix. c. vi. p. 834 n. 60.

[9] BONAZZI, i. 297-298. See also *Bollettino* cited, x. 63-67 (Doc. cxxiv.-cxxx.).

and labour which she had endured "pro fidei puritate atque devotionis sinceritate servanda erga Romanam Ecclesiam matrem suam."[1]   Moreover, during those prosperous years, Perugia reasserted her authority over many towns which through fear of the Emperor she had permitted to throw off their allegiance.   Among the rest, Gualdo and Nocera renewed their submissions, through terror rather than good-will;[2] and no doubt Dante's celebrated lines accurately describe their subsequent servitude.[3]   Perugia was not easily forgetful of injuries.

The Guelf party was everywhere triumphant, when the night ride of Manfred out of Acerra and his appearance, on the 2nd of November, 1254, with a mere handful of followers, before the walls of Lucera, changed the aspect of affairs throughout the length and breadth of Italy.   News shortly arrived that Foggia had been taken by storm and that the papal army had abandoned Troia in headlong flight, without striking a blow.   Barletta, Venosa, Acerenza, Melfi, Bari, Trani, Rapolla were either taken by force or voluntarily opened their gates; and well-nigh all Apulia submitted to the conquering arms of the Prince of Taranto. As a natural consequence of these successes, the Ghibelline faction began to take heart.

In August, 1256, Perugia entered into an alliance with Orvieto, to the honour of God, of the Virgin Mary, of the Roman Church, of the Pope and of the Cardinals, *et ad honorem matris nostre alme Urbis*;[4] and, in January, 1259, when Manfred invaded the March of Ancona, Alexander IV. turned to the Perugians for aid, belauding their valour and fidelity in no measured terms; describing them as "ever famous athletes, robust pugilists and elect champions of the Church," and summoning them to fight the battle of the Lord against her persecutors.[5]

---

[1] The document is published by BARTOLI, i. 411-412.

[2] R. GUERRIERI, *Storia di Gualdo Tadino, op. cit.*, pp. 53-58; *Bollettino* cited, ii. 139-141 (Doc. xxii.-xxiii.), 143-145 (Doc. xxvi.-xxvii.).

[3] *Paradiso*, xi. 47-48.   Compare GUERRIERI, *op. cit.*, p. 65.

[4] FUMI, *Codice Dipl., op. cit.*, pp. 208-209 (Doc. cccxxxi.).

[5] *Arch. Stor. It.*, XVI. ii. 484.   This Bull is also printed by CIATTI, *op. cit.*, iii. 382-383.

In the following year, the Ghibelline predominance in Central Italy was temporarily assured by the glorious victory of Montaperto (4 Sept. 1260),

Che fece l' Arbia colorata in rosso.[1]

It seems that there was a Perugian contingent in the defeated army,[2] though so small a one that Bonazzi gratuitously asserts that, at this period, " the Guelfism of Perugia had notably cooled." [3] Certainly, there are no signs of such a change either before or afterwards ; and there was danger enough nearer home to make her fearful for her own safety. Jesi, Cingoli and Recanati had rebelled from the Church ; Camerino and Fermo were in the hands of Manfred's Vicar ; Gubbio, whose *contado* had been given to Perugia by the Pope, in 1257,[4] and with whom she had recently been at war, was now her deadly enemy,[5] while Città di Castello was torn by intestine discords.[6] In 1261, we find the Sacred College appealing to the Perugians " tamquam domus Dei propugnatores fortissimi " ; [7] in 1264, Urban IV. took refuge in Perugia to escape falling into the hands of Pietro Di Vico, who was plotting to surprise him and his Curia in Orvieto ; [8] at the Battle of Benevento (26 Feb., 1266) Perugian knights fought on the side of the victor,[9] and Perugian hands probably helped to raise the *grave mora* [10] which covered all that remained of the blond and beautiful Manfred,

> lo cavalero più fino,
> ch' è fiore gibellina
> sovr' ogn' altro latino.[11]

---

[1] *Inferno*, x. 86.   [2] G. VILLANI, vi. 79.   [3] BONAZZI, i. 302.

[4] *Bollettino* cited, x. 75 (Doc. cxl.) ; PELLINI, i. 264 ; BRIGANTI, p. 98 ; *Arch. Stor. It.*, XVI. ii. 483.

[5] P. CENCI, *Le relazioni fra Gubbio e Perugia*, etc., *ubi cit.*, pp. 547-559, and compare *Bollettino* cited, iii. 202 (Doc. xliii.).

[6] MUZI, *Memorie civili, op. cit.*, i. 65.

[7] The document is printed in *Arch. Stor. It.*, XVI. ii. 486-487.

[8] CALISSE, *I Prefetti Di Vico* (Roma, A cura della R. Società Romana di Storia patria, 1888), p. 39 ; GREGOROVIUS, *op. cit.*, Vol. II. Lib. x. cap. i. p. 884.

[9] PELLINI, i. 272, 273.   [10] *Purgatorio*, iii. 129.

[11] *Rime antiche senesi* (published by the Società Filologica Romana, 1902), p. 31.

Moreover, the sheer savagery of the Perugian enactments against the defeated and disheartened Imperialists is enough to make the blood run cold with horror. In December, 1269, more than a year after the brutal murder of Corradino on the Piazza del Mercato at Naples, it was decreed in the General and Special Councils that " whosoever shall make a ballad (*cantionem*) against King Charles of Anjou, or say or sing it, or shall speak any evil of him, shall, for each offence, pay a fine of a hundred pounds of money ; and, if he be unable to pay the same, shall have his tongue torn out." Proclamation to this effect was to be made monthly through the city.[1] Thus, the penalty which was ordinarily reserved for blasphemy against the Almighty was inflicted upon defamers of the Angevin usurper ; while, lest any mercy should be found in the judgment seat, it was provided by the Statute that the Potestà must be *amator et fidelis Ecclesie et de parte Ecclesie*, and that his election should be null and void *si esset vel fuisset de parte olim Regis Manfredi et de parte seu voluntate Uberti Pelavigini seu etiam Corradini vel eorum heredum vel eorum sequacium in civitate de qua esset electus.*[2]

If, however, Perugia was, as Bartoli declares, " Guelf in her sinews, in her blood and in her marrow," [3] her allegiance to the Pope was never servile ; and, though a true and faithful feudatory of the Church, she often proved a refractory and impatient one. Thus, in two Bulls of the 15th of May and the 15th of July, 1258, Alexander IV. bitterly laments the hostility of the Perugians to his nephew Anibaldo, Rector of the March of Ancona, and complains of the assistance which they had given to the citizens of Fermo, rebels of the Church and enemies of the said Anibaldo. In the first Bull, after recounting the benefits

---

[1] " Quicumque fecerit cantionem contra regem Karolum vel dixerit vel cantaverit solvat pro qualibet vice C libras den. vel aliquam injuriam contra eum dixerit, et si non posset solvere dictam penam amputetur ei lingua secundum quod amputari debet nitenzantibus pro Churradino ex forma Statuti. Et hoc banniatur quolibet mense per civitatem et burgos." *Annales variorum annorum*, c. 310, r., cited by V. ANSIDEI, *Alcune notizie*, etc., *ubi cit.*, p. 597 n.

[2] Statute of 1279, Rubric 4 ; BRIGANTI, *op. cit.*, pp. 189-190.

[3] BARTOLI, i. 413.

which the Apostolic See had heaped upon the Commune, he continues, " But ye, with grief do we say it, as if forgetful of the favours of the aforesaid See, seek to obscure the brightness of your name with dark deeds of impiety"; and finally exclaims, " Are these the works of faithful lieges ? Is this the example of devotion which ye set to other cities ? Is this the return which the Church has deserved for the many benefits which ye have received from her ? Where is that ancient loyalty which ye were wont to have for us and for the Church ? Where is your accustomed prudence ? Where is that boasted fidelity of yours which was noised abroad through all the borders of Italy, yea, almost to the uttermost ends of the World ? " [1]

Moreover, the Perugians were determined not to be priest-ridden. As early as January, 1256, we find the Special and General Council of the Rectors of the Arts and of the *xx boni homines* elected for each Porta, deliberating concern-ing an embassy to be sent to the Pope to demand that the clergy should be subject to lay tribunals—*quod clerici debeant respondere in curia Perusij sicut in statuto contenetur.*[2] According to Pellini, Clement IV. expressed his grief and surprise that the Perugians, who were so loyal to the Apos-tolic See, held the clergy in such small esteem, and especially the Canons of the Cathedral, whose palaces and houses they took for their own use and whom they burdened with enormous taxes;[3] while, a little later, after the death of that Pontiff, the Cardinals wrote from Viterbo, where they were assembled to elect his successor, exhorting the Perugians to desist from forcing the Bishop and clergy to contribute towards the reparation of the walls of the city.[4] So jealous were the citizens of their rights that, when John XXI. re-quested them to send fish from Lake Trasimeno, that he and his Cardinals might eat thereof on Holy Thursday, they forthwith suspected that he was endeavouring to revive, on behalf of the Church, the old imperial claim to the Lake ; [5]

---

[1] ANSIDEI, *Alcune notizie*, etc., *ubi cit.*, p. 598.
[2] *Consilia variorum annorum*, sæc. xiii., c. 82, t.; ANSIDEI, *loc. cit.*, p. 598 n. 3.
[3] PELLINI, i. 274.　　　　　　　[4] *Arch. Stor. It.*, XVI. ii. 488.
[5] "Lacus quoque perusinus totus in nostra et successorum nostrorum erit potestate." See p. 28 *supra*.

and, although the Magistrates finally resolved to send him the fish, they appointed a syndic to accompany it and to explain that it was a free gift and not a tribute.[1]

By the solemn charter of 1278, Rudolf of Hapsburg confirmed all the territorial pretensions of the Popes, and thenceforward the communes and feudatories of Emilia, Romagna, the March of Ancona, the Patrimony of St Peter and the Campagna of Rome held of the Holy See and not of the Empire. This was the great achievement of Nicolas III., and established the temporal authority of the Papacy on a solid legal basis.[2] Even Bologna acknowledged the suzerainty of the Church.[3] So far as Perugia was concerned, the position remained unchanged ; the cities and seigniors who now swore fealty were doing no more than she herself had done over three-quarters of a century earlier ; but, since she could not fail to perceive that the increased power of the Papacy might prove dangerous to her liberties, she grew yearly more watchful and more suspicious, not only of the Popes, but also of the French influence in Italy.[4] We have already seen how she flouted the French Martin IV. ;[5] while, in 1286, by the terms of her alliance with Todi, Spoleto, and Narni, the right of the Ultramontane Popes to assistance in men or money was categorically denied.[6] Neither, after the

---

[1] PELLINI, i. 291 (ad ann. 1277). The request was no new one. See BEL-FORTI, *Bolle e Diplomi*, saec. xiii. Ni 21, 25, 40, 41, 48, 49, 53, 59, and *Arch. Stor. It.*, XVI. ii. 483.

[2] GREGOROVIUS, *op. cit.*, Vol. III. Lib. x. cap. iv. p. 68 ; MURATORI, *Annali*, ad ann. 1278 ; SISMONDI, *op. cit.*, Vol. II. cap. xxii. p. 20.

[3] VITO VITALE, *Il Dominio della Parte Guelfa in Bologna*, *op. cit.*, p. 23. Compare L. TONINI, *Rimini nel Secolo XIII.* (Rimini, Tip. Malavolti ed Ercolani, 1862), pp. 129-130. The first Count of Romagna for the Church was Bertoldo Orsini, the Pope's nephew.

[4] This sentiment of antipathy to the foreigner was general throughout Italy, and the French were cordially hated even by the party to whose political purposes they directly ministered. Compare COULTON, *op. cit.*, p. 237.

[5] See p. 74 *supra*, and the various Bulls of 1283 and 1284 recorded in *Arch. Stor. It.*, XVI. ii. 489-490. GREGOROVIUS (*op. cit.*, Vol. III. Lib. x. cap. iv. p. 75) speaks of this outbreak as a desertion of the papal cause and considers it as a result of the Sicilian Vespers. Personally, I cannot agree with him. His theory, as I conceive it, confounds *post hoc* with *propter hoc*.

[6] Although there is, as far as I am aware, no record of this alliance to be found among the Perugian Archives, its existence is amply proved by the *Registrum vetus instrumentorum* of Todi, which, however, I have had no opportunity of

removal of the Papal See to Avignon, did she abate one jot
of her vigilance ; and we find that, in 1308, when the Apostolic Legate at Orvieto was invited to take up his residence
in Perugia, he was informed that, if he did so, he must come
as Cardinal Napoleone Orsini and not as Apostolic Legate,
since the citizens had no mind to permit his visit to prejudice their liberties.[1]   In like manner, in the following year,
when Cardinal Arnaud de Pellagrue demanded troops for the
war against the Venetians, it was solemnly debated in the
Collegio de' Dottori, whether, if his request were complied
with, such compliance could be construed as an admission
that the Church had a right to demand the assistance
granted.   Nor was it until this question had been answered
in the negative that the Magistrates proceeded to consider
the nature of the aid which they were prepared to give.
They eventually sent a subsidy of five hundred and fifty
golden florins.[2]

examining.   The Bull of Boniface VIII., whereby it was annulled, in December,
1300, is published by FUMI, *Codice Dipl.*, etc., *op. cit.*, p. 379 (Doc. dxci.).   For
the clause above mentioned, referring to the Ultramontane Popes, the only
authorities which I have found are BONAZZI, *op. cit.*, i. 309, and CECI, *Todi nel
Medio Evo*, *op. cit.*, vol. i. p. 179.   It is presumable that the latter writer has
verified his assertion by consulting the original document ; but, it is sufficiently
obvious that he has copied his phraseology from Bonazzi ; and, as I have already
hinted, Bonazzi's statements will always bear examination.

[1] PELLINI, i. 351.
[2] PELLINI, i. 358.

6

CHAPTER VI

TO THE END OF THE CENTURY

THE latter half of the thirteenth century sparkles and coruscates with illustrious names—great sovereigns, great pontiffs, great warriors, great statesmen, great lawyers, great men of science, great philosophers and divines, great architects, great poets and painters. There were giants in the Earth in those days and they wrought as giants. It was an epoch of unparalleled achievement, of excessive, because premature activity, intellectual and political.[1] Nothing was done upon a small scale ; its crimes were as magnificent as its virtues, its sinners as splendid as its saints. Through all the wars and pestilences of the dark ages the law of the survival of the fittest had not been tampered with ; feeble organisms were doomed to speedy destruction, and character had an energy unknown to-day. The " strenuous life " was not only talked about, it was lived ; and the most terrible outrages against God and man were held scarcely blameworthy, if only they were done " manfully." [2] " The men of that time had all the vices except triviality, all the virtues except moderation." Dante's *Inferno* is peopled with heroic figures—men who, like Farinata degli Uberti, " had Hell itself in great despite," [3] or, like the grandson of the good Gualdrada,

"Wrought mightily alike with brain and sword." [4]

There is the second Frederick, the brilliant, the chivalrous,

---

[1] See J. B. LIGHTFOOT, D.D., *Historical Essays* (London : Macmillan & Co., 1895), pp. 94 *et seq.*

[2] Thus when Guy de Montfort murdered Prince Henry "in grembo a Dio" (*Inferno*, xii. 119) there did not lack a contemporary chronicler to praise the deed, as being a manfully executed vengeance : " Occiditur in ultionem viriliter paternæ mortis." Compare GREGOROVIUS, *op. cit.*, Vol. III. Lib. x. cap. iv. p. 78 n. 9.

[3] *Inferno*, x. 36.   [4] *Inferno*, xvi. 39.

the wonder of the World ;[1] there Pier della Vigna, his chancellor ;[2] there Guido of Montefeltro, the great Ghibelline chieftain,[3] and there Paolo Malatesta, who gave all for love.[4] Alone of contemporary sinners, we encounter Celestine V. in the dark plains of Ante-Hell, a miserable weakling, and, as a weakling, disdained alike of Justice and of Mercy.[5]

As a result of this universal and all-pervading energy, the material progress of the communes was enormous, and for Perugia, in particular, it was a period of ever-increasing power and prosperity. The destruction of the House of Hohenstaufen and the triumph of the Guelf cause had left her supreme in Umbria ; and, strong in her alliance with Rome and with the Papacy, she was able to devote much of her energy to administrative reforms, to the erection of splendid edifices within her walls, and to the consolidation of her dominion in the *contado*. Taxation was systematized, and the property of the citizens was assessed and registered ;[6] an *Archivio*, or Records Office, was established with suitable officials for the custody of the public documents;[7] the length of the mile was fixed and measured from each of the principal gates of the city ;[8] the *piazze* and streets were

---

[1] *Inferno*, x. 119.   [2] *Inferno*, xiii. 58 *et seq.*

[3] *Inferno*, xxvii. 67 *et seq.* In this connection I may mention that a very excellent study of Guido of Montefeltro has been published by R. HONIG, *Guido da Montefeltro*, Bologna, Tip. Zamorani e Albertazzi, 1901.

[4] *Inferno*, v. 73-142.   [5] *Inferno*, iii. 59-60.

[6] PELLINI, i. 275-276 : " Et si soggionge che del presente anno [1266] fossero fatti i contrasti e allibrati i bene di tutti i Cittadini di Perugia." The earliest notice which I have found of the *catasto* in the Perugian *contado* belongs to the year 1310. See PELLINI, i. 371, and compare BRIGANTI, *L' antico comune della Spina* (Perugia, Tip. Umbra, 1904), p. 19.

[7] PELLINI, i. 307. See also G. DEGLI AZZI, *Per la storia dell' antico Archivio del Comune di Perugia*, in *Bollettino* cited, Vol. VIII. fasc. 1, and especially the documents there published on pp. 44-50.

[8] PELLINI, i. 283, ad ann. 1273 : " Et fu deliberato che si determinasse quanto havesse à stendersi il Miglio, e che se ne dovesse prendere la misura dello spatio che dovea contenere, e si terminasse da huomini esperti e intelligenti." Compare the Statute of 1342, Lib. iii. Rubrics 118 and 213. At this period the mile measured 1275 *passi*, each *passo* containing five feet. In the sixteenth century, however, it seems to have been reduced to 1000 *passi*, each *passo* containing five feet, and each foot consisting of fifteen inches (*quindecim digitorum*). Statute of 1528, Vol. I. Rubric 25. It is said that, judging by the old mile-stones in the neighbourhood of the city, the Perugian mile must have exceeded 2000 metres in length. BONAZZI i. 310 n.

paved,[1] and roads were constructed to Città di Castello, to Marsciano and to Castel della Pieve ;[2] the Carpena was bridged between Fratta and Montone and the Nestore at Compignano ; the Ponte Nuovo was built above Deruta and the other bridges over the Tiber were repaired and protected by towers upon the further side.[3]   Many villages of the *contado* were fortified, either at the public expense or by individual enterprise ;[4] for the old short-sighted policy which had ruined Castiglione del Lago had long ago been abandoned, and the right of every *universitas* to surround itself with walls was freely acknowledged.[5]   Castiglione itself was now a fortified town with a strong citadel, and a project was on foot for converting it into an island by means of a wide and deep ditch to be cut through the base of the promontory upon which it was situated[6] ; while the western frontier of the State was protected by the erection of the fortress of Beccatiquello on the Chiana.[7]   Commerce flourished and commercial treaties were entered into with

[1] The work of paving the Piazza seems to have begun in 1253 (*Brevi Annali, ubi cit.*, p. 56).   As to the paving of the streets, compare PELLINI, i. 279 ; MARIOTTI, *Saggio, etc., op. cit.*, i. 18.   I shall have occasion to refer to the subject again in a subsequent chapter.

[2] PELLINI, i. 317, 318, 319.   Compare GIGLIARELLI, *Perugia antica e Perugia moderna Indicazioni Storico-Topografiche* (Perugia, Tip. Cooperativa Editrice, 1907-1908), pp. 129-130.

[3] PELLINI, i. 287, 314, 315, 327.   Such a tower is still to be seen at the southern extremity of the Ponte Nuovo.

[4] PELLINI, i. 287, 292, 316, 317, etc. ; BRIGANTI, *Citta Dominanti*, etc., *op. cit.*, pp. 127-128.

[5] Statute of 1279, Rubric 408: " Quelibet universsitas castri seu ville comitatus perusii possit se reducere ad fortilitiam et castrum facere et murare eorum espensis sine alicuius contraditione et potestas et capitaneus teneantur eis dare si voluerint suprastantes pro operibus faciendis et dare debeant universsitati auxilium et favorem contraditione aliqua non obstante."   Compare the Statute of 1342, Lib. iv. Rubric 29 : " *Che glie casteglie del contado de peroscia se mureno.*"

[6] PELLINI, i. 321-322.   Compare the Statute of 1279, Rubric 216: " *De custodia arcis Castilionis clusini,*" etc., and Rubric 217 : " *De CC. lib. expendendis in arce Castilionis clusini.*"

[7] PELLINI, i, 314.   The *Rocca* was built in the last decade of the thirteenth century, but the name of *Beccatiquello* was, perhaps, bestowed upon it at a later date.   Over against it, in Sienese territory, was another tower called *Beccatiquesto*.   The remains of both of them are still to be seen.   (Compare F. PETRUCCI, *I confini Senesi di Val di Chiana* in the *Bullettino senese di Storia Patria*, ii. 284.)   There was another *Beccatiquello* in the Spoletino.   See *Arch. Stor. It.*, XVI. i. 72.

Florence [1] and other cities ; [2] the *Arti* were classified ; [3] an annual fair was decreed which lasted a full month, from the 17th of October to the 16th of November ; [4] and an immense impetus was given to the manufacture of woollen fabrics by the summoning of the Frati Umiliati from Lombardy. [5] The coinage was improved, skilled work-men being brought from Lucca ; and, ere long, the gold florin of Perugia rivalled that of Florence. [6] Boni-fazio da Verona was commissioned to write his " *Eulistea*," [7] and a tame lion, the living emblem of the Guelf Party, was maintained at the public expense. [8] The Statute was

---

[1] *Bollettino della R. Dep. di Storia patria per l'Umbria, op. cit.,* ix. 122-124 (Doc. cix.—"Capitula cum comunitate Florentie," 1235, Marzo 14). The document is published in its entirety by BARTOLI, i. 415-424. Compare also the *Concordia tra Firenze e Perugia* of 1218, printed by A. DEL VECCHIO and E. CASANOVA in the appendix to their work on *Le Rappresaglie nei Comuni medievali e specialmente in Firenze* (Bologna, Zanichelli, 1894), pp. 285-287.

[2] Compare BRIGANTI, *op. cit.,* cap. viii. In the *Constituto del C. di Siena* (edition ZDEKAUER), Dist. III. Rubrics 385 and 387, allusion is made to a treaty with Perugia, and the terms of the *Societas* in question may be gathered from the *Caleffo Vecchio,* ad ann. 1237. See LISINI, *Inventario generale del R. Arch. di Stato in Siena* (Siena, Lazzeri, 1899), Parte I. p. 91.

[3] BONAZZI, i. 311. The Statute of 1279 makes honourable mention of both the *Arte della Mercanzia* and the *Arte del Cambio* (Rubric 48) ; while PELLINI (i. 316) records the fact, that in 1295, the *Arte degli Orefici* was included among the other *Arti* of the city. See BONAINI, *Prefazione* cited, pp. xlvii-xlviii and DEGLI AZZI, *Il Collegio della Mercanzia,* Perugia, Terese, 1901.

[4] PELLINI, i. 289 (ad ann. 1276) : " Fu ordinato che si publicasse et intimasse la Fiera di Ogni Santi libera et immune d' ogni gravezza per 15 giorni innanzi, e 15 doppo, et che fosse lecito ad ogn' uno di venirvi non ostante la represaglie che v' erano in alcune città vicine," etc. Compare BRIGANTI, *op. cit.,* cap. viii. § 82.

[5] BONAZZI, i. 311. See also the Statute of 1279, Rubric 193 : " *De fratribus humiliatis havocandis pro drapparia facienda.*"

[6] VERMIGLIOLI, *Della Zecca e delle Monete Perugine* (Perugia, Tip. Baduel, 1816), p. 12 and Doc. i. The silver money was to be made "ad modum ponderis et ligæ comunis Senæ," while the gold coinage was to be based on that of Florence. *Cf. Brevi Annali, ubi cit.,* p. 56.

[7] See page 3 *supra,* and compare PELLINI, i. 313.

[8] PELLINI, i. 319 : " And a lion was brought to Perugia, and it was resolved by the Council that a dwelling-place (*stanza*) should be built for it at the expense of the City, and that a man should be appointed to take care of it, and that he should receive 50 *libre di danari* for his salary every year." The lion's quarters seem to have been in the *Via dell' Ospedale,* "nel popolo di S. Errico verso il Campo di Battaglia, tra la chiesetta di S. Giuseppe e la bella fabbrica inalzata

compiled,[1] the University created [2] ; water was brought
from Monte Pacciano ; [3] the *platea comunis* was adorned
with a noble fountain [4] ; the Palazzo Pubblico was commenced,[5] and, in the last year of the century, it was resolved
wholly to rebuild the Cathedral, that same Fra Bevignate
who had been employed upon the Fountain being appointed
sovrastante, as one " ad hujusmodi opera facienda solicitus et
expertus." [6]   And these achievements are all the more
marvellous when we remember the wars which were waged
with neighbouring cities and the constant assistance
demanded by the Popes and by the allied communes.   The
Perugians wrought as did the Jews in the days of Nehemiah,
when every man builded with his sword girded by his side,
and half of them held the spears, from the rising of the
morning till the stars appeared.   There were Perugians in the
Guelf army which dictated terms to Siena, in 1270 ; [7]
Perugian cavalry fought at Campaldino [8] and against Guido
da Montefeltro in the Romagna,[9] and doubtless there were

dal Cardinale Armellini ad uso di pesceria."   The position of *custos leonis* in the
Mediæval Communes was one of some importance and responsibility, and,
among his other privileges, seems to have been that of exemption from military
service (compare *Il Libro di Montaperti*, edited by C. PAOLI, Firenze, Vieusseux,
1889, p. 54).   In 1304, there were two lions and a leopard in Perugia
(PELLINI, i. 334) and, in 1434, we read that two young lions escaped from their
stanza and out of the Porta S. Susanna (*Arch. Stor. It.* XVI. i. 382).   Later on
the Baglioni kept lions.   On the subject in general compare my *Palio and Ponte*,
op. cit., p. 13 n. 2.

[1] In 1279.   Compare *Bollettino* cited, ii. 5 *et seq.*

[2] Attempts have been made to trace the origin of the Perugian University back
to the eleventh century, but according to the better opinion it owes its existence
to a decree of 1276.   The principal work on the subject is, of course, the
*Memorie istoriche della perugina Università degli studî e dei suoi professori raccolte
dal* P. D. VINCENZIO BINI, Monaco Cassinese (Perugia, 1816).

[3] PELLINI, i. 294 ; *Brevi Annali, ubi cit.*, p. 57.

[4] See BARTOLI, i, 438 *et seq.* ; BONAZZI, i. 365, and above all BELFORTI,
Memorie istoriche della Fonte di Piazza, Ms. N. 1348 in the Communal Library of
Perugia.

[5] Statute of 1279, Rubric 215 ; A. BELLUCCI, *I Palazzi della Comunità di
Perugia nel secolo XIII.* in *Bollettino* cited, v. 793-796.

[6] See the document published by Can. L. ROTELLI, *Il Duomo di Perugia*,
op. cit., pp. 13-16.

[7] PELLINI, i. 281.

[8] PELLINI, i. 302.

[9] *Brevi Annali, ubi cit.*, ad ann. 1281 ; PELLINI, 295, 296.

THE FONTE MAGGIORE

Perugians with Messer Giovanni di Appia before Forlì, when the wily Ghibelline chieftain made horrible slaughter of the Guelfs

e di Franceschi sanguinoso mucchio.[1]

Perugian, as well as Florentine levies, were to be found in the ranks of Charles of Anjou before Messina,[2] and Perugian knights rode to the aid of their suzerain when he beleaguered Palestrina.[3] From 1282 to 1296, Perugia was on ill terms with Foligno, and often at open war with her ; [4] in 1291, an expedition was sent against Assisi,[5] and, in 1295, hostilities were commenced against Nocera for the protection of the lords of Somareggio,[6] while, in 1298, war with Gubbio was scarcely averted.[7]

Nevertheless, if the times were still troublous, men were weary of conflict and longed for peace.[8] There was an ever-increasing willingness to settle disputes by arbitration, and we find Perugia continually exerting herself to compose dissensions. She mediated between Assisi and Bettona when they quarrelled about the body of S. Crispolto ; between Foligno and Nocera and Foligno and Montefalco ; between Terni and Narni and Narni and Stroncone ; between Todi and Amelia, Todi and Orvieto, and Spoleto and Todi ; while, in her turn, she did not disdain to accept the mediation of her neighbours, and especially of the Orvietani and Todini. So successful was her diplomacy and so equitable were her decisions that she began to be looked upon as the natural arbitrator between the Umbrian communes. Intestine discords were often allayed by the election of a Perugian Potestà ; and, in 1293, when Todi was torn with civic strife, ambassadors were sent to seek the aid of Perugia, openly declaring that she was " the one true

---

[1] *Inferno*, xxvii. 44.   Compare HONIG, *Guido da Montefeltro, op. cit.*, pp. 34 *et seq.*
[2] PELLINI, i. 295.
[3] PELLINI, i. 318.
[4] PELLINI, i. 296, 302, 304-305 ;   *Arch. Stor. It.*, XVI. ii. pp. 489-490.
[5] GRAZIANI, *ubi cit.*, 520-522.   *Cf. Brevi Annali*, ad ann.
[6] PELLINI, i. 316.
[7] PELLINI, i. 321 ; P. CENCI, *ubi cit.*, pp. 561-562.
[8] Compare ZDEKAUER, *La Vita pubblica nel Dugento, op. cit.*, p. 20.

leech " who could heal their city of the disease from which
it suffered.[1]

It was Umbria's golden age, but destined, in the opening
years of the fourteenth century, to be followed by an age
of iron.

[1] " Quare affectuose rogant quod, prudenter ac sine mora, per commune
Perusij, qui MEDICVS VERVS est, hæc plaga valeat liberari." PELLINI, i. 312.
Read also pages 277 to 322, and compare BONAZZI, i. 311-312.

CHAPTER VII

THE ECCLESIASTICAL STATE

A T the beginning of the fourteenth century, the
supreme administrative and executive authority in
each of the Provinces of the Ecclesiastical State was
the Papal Rector, whose *curia* exercised its functions in the
name of the sovereign Pontiff. The power of the Rector
was, however, far from being absolute ; apostolic privileges,
acts of submission, customary rights and ancient traditions
of free government combined to limit and vary his jurisdiction ; and although, here and there, cities and feudatories
had been reduced to almost complete subjection, many of
the communes still maintained their independence practically
unimpaired. Yet, for all its limitations, the sovereign
authority of the Rector was a fact which, in theory at any
rate, was rarely disputed ; and its existence constituted a
strong element of union and order, completing and har-
monizing the various local governments of the feuds and
communes, without destroying their autonomy. To this
system the removal of the Apostolic See to Avignon gave
an irreparable shock. Like weeds in an abandoned garden,
petty despots sprang up on every hand to dispute the jurisdiction of the Church ; the whole Papal State was in revolt,
and, in Italy, the authority of the Popes was reduced to wellnigh nothing. The French Legates and Rectors, who were
sent by Clement V., were not only ignorant of and
indifferent to Italian susceptibilities, but cared for nothing
but the filling of their own pockets ; and, at the very
moment when mediæval institutions were crumbling into
ruin, and the violent clashing of interests and passions
demanded an unusually wise and strong government, their

tyrannies and exactions were all too often the direct cause of anarchy and rebellion.[1]

Already, in 1305, Florence had treated the Papal anathemas with contemptuous indifference,[2] and, in 1306, the Apostolic Legate was not only compelled to flee from Bologna to save his life, but was shamelessly plundered as he fled.[3]   In the Patrimony, the extortions and oppressions of the papal representatives drove even the faithful Orvieto to revolt;[4] while, to the southward, Rome was steadily substituting her own authority for that of the Church. As early as 1300, Toscanella had submitted to the Republic,[5] and the subjection of other cities followed.   In 1307, the Romans made themselves masters of Amelia, which attempted resistance, but, receiving no succour from the Rector, was forced to come to terms, agreeing to render military service and to send six *iocatores* to the annual games on Monte Testaccio.[6]   A little later an expedition was undertaken against Corneto, and, in 1311, Sutri, which had long been immediately subject to the Church, transferred her allegiance to the Republic, whose *missi* were continually travelling through the towns of the Patrimony.   In April, 1312, they actually presented themselves before Montefiascone, the seat of the Curia and the residence of the Rector. Against those who refused to obey them the Romans promptly took up arms, and, in September of the same year, they moved against Montalto, Canino and other places in the Maremma.   Thence they passed into the *contado* of Viterbo, advancing as far as the hospital of S. Giovanni in

[1] M. ANTONELLI, *Vicende della Dominazione Pontificia nel Patrimonio di S. Pietro in Tuscia dalla Traslazione della Sede alla Restaurazione dell' Albornoz.*   Estratto dall' " Arch. della R. Soc. Romana di Storia patria," Vol. XXXV. e XXXVI. (Roma, 1904), pp. 3-4 ;   GREGOROVIUS, *op. cit.,* Vol. III. Lib. xi. cap. i. pp. 212-213.

[2] G. VILLANI, *Cronica,* viii. 82-85.

[3] G. VILLANI, viii. 85 ;   DINO COMPAGNI, *Cronica,* Lib. iii. c. 17 ; MURATORI, *Annali,* ad ann. 1306.

[4] *Le antiche cronache d' Orvieto,* in the *Arch. Stor. It.,* Serie v. (1889), iii. 30 ;   FUMI, *Codice Dipl., op. cit.,* pp. 416-419 ;   ANTONELLI, *op. cit.,* pp. 6-7.

[5] GREGOROVIUS, *op. cit.,* Vol. III. Lib. x. cap. vi. p. 124.

[6] G. PARDI, *Relazioni di Amelia con il Comune di Roma ed i Nobili Romani,* in *Bollettino* cited, i. 579 and Doc. i. pp. 585-587.   For " *iocatores cestare,*" in line 72 of the document, read " iocatores Testace."

of showing himself austere and unbending to ancient allies and vassals, " ex mala informatione assumpta." [1] Strange, indeed, was the dilemma of the Papacy, constrained to seek assistance and protection from the very men whom it distrusted and feared ! [2]

The descent of Lewis of Bavaria, in 1327,[3] had added enormously to the general confusion, and his departure failed to extinguish the fires which he had kindled. Amelia and Todi continued in open revolt, and, as late as 1340, we find the Rector imploring the assistance of Perugia against the rebels ; [4] while the death of Robert of Naples, in 1343, followed by the murder of Andrea, in 1345, was a heavy blow not only to the papal authority, but also to the Guelf party. At Viterbo, there were scenes of wild exultation. In opprobrium and derision of the memory of Robert, the Imperial Eagle was set up in the Piazza with the arms of Anjou beneath its feet, while the populace kneeled before it in adoration, offering candles and oblations.[5] However, the two events which, above all else, contributed to divest the Pope of every shadow of authority in the Ecclesiastical State were the revolution of Cola di Rienzo and the Great Pestilence of 1348. The former undermined the very foundations of the temporal power, disclosing the weakness of the Papacy and its utter incapacity for the direction of public affairs ; while the general dissolution of society, and the loosening of all the bonds of law and order

[1] CANESTRINI, *Alcuni documenti risguardanti le relazioni politiche dei Papi d' Avignone coi Comuni d' Italia*, etc., Doc. vi., in the *Arch. Stor. It.*, Serie i. Tom. vii. App. pp. 356-359.

[2] FILIPPINI, *ubi cit.*, p. 175. Compare, as to Perugia, the alternate entreaties and lamentations of the Popes in " *Regesto e Documenti* " at the end of the *Cronache Perugine*, in *Arch. Stor. It.*, XVI. ii. pp. 493 *et seq.*

[3] See Chapter XI., *infra*.

[4] ANTONELLI, *Notizie Umbre tratte dai registri del Patrimonio di S. Pietro in Tuscia*, in *Bollettino* cited, ix. 381-398, 469-506. Compare SCALVANTI, *I Ghibellini di Amelia e Lodovico il Bavaro*, in *Bollettino* cited, xii. 235 *et seq.*

[5] CALISSE, *I Prefetti Di Vico, op. cit.*, p. 71, and App. Doc. xc. : " . . . quandam non modicum aquile ymaginem, signum rastelli et florum lilii tenentem subtus pedes, in opprobrium seu derisionem memorie inclite recordationis Roberti regis Sicilie in platea civitatis Viterbiensis de novo positam tamquam ydolum flexis genibus et amotis caputiis adorarunt et adorant, publice offerendo eidem ymagini candelas et alias," etc.

which followed the latter, afforded an opportunity for new usurpations and for the creation of new signories. The revolt of Michael of Cesena, and the writings of William of Occam, "the Invincible Doctor," of Marsiglio of Padua and John of Jandun had completely revolutionized human thought ; and the consequent decay of Ecclesiastical and Imperial authority was taken advantage of by the Italian communes, which now aspired to complete independence.

Thus Cola di Rienzo owed his success to the fact that he translated into action the aspirations of the age in which he lived. The principles which he enunciated were equally subversive of the authority of the Empire and of the Church ; and albeit he, at first, professed the most profound devotion to the Holy See, there can be no doubt that, in Rome at any rate, he aimed at substituting his own government for that of the Pope and only delayed putting himself in open opposition to his sovereign until he should be strong enough to do so with impunity. As soon as his power was increased by the support and favour of the communes, he published the famous edict of the 1st of August, 1347, whereby he revoked all the privileges which the Emperors had granted to the Church, thus dealing a terrible blow to the papal jurisdiction ; he occupied the Sabina and the Patrimony, declaring that, in so doing, he was obeying the will of the People ; he exacted tribute from the communes, and, having expelled the Papal Vicar, ruled as a true and absolute despot.[1]

Then it was that he formed the idea of a confederation of the communes and seigniors of all Italy, which should enable him to assert her independence against both Pope and Emperor. He invited the cities to send their syndics to Rome, and, at the same time, he despatched letters to the despots of Lombardy and of the Ecclesiastical State, promising the legitimation of their sovereignties.[2] Many,

[1] FILIPPINI, *op. cit.*, pp. 177-178 ; ANTONELLI, *op. cit.*, p. 111 ; GREGOROVIUS, *op. cit.*, Vol. III. Lib. xi. cap. vi. ; FUMI, *I Registri del Ducato di Spoleto*, *op. cit.*, p. 182, xvii. § 58.

[2] See FILIPPINI, *ubi cit.*, p. 178, where the *Epistolario di Cola di Rienzo* a cura di A. GABRIELLI (Roma, 1890), n. 35, i. 340, is cited : " sub illo

who at first had been doubtful and diffident, hastened to send solemn embassies, as, for example, the Malatesta, who, doubtless, had a fellow-feeling for one who was a rebel like themselves, who had taken the title of Tribune and Liberator of Rome, even as they had taken the title of Liberators of the People, and in whom they hoped to find a defender of their cause and of their rights.

Among the earliest of his allies was Perugia, who had been deeply offended by news which arrived from Avignon, on the 8th of July, 1346, that Clement VI. had declared the Commune immediately subject to the Holy See. The announcement seems to have been made in the course of a decision touching the Church of S. Giovanni in Marsciano, and was, probably, a mere *obiter dictum*; but that fact did nothing to mitigate the indignation of the Perugians. For nearly half a century they had been accustomed to regard the Pope as little more than a useful pawn in the game which they were playing, and their wrath was only equalled by their surprise.[1] In October, Clement wrote exhorting them to assist the Rector against the rebels of the Patrimony;[2] but they appear to have paid no attention to his prayers; while their resentment naturally led them to acquiesce in the establishment of "the good estate," and to lend a willing ear to the overtures of the Tribune. They assisted him in his war against Giovanni Di Vico,[3] and sent a splendid embassy to Rome, consisting of ten ambassadors, two for each Porta, with an escort of a hundred men-at-arms, accompanied by "quinquaginta pueris cum equis indutis et armatis et aptis ad solatia et hastiludia facienda."[4] Florence and other communes hesitated to accept the banners which Cola offered them, lest the ceremony should be regarded

pretextu citationis . . . sinodum constitueram celebrare ubi omnes tyrannos Italiæ dulcissimis litteris convocaram illis distributionem honorum et iustificationes dominatuum pollicendo." Unfortunately, it appears that all these letters have been lost.

[1] GRAZIANI, ad ann. ; PELLINI, i. 569-570.
[2] *Arch. Stor. It.*, XVI. ii. 533.
[3] CALISSE, *op. cit.*, p. 74 ; GREGOROVIUS, *op. cit.*, Vol. III. Lib. xi. cap. vi. p. 375.
[4] *Chronicon Mutinense*, in MURATORI, *Rer. Italic. Script.*, xv. col. 608.

as an infeudation ; [1] but Perugia, now as ever proud to proclaim herself the daughter of Imperial Rome, was deterred by no such scruple. According to the chronicler, "the Tribune espoused the ten ambassadors with a single ring ; and, lastly, he gave them a gonfalon or standard with the arms of Constantine, the Emperor, to wit a White Eagle with an Olive Garland in its beak, upon a red field ; and at its feet were letters written : ASIA, AFRICA ET EVROPA ; the which gonfalon the said Tribune gave unto the Commune of Perugia for greatness and for magnificence, saying, 'Bear this, on my behalf, to the Commune of Perugia in token of fraternity and love.' Wherefore it was held in great honour. And, after our ambassadors had tarried in the City of Rome for about the space of a month, making jousts and tournaments with other very solemn feasts, they took their leave and returned to Perugia." [2]

It is true that, later on, Cola di Rienzo gave proof of inexcusable weakness, openly retracting everything that he had said, and pretending that he had invited the despots to Rome only to hang them all ; [3] but the movement to which he had given so vigorous an impulse could not be arrested by his fall. His work was continued, though with other and less noble motives, by Giovanni Di Vico, who, taking advantage of the propitious moment, established a principality and proceeded to conquer all the cities of the Patrimony. The Malatesta, already lords of Rimini, Pesaro, Fano and Fossombrone, possessed themselves of Ancona, Sinigaglia, Osimo, Recanati, Jesi, Ascoli, and thus became masters of nearly all the March. Giovanni di Ricciardo Manfredi made himself despot of Faenza, and Francesco Ordelaffi, who had for some time been the acknowledged master of Cesena and Forlì, occupied Medula, Castrocaro, and Brettinoro, with the secret assistance of Manfredi and the Pepoli of Bologna ; while the military incapacity and overweening ambition of Astorgio di Durafort, Count of

---

[1] GREGOROVIUS, *op. cit.*, Vol. III. Lib. xi. cap. vi. pp. 382 and 404 n. 41.

[2] *Arch. Stor. It.*, XVI. i. 144-145 ; FABRETTI, *Cronache*, i. 97 ; PELLINI, i. 879 ; *Chronicon Estense* in MURATORI, *Rer. Italic. Script.*, xv. col. 441 ; G. VILLANI, xii. 90.

[3] FILIPPINI, *ubi cit.*, p. 179.

Romagna and Papal Legate, only resulted in the acquisition of Bologna by the Visconti of Milan. On the 23rd of October, 1350, Galeazzo, the nephew of the Archbishop, entered the city with twelve hundred men-at-arms ; and, on the following day, the *Consilium populi et masse populi Civitatis Bononie* accepted the signory of their new masters by 486 votes to 43.[1] The consequences were far-reaching, for Bologna had hitherto constituted a " buffer-state" between the Lombards, the Venetians and the Emiliani, on the one hand, and the communes of Central Italy on the other ; whereas, now that it had fallen into the hands of a Lombard despot, its neutral character was lost, and it at once became a serious menace to the Tuscan provinces. Indeed, hardly had Giovanni Visconti set foot in the Ecclesiastical State than he attempted to extend his dominion to the southward ; while the Florentines, fully conscious of their peril, sought to interpose a barrier to his ambition in the shape of a league with Perugia and Siena. In the war which followed, the Pope deserted his ancient allies, and, by his reconciliation with the Visconti, almost drove the communes of Perugia and Florence to rebellion. Indeed, it is certain that, for a time, those two powerful cities, which " in devotion to the Church and in defence of its vassals, had been wont to shine like two great lights, set not under a bushel but upon a candlestick by the hand of a perfect artificer," [2] aimed at overthrowing the papal sovereignty in Italy.[3]

Before he died, Clement saw the whole of the Ecclesiastical State in hopeless revolt ; and only with the coming of the great warrior-priest, Albornoz, did the Church begin to regain something of that which she had lost.

Of the wars and conquests of Perugia during this period

---

[1] SORBELLI, *La Signoria di Gio. Visconti a Bologna e le sue relazioni con la Toscana* (Bologna, Zanichelli, 1901), pp. 33-35.

[2] *Arch. Stor. It.*, XVI. ii. 515 : " Habet antiquorum fida relatio quod dicta comunia civitatum Florentie et Perusii que pre ceteris de Italia in Ecclesie devotione ac fidelium ac devotorum ipsius defensione perlucent velud duo magna luminaria, non sub modio sed super candelabro posita manu perfecti opificis," etc.

[3] FILIPPINI, *ubi cit.*, p. 184.

I shall treat with some detail in the following chapters. Enough in this place to emphasize the fact that the utter weakness of the Papacy during the whole of the first half of the fourteenth century should alone suffice to cast considerable doubt on the assertion of certain English writers that Perugia was never an independent commune in the same sense that Florence and Siena were independent.[1] The contrary is the case ; and the great jurist, Bartolo da Sassoferrato, stated only the simple truth when he declared " *quod Civitas Perusina non subsit Ecclesiæ nec Imperio.*" In the heyday of her power, Perugia owned no temporal suzerain and brooked no interference, but treated Pope and Emperor alike as mere pawns in the great game which she was playing for the lordship of Umbria.

[1] See, for example, SYMONDS and DUFF GORDON, *The Story of Perugia, op. cit.,* p. 17, and W. BOULTING, *History of the Italian Republics, op. cit.,* p. 446. Both these works stand sadly in need of thorough revision ; while a large part of the former, at any rate, should be wholly rewritten. It has already gone through five or six editions, apparently without correction, and the time has surely come when, if it is to continue to be of any use to the serious student, it should be brought into line with the results of modern research.

TOMB OF POPE BENEDICT XI IN THE CHURCH OF S. DOMENICO

CHAPTER VIII

FROM BONIFACE VIII. TO HENRY VII.

ON the 11th of October, 1303, Boniface VIII. "died of
rage, like a poisoned rat in a hole." With him fell
the mediæval Papacy; and it has been well said that the
drama of Anagni is to be set against the drama of Canossa.
His successor, the mild and gentle Benedict XI., took refuge
in Perugia, where he died in the following July, not without
suspicion of foul play, and for eleven weary months the
discordant Cardinals wrangled in the " Palazzo del Papa." [1]
Finally, the patience of the Perugians was exhausted, and
steps were taken to force the Conclave to a decision.   The
election of Clement V. (5th June, 1305) was the result of a
compromise, and was speedily followed by the removal of
the Papal See to Avignon, with the disastrous consequences
which I have already indicated.

Perugia was almost immediately involved in war with the
neighbouring communes; and, by a cruel irony of fate,
those same allies who had stood shoulder to shoulder with
her for wellnigh half a century, became her earliest and
bitterest foes.   Scarcely had Clement announced his intention of remaining in France, than the Ghibellines of Spoleto
took up arms, and, captained by Abrunamonte da Chiavano,
expelled the Guelfs.   This was in the late summer or early
autumn of 1305.   In the following year, the *fuorusciti*,
who had taken refuge in Trevi, received such effectual
succour from Perugia that they routed their enemies with
considerable slaughter, and returned in triumph to their
homes.   Of the details of the conflict we know nothing.
Pellini's narrative is demonstrably apocryphal, being based

---

[1] A. LUPATTELLI, *Benedetto XI. in Perugia.   Suo monumento sepolcrale.
Sue reliquie*, Roma, Desclée, Lefebvre e C., 1903.   Compare SYMONDS and
DUFF GORDON, *op. cit.*, pp. 164-167.

upon documents which are referable to 1323 instead of
1306.[1] Minervio's chapter *de seditionibus quæ Spoletii inter
Guelfos et Gibellinos fuerunt* begins with the year 1310,[2]
and albeit the annalist Parruccio Zampolini speaks of an
ambush laid by the Guelfs at the village of S. Brizio, it is
almost certain that he is recounting, under an earlier date,
a feat of arms which actually occurred in 1312.[3] Giovanni
Villani keeps silence, and the chronicle attributed to
Graziani[4] only opens with the year 1309. Under these
circumstances we must content ourselves with the knowledge
that, while many of "the Guelfs returned to Spoleto and
abode therein for divers years," others, more wary, preferred
to remain in Trevi.[5] Neither, as the event proved, was
their caution excessive, since, ere long, the smouldering
fires of civic discord broke out afresh and raged more fiercely
than ever.

The election of Henry of Luxembourg, in November,
1308, and the death of Charles II. of Anjou, in the following
May, raised high the hopes of the Ghibellines, and, throughout the year 1309, they displayed exceptional activity. In
April, the Tarlati returned to Arezzo and renewed the war
with Florence ;[6] in October the Orsini were routed by the
Colonna beneath the walls of Rome ;[7] while, nearer home,
Foligno, now Guelf, was threatened by Corrado di Anastasio
of the noble family of the Trinci, at the head of a large
body of Ghibellines from Todi and the March. He had
been expelled from the city in 1305.[8] The measure of

---

[1] PELLINI, i. 342 *et seq.* ; ANSIDEI, *Su alcuni rapporti fra Perugia e
Spoleto nel Sec. XIV.*, in *Bollettino* cited, iii. 554-556.

[2] S. MINERVII, *De rebus gestis atque antiquis monumentis Spoleti*, cap. x.
This work will be found among the *Documenti*, etc., *op. cit.*, published by
A. SANSI, Parte I. pp. 11 *et seq.*

[3] A. SANSI, *Documenti*, etc., *op. cit.*, Parte I. p. 111 and n. 1 on
p. 112.

[4] The chronicle attributed to Graziani is published in the *Arch. Stor. It.*,
XVI. i. pp. 69-750. According to Professor O. Scalvanti, Antonio di
Andrea di Ser Angelo dei Guarneglie is the true author of the manuscript
up to July 1450 ; his work being continued, after his death, by Pietro
Angelo di Giovanni (see *Bollettino* cited, iv. 65). I shall, however, con-
tinue to cite it by its old familiar title of " GRAZIANI."

[5] SANSI, *Storia del C. di Spoleto, op. cit.*, i. 176.

[6] G. VILLANI, viii. 107.   [7] *Ibid.*, viii. 117.   [8] PELLINI, i. 341.

Foligno's peril may be gauged by the urgency of her cry to Perugia for succour : *Datum Fulginei, etc., de nocte, succurrite succurrite, succurrite sine mora.*[1]

A little earlier, help had been implored by Spoleto, which (says Pellini) was " in very great discord " ; and it seems that cavalry and infantry were sent thither,[2] though apparently not in sufficient numbers to maintain order, since, in March, 1310, the Ghibellines, having been reinforced by Corrado di Anastasio and the Todini, succeeded in once more expelling the Guelfs, who, as in 1306, took refuge in Trevi, only to be driven thence on the following day. " Thereafter, on the 28th day of March, the knights of Perugia rode to the town of Trevi, and by battle reinstated the Guelfs in the said town and drove out the Ghibellines." [3] As yet, however, the Perugians were not strong enough to attack Spoleto itself, and the next three months were devoted to warlike preparations. Orders were issued that every family in the city and in the *contado* should furnish a man ;[4] a company of "*Catalans*" under Tomaso da Lentino was taken into the pay of the Commune, and Messer Gentile Orsini was appointed general-in-chief at a salary of two thousand florins of gold for six months.[5] The army mustered at Foligno, on the 3rd of July, and, on the 5th, the *contado* of Spoleto was invaded, the line of march being along the *strada vecchia*, which lay upon a somewhat lower level than the modern road and was guarded by a fortress with the defiant title of *Beccatiquello*. The Griffin accepted the challenge contained in the name, and " pecked " so shrewdly that, on the 6th, Beccatiquello surrendered. On the 9th the Guelfs advanced to within a mile of Spoleto, burning and wasting all the country side, until the

[1] PELLINI, i. 357.　　　　　　　　　　　[2] PELLINI, i. 356.

[3] G. VILLANI (ix. 6), who is followed by MURATORI (*Annali,* ad ann.), places these events in July ; but all the other chroniclers agree that they happened in March. GRAZIANI, *ubi cit.,* pp. 71-72 ; PELLINI, i. 361 ; MINERVIO, *ubi cit.,* Lib. i. c. ix. ; SANSI, *Storia del C. di Spoleto, op. cit.,* i. 179.

[4] GRAZIANI, *loc. cit.* : " . . . e fu comandato uno homo per casa in citade e in contado." On the other hand PELLINI has, " un' huomo per casa nella città, e uno fra due famiglie per lo contado."

[5] PELLINI, i. 361.

Spoletini came forth to give them battle ; "and there were with them Todini and Narniesi and Ternani and men of Amelia and of S. Gemini, and the Duke of the Ducato with many knights." On the side of Perugia were levies from Gubbio, Città di Castello, Camerino, Assisi, Foligno, Spello and Trevi, as well as the mercenaries of Tomaso da Lentino and the *fuorusciti* of Spoleto. The battle joined at the village of Maiano, on the morning of the 10th, and, after a fierce and bloody conflict, which raged through the hottest hours of a long summer day, the combatants were finally compelled to abandon the struggle through sheer exhaustion. That night the Guelfs retired towards Clitunno (*Clitumnus*), and, on the 12th, encamped at Marsciano, whence they raided the *contado* of Todi and returned loaded with spoil. In this incursion they seem to have encountered no resistance ; and the Perugians, believing, apparently, that the enemy, though, perhaps, technically victorious in the recent battle, had been too roughly handled to have any stomach for further fighting, garrisoned Marsciano with two hundred men-at-arms and a number of cross-bowmen, dismissed their allies, and disbanded their army.[1]

Meanwhile, however, the Ghibellines had been reinforced by the Marquis of the March with a great company of horsemen ; and, on the 19th of July, they suddenly crossed the Perugian frontier, "burning and pillaging even to the Fratta of the Sons of Azzo." When the news reached the city, there was saddling and bridling in haste ; messengers were sent to recall the troops to their standards, and, on the same day, the knights of Perugia rode to Cerqueto and to Marsciano ; but, in spite of every effort, it was found impossible to gather an army strong enough to take the field until the end of August. Marsciano was the trysting place, and thither came Messer Pietro Tolomei of Siena, the Potestà, eight of the Priors, and twenty-five Rectors of the

---

[1] GRAZIANI, pp. 72-73 ; FABRETTI, *Cronache*, i. 3 ; MINERVIO, *loc. cit.* ; PELLINI, i. 362 ; SANSI, *Storia del C. di Spoleto, op. cit.*, i. 181-182 ; BONAZZI, i. 385. Pellini tells us that the Battle of Maiano was fought on the 6th of July, but if, as Graziani declares, the Perugian army encamped for five days at Beccatiquello, it can hardly have taken place before the 10th. The 10th is the date accepted by Baron Sansi.

Arts; and there they held a council, in the Church of S. Giovanni, to provide for the prosecution of the war and to elect the civic magistrates for the next two months.[1] On the 29th the muster was completed, and, on the 31st, the territory of Todi was again invaded. The following day Fratta del Vescovo (now Fratta Todina) was taken by storm, and twenty-eight prisoners were sent bound to Perugia; while, on the 3rd of September, the army advanced to the Bridge of Montemolino and there encamped on the western bank of the river. "And," says Graziani, "on the 5th day of September, in the Octave of St John, the Commune of Perugia being encamped at the Bridge of Monte Molino in the *contado* of Todi, the Todini came with much folk, both horse and foot, and drew nigh unto the host of Perugia, whereupon the men of Perugia forthwith crossed the Tiber and advanced to meet the said Todini, who incontinently turned back; but our knights and footmen followed hard after them and pursued them and discomfited them; and they followed them even unto the going up to Todi, slaying and burning everything. Now there were with the said Todini knights of Spoleto, of Terni, of Narni, of Amelia, mercenaries (*soldati*) of Pisa and the Duke of the Ducato with many knights. And thereafter the folk of the Commune of Perugia took the Bridge of Montemolino and Ilci; and many other walled places and villages and houses were burned even unto the hill of Todi. In the which discomfiture was slain the Duke of the Ducato with many other folk, both gentlemen and common people. There were brought to Perugia eight banners of the men of Todi and many bells which had been in the walled places which were taken. The host abode in the *contado* of Todi twenty and two days." [2]

According to Giovanni Villani, the Perugians owed their victory to the Mareschal of King Robert of Naples, who had been sent to their assistance by the Florentines with three hundred men-at-arms; [3] and certainly, if he was

---

[1] PELLINI, i. 363; GRAZIANI, p. 73.

[2] GRAZIANI, *ubi cit.*, pp. 73-74. Compare FABRETTI, *Cronache*, i. 4.

[3] G. VILLANI, ix. 5. According to him the battle was fought in July.

present at the battle,[1] he may well have contributed to the winning of it; for we are told that so enamoured was he of the game of war that, when his sovereign, on the occasion of his coronation, sent him a new banner, he forthwith made a hazardous incursion into Aretine territory for the mere purpose of handselling it—*per provare la bandiera.*[2]

On the 26th of September, the victors ceased from ravaging the *contado* of Todi and returned to Perugia, loaded with spoil and bringing with them innumerable prisoners. Their work, however, was not yet finished. *Vendetta boccon di Dio* runs the Italian proverb, and there was vengeance to be wrought on the Marquis of the March before the Perugians could possess their souls in peace. " Now it befel that Messer Arnaldo, Lord of Ancona, who had fought in the Guelf army since the beginning of the war, was minded to return to his own city; and when he departed from Perugia, many knights of Porta Sole and Porta Borgne went with him, ostensibly to do him honour and to serve as his escort, but really to take vengeance for the incursion which the Marquis of the March had made through the *contado* of Perugia with the Todini. And they went by the way of Pergola even unto Sinigaglia, and there they abode eighteen days; and they rode through the *contado* of Jesi, burning and slaying men, and gathering spoil and prisoners; and there went with them knights of Gubbio and of Ancona and of many other towns. Thereafter they rode to the gates of Fano, wasting all the land; and when they might not enter into the city, the Trumpeter of Perugia made proclamation beneath the walls thereof that these were Perugians who went from town to town seeking the Marquis. And they did the like beneath the walls of Fermo." [3]

---

[1] BONAZZI (i. 386) seems to doubt the fact, and maintains that the victory was " won by the Perugians alone." As usual, however, he gives no adequate reason for the faith which is in him.

[2] G. VILLANI, viii. 118.

[3] GRAZIANI, *ubi cit.*, pp. 74; PELLINI, i. 366-367. As to the mediæval feeling with regard to revenge, compare G. ARIAS, *Le istituzioni giuridiche medievale nella Divina Commedia* (Firenze, Lumachi, 1901), cap. ii. pp. 31-62.

In December, hostilities recommenced, and the *contado* of Todi was invaded by the way of Deruta. There was, however, no decisive battle, and I do not greatly care to tell of the farms and villages which went up in flame, of devastated fields and trampled vineyards, of fortresses taken and retaken, of ambushes, massacres, treasons, wounds, of furious clamour of bells for aid which never came, of cries of lamentation and of wrath, ringing through all that pleasant country side, which, to-day, echoes to no harsher note than the call of the ploughman to his oxen and the twittering of birds among the apple branches. Suffice it to say that neither the Todini nor the Perugians obtained any conspicuous advantage, and that the war resolved itself into a series of raids and counter-raids which were almost equally disastrous to either Commune, and were continued throughout the spring and summer of 1311.[1]

During all this time, it would seem that Todi received but scant assistance from the Ghibellines of Spoleto, who were, probably, fully occupied in repelling the attacks of their own *fuorusciti*. These, as we have seen, had occupied Trevi; there they formed an *universitas*, governed by a Council and two Heads (*Capi*), to which they gave the name of "The University of the Excluded from Spoleto," and thence they descended to harry the plain below. Trevi, on its high-peaked hill and filled with fighting men, was practically impregnable, and it was scarcely ten miles from Spoleto. Hardly was a foray repulsed than the raiders were at work again, and, night after night, the flare of burning villages lit up all the valley of the Maroggia. In vain the Ghibellines strove to defend their *contado*; the only salvation for the country folk lay in agreement with the *fuorusciti*, and an instrument was long preserved among the archives of the Monastery of Sassovivo, whereby, in October 1310, the University of the Excluded granted to the *coloni* of S. Andrea of Maiano and to those of the Trinità and of S. Apollinare of Spoleto, to till the lands of those churches unmolested, because they were subject to the

---

[1] GRAZIANI, *ubi cit.*, pp. 75-77. If the reader will study the chronicle with a good map, his time will not be wasted.

said monastery.[1]   Finally, in February, 1312, the Ghibellines resolved to attempt the wellnigh impossible task of expelling the Guelfs from Trevi, and, on the 25th of that month, they took the field.   The *fuorusciti*, however, had been reinforced by the Perugians, and, instead of waiting to be attacked, marched out to meet the enemy and routed them with great slaughter in the Piano di S. Brizio.   Among the slain was that Abrunamonte da Chiavano who captained the Ghibelline revolt in 1305, and whom Graziani calls the "seignior of Spoleto."   The messengers who brought the good tidings to Perugia were richly rewarded, and ambassadors were sent to carry the news of the victory to Siena and Florence."[2]

Meanwhile, the Emperor had sailed from Genoa, and, after having been delayed at Portovenere by contrary winds for eighteen days, finally reached Pisa, on the 6th of March, 1312.   Thence, on the 23rd of April, he set out for Rome at the head of two thousand men-at-arms and a considerable body of infantry.   Advancing along the sea-coast, through the Sienese Maremma, he crossed the Ombrone near Grosseto, and on the 1st of May reached Viterbo, where he was joined by the Aldobrandeschi of S. Fiora and other feudatories, as well as by the militia of Todi, Amelia, Narni and Spoleto.   He continued his march through Sutri, along the Via Claudia, and, having crossed the Ponte Molle on the 6th of May, entered Rome on the 7th.   Here, however, he met with so obstinate a resistance that, although he soon made himself master of the greater part of the city, he could make no impression on the quarter of the Vatican, which was held by Prince John of Naples, who was reinforced, on the 21st of May, by a considerable body of troops

[1] SANSI, *Storia del C. di Spoleto, op. cit.*, i. 184.   The monastery of Sassovivo is situated some four miles to the east of Foligno.

[2] GRAZIANI, *ubi cit.*, p. 78 ; PELLINI, i. 386 ; G. VILLANI, ix. 38 ; SANSI, *op. cit.*, 185.   I have followed Graziani.   The date given by Villani is the 28th of February.   As to the death of Abrunamonte da Chiavano, both Pellini and Fabretti, following Minervio, would have us believe that he was killed at the Battle of Maiano, in 1310 (compare *Arch. Stor. It.*, XVI. i. 78 n.) ; but Baron Sansi has demonstrated that this is impossible, since, as late as November, 1311, he was Potestà of Monteleone (*op. cit.*, p. 182).

from the Guelf cities of the Tuscan League, and, among the rest, by a hundred and fifty Perugian knights.[1] During the next few days a series of battles was fought near the Capitol, in which the Germans were worsted, and, on the 29th of June, Henry was compelled, contrary to all precedent, to have his coronation performed in the Lateran.

On the 20th of August, he left Rome, and passing through Viterbo reached Todi on the 27th. The alarm of Perugia was great; for her there could be no forgiveness, and her enemies gave her no time for preparation. On the 30th, the Imperial armies poured into her *contado*, irresistible as lava down Etna, devastating as a tornado. Marsciano was taken and sacked; Casalina, Cerqueto, La Morcella, S. Ellera, S. Martino in Colle, Celle, Compignano, La Spina, S. Enea, S. Apollinare, and many other villages were burned to the ground. Only Marsciano and Castiglione del Lago made any resistance. Of the latter we are told that " the town (*castello*) they took, but the citadel (*rôcca*) they might not have; and all the walled places which they took they took without any difficulty, because the folk which were therein fled away or ever the enemy came thither. . . . They encamped in the *contado* of Perugia six days; and, on the 4th day of September, the Emperor Henry departed out of the *contado* of Perugia with all his folk and went to Cortona." [2]

Ten days later, the Perugian territory was again invaded; and this time by "the Spoletini and Todini and all their league, and with them were three hundred German men-at-arms of the folk of the Emperor" who had remained in Todi; "and they encamped against Marsciano and destroyed it, and wasted Colle Baruccio." Apparently it had been the intention of the German men-at-arms to continue their

[1] GREGOROVIUS, *op. cit.*, Vol. III. Lib. xi. Cap. i. p. 229 ; GRAZIANI, *ubi cit.*, p. 78 ; PELLINI, i. 389. In February, the Florentines had requested the Perugians to send ambassadors to take part in a " parlamentum " in Florence, " super formanda tallia " ; and, on the 19th of May, we find them exhorting them to send troops to Rome. See DEGLI AZZI, *Le Relazioni tra la Rep. di Firenze e l' Umbria nel Secolo XIV.*, *secondo i documenti nel R. Archivio di Stato di Firenze, op. cit.*, Vol. I. pp. 7-8, §§ 9, 12.

[2] GRAZIANI, *ubi cit.*, 79-80 ; FABRETTI, *Cronache*, i. 6, 70 ; PELLINI, i. 392-393.

march through the Perugian *contado* to Arezzo; but learning that the Perugians had been reinforced by troops which the Florentines had despatched from Rome,[1] and that a considerable body of cavalry had occupied Monte Vibiano and was prepared to contest their passage, they turned back and entered the *contado* of Orvieto, where they halted at Fabro, in the Val di Chiana. Instead of being content to let well alone, the Perugians seem to have ridden after them and to have sustained a defeat, somewhere to the westward of the Lake, in the district of *Il Chiugi*.[2]   And thus, says Giovanni Villani, the Germans who had been left behind at Todi "passed with damage and shame to the Perugians."[3]

If, however, the Commune had offered but slight and ineffectual resistance to the Emperor, his departure was the signal for renewed activity. The ruined and deserted villages were restored and repopulated with incredible celerity and at vast expense;[4] while, early in November, the Perugians were in a position to repay the services of the Florentines in kind by sending troops to their assistance under the command of Brasco "Peri" and Tommaso da Lentino.[5]   In June, 1313, the territory of Todi was once more invaded;[6] and, a few weeks later, Perugian succour alone saved Orvieto from Ghibelline domination.

For four days the rival factions of the Filippeschi and Monaldeschi had fought through the streets of the city with varying fortunes, until at last, on Sunday the 19th of August, the defeat of the former seemed inevitable. The greater part of the town was already in the hands

---

[1] That the Perugians had received reinforcements I infer from DEGLI AZZI, *op. cit.*, p. 12, § 29, where we have a synopsis of a letter of the 3rd of September from the Florentine Signoria to their captains in Rome, urging them to hasten to the assistance of the Perugians against the Emperor. Compare BONAINI, *Acta Henrici VII. Romanorum imperatoris et monumenta quædam alia suorum temporum historiam illustrantia*, Doc. 202.

[2] GRAZIANI, *ubi cit.*, p. 81 ; FABRETTI, *Cronache*, i. 7 ; BONAZZI, i. 389-390.

[3] G. VILLANI, ix. 47.

[4] GRAZIANI, *ubi cit.*, p. 82 ; PELLINI, i. 397 ; BONAZZI, i. 391.

[5] DEGLI AZZI, *Le Relazioni*, etc., *op. cit.*, i. 12, § 30. They appear to have sent further succours in March and May, 1313 (see §§ 31, 33).

[6] *Arch. Stor. It.*, XVI. i. 82.

of the Guelfs and the Filippeschi were on the point of
abandoning the conflict, when they were reinforced by
Bindo da Baschi and his brethren, with the knights of
Spoleto, of Narni, of Amelia, of Terni, *et omnibus aliis
Gibellinis de provincia*, among them Bernard de Coucy,
Canon of Nevers and representative of the Papal Rector.
There, too, were the Counts of Santa Fiora, the Seigniors
of Bisenzo and that Sciarra Colonna who struck the deadly
blow against Boniface at Anagni. They entered Orvieto
by the Porta Vivaria, about the ninth hour, "cum tubis
argenteis et aliis multis et variis instrumentis et cum magno
gaudio"; and so confident were they of their overwhelming
strength that they did not at once attack the Monaldeschi,
whom they apparently expected to escape from the town
during the night. In this they were disappointed; but,
after a few hours' fighting on the morning of the 20th,
the Guelfs broke and fled and were already streaming
through the gates of the city in headlong rout, when "a
great voice spake out of Heaven, saying, 'All ye who flee,
return to your homes, return, for lo! the hosts of Perugia,
both horse and foot, come hither to protect the Cathedral
of the Blessed Virgin Mary and to give aid to the Guelf
Party.'"[1] According to one account the Perugian succours
numbered no fewer than twelve hundred men-at-arms and
as many foot-soldiers; and scarcely had they passed
through the Porta Maggiore than they entered into the
battle, ever shouting, *Viva el populo de Peroscia!* "Wherefore the Ghibellines, beholding this, incontinently fled; and
on this wise were they driven forth and discomfited; and
there died in that battle many of the men of Todi, both
horse and foot, among the which was slain Bindo da Baschi,
captain of the Ghibellines of Todi."[2]

[1] ". . . facta est vox de celo magna, dicens: Omnes qui fugitis civitatem
propriam revertimini securi, revertimini, quoniam ecce stipendiarii de
Perusiis equites et pedites, qui ad tuendum domum b. Virginis Marie
veniunt et in auxilium partis Guelfe."

[2] GRAZIANI, *ubi cit.*, p. 83; FABRETTI, *Cronache*, i. 8; PELLINI, i. 400.
The chronicles of Orvieto are fuller and more picturesque than those of
Perugia. See the extracts published by FUMI, *Codice Diplomatico*, etc.,
op. cit., pp. 412 *et seq.* Compare also G. PARDI, *Dal Comune alla Signoria
in Orvieto*, in *Bollettino* cited, xiii. pp. 406-410; ANTONELLI, *Vicende della*

Four days later, Henry of Luxembourg passed away at Buonconvento in the Senese, and the great army which he had gathered melted like snow in the springtime. The Ghibellines of Arezzo, of the March and of the Romagna abandoned the camp, and, full of suspicion and terror, scattered to the four winds of heaven, while the hearts of the men of Todi and of Spoleto became as water. In December negotiations were opened, and " on the 20th day of April, 1314, peace was made between the Commune of Perugia and the Commune of Spoleto after this manner, to wit, that the Syndic of those within Spoleto came to Perugia with sixteen ambassadors, and likewise the Syndic of the exiles ; and they made the said peace at the foot of the Campanile of S. Lorenzo, with great solemnity and love ; and the Syndics of the one party and of the other kissed together on the mouth ; and all the covenants which they made appear in the Chancery of our Commune in the contract which was written by the hand of Ser Cellolo of Porta S. Susanna of the parish of S. Gregorio."[1]

In August, the Todini followed the example of the Spoletini, and the exiles returned to their homes.[2]

Throughout these negotiations the conduct of Perugia seems to have been beyond praise. She acted primarily as arbitrix between the contending factions, the *intrinseci* and *extrinseci*, and was scrupulously careful not to arrogate to herself any unnecessary dominion over her old allies. The documents prove it.[3] Again and again she protests that all she desires and seeks is " pacem solidam et firmam et comunem " ; and her actions corresponded with her words. If, later on, she was compelled to reduce Spoleto to the condition of a vassal state, the fault was none of hers.

Dominazione Pontificia, etc., *op. cit.*, pp. 7-8, and CALISSE, *I Prefetti Di Vico*, *op. cit.*, p. 59.

[1] GRAZIANI, *ubi cit.*, p. 83. The treaty itself is lost, but Count V. ANSIDEI, in his article *Su alcuni rapporti fra Perugia e Spoleto nel Secolo XIV.* (*ubi cit.*), has published the *Capitoli* of the 22nd of February, which are still preserved in the ARCH. COM. DI PERUGIA, *Annali Decemvirali*, ad ann. 1314, c. 280 t. Compare also PELLINI, i. 407.

[2] *Arch. Stor. It.*, XVI. i. 84.   [3] See *Bollettino* cited, iii. 551.

CHAPTER IX

THE SUBJECTION OF ASSISI AND SPOLETO

THOUGH the death of Henry of Luxembourg was a heavy blow to the Ghibellines, the long vacancy of the Papal See, which intervened between the Pontificates of Clement V. and John XXII. gave them breathing space, and the Imperial Standard was still raised high in four regions of Italy. To the southward Frederick of Aragon continued to hold his own without much difficulty ; in Milan, the strong signory established by Matteo Visconti upon the ruins of the House of Torriani remained unshaken ; in Verona, Can Grande della Scala, upon whom the mantle of the greatest of the Hohenstaufen seemed to have fallen,[1] reigned with more than Oriental splendour ; while, in Tuscany, the Eagle Banner of Pisa, in the hand of Uguccione della Faggiuola, once more became a terror to all the neighbouring communes ; the slaughter of Montecatini (August, 1315) rivalled that of Montaperto. In the defeated army was a considerable body of Perugians, who seem to have suffered very heavily. One chronicler estimates their loss at over two hundred left dead upon the field of battle, besides numerous prisoners who were carried to Pisa by the victors and perished miserably in the Torre della Fame.[2] The news of the disaster was received with

---

[1] Compare *Decamerone*, i. 7 : "Messer Cane della Scala . . . fu uno de' più notabili e de' più magnifici Signori che dallo Imperadore Federigo secondo in qua si sapesse in Italia."

[2] GRAZIANI, ad ann. ; PELLINI, i. 412 ; FABRETTI, *Cronache*, i. 9, 71-72 ; BONAZZI, i. 393. Compare also the *Cronica Sanese* in MURATORI, *Rer. Italic. Script.*, xv. 58, where, after giving a list of the principal men who fell in the battle, the chronicler continues : " E morivvi altra gente di Perugia e del contado più di 200 altre persone." In October, we find the Perugians beseeching the Orvietans to exchange certain Aretine prisoners, whom they had in the dungeons of the Palace of the Commune, for Cencio di Montemelino, Pellolo di Uguiccionello and Bolgaruccio Count

something approaching consternation and the whole city put on mourning.[1] The general alarm was still further increased by disquieting rumours of Ghibelline activity in the March of Ancona,[2] and Perugia abandoned all thought of further intervention in Tuscany, till she should have set her own house in order. A severe law was passed for the suppression of civic tumult;[3] ten officials, the majority of whom were nobles, were appointed for the defence of the city, with the title of *Capitani delle Porte*;[4] and all the towers and fortresses, whether in town or country, instead of being left as formerly to the care of their owners, were garrisoned by troops in the pay of the Commune.[5] The bare suspicion of Ghibellinism was made an absolute disqualification for the *Priorato*,[6] and the old law which provided that the Potestà must be "amator et fidelis Ecclesie et de parte Ecclesie"[7] was strictly enforced to the exclusion of Messer Maggino de' Maggi of Brescia, who was believed

of Marsciano, Perugian citizens who had been captured by the Pisans. Bolgaruccio died shortly afterwards in the Torre della Fame. See FUMI, *Codice Dipl.*, *op. cit.*, p. 431. A good example of the terrible treatment of prisoners of war in the Middle Ages is to be found in the Chronicle of Fra Salimbene of Parma, where he tells us how, after the Battle of Meloria, "many women of Pisa, fair ladies and noble and rich, went on foot to Genoa to seek out and visit their captives; but the jailers answered them saying, 'Yesterday thirty died and to-day forty. We cast them into the sea, and thus do we daily with the Pisans . . .' For the Pisans died in prison of hunger and famine and poverty and misery . . ." See COULTON, *From S. Francis to Dante*, *op. cit.*, p. 216, and compare pp. 124, 126, 127.

[1] AMMIRATO, *Istorie Fiorentine* (Firenze, Battelli e C., 1847), Vol. II. Lib. v. p. 51: "In Firenze, in Bologna, in Siena, in Perugia e in Napoli, per il pianto de' cittadini perduti, tutto il popolo si vestì a bruno."

[2] TONINI, *Rimini nella Signoria de' Malatesti*, P. I. § 14, p. 32; PELLINI, i. 413.

[3] PELLINI, i. 413: ". . . ordinò co'l consiglio d' alcuni huomini prudenti, che si elesse per consiglieri, che qualunque fosse auttore d' alcun romore, ò tumulto nella città, fosse in pena dell' ultimo supplicio, e nella perdita della robba caduto."

[4] PELLINI, i. 413, 424.

[5] PELLINI, i. 413; MARIOTTI, *Saggio*, etc., *op. cit.*, i. 17. Compare also the list of garrisoned towers given by Dott. R. GIGLIARELLI, *Venere: Racconto storico della metà del Secolo XIV.*, pp. 67-68 n. The work in question is an historical novel, of which the less said the better. The notes, however, are extremely valuable, and no serious student of mediæval Perugia can afford to neglect them.

[6] PELLINI, i. 415.   [7] Statute of 1279, Rubric 4. See page 78 *supra*.

to have displayed Ghibelline leanings, and, although Potestà
elect, was informed that his services would be dispensed
with.[1]

The overtures of Florence, Bologna and Siena, who
wished Perugia *esse in societate et tallia Tuscorum*, were
rejected, and a league was entered into with Orvieto, Assisi,
Spoleto, Gubbio, Foligno, Cagli, Sassoferrato, Spello,
Bevagna, Montefalco, Bettona, and other Umbrian communes, for the purpose of providing a body of ultramontane
mercenaries with an ultramontane captain for the common
defence.[2]   Unfortunately, however, the new League rested
on no very firm basis, and although Perugian ambassadors
and Perugian jurists were continually travelling from place
to place, seeking to compose the differences of the confederated cities, and to keep peace between them and their
neighbours, the task proved a hopeless one.[3]   The end
came in 1319, when the defection of Assisi, shortly followed
by that of Spoleto, shattered the Umbrian League and gave
the signal for renewed hostilities.

Earlier in the year, Perugia had had cause to complain
of certain raids which the Assisani had made in the territory
of Nocera ; but her intervention proved successful, and the
aggressors consented to make reparation, declaring that " to
be at discord with the people of Perugia was a perpetual
inquietude and perturbation of mind to the City of Assisi." [4]
These sentiments, however, naturally found no echo in the
breasts of the Ghibelline *fuorusciti*, who, led by Muzio di
Francesco, succeeded in surprising the town on the night of
the 29th of September.[5]   And here it is to be observed
that the overthrow of the Guelf government in Assisi was
no mere sporadic outbreak of intestine discord, but part and
parcel of a far larger movement, forming, in fact, the prelude

[1] PELLINI, i. 413 ; MARIOTTI, *Saggio*, etc., *op. cit.*, ii. 247 ; BONAZZI,
i. 394.

[2] PELLINI, i. 414-415 ; FUMI, *Codice Dipl., op. cit.*, pp. 428-430 ; Doc.
dcxxi.

[3] BONAZZI, i. 395-396, and read PELLINI, i. 414-434.

[4] PELLINI, i. 434.

[5] GRAZIANI, *ubi cit.*, p. 87 ; CRISTOFANI, *op. cit.*, i. 209 ; FUMI, *Eretici
e Ribelli*, etc., *op. cit.*, in *Bollettino* cited, iii. 271.   The date there given,
" 19 September," is an obvious misprint.   Compare *Bollettino*, iv. 228.

to a general rising of the Ghibellines which extended far beyond the limits of Umbria and menaced the very existence of the Ecclesiastical State.[1] The head and soul of the rebellion was, as I have said, Frederick of Montefeltro. With him were his two brothers, the Counts Guido and Speranza, Pauluccio della Faggiuola, Uberto, Count of Ghiaggiuolo, Lupaccio and Andrea of Osimo, and, last but not least, the Aretine Bishop, Guido de' Tarlati of Pietramala. Large bodies of troops, both horse and foot, were brought from Arezzo, from Lucca and from Pisa ; and the whole of the Romagna and the March flamed out into war.[2] We are, therefore, not surprised to learn that Muzio and the *fuorusciti* who attacked Assisi were aided by the men-at-arms of Frederick of Montefeltro, and that, after the expulsion of the Guelfs, Fra Vanne da Poppi was sent thither by Bishop Guido to fill the office of Potestà.[3] Muzio himself became Captain of the People ; and, although the outward forms of communal government continued to be observed, he seems, in fact, to have exercised almost uncontrolled authority. Graziani does not hesitate to speak of him as " Despot of Assisi." [4]

From the nature of the case his policy was a policy of aggression. The continued assistance of the Ghibelline leaders was no doubt strictly conditioned on his activity and zeal for the common cause ; and therefore, obviously, one of his earliest cares must be the filling of his war-chest. To this end he did not scruple to violate the Monastery of S. Francesco or to lay hands upon the vast treasures which were there accumulated. Not only did he appropriate the tithes of innumerable churches and the monies deposited with the friars by Cardinals and other ecclesiastics, but also the relics of the Saints, crosses, chalices, censers, candlesticks, and images, vessels of gold and silver, rich vestments and

---

[1] See pages 92-93 *supra*.

[2] TONINI, *op. cit.*, P. I. § 19, p. 41.

[3] *Bollettino* cited, iv. 266 : " Epūs aretinus . . . ad requisitionem et petitionem dicti Mucii, misit fratrem Vannem de Poppio, familiarem et sotium suum ad regimen potestarie dicte Civ. . . . "

[4] GRAZIANI, *ubi cit.*, p. 87 : " . . . remasene signore Muccio de ser Francesco."

precious stones of enormous value. Nor did he treat the ecclesiastics themselves with any more respect than he did their churches. A priest who offended him was thrown headlong from the window of the Communal Palace, to perish miserably on the pavement below; the Prior of the Cathedral was imprisoned in a loathsome dungeon, whence he barely escaped with his life; while the Bishop was despoiled of all his possessions and compelled to flee from the city.[1] Meanwhile, a large body of horse arrived from Arezzo;[2] the Perugian *contado* was invaded,[3] and the Ghibellines of Spoleto were urged to follow the example of Assisi. At this time, according to Baron Sansi, the Potestà of Spoleto was Messer Ruggero da Fabriano, a Ghibelline, while many of the other offices of the Commune were filled by men of the same political faith. Negotiations were secretly entered into with Muzio; and before daybreak on the 30th of November, all Assisi was under arms and on the march for Spoleto.[4]

As their allies drew near to the city, Messer Ruggero and his accomplices in the Palazzo caused the trumpets to be

---

[1] See the "*Sentenza di scomunica contro Muzio,*" in *Arch. Stor. It.*, XVI. ii. 495-501; CRISTOFANI, *op. cit.*, i. 218-219; FUMI, *Eretici e Ribelli nell' Umbria*, etc., cap. i. in *Bollettino* cited, iii. 271. Compare also iv. 222-223. The date of this robbery and sacrilege seems to have been 1 October, 1319. See FUMI, *I Registri del Ducato di Spoleto, op. cit.*, p. 242.

[2] FUMI, *Eretici e Ribelli*, etc., *op. cit.*, App. iii. Doc. ii. (*Bollettino* cited, iv. 266-271): ". . . et quod ope et operatione ipsius Epi aretini multi equites venerunt Asisium ad rebellandum et depredandum totam ducalem provinciam, et etiam ipsi equites missi ab ipso Epo aretino intraverunt civ. Spoleti . . . et eandem civ. invaserunt et homines et mulieres quam plures interfecerunt et plures depredationes et domorum concremationes fecerunt et conmiserunt et ipsam civ. contra R. E. in rebellione posuerunt."

[3] ". . . comburendo et destruendo comitatum P. et personas de dicta Civ. et Comit. P. capiendo et occidendo." See the important extract from the *Annali Decemvirali* printed in *Bollettino* cited, iii. 273 n.

[4] GRAZIANI, 88; G. VILLANI, ix. 104. MURATORI (*Annali*, ad ann. 1319) follows Villani, while PARUCCIO (*Annali, ubi cit.*, p. 112) tells us that the year *che fo romoreggiatu Spoliti . . . fo nel 1319 vel circa.* On the other hand, SANSI (*Storia del C. di Spoleto, op. cit.*, i. 192 n. 2) accepts the view of PELLINI and CAMPELLO, who state that the rebellion of Spoleto occurred in 1320. Recent researches, however, seem to have established the accuracy of the earlier date. See FUMI, *Eretici e Ribelli*, etc., in *Bollettino* cited, iii. 435 n.

sounded and the great bell of the Commune to be rung to summon the citizens to the Council Chamber. Thither came the Ghibellines, seven hundred in number and fully armed ; and, having excluded by force all such as were not of their own faction, they forthwith decreed the expulsion of the Guelfs and " the reformation of Spoleto to the Ghibelline Party."   Among the leaders of that violent assembly were Enrico di Messer Abrunamonte da Chiavano, Vanni, Pietro, Andrea, Tommaso and Ranotto, Seigniors of Ancaiano, Rinaldo di Lapparino, Chino and Rinaldo di Simone Fidanza, Petruccio Castelli, Matteo and Paolo Transarici, Alleuro Petroni, Bartoletto Bancaroni, Matteo Galli, Matteo and Ottaviano, Seigniors of Arrone, and Nicolò of Rocca Accarini.[1]   Seizing the gonfalon of the Republic, they issued forth from the Palace and raised the city against the Guelfs.

At the first alarm, the latter had sent to Perugia for succour ; but Perugia was far away, and the Assisani, with the men-at-arms of Montefeltro and Arezzo, were even now at the gates.   Resistance was hopeless, and the conflict soon became a massacre pure and simple.   That night the Cathedral was thronged with fugitives ; but neither the sanctity of the place nor its massive walls availed them anything.   It was stormed by the Ghibellines on the following morning.   Many of the Guelfs were put to the sword and many taken.   Among the slain were the Prior of the Duomo and Messer Simone, Prior of S. Erasmo ; among the captives two canons and eleven other ecclesiastics.   These latter, with about a hundred of the wealthiest citizens, were permitted to ransom themselves and to leave the town ; the remainder, men, women and children, were dragged away to prison ; part of them being immured in the great tower of the Anselmi, hard by the Church of S. Benedetto, and part in subterranean vaults near the Monastery of S. Agata.   Then, while the soldiery and the mob despoiled the altars and broke into the sacristy of the desecrated Cathedral, the victorious Ghibellines, no longer finding any foe to slay, wreaked their fury upon

[1] SANSI, op. cit., i. 190. These must have been the vigintiquinque tiranni vel ibi circa, referred to in the Annali Decemvirali, D. c. 279 r. See Bollettino cited, iii. 564.

senseless stones and mortar. No fewer than sixty great
palaces were sacked and burned, among them those of the
Manenti, below the Duomo, and of the ancient and powerful family of the Agurri : while of humbler dwellings more
than two hundred were destroyed. Traces of these devastations are still to be found in Spoleto ; " and," says Baron
Sansi, " he who, wandering through certain remote streets,
observes the walls which enclose the gardens of the city
will see how many bricked-up doorways there are to bear
witness to the bestiality of those factions."

Meanwhile, the Perugians were hastening to the assistance of the Guelfs ; but the conflict was over almost before
the news of any disturbance in Spoleto reached them ; and
hardly had they passed their own frontiers when they
encountered the troops of Muzio on their return march.
A stubbornly contested battle followed, in which the
Ghibellines were worsted with considerable slaughter and
with the loss of many banners and many prisoners.[1] Such
a victory, however, could do nothing to counterbalance the
alienation of Spoleto from the Guelf cause ; and, a few
months later, the rebellion of Nocera rendered the position
still more critical. Not only were the Guelfs expelled, but
the *greve giogo* of Perugia was broken and the Perugian
Potestà, Messer Cucco di Gualfreduccio de' Baglioni was
sent prisoner to Assisi.[2] This too was the work of
Muzio, who " together with Frederick, Count of Montefeltro,
excommunicate, heretic and false idolater, the open enemy
of God and of the Roman Church, was sowing discord,
fomenting wars, exciting dissentions and stirring up
scandals in all the Duchy of Spoleto, to the manifest
increase of heresy and schism and the imperilling of men's
souls and bodies." [3] With them, as we have seen, was

[1] PELLINI, i. 435. Compare the document published in *Bollettino* cited,
iii. 273 n.

[2] PELLINI, i. 443 ; FABRETTI, *Cronache*, i. 10, 73 ; *Arch. Stor. It.*, XVI. i.
88. This insurrection is said to have taken place in July, 1320.

[3] *Sentenza contro Muzio, ubi cit.*, p. 497. MURATORI (*Annali*, ad ann.
1322) appears to consider that the words " heretic and idolater " as applied
to Frederick were mere " common form " ; but, if we may accept the
opinion of FUMI (*Eretici e Ribelli*, etc., in *Bollettino* cited, iii. pp. 435 *et seq.*)
there was a very definite meaning in the accusation of idolatry. In the

leagued the warrior Bishop of Arezzo, Guido Tarlati, who "represented in Umbria the authority and force of the Ghibellines."[1]

At first sight, it seems incomprehensible that Perugia should have been able to make head against so many and such powerful enemies ; but a closer view of the situation will, I think, convince us that the odds against which she fought were more apparent than real. Where her opponents were weakest she was strongest, and her principal strength lay in the fact that she alone of all the cities of Umbria, nay, perhaps of all the cities of Italy, was not divided against herself. For many years, Nobles and People alike had been whole-heartedly and consistently Guelf. If there were Ghibellines in Perugia, they were far too few to dream of overthrowing the Government, and, as a consequence, her citizens lived at peace among themselves. Menaced by no horde of wronged and vengeful *fuorusciti*, life within her gates must, at this time, have been exceptionally secure ; and, even if she had denuded herself of all her troops, she would have had but little reason to fear any such disaster as that which overtook the Guelfs of Rieti, when they went forth to besiege Arrone, in 1320.[2] Whatever might befall Perugia abroad, she was safe at home ; and the advantage which this security gave her was as tremendous as it was unique.[3] In Spoleto and Assisi, on the contrary, the population must have been pretty equally divided between

language of the ecclesiastics, *Idolatria* and *Maleficium* were one and the same thing ; and it is probable that the Count of Montefeltro was believed to be a magician and necromancer in league with the Powers of Darkness.

[1] See the letter of Pope John XXII. to the Bishop of Arezzo, printed in *Bollettino* cited, iii. 469-471.

[2] G. VILLANI, ix. 125 : " Essendo i detti guelfi di Rieti all' assedio del castello d' Arrone nel contado di Spoleto, i ghibellini di Rieti usciti, coll' aiuto e forza di Sciarra della Colonna, per forza rientrarono in Rieti e cacciarne i guelfi che non erano all' oste."

[3] The fact that this security did not render the Magistrates careless or over confident, and that they constantly took precautions against possible disturbances (see PELLINI, *passim*, and page 114 *supra*) does not seem to me to militate against the accuracy of the statement made in the text. That their precautions proved unnecessary is good evidence that Perugia differed profoundly from her neighbours. Compare COULTON, *From St Francis to Dante*, op. cit., pp. 205 et seq.

Guelfs and Ghibellines, and the expulsion of the former entailed an enormous accession of strength to the Perugian army, which at once became more than a match for any force which could be brought against it.   In the war which followed, the Ghibellines never ventured to fight a pitched battle ; the advantage was Perugia's from the very beginning, and, whatever the vicissitudes of the struggle might be, the ultimate result was scarcely doubtful.

These facts were fully realized by the neighbouring towns and villages, and no sooner were preparations made for invading the territory of Assisi than, by common consent, the inhabitants of Valfabbrica, Castel della Torranca, Coltraticcio and S. Gregorio hastened to transfer their allegiance to Perugia.[1]   In the spring the Guelfs took the field under the command of the veteran Cante de' Gabrielli of Gubbio,[2] and advanced to Isola Romanesca,[3] the modern Bastìa.   The *borgo*, the unwalled suburb, was taken by assault, but the town itself (the *castello*) had been strongly garrisoned, and offered so strenuous a resistance that it was found necessary to construct a *battifolle* and to invest it in due form.[4]   The siege lasted seven months, and the defenders only surrendered in October, 1320, when famine stared them in the face.   They obtained favourable conditions, which, however, seem to have been shamelessly violated.   The place was sacked and destroyed, and the body of the Blessed Conrad of Offida, which lay in

---

[1] PELLINI, i. 434 ; CRISTOFANI, i. 211.

[2] " *Dominus Cantis, Capitaneus guerre et Priorum Artium civitatis Perusij.*"   This was the same Cante Gabrielli who, as Potestà of Florence, passed sentence of exile on Dante Alighieri, eighteen years earlier.   See DEGLI AZZI, *Le Relazioni*, etc., *op. cit.*, ii. 29, § 95 n., and authorities there cited.

[3] In the name *Isola Romanesca* we have a record of the period when the central basin of Umbria was covered by an immense lake.   See SYMONDS and DUFF GORDON, *op. cit.*, p. 3.

[4] We may define a *Battifolle* as a sort of redoubt, with towers and ramparts, generally built of timber, and used as a blockading station against a besieged place.   In Simone Martini's affresco of Guido Riccio Fogliani at the siege of Montemassi, in the Palazzo Comunale of Siena, we have a representation of a *battifolle* complete in all its parts.   Compare Miss L. OLCOTT's *Guide to Siena* (Siena, Torrini, 1903), p. 207 n.

S. Croce, the church of the Minor Friars, was carried away to Perugia.[1]

A few weeks later Nocera was once more occupied by the Guelfs;[2] and thereafter the siege of Assisi itself was pushed forward with vigour. Divers *battifolli* were constructed round about it,[3] and, early in 1321, considerable reinforcements arrived from Perugia, together with a *spingarda*, or small cannon, which was probably used to batter down the gates, since as yet artillery was quite useless for breaching the massive walls of a mediæval town.[4] All

---

[1] PELLINI, i. 437, 442; *Arch. Stor. It.*, i. 88; FABRETTI, *Cronache*, i. 73; CRISTOFANI, i. 211-212; BONAZZI, i. 399.

[2] PELLINI, i. 442.

[3] On the 7th of December, 1320, the Priors of the Arts of the City of Perugia ordered the *Massaio* of the army before Assisi " quod solvat Ambrosio magistro qui stetit in battifolle pro xiiij diebus quibus stetit in exercitu comunis perusij ad faciendum fieri battefolle novum contra civitatem Asisii pro Comune Perusij et ad faciendum steccatum breteschas et alia edifitia in dicto exercitu ad rationem xx sol. den. pro qualibet die, viginti tres libras et xv sol. den" (*Annali Decemvirali*, ad ann., a c^ta 180 t). This " Ambrosius magister " was, of course, Ambrogio Maitani of Siena, the brother of the more famous Lorenzo.

[4] PELLINI, i. 444: " . . . et ad uno di quei forti intorno ad Ascisi vi fu mandato un pezzo d' artigliaria, da essi chiamato *Spingarda*, pur all' ora per quella occasione fatta dal publico." There can, I think, be no doubt that Pellini here uses the word *artigliaria* in the modern sense of " ordnance " or " cannon," though it is, of course, indisputable that the Italian *artiglieria*, like the English *artillery*, was also used to mean any engine for projecting missiles, even to a bow and arrows (compare ARIOSTO, *L'Orlando furioso*, x. 55, and 1 Samuel xx. 40- Authorized Version). Certainly, it is thus that CRISTOFANI understands him (*op. cit.*, i. 213); but, on the other hand MARIOTTI (*Saggio*, etc., *op. cit.*, p. 252) flatly negatives this theory, asserting in so many words that " quest' arme non era da fuoco come sono l' odierne Spingarde." I fancy, however, that the question is quite an open one. The Genoese are said to have possessed cannon as early as 1306, while towards the middle of the century the use of artillery became quite common. Thus Petrarca, writing not later than 1344, tells us that *haec pestis, nuper rara, . . . nunc . . . ita comunis est ut quodlibet genus armorum* (see MURATORI, *Dissertazione*, xxvi.). According to G. VILLANI (xii. 66, 67) the English, at the Battle of Crecy, in 1346, made use of *bombarde* " che saettano pallotte di ferro con fuoco, per impaurire e disertare i cavalli de' Franceschi "; while a curious picture of a *spingarda* in its most primitive form may be seen in the portico outside the Church of the Convent of Lecceto, a few miles from Siena. There, among other incidents of mediæval life, is depicted the storming of a castle, and, in the foreground, is the *spingarda* in question. It is a small cannon,

citizens from sixteen to sixty were required to take up arms, and to obtain money for the prosecution of the war, the crops of Il Chiugi were sold for a year and the fisheries of the Lake for five years.[1] In April Assisi was excommunicated by the Pope, and, shortly afterwards, proclamation was made by the besiegers that 10,000 florins of gold would be paid to whomsoever should deliver Muzio, alive or dead, into the hands of the Potestà or Captain of Perugia.[2] Nevertheless, the Ghibelline leader was still strong enough to defy the thunders of the Vatican ; the terrified clergy continued to celebrate all the sacraments of the Church ; and, when the Guardian of S. Maria in Porziuncula attempted to affix a copy of the interdict to the door of the Cathedral, he and the friar who accompanied him were not only savagely beaten, but were actually forced to eat the Papal Bull with its leaden seal, and to wash it down with their own urine.[3]

Such outrages, however, only tended to increase the ever-growing discontent, and the anathemas of the Church, though treated by Muzio himself with the utmost scorn, can hardly have failed to shake the loyalty of some of his more superstitious adherents. The price which the Perugians set upon his head was a fresh blow to his already waning authority, and ere long, despairing of effectual succour from without, he stole through the besieging army

perhaps five feet in length, inclined at a considerable angle, and resting upon what might be taken for a thick plank, were it not for the fact that a fire is lighted underneath it, apparently for the purpose of heating the barrel. The ball, which is about to be discharged, may be seen protruding from the bell-shaped mouth of the *spingarda*, being, indeed, too large to go down any further. A gunner is bending over the touch-hole. This painting is attributed to the year 1343, and is said to be the work of Paolo di Maestro Neri, a pupil of Ambrogio Lorenzetti (see G. MILANESI, *Documenti per la storia dell' Arte Senese*, T. i. p. 30). In connection with this affresco the reader may profitably examine a document of 1358, published by TONINI, *op. cit.*, Parte I. App. cxxiv. pp. 234 *et seq.*, where some curious details are to be found touching a great cannon which was used in the war with Forlì.

[1] PELLINI, i. 446 ; BONAZZI, i. 400.
[2] PELLINI, i. 447 ; CRISTOFANI, i. 213-214.
[3] See the *Sentenza contro Muzio, ubi cit.*, p. 496 ; CRISTOFANI, i. 219.

and made good his escape to Todi. Deprived of their leader, the Assisani had no longer any heart for resistance, and, on the 19th of August, they sent two syndics to Perugia to treat for peace. So abject was their surrender that they appeared before the Priors and other magistrates of the Commune, in the Piazza Maggiore, bringing with them a blank sheet of paper upon which the victors might write such conditions as they chose. The Perugians did not abuse their power ; they were still bent on conciliation and peace ; milder terms could hardly have been offered.[1] It was only after the Ghibellines had once more taken up arms, and, as Pellini phrases it, "returned to their vomit," that they learned how heavy the hand of Perugia might become. Then, indeed, if we may credit Giovanni Villani, their bad faith was repaid in kind, and although, on the 29th of March, 1322, they once more surrendered on conditions which, at the worst, should have insured their persons and property from violence,[2] the Perugians no sooner entered the city than they "*corsono la terra*,[3] and slew more than a hundred citizens who had been their rebels." The *contado* of Assisi was taken from her "even unto the river Chiaggio ;"[4] her outer circuit of walls was destroyed, and her gates, with their massive chains and bolts, were carried as trophies to Perugia.[5] Henceforward the Guelfs alone were permitted to inhabit the still fortified *Città Vecchia*, the Ghibellines being compelled to live in the unprotected *borghi*.[6] For wellnigh half a century Assisi remained a vassal state, sending her yearly *palio* to the

---

[1] PELLINI, i. 448-449 ; BONAZZI, i. 401.

[2] See *Arch. Stor. It.*, XVI. i. 88 and note 3.

[3] I apprehend that the fundamental idea contained in the expression *correre la terra* is that of ironclad warriors galloping through the streets of the city slaying as they go. (*Cf.* FRANCO SACCHETTI, *Nov.* 79.) In fact, it was to make it impossible to *correre la terra* that the burghers were so careful to *porre le catene per le strade*.

[4] VILLANI, ix. 139 ; FABRETTI, *Cronache*, i. 10-11.

[5] In the *Annali Decemvirali*, under the date of 16 April, 1322, a payment is registered " pro hominibus habendis et mictendis ad civitatem Assisii qui haberent et traginarent portas Civ. Assisii ad Civ. Perusii pro honore comunis Perusii causa dicte guerre."

[6] PELLINI, i. 464 ; CRISTOFANI, i. 217 ; *Bollettino* cited, iv. 230.

feast of S. Ercolano,[1] and receiving her Potestà and even her laws from her conqueror.[2]

Meanwhile, however, the Ghibellines of Spoleto continued " in obstinate rebellion against the holy Roman Church." Not content with expelling the Guelfs, they filled the offices of the Commune with heretics, some of whom had actually been condemned by the Inquisitor ;[3] they set the papal ministers at open defiance, and, " *quasi novum balaam ydolum*," they welcomed to their city the excommunicated Count Frederick of Montefeltro, " with damnable temerity " proclaiming him their Captain-General and Duke.[4]

In March, 1320, Pietro Tarlati, " il Saccone," arrived with a large body of horse *ad regimen capitaneatus guerre Spoleti*, while, three months later, the Bishop of Arezzo sent " multitudinem gentium equitum in subsidium et favorem rebellium de Spoleto."[5] The Rector of the Ducato was helpless ; he had no such force at his disposal as might enable him to attack the revolted city with any prospect of success, and the Perugians, to whom he naturally turned for aid, were fully occupied with Assisi. The first efforts of the Pope were, therefore, devoted to obtaining allies. On the 23rd of March, he wrote to Orvieto, exhorting her to assist the Rector " potenter et viriliter " ;[6] while, a few days later, we find him urging the Duke of Calabria to send *oportunum sufragium gentis armigere de terris Regni* for the suppression of a rebellion which, if left unchecked, might well spread to his own dominions. At the same time, he plied the Spoletini themselves with prayers, entreaties, menaces, and severely admonished the Bishop of Arezzo,

[1] " . . . et quod anno quolibet in festo beati Herculani in Kal. mensis martii comune dicte civitatis Asisii mictet et presentabit per legitimum sindicum, nomine census et reverentie ac subiectionis comuni Perusii, unum pallium de serico distensum ad pedes Campanilis sancti Laurentii in civitate Perusii." *Arch. Stor. It.*, XVI. i. 89.

[2] See CRISTOFANI, i. 221, and the document published in *Bollettino* cited, iv. 230 n.

[3] See the document published in *Bollettino* cited, iii. 481-485.

[4] *Bollettino* cited, iii. 435, 479, 482 ; iv. 268.

[5] See the *Informatio Rectoris Ducatus Spoletani contra Guidonem Episcopum Aretinum*, published in *Bollettino* cited, iv. 266-271.

[6] FUMI, *Codice Diplomatico*, etc., *op. cit.*, pp. 447-448 ; Doc. dcxxxi.

whom he ordered to forsake his allies and to return to the obedience of Holy Church.[1]

Spoleto, however, had but little to fear so long as Muzio remained unconquered. Not only did she turn a deaf ear to the papal admonitions but, in December, 1320, she added to her other crimes by the cold-blooded murder of the Guelf prisoners. Some of them were burned alive in the tower of the Anselmi, while others were butchered like sheep in the subterranean vaults where they had been herded together for twelve weary months. The strongest among them fought desperately, and a few of them succeeded in snatching the weapons from the hands of their assailants and cutting their way out of the city; but the weaklings, the aged, the women and the children were all slaughtered in those caverns.[2]

The news of the massacre was carried to Perugia by the fugitives and filled the exiles of Spoleto with a yet keener desire for vengeance; but Perugia would not loosen her grasp upon Assisi, and without the help of Perugia nothing could be effected. Only in the autumn of 1321 was any serious attempt made to put an adequate army in the field. Then, after a conference at Foligno between Messer Cante

---

[1] *Bollettino* cited, iii. 468-471. Compare FUMI, *I Registri del Ducato di Spoleto, op. cit.*, p. 17, §§ 51, 52, 53, 55, 56, 57, etc.

[2] G. VILLANI, ix. 104 ; PARRUCCIO, *Annali, ubi cit.*, p. 112 ; MINERVIO, *De rebus gestis*, etc., *op. cit.*, p. 40 ; PELLINI, i. 462 ; SANSI, *op. cit.*, i. 195 ; MURATORI, *Annali*, ad ann. 1320. The fullest and most picturesque account is that of Baron Sansi, who, however, attributes the massacre to the winter of 1322-1323. I have preferred to follow the contemporary Villani, whose statement is substantially borne out by Parruccio, when he tells us that the Guelfs were imprisoned " da un anno in su, e poi ci misero focu e arseroli tutti." The following terrible details are given by Minervio : " Gibellini postea captivos omnes horrendis suppliciis affecerunt, magnaque lignorum circumjecta strue ad nefandae crudelitatis memoriam incendio consumpserunt. Fuitque tale incendium in turre Cioli dñi Anselmi, quæ sita erat in regione S. Benedicti, ubi mulier quædam, Aurienta nomine, patre gibellino orta, et guelfo cuidam nupta, cum duobus nondum ablactatis parvulis liberis, quos dextera laevaque trahebat, sinu fovens, ex altiori fenestra flagrantis turris, fratres suos conspicata, ipsos rogavit, ne cum filiis eam incendio consumi sinerent. Cui fratres responderunt, quod si ipsa a suis excipi vellet filios guelfi seminis in flammis relinqueret. Cumque illa generoso spiritu abundans, filios deserare negasset, incendio absumpta, periit."

de' Gabrielli and the Treasurer and Mareschal of the Ducato,[1] the communes of Foligno, Spello, Bevagna, Montefalco, Trevi, Cerreto, Cascia, Visso, Bettona, Cannara, Nocera, Gualdo and Sassoferrato were commanded to take up arms and simultaneously to make war upon Spoleto, following the banner of the Church under the command of Rinaldo di S. Artemia, Rector of the Ducato.[2] The rebellious city was laid under an interdict, and, in December, a crusade was proclaimed against Frederick of Montefeltro and his brethren, as well as against all those who favoured that "pestilent spawn of vipers," and in particular against Spoleto, Urbino, Osimo and Recanati.[3] The interdict, however, was fulminated in vain ; the Spoletini paid no manner of attention to it, and the Magistrates prevented its observance by the clergy. Priests and friars alike continued to officiate in the churches, with open doors and ringing of bells, and to bury the dead in holy ground *in contemptum clavium*.[4]

The fall of Assisi, in March, 1322, and the death of Frederick of Montefeltro a few months later,[5] were two staggering blows to the Ghibelline cause ; and when, after devastating the Val di Spoleto, the armies of Perugia and the Rector advanced to the siege of the city, the Spoletini may well have felt serious misgivings as to the ultimate result of the war. They had already sent orators to Avignon to endeavour to pacify the papal indignation, declaring that they had acted from no hostility to the Church, but had expelled the Guelfs as disturbers of the

[1] Fumi, *I Registri del Ducato di Spoleto, op. cit.*, p. 18 § 65 : " 1321—Ag. 25—Jacobo quem expendiderat quando de mandato ducis ivimus Fulginium ego et marescallus una cum d. Masseo de Montefalco pro ambasiatoribus domini ducis ad dominum Canti Capitaneum guerre, cum quo habebamus conferre multa tangentia statum provincie in Fulgineo, quia eramus duodecem in equis—*1 fl. a.*"

[2] Arch. Vaticano, *Secret Joan. XXII.* An. vi. Cta 122 (25 Ottobre, 1321) ; *Bollettino* cited, iii. 456-457.

[3] *Bollettino* cited, iii. 457, 471-481.

[4] *Bollettino* cited, iii. 483.

[5] According to Muratori (*Annali,* ad ann.), Ugolini (*Storia de' Conti e Duchi d' Urbino,* Vol. I. p. 122) and the various writers who have followed G. Villani (ix. 141), the death of Frederick occurred in April, 1322 ; whereas, as a matter of fact, the true date is either September or October. See Tonini, *Rimini nella Signoria de' Malatesti,* P. I. pp. 46-47.

public peace, who were seeking to tyrannize over their fellow-citizens and to take Spoleto from the Pope and subject it to Perugia.[1]   In July they released fourteen Guelf prisoners who had been confined *in carceribus comunis*; they made proclamation inviting the *fuorusciti* to return to their homes, and they appointed a *sapientem et discretum virum* as their Syndic and Procurator to swear submission to the will of the Pope;[2] but they none the less continued to defend themselves valiantly, and, at the approach of winter, the besiegers withdrew, having accomplished nothing.

Meanwhile, the Pope, who had " received and heard the ambassadors of Spoleto patiently,"[3] showed himself not unwilling to grant a pardon, if he could be sure of the penitence of those who sent them.   He deputed Messer Ademaro Farga, Archpriest of S. Africano, and Falcone da Siscarico, a Dominican friar, to examine whether their professions corresponded with their intentions, bidding them, together with the Rector of the Ducato, go to the Spoletini *intrinseci*, and ascertain whether they were ready to submit themselves, their goods and persons, their city and its territory, to the good pleasure and commandment of the Holy Roman Church, to recall their exiles and to live at peace among themselves.   If they were willing to do so, the papal *nuntii* were instructed to take possession of Spoleto in the name of the Church, and to concert measures *cum dilectis filiis civibus perusinis* for preserving peace between the Guelfs and Ghibellines, the *extrinseci* and *intrinseci*; while to the end that the Holy See might not be deceived or defrauded of any of its rights, both factions

[1] SANSI, *Storia del C. di Spoleto, op. cit.*, i. 194.

[2] See the *Atti del Consiglio di Spoleto relativi alla liberazione de' prigionieri Guelfi*, published by FUMI, *Bollettino* cited, vii. pp. 103-116.   The document is a most interesting one, and will bear careful study.   It admits us to the " arengna generalis et contio sive parlamentum comunis civitatis Spoleti," convened " in platea sancte Marie, ut moris est."   We are privileged to be present at the liberation of the prisoners " in via Pretenga ante carceres comunis," and to hear the proclamation for the readmission of the *fuorusciti*, made by the " preco pubblicus comunis " within the hearing of the besieging army.

[3] " . . . nuncios recepimus et audivimus patienter."

were to make oath of fealty. These instructions bear date the 31st of October, 1322, and were communicated to the Rector and to the Perugians as well as to the Spoletini.[1]

At about the same time, the Pope secretly summoned the Rector to Avignon, appointing Messer Giovanni di Amelio, the Treasurer of the Ducato, vice-rector during his absence. He provided for the levying of troops, and placed at the disposition of the Perugians, those "strenuous pugilists and athletes of God and of the Church," the tithes of the Ducato, of the Diocese of Perugia and of divers other parts, for the period of three years, "ad hoc ipsorum Spoletanorum astutiam inde credimus non eludi."[2] Orders were issued to recover and fortify the Fortress of S. Giuliano, Castel Litaldo, "Terra Arnulphorum," and the Rocche de' Cesari; while many towns and villages were withdrawn from the jurisdiction of the Ducato and included in that of the Patrimony.[3]

Although the rebels continued to negotiate throughout the summer and autumn of 1323,[4] they showed no real desire to come to terms, and, in May, the siege of Spoleto was resumed and pushed forward with the utmost vigour. Surrounded by nine *battifolli* and five camps,[5] it seemed impossible that the city could resist much longer; and, in September, the Papal Legate, the Vice-Rector and the Priors of the Arts and *sapientes* of Perugia were already discussing the "capitula que videntur utilia pro reformatione, reconciliatione et pacificatione civitatis Spoleti."[6]

---

[1] *Bollettino* cited, iii. 459-461 and notes.

[2] *Bollettino* cited, iii. 462, and compare FUMI, *I Registri del Ducato*, etc., *op. cit.*, i. § 117, pp. 25-26.

[3] *Bollettino* cited, iii. 462.

[4] FUMI, *I Registri del Ducato*, etc., *op. cit.*, pp. 19-21, i. §§ 74, 75, 76-79, 84, 90, 92, etc.

[5] SANSI, *Storia del C. di Spoleto, op. cit.*, i. 196; PARUCCIO, *ubi cit.*, 112; PELLINI, i. 467. In May, *Magister Laurentius de Senis* was summoned "ad consulendum . . . de loco novi bactifollis" (FUMI, *Registri del Ducato*, etc., *op. cit.*, i. § 71, p. 19); while, as we learn from the *Annali Decemvirali* (ann. 1323, c[ta] 246), Ambrogio Maitani was in the camp of the besiegers in June, "ad laborandum in factis et operibus necessariis in dicto exercitu et in expeditione guerre predicte."

[6] The document is published by V. ANSIDEI, *Su Alcuni Rapporti fra Perugia e Spoleto nel Secolo XIV.* in *Bollettino* cited, iii. 564-566.

9

The Spoletini, however, were not yet conquered, and their hopes were kept alive by the Bishop of Arezzo, who was in constant communication with the Ghibellines of Todi and of Narni, with Castruccio Castracane, and even with the Emperor, and who was straining every nerve to gather troops enough to raise the siege and destroy the *battifolli*.[1] Rebellion still smouldered in the March of Ancona,[2] while the capture of Città di Castello by the Tarlati, on the 2nd of October, must have served to inspire the Ghibellines with fresh courage.[3] "Et," runs the old record, "ipse Epũs aretinus scribebat Spoletinis alia multum bona."[4] Thus the defenders continued to hold out, hoping against hope, until the spring of 1324, when, besides the Perugians and the papal levies under Ugolino Trinci and Poncello Orsini, the blockading army contained troops from Siena, Florence, Montepulciano, Orvieto and Camerino.[5] So closely was the city invested that "not only was it impossible for the Spoletini to issue forth from the gates, but the arrows which they shot from their bows almost always fell within the camp of the besiegers."[6] At last, on the 9th of April, famine accomplished that which force had failed to do, and, after having gallantly defended herself for more than two years against overwhelming odds, Spoleto "surrendered freely to the Church and to the Commune of Perugia, without any condition save only that the lives of her citizens should be spared." For greater security the first to enter the town were two hundred and fifty knights of Florence and Siena, "the which protected the place"; and thereafter followed the Perugians without doing any wrong to any man. And on this wise, says Muratori, Spoleto "was brought back to the Guelf party and remained

[1] Compare the *Informatio Rectoris Ducatus Spoletani contra Guidonem Episcopum aretinum*, published by FUMI, *Bollettino* cited, iv. 266-271.

[2] As late as August, 1323, we find the Pope thanking the Perugians for the help which they had given to the Rector of the March against the Fabrianesi. *Arch. Stor. It.*, XVI. ii. 494.

[3] See the next chapter.

[4] *Bollettino* cited, iv. 270.

[5] PELLINI, i. 467; G. VILLANI, ix. 244; *Cronaca Sanese* in MURATORI, *Rer. Italic. Script.*, xv. 65; *Bollettino* cited, iii. 463 *et seq.*

[6] PELLINI, *ubi cit.*

distrettuale of Perugia."[1]   Parruccio Zampolini tells us that the arms of Perugia were painted over all the gates of the city.[2]

The *capitula* which were drawn up by the victors for the pacification of Spoleto provided that the Guelfs should return freely to their homes and should assume the government of the city.   The Ghibellines, on the other hand, were condemned to perpetual banishment ; and, although the Commune was left in possession of all its wonted jurisdictions, customs, franchises and statutes, it was compelled to acknowledge its subjection to Perugia and to the Church, with all the covenants and provisoes usual in such submissions.   Then, when it had been "reformed to the Party Guelf," the allied army departed, leaving it "half burned, half demolished, and half emptied of its citizens."[3]

On the 22nd of April, the Syndics and *procuratores* of Spoleto appeared in Perugia, and, "in gradibus scalarum que sunt in pede campanilis sancti Laurentii," formally admitted her suzerainty.   By the Act of Submission, then drawn and attested, the Commune of Perugia undertook to protect and defend the Commune of Spoleto against every *universitas*, city or individual, save only against the Roman Church and its officials ; to maintain the said Commune "in bono, pacifico et integro statu," and to "interpose instant and effectual prayers" to the end that the processes and sentences against Spoleto might be annulled and that she might be reinstated in the good graces of the Pope.   On the other hand, the Commune of Spoleto recognized the *merum et mixtum imperium* and jurisdiction of Perugia which was to be exercised by a Potestà or "Reformator, Pacificator, Conservator et Depositor" ; undertook to follow her in war and to pay *datas et collectas* and all other imposts which the citizens of Perugia paid.   She further agreed to present a *palio* of silk, every year on the festival of S. Ercolano, by the hand of her lawful Syndic, "nomine census et reverentie ac

---

[1] MURATORI, *Annali* ; G. VILLANI, ix. 244.

[2] SANSI, *Documenti inediti*, etc., *op. cit.*, p. 113 : " et furono pinte l' armi del detto commune di Peroscia ad ogni porta."

[3] SANSI, *Storia del C. di Spoleto, op. cit.*, i. 198.

subiectionis Comuni Perusij." Finally, the following proviso was inserted : *Salvo semper et reservato iure et iurisdictione quod et quam habet et habuit Ecclesia Romana in civitate et comitatu Spoleti.*[1]

This document, which differs materially from the *capitula* of September, 1323,[2] constituted a distinct usurpation on the part of Perugia and gave great offence to the Rector of the Ducato. On April 14th he wrote to Avignon that Spoleto had come into the hands of the Perugians, and, on the 20th, he sent " many letters to the Lord Pope, the Chancellor and the Treasurer of the Pope, and to the Cardinals and other Prelates of the Church, informing them in what manner the Perugians had elected a Potestà in Spoleto on their own authority, without consulting the officials of the Church."[3] In subsequent letters he declared that the Holy See had been " delusa a Perusinis."[4]   The Commune, however, had no intention of relinquishing what it had gained, and the Pope was too well aware of his dependence upon Perugian assistance to take stringent measures against his strongest and most trustworthy allies. Various contemporary bulls leave no doubt of his displeasure.[5]   In 1326, he expressed himself as *contra eos multum didignatus* ;[6] he even excommunicated them ; but absolution quickly followed,[7] and Spoleto continued to be subject to Perugia up to 1359 ; while, in 1351, she headed the list of over thirty towns and cities which sent tribute and *palii* to S. Ercolano.[8]

---

[1] See E. Loevinson, *Intorno alla sottomissione di Spoleto a Perugia nel 1324*, in *Arch. Stor. It.*, Serie v., Tom. XIII. (1894), pp. 98-104, where the document is printed in its entirety.

[2] See page 129 *supra*.

[3] Fumi, *I Registri del Ducato*, etc., *op. cit.*, i. §§ 151-152, p. 31.

[4] *Ibid.*, i. § 162, p. 33.

[5] *Bollettino* cited, iii. pp. 553-554 ; *Arch. Stor. It.*, XVI. ii. 494 ; E. Loevinson, *ubi cit.*, p. 103.

[6] Fumi, *I Registri del Ducato*, etc., *op. cit.*, i. § 266, p. 50.

[7] *Bollettino* cited, iv. 221 and note.

[8] Pellini, i. 906 ; Bonazzi, i. 436.

CHAPTER X

THE WAR WITH CITTÀ DI CASTELLO

THE submission of Spoleto did not bring peace; for, while Spoleto was still battling desperately for independence, Perugia found herself involved in a new and disastrous war with another old ally. In the autumn of 1323, Città di Castello ranged herself in the Ghibelline ranks; and Città di Castello bred warriors every whit as valiant as those of Perugia.[1] Henceforward, there was to be but little wasting of hostile territory and building of *battifolli* round about beleaguered cities; rather were the Perugians forced to fortify their own walls and to strain every nerve to protect their own *contado*.[2]

The defection of Città di Castello seems to have been entirely due to the overweening ambition of Messer Brancaleone de' Guelfucci, the head of the Guelf Party, who had succeeded in making himself despot of the Commune, and (says Muratori) "grievously oppressed that people." Many of the principal citizens were driven into exile, and, rather than submit to the rule of Brancaleone, those who remained abandoned their political faith and appealed to the Bishop of Arezzo for assistance. On the night of the 2nd of October, 1323, three hundred Aretine horsemen, together with a considerable body of foot-soldiers, entered the town through the Porta S. Giuliana, which had been opened to them by the conspirators. They were led by Arrigo, Marquis of Petrella, Tarlatino and Pier Saccone, the brothers of the Bishop, and Gerio di Tano degli Ubaldini. The first warning which Messer Brancaleone had of his danger was, probably,

---

[1] See MUZI, *Memorie Civili*, etc., *op. cit.*, Vol. I. p. 10.
[2] See ANSIDEI e DEGLI AZZI, *Regesto di Documenti del Secolo XIV. relativi a Città di Castello esistenti nell' Archivio Decemvirale del C. di Perugia* in *Bollettino* cited, vi. 440; Doc. lxvi.

the thunder of the hoofs of the Ghibelline cavalry as they *corsono la terra* at daybreak. Resistance was useless, and he and his partisans sought safety in flight. Among the fugitives was the Potestà, Messer Pietro de' Vincioli of Perugia. Not content with the expulsion of the despot and his creatures, the Aretines proceeded to drive out all the Guelfs, including even the traitors who had admitted them.   Città di Castello became wholly Ghibelline.[1]

The news of this revolution was received with indignation and alarm by all the Guelf communes of Central Italy ; while the Perugians themselves were filled with consternation. All their available troops were besieging Spoleto, and it was feared for the moment that the enemy might even attempt to surprise Perugia. Measures were at once taken for the protection of the city, and, on the 3rd of October, the Priors resolved that five captains should be elected for each Porta "super custodia civitatis et burgorum Perusij," to whom should be given full authority and discretion in all matters touching the defence and fortification of the city and its suburbs.[2]   Ere long the ambassadors of Perugia, Siena, Bologna, Orvieto and Gubbio met in Florence to organize a league for the recovery of Città di Castello ;[3] it was agreed that three thousand men-at-arms should be enlisted for three years at the joint expense of the allies, and Guido, Marquis of Monte S. Maria, was appointed Captain-General for the first six months. He seems to have been a typical feudal seignior, violent and blood-stained ; among his other crimes was the murder of a monk, whom "ausu sacrilego interfecit."   The Pope, however, proved placable, and the warrior who was to lead the Guelf armies against the common enemy found but little difficulty in obtaining

[1] VILLANI, ix.   226 ;   FABRETTI, *Cronache*, i. 74 ; PELLINI, i. 467 ; MURATORI, *Annali*, ad ann. ; MUZI, *op. cit.*, i. 143-144 ; FUMI, *Eretici e Ribelli*, etc., *op. cit.*, cap. iv. (*Bollettino* cited, iv. 439 *et seq.*).

[2] ANSIDEI e DEGLI AZZI, *Regesto*, etc., *op. cit.*, Doc. lxvi. It may be noted as an indication of the alarm of the Perugians that whereas, in 1315, after the Battle of Montecatini, it had been deemed sufficient for the public safety to appoint ten *Capitani delle Porte* (p. 114 *supra*), the Priors now elected no fewer than five Captains for each Porta, or twenty-five in all.

[3] AMMIRATO, *Istorie Fiorentine* (edition cited), Tom. II. Lib. vi. p. 104.

absolution.[1] The League was published in Florence on the 21st of March, 1324 ;[2] and, on the 28th of May, the Florentine contingent of three hundred and forty horsemen set out for Perugia under the command of Messer Amerigo Donati.[3] Nothing, however, seems to have been accomplished ;[4] and, in the following year, the fall of Pistoia obliged the Florentines, in their turn, to call upon their friends and allies for assistance. Three hundred men-at-arms in the pay of Perugia fought in the Guelf army at the Battle of Altopascio, and, after Raimond of Cardona had been taken prisoner by Castruccio, Messer Oddo degli Oddi succeeded him as *Capitano di Guerra* in Florence.[5]

In the meantime, Monte S. Maria, which had become the centre of the war with Città di Castello, was strongly garrisoned [6] and furnished with new fortifications on the design of Ambrogio Maitani of Siena,[7] who, together with his more celebrated brother Lorenzo, was employed by the Perugians, during the spring and summer of 1325, to put their *contado*, and more particularly the northern and western portions of it, in a state of defence. In addition to Monte S. Maria, Ambrogio fortified La Zeppa di Valiano in the Val di Chiana ;[8] while Lorenzo was sent to examine and report on the condition of all the castles, towns and fortresses of the *contado* of Porta S. Susanna and Porta S. Angelo (*comitatûs porte sancte Susanne et porte Sancti Angeli*), and especially the town and citadel of Castiglione del Lago,[9]

---

[1] FUMI, *Eretici e Rebelli*, etc., in *Bollettino* cited, iv. 440, and note 2. Guido seems to have entered upon the discharge of his duties as " Captain of the Tallia of the knights of the communes of Florence, Siena, Bologna, Perugia, etc." on the 1st of March, 1324. See DEGLI AZZI, *Le Relazioni*, etc., *op. cit.*, ii. § 222, p. 56.

[2] PELLINI, i. 467 ; AMMIRATO, *ubi cit.*, p. 108 ; *Cronaca Sanese*, in MURATORI, *Rer. Italic. Script.*, xv. 65.

[3] G. VILLANI, ix. 253.

[4] In November they had not yet even selected the site on which to build the " terra nova sive battifolle, que fieri ordinata est pro recuperatione Civitatis Castelli." DEGLI AZZI, *Le Relazioni*, etc., *op. cit.*, ii. § 225, p. 56.

[5] G. VILLANI, ix. 320 ; PELLINI, i. 471, 473 ; DEGLI AZZI, *Le Relazioni*, etc., *op. cit.*, ii. §§ 234-237, pp. 58-59.   [6] PELLINI, i. 470.

[7] ANSIDEI e DEGLI AZZI, *Regesto*, etc., *op. cit.*, Doc. ciii., cxv.

[8] *Annali Decemvirali* del 10 aprile, 1325, a c^{ta} 13t.

[9] *Annali Decemvirali* del 16 novembre, 1325, a c^{ta} 125.

which he is said to have surrounded with *carbonaie*.[1] In Perugia, as in Orvieto, he was both a civil and military architect—" generalis superstes omnium operum comunis " —and to him must be attributed the restoration of the great aqueduct which supplied the Fonte Maggiore with water.[2]

No merely defensive preparations, however, could suffice to save Perugia from mortifying reverses, and the successive disasters which befell the Guelf arms in Tuscany reacted calamitously upon events in Umbria. In vain she summoned the Counts of Marsciano and Campiglia to join the armies of the League, in vain she demanded assistance from all the towns of the Ducato and imposed extraordinary taxes ;[3] her former victories had now turned to her disadvantage, and, when the Tarlati, strong in their alliance with Castruccio and the Visconti and vaunting their prerogatives of Imperial Vicars, called the Ghibellines of Umbria to arms, she beheld ranged against her all that vast company of exiles whom she had helped to drive from Assisi and Spoleto.

The object of the Tarlati was the isolation of Perugia. The Marquis of Petrella and the Bishop of Arezzo attacked Cortona and attempted to take it from the sons of

[1] FUMI, *op. cit.*, cap. iv. (*Bollettino* cited, iv. 440).   *Carbonaia* is said to be equivalent to the Latin *pomœrium*, and was, in fact, a fosse constructed below the walls of a town or fortress to render an escalade more difficult. In time of war the *carbonaia* was filled with faggots which were set on fire as soon as the enemy commenced their assault, and the name is probably derived from the quantity of charcoal which resulted. See *Il Costituto del Comune di Siena* (1309-1310), *op. cit.*, Vol. II. p. 622. In the *Glossario*, s.v. " Carbonaia."

[2] See A. ROSSI, *Lorenzo ed Ambrogio Maitani al servizio del C. di Perugia,* in the *Giornale d' Erudizione Artistica* pubblicato a cura della R. Commissione conservatrice di Belle Arti nella Provincia dell' Umbria, Vol. II. fasc. iii. Marzo, 1873.   It has been justly remarked that, in the Middle Ages, no vocation was more laborious or varied than that of the architect. " Uniting the practice of arms with an intimate knowledge of design, their services were sought for in every part of Europe, either to plan fortresses, build palaces, cast statues, paint frescoes, execute hydraulics, or command troops." See E. HUTTON'S new edition of DENNISTOUN, *Memoirs of the Dukes of Urbino* (London : John Lane, 1909), Vol. III. p. 265.

[3] PELLINI, i. 476.

Guglielmino, the friends of the Perugians.[1] They kept alive the discords of the Ducato; they fomented disorders in Il Chiugi, and sowed dissensions in the Guelf army. Ere long Castel della Pieve revolted and expelled Messer Tillo de' Vincioli, the Perugian Potestà, together with many of the Guelfs;[2] while, as early as March, 1325, the conduct of the mercenaries in the pay of the Commune gave cause for great uneasiness. In that month Ferrantino Malatesta actually ravaged the *contado* of the friendly Cortona, already in deadly peril from the incursions of the common enemy.[3] The Cities of the League, each of which had its own troubles nearer home, left all the burden of the war on the shoulders of the Perugians, who, in their turn, began to grow weary and demanded a subvention from the Pope " de pecunia Ecclesie et decimarum circumstantis provincie et de aliis remediis oportunis pro expensis dicte tallie."[4] Hostilities languished, and when, in February, 1326, " many noble and notable men of the Ghibelline faction" were taken prisoners in an engagement between the garrison of Città di Castello and the Perugian mercenaries,[5] the Guelfs, with that precious pledge in their hands, were perfectly ready to treat for peace. Not only was the treasury of Perugia practically empty, but the Marchesi del Monte were wellnigh ruined, their lands laid waste, their farms and villages destroyed, their vassals " taken, slain, burned,

---

[1] *Bollettino* cited, iv. 441 and note 2, where a long extract is printed from the *Annali Decemvirali* of 17th November, 1325. It is probably unnecessary to remind the reader that the animosity which Bishop Guido displayed towards Cortona was largely due to the fact that the Pope had just constituted that city the seat of a new bishopric, thus materially diminishing the diocese of Arezzo; while insult had been added to injury by the choice of Ranieri degli Ubertini as the first Bishop. Compare MANCINI, *Cortona nel Medio Evo, op. cit.*, pp. 97-98.

[2] PELLINI, i. 477. See also the document published in *Bollettino* cited, iv. 442 n.

[3] *Annali Decemvirali* del 7 Marzo, 1325, a c^{ta} 8^t; *Bollettino* cited, iv. 441 n. 2, and compare ANSIDEI e DEGLI AZZI, *op. cit.*, Doc. lxx.

[4] *Annali Decemvirali* del 28 Dicembre, 1325, a c^{ta} 150^t; *Bollettino* cited, iv. 442-443 notes.

[5] G. VILLANI, ix. 341; PELLINI, i. 478-479. The document to which Pellini refers is published in *Bollettino* cited, iv. 444 n. 1. See also ANSIDEI e DEGLI AZZI, *op. cit.*, Doc. ccxviii., ccxix.

mutilated and despoiled." [1]   In April, the dissensions among
the *fuorusciti* of Città di Castello became so violent that
special enactments were passed, inflicting a fourfold penalty
on disturbers of the peace and invoking the *lex talionis* in its
crudest form.[2]   The negotiations, which dragged on until
December, were rendered abortive by the refusal of the
Tarlati to abandon the seigniory of the revolted town.
The Magistrates of Perugia, indeed, seem to have been
willing to consent to almost any terms if only they might
have peace ; but the rest of the citizens refused to accept
their decision, and, having forced their way into the Palazzo,
compelled the Priors to summon a *parlamentum*.   The
capitula which had been drawn up were torn to pieces and
scattered to the four winds of heaven amid deafening
shouts of " Guerra ! Guerra ! " [3]   The war was resumed, and
Ugolinuccio d' Ufreducciolo d' Alviano, of the noble family
of the Atti of Todi, was appointed Captain.[4]

Meanwhile, the aid of Perugia had been demanded by
the Rector of the Patrimony against the rebels of Narni ; [5]
while, early in 1327, the revolt of Fermo and Fabriano
compelled her to send Messer Oddo degli Oddi with two
hundred men-at-arms into the March of Ancona.[6]   The
Pope was prodigal in praise and thanks, but neither praise
nor thanks could fill the exhausted coffers of the State.   In
March, Spoleto, grown weary of servitude, presented the
silken *palio* without due words of vassalage and had to be
coerced into obedience ; [7]   Assisi showed signs of disaffec-

---

[1] *Annali Decemvirali* del 21 luglio, 1326, a c^{ta} 154 ; *Bollettino* cited, iv.
445 n. 1 ; ANSIDEI e DEGLI AZZI, *op. cit.*, Doc. cclxxvii.

[2] *Annali Decemvirali* del 4 aprile, 1326, c^{ta} 64^t ; *Bollettino*, cited, iv.
441 n. 1 ; ANSIDEI e DEGLI AZZI, *op. cit.*, Doc. ccxlii.

[3] FABRETTI, *Cronache*, i. 13, 76 ; PELLINI, i. 487-488. See also *Frammenti di cronaca Perugina inedita*, published by O. SCALVANTI, *Bollettino*
cited, xi. 579.

[4] PELLINI, i. 489.

[5] PELLINI, i. 489 ; ANTONELLI, *op. cit.*, pp. 47-50 ; *Bollettino* cited, iv.
447 *et seq.*

[6] PELLINI, i. 489, and documents in *Arch. Stor. It.*, XVI. ii. 501-503.

[7] FABRETTI, *Cronache*, i. 14, 77 ; PELLINI, i. 491 ; SANSI, *Storia del C
di Spoleto, op. cit.*, i. 200. Compare also *Arch. Stor. It.*, Serie v. Tom.
XIII. (1894), pp. 103-104.

tion,[1] and, in May, there were fresh tumults in Castel della Pieve.[2]

In September, Pier Saccone sat down before Monte S. Maria, and though, owing to the disheartenment caused in the Ghibelline ranks by the news of the death of the Bishop of Arezzo,[3] the Perugians were enabled to raise the siege and to destroy the *trabocchi* and *battifolli* which had been constructed round about the place,[4] they were forced to make peace a few months later, leaving Città di Castello to the Tarlati. "And this they did (says Giovanni Villani) because they were utterly weary of the said war, and because, by reason of the coming of the Bavarian, they could get no help from the Florentines and the other Tuscans."[5]

[1] PELLINI, i. 492.
[2] GRAZIANI, *ubi cit.*, p. 94 ; PELLINI, i. 493.
[3] G. VILLANI, x. 35.
[4] GRAZIANI, *ubi cit.*, p. 96 ; FABRETTI, *Cronache*, i. 16 ; PELLINI, i. 495.
[5] G. VILLANI, x. 51.

CHAPTER XI

THE COMING OF LEWIS OF BAVARIA

FOR years the Ghibellines of the Ecclesiastical State had looked forward to the coming of the Emperor as to that of the Messiah;[1] and the march of Lewis of Bavaria from Tuscany southward was one long triumphal progress. It is true that Montalto opened her gates to him reluctantly and only paid the *fodrum* for fear of destruction, but Corneto and Toscanella hailed him with enthusiasm and Viterbo welcomed him royally. On the 2nd of January, 1328, the keys of that city were consigned to him by Silvestro Gatti, and, on the 5th, he left for Rome,[2] there to be acclaimed by the populace *ut Deo ab excelsis veniente.*[3] Yet nowhere in all Italy was the rejoicing greater than in the Ghibelline strongholds of Amelia and Todi. As fresh tidings of the Emperor's advance arrived from Pisa, from Viterbo and from Rome, the streets and squares of Amelia flamed with bonfires and rang with delirious shouts of joy and triumph: "Long live the holy Emperor! Death to John of Cahors, heretic, paterene, sodomite and false Pope!" A dog, which the populace had christened "*Papa Johagne,*" was dragged through the city, beaten and drowned; while, as we learn from the *Processus contra Amelienses* which was opened in Perugia on the 26th of October, 1329,[4] on the

---

[1] "Quem in ipsis partibus velut adventum Messie dicuntur vanis cogitationibus expectare." So wrote John XXII. to the Rector of the Patrimony, in December, 1325, speaking of the Viterbesi, Cornetani and other rebels who accepted Lewis as Emperor and King of the Romans in spite of the sentence which the Vatican had fulminated against him. RIEGLER, *Vatikanische Akten zur deutschen Geschichte in der Zeit Kaiser Ludwigs des Bayern* (Innsbruck, 1891), Doc. dxcviii., cited by ANTONELLI, *La dominazione pontificia nel Patrimonio*, etc., *op. cit.*, p. 52 n. 1.

[2] ANTONELLI, *op. cit.*, p. 52.   [3] MILMAN, *op. cit.*, Vol. VII. p. 415 n.

[4] Published in *Bollettino* cited, v. 340-349.

very day that the Emperor entered Rome (7th January, 1328) a vast crowd assembled in a suburb of Amelia *quod dicitur spiazo*,[1] and having filled a sack with straw and labelled it "Pope John," burned it with every manifestation of hatred and loathing, as if burning a heretic. When news came of the election of the Antipope, Pietro di Corbara (12th May, 1328), more than two hundred citizens were seen *euntes per terram, saltando in choreis*, with lighted candles in their hands, leaping and rejoicing and crying aloud : "Death to the Roman Church, prostitute, harlot, simoniac ! "[2]

Nor was the enthusiasm of Todi one whit less fervent than that of Amelia; for, of all the Umbrian communes administered by the Rector of the Patrimony, these two were the most rebellious. Especially was the City of Jacopone the centre of Ghibelline revolt and of the religious movement which accompanied it. Set between the Guelfic communes of Perugia and Orvieto, her geographical position alone would probably have sufficed to make her anti-Guelf; and when, together with Terni, Narni and Rieti, she was severed from the Ducato to form a *Commissariato* under the jurisdiction of the Rector of the Patrimony,[3] her Ghibellinism grew fiercer and more inflexible. None of the communes affected by the new arrangement were contented, but Todi absolutely refused to accept it. She allied herself with Viterbo, Arezzo and Pisa, and became a terrible thorn in the side of the Rector, whose authority she declined to acknowledge, declaring that even the Holy See itself possessed no temporal jurisdiction within her territories.[4]

---

[1] *Spiazo*, or, as it is elsewhere written in the same document, *spazo*, is equivalent to the modern *piazzetta*. Compare GRAZIANI, *ubi cit.*, p. 324 : "A queste tempe sempre se predicò a Santo Francesco nella *spiaza* de fuora."

[2] Compare FUMI, *Eretici e Ribelli*, etc., *op. cit.*, cap. v. (*Bollettino* cited, v. 20-21,) and see SCALVANTI, *I Ghibellini di Amelia e Lodovico il Bavaro*, in *Bollettino* cited, xii. 235-265.

[3] See page 94, n. 1 *supra*. The first Rector of the Patrimony to be invested with this "Commissariate" was Guglielmo Costa. See the Brief of Pope John XXII. of the 27th October, 1318, in the *Arch. di S. Fortunato di Todi*, A. I. C., iv. n. 160, and *Bollettino* cited, v. 1, in nota.

[4] FUMI, *Eretici e Ribelli*, etc., op. cit., App. v. Doc. i., in *Bollettino* cited, v. 24-32.

In spite of the entreaties and menaces of the Pope she gave sanctuary to Muzio of Assisi and to numerous other heretics and rebels condemned by the Inquisition, while her open adherence to the schism of Michael of Cesena proves how easy it is to pass from political to religious antagonism when the Church,

> Per confondere in sé due regimenti,
> Cade nel fango, e sé brutta e la soma.[1]

By the publication of the Bull *Cum inter nonnullos,* John XXII. had arrayed against himself the whole body of earnest Franciscans ; and thenceforward the Ghibelline ranks included all that was most puritanical [2] as well as all that was most licentious in mediæval society.   There were the Fraticelli, the Spirituals and the Michaelists, ruthlessly persecuted for their loyalty to the Rule of their Founder and to the ideals of the *Fioretti* ; and, because human nature is what it is and mysticism in all ages has been the parent of sensuality and general corruption,[3] there too were innumerable renegade friars who, under the cloak of religion, indulged in such abominations as, even in the so-called Ages of Faith, when the morality of the monastic orders was, perhaps, at its lowest, the Church might hardly endure. The worst of the *novelle* of Boccaccio and Sacchetti are no worse than the actual facts.[4]

While yet the Emperor was at Trent, Todi had sent him letters of felicitation, and no sooner had he entered Lombardy than she hastened to acclaim him her suzerain.[5]   True it is

---

[1] *Purgatorio,* xvi. 128-129.

[2] I use the word " puritanical " advisedly.   Compare G. G. COULTON, *The High Ancestry of Puritanism* (*Medieval Studies,* No. 4, Simpkin, Marshall & Co.).

[3] See MAX NORDAU, *Degeneration* (English translation, 1895), p. 89, and compare an excellent article on *The Inner Life and its Dangers,* in *The Spectator* of February 23, 1901.

[4] Compare, for example, *Processo originale dell' Inquisizione contro Paolo Zoppo,* published by FUMI in *Bollettino* cited, v. 349 *et seq.,* with F. SACCHETTI, *Nov.* 101, and *Decamerone,* iii. 10.   As to the Franciscan revolt in general, see F. TOCCO, *L'Eresia nel Medio Evo* (Firenze, Sansoni, 1884), Lib. ii. cap. ii.

[5] " . . . pars Gebellina de Tud. scripsit dicto Bavaro dum erat Tridenti, et quando d. B. venit in Lombardia vocaverunt eum dominum in d. Civ. Tud." FUMI, *Eretici e Ribelli,* etc., App. vii. in *Bollettino* cited, v. 321.

that she was not very prompt in furnishing the *subsidium armatorum* which he demanded for his march to Rome:[1] but many of her nobles joined his standard.   The Counts of Marsciano and of Baschi, the Alviano and the Chiaravallesi welcomed his coming as they had welcomed that of Henry of Luxembourg eighteen years before, while Ugolinuccio di Baschi and Baldino di Marsciano, in particular, were among his most intimate familiars and councillors.[2] The former, at any rate, was with him at Pisa, and, together with the Imperial *maliscalco* and the Counts of Santa Fiora, was sent forward to seize the passes of the Maremma and to provide food and forage for the army.[3]

At this time the chiefs of the Ghibelline faction in Todi were Bartolello di Corrado and Matteolo di Gentiletto de' Chiaravallesi.   The Commune was governed by twelve "Conservators" called *del pacifico stato*; and the Potestà was the excommunicated Borgaruccio da Matelica, one of the fiercest Ghibellines of the March.   Both Borgaruccio and his son Ranuccio had incurred the enmity of the Inquisition by their zealous support of Luppaccio and Andrea of Osimo, "public and manifest heretics and persecutors of the Church," whom we have seen leagued with Frederick of Montefeltro;[4] and no sooner was Borgaruccio elected Potestà than Fra Servo della Penna, the Inquisitor of Ancona,[5] took steps to have him expelled from that office.   The Bishop of Todi was ordered to publish the excommunication of both father and son with bell, book and candle in the Cathedral Church, *publice coram populo*. The election was declared null and void, and the Magistrates were admonished that no obedience was to be paid to

---

[1] See the letter of Lewis the Bavarian to the Commune of Todi, "data Viterbii die iiij Januarij regni nostri anno xiiij (January 4, 1328)." It is published by FUMI in *Bollettino* cited, v. 38.

[2] See the *Processo dell' Inquisizione contro Todi*, published by FUMI, *Eretici e Ribelli*, etc., *op. cit.*, App. vii. (*Bollettino* cited, v. 269-340).

[3] G. VILLANI, x. 48.

[4] See page 116 *supra*.

[5] Fra Servo della Penna was himself a Minor Friar. Even after the revolt of the Michaelists, the "superficially correct and self-satisfied majority" were, probably, still faithful to the Church. See G. G. COULTON, *The Failure of the Friars* (*Medieval Studies*, No. 9).

Borgaruccio, whose arms, horses, gear and salary were to be sequestrated.   If the Bishop refused to obey, he was to be threatened with suspension *a divinis* and, finally, with ex-communication : while, if the Magistrates proved recalcitrant, the city was to be laid under an interdict.   The Council assembled.   Gualterello Pennazza "consuluit" in favour of the Potestà and carried his motion by 191 votes to 48— a sufficient indication of the state of parties in Todi.   The majority against the Church was wellnigh four to one.[1]

On the following day (17th January, 1328) Lewis of Bavaria was crowned in Rome by Sciarra Colonna.

Towards the middle of February, a body of fifteen hundred German horse, under the command of the Imperial Chancellor, moved against Orvieto, and, after receiving re-inforcements from Viterbo, swept down the fertile slopes which surround the Lake of Bolsena, burning, ravaging and destroying.   Bolsena itself withstood their attack, but Latera, Gradoli and Valentano went up in flames.   Many of the inhabitants were slain and many more were led captive to Viterbo.   At Gradoli, for example, the dead numbered sixty, the prisoners a hundred and ninety. Terrified by the fate of her neighbours, the Commune of S. Lorenzo sent the keys of her gates to the Imperial Chancellor at Gradoli ; while Montefiascone, in hourly ex-pectation of attack, besought assistance from Orvieto, who in her turn, called upon Perugia for aid.   However, on the 4th of March, the troops of the Emperor were recalled to Rome to suppress a revolt which had been provoked by the excesses of his German followers, and before Messer Becello de' Baglioni reached Orvieto with the Perugian succours, the danger was over.[2]   In the meantime, another

[1] ARCH. COM. DI TODI, *Rif. ad ann.*, c. 71t (*Bollettino* cited, v. 34-38) The word *consuluit* was the technical term for moving a resolution. The presiding officer asked counsel (*consilium petiit*) and thereupon one of the councillors rose to his feet and *consuluit*. He was said to *arengare* while, finally, the agreement of the majority to the motion before the house was expressed by the word *acordare*. Compare L. ZDEKAUER, *La vita pubblica nel Dugento, op. cit.*, p. 12.

[2] G. VILLANI, x. 65 ; ANTONELLI, *op. cit.*, pp. 52-53, and authorities there cited ; GRAZIANI ,p .98 ; PELLINI, i. 499-500. Messer Becello di Messer Gualfreduccio de' Baglioni left Perugia on the 10th of March at the

body of Germans under Tebaldo di S. Eustachio occupied almost the whole of the Sabina ;[1] while according to the chronicle attributed to Graziani, "in the said month of March, the Vicar of the Duke of Bavaria entered Todi with a great multitude of horse."[2]   We also have record of a skirmish beneath the walls of Narni, on the 4th of June, when three hundred men-at-arms in the pay of Perugia routed a larger German force ;[3] but it was not until the Emperor himself left Rome (4th August) that serious hostilities recommenced.   On the 6th he reached Viterbo at the head of more than 2500 German horse, without counting his Italian allies, and thence he invaded the *contado* of Orvieto, trusting to the promise of the Filippeschi that the city itself would be betrayed into his hands on the Vigil of Our Lady of Mid-August, when, as in Siena [4] and Pisa,[5] all the citizens were wont to carry their offerings of wax candles to the Duomo.[6]

In pursuance of this plot, the Emperor sat down before Bolsena with his main army, while the rest of the troops ravaged the country up to the walls of Orvieto. Bolsena, however, once more resisted valiantly, and when, on the 14th of August, "the Imperial Mareschal, with a thousand men-at-arms appeared before the gate of Orvieto which goeth toward Bagnorea, as it pleased Our Lady, ere yet he had come thither, the aforesaid conspiracy and treason were made manifest and the traitors were put to death."   Wherefore, continues the chronicler, "after that the Bavarian had failed of his purpose, he departed from Bolsena, on the following day, he and all his host, and

---

head of " 200 cavaliere inglese e francesche."   At this time the Floren-tines also seem to have continually demanded aid from Perugia.   See DEGLI AZZI, *Le Relazioni*, etc., *op. cit.*, i. §§ 47, 48, 49, 50, 57, 58, pp. 17-18.

[1] ANTONELLI, *op. cit.*, p. 53.

[2] GRAZIANI, *ubi cit.*, p. 98.   Compare FABRETTI, *Cronache*, i. 18, 79.

[3] G. VILLANI, x. 76 ; GRAZIANI, p. 99 ; PELLINI, i. 501-502.

[4] See my *Palio and Ponte*, *op. cit.*, Book I. chap. iii.

[5] *Ibid.*, p. 14.   See also E. HUTTON, *Florence and Northern Tuscany* (Methuen, 1907), pp. 90-93, and compare P. VIGO, *Una festa popolare a Pisa nel Medio Evo* (Pisa, Tip. Mariotti, 1888), p. 9 and Doc. xi.

[6] Compare FUMI, *Codice Diplomatico*, etc., *op. cit.*, p. 765 nota.

returned to Viterbo with his false Pope and his Cardinals and all his folk, and came to the City of Todi." [1] Ghibelline Todi received him with open arms. In vain the Bishop Ranuccio, praised and exhorted by the Pope and zealously supported by the doughty old knight Andrea di Ranuccio, his father, sought to persuade the citizens to close their gates against the foreigners. [2] In vain two merchants were sent to the Imperial camp, " in plano Paterni " in the *contado* of Orvieto, to offer four thousand golden florins if only Lewis would consent not to enter Todi; the Chiaravallesi outbid them, promising more than ten thousand florins, [3] and the impecunious Bavarian accepted the larger bribe.

On the 19th of August, at Ponte Martino on the Naia, he was welcomed by a noble company which had come forth to do him honour. [4] Barons and knights vied with one another in carrying the silken baudekins which, " ut est moris," were held above the heads of the Emperor, the Empress and the Antipope, and in leading their horses. Ugolinuccio di Baschi and Baldino di Marsciano preceded their guests with the German men-at-arms, and, in order to prevent any hostile demonstration on the part of their adversaries, occupied every point of vantage in the city. As the procession approached the gates it was met by the Friars Minor of S. Fortunato, walking two and two and bearing the Cross before them. Fra Francesco della Bionda offered it to the Empress to kiss. The people, who thronged the streets, uncovered their heads and bent their knees, and, when the Emperor dismounted before the Palazzo Pubblico,

---

[1] G. VILLANI, x. 95 ; GRAZIANI, p. 100 ; ANTONELLI, *op. cit.*, pp. 55-56.

[2] FUMI, *Eretici e Ribelli*, etc., in *Bollettino* cited, v. 10.

[3] *Processo contro Todi, ubi cit.*, p. 276. This document enables us to correct the narrative of G. VILLANI (x. 95), who, as usual, when writing about the enemies of Florence, deals in those half truths which are the worst of lies. For him, " il Bavaro " was capable of every iniquity.

[4] Compare the original document (*Processo contro Todi, ubi cit.*, pp. 277-278), where we have a vivid touch in the words " in quodam alboreto." It was August, and doubtless the " multi barones et domini " who were waiting for the Emperor and the Antipope were glad enough to be able to take advantage of the shade while they " ordinaverunt et se ad invicem diviserunt . . . qui eorum deberent portare bravium sive pallium et qui predictos adestrare deberent."

the great square rang with shouts of *Viva! Viva!* Doubtless some among the crowd shouted rather from fear than love,[1] but Ugolinuccio was in the Piazzi, bestriding his warhorse and armed to the teeth. Even for a Guelf, to shout were wiser.

The Antipope, who was lodged in the Monastery of S. Fortunato, proceeded pontifically to the Duomo, where he celebrated the divine offices and gave his blessing to the people. A plenary indulgence was granted, and from the pulpit of S. Fortunato the Minor Friars preached continually that he, Nicolas V., was the true Pope and John of Cahors a heretic, paterene and excommunicate. The Abbeys and Monasteries which remained faithful to the Church were forcibly occupied, and canonries, prebends and benefices were freely distributed to Ghibelline ecclesiastics. Among the most favoured were the kinsfolk of the Chiaravallesi and the Counts of Marsciano.[2] If, however, the great feudal families profited by the coming of the Bavarian and his Antipope, the Imperial sojourn in Todi was a heavy burden to the citizens generally, for, " in those days, nothing was done save to seek and squander money : money for the Procurator-General of the Treasury ; money for the Emperor ; money for his *ostiarî* and for Ugolinuccio ; money for Sciarra Colonna, *commannatore* of the Germans ; money for the Imperial Chancellor." At first, the Secret Council of the Commune was obstinate and refused to allow the citizens to be despoiled ; but its resistance was overcome when the Potestà ordered the two urns in which the votes of the Councillors were deposited to be placed at some distance from one another, so that it might be plainly seen who voted for the motion and who against it.[3] Andrea di

---

[1] Many of the witnesses examined by the Inquisitors declared that they acted " *propter timorem,*" " *propter timorem mortis,*" " *propter timorem jam dictum,*" etc. etc.

[2] *Processo contro Todi, ubi cit.,* pp. 274, 313, 314, 328, *et passim.*

[3] Mannuccio " Marchelli " testified *quod interfuit Consilio quando fuit deliberatum de dandis .x. milibus flor. Bavario, in quo Consilio semper dixit contrarium, donec Potestas dividi fecit bussulas ubi mictebantur pallocte et tunc postmodum propter timorem posuit palloctam quod sic, sil : quod darentur B. dicti floreni.* See also more fully in the evidence of Gualterello " Vivieni." *Processo contro Todi, ubi cit.,* p. 323.

Ranuccio, who had the courage to oppose a resolution that the city should be freely given to the Emperor, was fined four hundred lire, and *The Council of One Hundred* was superseded by a Commission or *balìa* of eighteen citizens, who forthwith levied an extraordinary tax " pro dono domino Imperatori." [1]

During the twelve days which Lewis remained in Todi, he sent the Count of Oettingen into the Romagna with five hundred horse, " the which, with the force of the Ghibellines of the Romagna, rode even unto the gates of Imola, burning and wasting everything." Meanwhile his Mareschal ravaged the *contado* of Bevagna, and attempted to surprise Foligno at the head of a thousand men-at-arms, only to find himself thwarted by the vigilance of the Trinci ; " wherefore he returned to Todi, burning and consuming and gathering spoil from the towns of the Ducato." [2] Finally, on the last day of August,[3] " the Bavarian departed from Todi with all his folk and with his Pope and the Cardinals which he had made," leaving the citizens the poorer by more than 25,000 florins, and the Church of S. Fortunato despoiled of all its jewels and reliquaries even to its costly silver lamps which were taken away by the Antipope.[4]

The intention of the Emperor had been to march through the Perugian *contado* to Arezzo, as Henry of Luxembourg had done, and thence to advance upon Florence by the way of the Val d' Arno. At the same time Castruccio was to invest it from the west, while the Ubaldini and the Count of Oettingen with the Ghibellines of the Romagna were to raise the standard of revolt in the Mugello. The enterprise,

---

[1] Fumi, *Eretici e Ribelli*, etc., in *Bollettino* cited, v. 12-13. In giving the number of the members of the *balìa* as 18, I have followed the *Processo contro Todi*. According to the *Riformagioni Comunali*, they were 24.

[2] G. Villani, x. 95 ; Graziani, p. 100 ; Pellini, i. 503. See also V. Jacobilli, *Cronache Mss. di Foligno*, cited by Fumi in *Bollettino* cited, v. 14 n. 1, and the *Cronica Sanese* in Muratori, *Rer. Italic. Script.*, xv. 83.

[3] The *Processo contro Todi* not only supplies the documentary evidence of which Bonaini laments the lack, in his note to Graziani, p. 101, but it also proves the accuracy of that chronicler, for, in the deposition of Fra Paolo Telli, we read that the Emperor abode in Todi " per dies xij continuos " (*Bollettino* cited, v. 278).

[4] G. Villani, x. 95.

however, was abandoned owing to the mortal sickness of Castruccio ; and on the arrival of ambassadors from Don Pedro of Aragon, who was lying off Corneto with the Sicilian fleet, Lewis marched to meet him.[1] Thence he withdrew to Pisa, to Pavia, to Cremona and to Parma, and slowly abandoned Italy, "leaving behind him (says Gregorovius) no other results of his coming than the ruin of the ancient Ghibelline Party and an infinite confusion."[2] Yet, peradventure, the statement must not be taken absolutely literally, for out of that "infinite confusion" sprung those principles of popular sovereignty which rendered possible the splendid vision of an Italy confederated *pro bono et pacifico statu totius humanitatis* and capable of maintaining its independence against both Pope and Emperor.[3]

Already, in his *Defensor Pacis*, Marsiglio of Padua had asserted the rights of the State as against the Church. Law he there defined as "knowledge of what is just or useful, concerning the observance of which a coercive precept has been issued." The legislator is "the people or community of the citizens, or the majority of them, determining, by their choice or will, expressed by word in a general assembly, that anything should be done or omitted regarding men's civil acts under pain of temporal punishment"—a definition which, as Dr Creighton remarks, could hardly be improved upon at the present day. Nor did Marsiglio shrink from the logical consequences of his position. He declared the legislative power to be the source of the authority of the prince or ruler, and asserted that, if the prince set himself above the laws, he ought to be corrected by the legislative power which he represents.[4]

This teaching was eagerly welcomed by the Italian communes, and in Perugia found its most characteristic expression in the concise declaration of Bartolo da Sassoferrato : *Civitas perusina non subsit Ecclesie nec Imperio* ;

---

[1] G. VILLANI, x. 96, 100 ; NAPIER, *Florentine History*, Vol. I. p. 524.

[2] GREGOROVIUS, *op. cit.*, Vol. III. Lib. xi. cap. iv. p. 315.

[3] See pages 95-96 *supra*, and FILIPPINI, *La Riconquista dello Stato della Chiesa*, etc., *ubi cit.*, pp. 176-177.

[4] CREIGHTON, *A History of the Papacy*, Vol. I. p. 43.

while his great disciple, Baldo degli Ubaldi, proclaimed the democratic sovereignty in no uncertain terms.[1]   The arms of the Bavarian were not successful, but, if indeed he ruined the Ghibelline party, he also struck a terrible blow at the papal authority, and left behind him a confusion in which the seeds of popular independence germinated and out of which there grew new thoughts and new ideals.

The conflict with Lewis of Bavaria ends the Mediæval period of the history of the Papacy.

[1] O. SCALVANTI, *I Ghibellini di Amelia*, etc., *op. cit.*, in *Bollettino* cited, xii. 247-248.

CHAPTER XII

THE "RED BOOK"

THAT war has often proved the school of all the virtues and peace the breeding-ground of all the vices, can hardly be denied by any impartial student of history; and, after the passing of the Bavarian, for a few years Perugia had peace. The result, or, at any rate, the sequel, was an open rupture between the classes and the beginning of a blood feud between the great houses of the Baglioni and the Degli Oddi which endured for over two centuries.

At the close of the thirteenth century, these two families had acquired a notable preponderance in Perugia,[1] and there can be no doubt that, during the first quarter of the Trecento, the Nobles continued to occupy an honoured and honourable position in the State.[2] Many of them dedicated themselves to the study of law, and the toga of the *doctor* was often joined to the sword of the *miles*.[3] They served upon important embassies to Kings and Princes;[4] they were summoned to rule as Captains of the People or Potestà in allied and friendly Republics,[5]

---

[1] ANSIDEI, *Alcuni appunti per la storia delle famiglie perugine Baglioni e Degli Oddi*. Per le nozze Manzoni-Degli Oddi (Perugia, Unione Tip. Cooperativa, 1901), p. 10.

[2] Thus, for example, we find that, in 1308, the *nobilis et potens milex dominus Gualfredutius domini Johannis domini Balionis* was a member of the Consiglio Generale, and that, later on, when he was elected Potestà of Fermo, the Priors refused to permit him to accept that office "quod presentia nobilis militis domini Gualfredutij de Ballionibus est in civitate Perusij nimium fructuosa et absentia eius a civitate predicta hoc tempore Comuni et populo perusino posset essere dampnosa." *Annali Decemvirali*, 1308, c.ta 32t; 1310, c. 67 e 68r.

[3] BONAZZI, i. 540.   [4] ANSIDEI, *op. cit.*, pp. 10-15.

[5] See, for example, G. PARDI, *Serie de' Supremi Magistrati e Reggitori di Orvieto*, etc., in *Bollettino* cited, i. 383-387, and the chronological series

and by them were filled the majority of the vicariates
and potestarie of the subject towns and communes;[1]
while, lastly, the military offices were almost exclusively
in their hands.   It is true that the general employment
of mercenary troops had already done much to weaken
their position; and, as early as 1325, we find a first sign
of the coming change in the appointment of Ceccolino
de' Michelotti, a *popolare*, to the post of Councillor to the
Captain-General of the *Taglia* against Città di Castello;[2]
but, as long as Perugia was at war, the Nobles were far
too useful to be needlessly antagonized.   Moreover, they
were not without powerful allies.   From its foundation
by Pietro Vincioli, in the tenth century,[3] the Monastery
of S. Pietro had jealously maintained its independence
alike of the Bishop and of the Commune, acknowledging
no other suzerain than the Pope alone.   A great ecclesiastical feudatory, its dominion extended over many
churches and villages in the Perugian *contado*, and, from
1270, all its Abbots, without exception, had been drawn
from the Perugian nobility.[4]   Nor is there any reason
to suppose that these *Magnates de prole militari* put off
the habits and prejudices of their class with their lay
garments.   The warrior was hardly less a warrior and
the noble no whit less a noble because he had assumed
the cowl.   Witness the vengeance taken by Abbot

of Umbrian Magistrates in Florence during the fourteenth century,
published by Degli Azzi as an appendix to his *Le Relazioni*, etc., *op. cit.*,
i. pp. 255 *et seq.*

[1] Ansidei, *ubi cit.*; Pellini, *passim*.

[2] Ansidei e Degli Azzi, *Regesto di Documenti del Secolo XIV. relativi
a Città di Castello, op. cit.*, Doc. cxi.-cxii.   The reasons given for the appointment are significant: " quod honera tam pro factis guerre quam etiam
aliis et tempore guerre et pacis comuniter suportantur tam per nobiles
et magnatos quam etiam [per] populares civitatis eiusdem et propter hoc
equitas suadit et unitas civium perusinorum hoc exposcit quod offitia et
emolumenta offitiorum inter eos participentur et comuniter distribu-
antur. . . ."

[3] See Bartoli, i. 189.

[4] L. Brunamonti Tarulli, *Appunti storici intorno ai Monaci Bene-
dettini di S. Pietro in Perugia*, etc., in *Bollettino* cited, xii. 385 *et seq.*   For
the possessions of the Monastery in the Perugian *contado*, see Bartoli,
i. 200 n.

Raniero II., of the ancient house of Coppoli, upon the rebels of Casalina, when, in spite of the fact that they were protected by the Commune, he destroyed "manu armata dictum Castrum, asportando seu asportando faciendo exinde omnia bona mobilia hominum predictorum."[1]   This Raniero, the first of a long series of noble Abbots, was twice nominated by the Canons of the Cathedral to the Bishopric of Perugia and twice refused the proffered honour.   During his rule, many illustrious guests were magnificently entertained in the Monastery, and, among the rest, the two Cardinal Legates who were sent by Pope Nicolas IV., in 1289, to negotiate peace between Perugia and Foligno.   Together with several of his monks he was present at the submission of the latter city, on the 22nd of August.[2]

Raniero was succeeded, in 1290, by Orlandino of the Nobles of Montevibiano, a stanch adherent of the Baglioni,[3] then allied with the Raspanti, and sharing with the Degli Oddi the honours and emoluments of the Commune.[4]   Nor, as touching the power of the nobles at this time, is the fact without significance that it was not until the third decade of the fourteenth century that the streets and piazze of Perugia were "incatenate" or furnished with chains, to the end that they might be barricaded at a moment's notice against the charge of an ironclad feudal cavalry, thus putting the *pedites* on terms of equality with the *milites* in the event of a conflict.[5]

[1] L. BRUNAMONTI TARULLI, *ubi cit.*, p. 408.   As we learn from a diploma of the Emperor Henry III., the Corte di Casalina was granted to the Monastery by Pope Benedict VIII. : "et massam Casalini a Benedicto Papa per privilegium datam eidem Monasterio, et a Patre meo et a me modis omnibus eidem confirmata" (MARIOTTI, *Mem. delle Chiese di Perugia Mss.*).

[2] PELLINI, i. 303, 305 ; *Bollettino* cited, xii. 409 and n. 5.

[3] *Bollettino* cited, xii. 410-411.

[4] *Brevi Annali, ubi cit.,* pp. 59-60.   The passage is obscure ; but it seems that Messer Giovanni de' Baglioni was "caporale" of one section of the Raspanti, while Messer Giapeco Degli Oddi and Messer Piero de' Vincioli were "caporali" of the other.   Compare PELLINI, i. 329.

[5] *Brevi Annali, ubi cit.,* pp. 64-65 ; GRAZIANI, pp. 95, 99 ; FABRETTI, *Cronache,* i. 16, 18 ; PELLINI, i. 494.   In the neighbouring Orvieto there had been chains since about 1316, and their numbers were increased in

Even during the period when the popular party was at its strongest, not only the Potestà and the Captain of the People, the two chief Magistrates of the Republic in whose hands was concentrated almost the whole executive power of the State, but also the *Maggior Sindaco*, the judges and all the other foreign officials were invariably Nobles and *cavalieri* ;[1] and it was only natural that, with the best intentions in the world, they should often display bias towards members of their own class. It is, probably, to this state of things that we owe the earliest legislation against the Nobles, who seem to have taken advantage of their influence with the Magistrates to interfere with the administration of justice and with the government of the city generally. According to Pellini, a law existed, as early as 1306, which provided that neither Jurisconsults (*Dottori*), Knights nor Nobles should enter the Palaces of the Commune.[2] In 1317, provisions were discussed in the Councils to prevent many crimes remaining unpunished " propter familiaritatem frequentiam quam Magnates civitatis Perusij et etiam alij perusini habent cum postestatibus et capitaneis civitatis Perusij ; "[3] while Pellini informs us that, in 1322, "the law was renewed that the Nobles . . . and Jurisconsults might not enter the Palace of the lord Priors, without the licence of at least seven of them."[4]   It was

1322 ; while in Siena, according to Andrea Dei, " si cominciarono a porre le catene per le vie di Siena nel mese di Giugno," 1312.   See FUMI, *Codice Dipl., op. cit.*, p. 770 ; *Cronica Sanese* in MURATORI, *Rer. Italic. Script.*, xv. 48, and my *Historical Introduction* to Miss L. OLCOTT's *Guide to Siena* (Siena, Torrini, 1903), p. 65.

[1] DEGLI AZZI, *I " Paria" delle Società democratiche medievali* in *Varietà Storiche perugine* (Perugia, Tip. Umbra, 1900), pp. 56-57.   See also the Statute of 1342, Lib. i. Rubrics 4, 20.   This state of things was, of course, not peculiar to Perugia.   Compare, for example, *Il Costituto del C. di Siena* (1309-1310), *op. cit.*, and DEGLI AZZI, *Le Relazioni*, etc., *op. cit.*, i. § 65, p. 21.

[2] PELLINI, i. 347.

[3] *Annali Decemvirali*, ad ann. c. 161t ; ANSIDEI, *Alcuni appunti*, etc., *op. cit.*, p. 13 ; PELLINI, i. 423.

[4] PELLINI, i. 461.   The enforcement of the law proved difficult, and we find that the Priors were often compelled to give the Nobles permission to frequent both the Palazzo del Popolo (the residence of the Captain) and the Palazzo del Comune (the residence of the Potestà).   Such permission was, however, invariably accompanied by some restriction, being limited, *e.g.*, to such Nobles as wished to go thither " tantum pro eorum causis " ;

not, however, until eleven years later that any systematic attempt was made to relegate the Nobles to a condition of legal inferiority. The loss of the *Annali Decemvirali* from 1327 to 1351 leaves us very much in the dark as to the immediate cause of this disastrous change of policy ; but this much is certain that the compilation of the *Libro Rosso*, in 1333, marks the point of time when that same poison which had so long been working in the veins of the Italian body politic, and which had produced the *Ordinamenti sacrati et sacratissimi* of Bologna and the *Ordinances of Justice* in Florence, finally permeated and corrupted the laws and institutions of Perugia.

The *Libro Rosso*, or " Red Book," was a register in which were inscribed the names of all the Nobles of Perugia : " Hic est liber sive registrum, continens in se nomina et prenomina Mangnatum et de prole militari ex paterna linea de civitate et comitatu Perusij, et aliorum Mangnatum civium perusinorum, pro qualibet Porta," etc.[1] Unlike the *Libro d' Oro* of the Republics of Venice and of Genoa, the *Libro Rosso* was not a record of merit and of privilege, but was compiled for the injury and oppression of those whose names were contained therein, to the end that they might be liable to a double penalty, whenever they were adjudged guilty of any transgression of the law.[2] Nor was this the only disability under which they laboured. The Statute of 1342 contains innumerable provisions which were obviously dictated by hatred of the military caste, and which were intended to reduce the *Magnati* to a condition of complete subservience to the Raspanti.[3]

and even then access was only granted " in salis inferioribus ubi generaliter jura redduntur " (*Annali Decemvirali*, 1326, c. 4ʳ e 147). Often too licence had to be given to single individuals, as, for example, in November, 1326, to " domino Oddoni domini Ungari entrandi pallacium et domos eorum habitationis " in connection with his appointment as ambassador to King Robert of Naples (*Annali Decemvirali*, cc. 223ʳ e 227ᵗ).

[1] The *Libro Rosso* is published in its entirety by A. Fabretti, *Documenti di Storia Perugina* (Torino, 1887), Vol. I. pp. 102-122.

[2] Pellini, i. 521.

[3] Thus, the Nobles were forbidden to speak with the Potestà or with the Captain of the People in specified places and at specified times (Lib. iii. Rubric 146) ; to give security for persons charged with offences against the

Of the events which preceded and induced this legislation we have, as I have said, no certain knowledge; but the chronicles, though they make no mention of the *Libro Rosso* nor of any contemporary struggle between the Nobles and the People, do something more than hint at a period of aristocratic insolence and lawlessness, which may well have provoked the *popolari* to reprisals.

On the 6th of November, 1330, Messer Francesco of Lucca, Bishop of Perugia, died; and, a few days later, the Chapter of the Canons of S. Lorenzo nominated as his successor Messer Ugolino de' Vibiani, Abbot of S. Pietro. Thereafter, on the 2nd of December, a great council was assembled in the Palace of the Potestà on the motion of Messer Vinciolo Novello, who produced certain letters which he had written to the Pope in the name of the Magistrates of the city, recommending the election of a kinsman of his own, a certain Fra Alessandro Vincioli.[1] These he demanded that the Priors should seal with the seal of the Commune. He was supported by Messer Baglione Baglioni and his partisans; while, on the other hand, Messer Oddo di Longaro Degli Oddi, "con molta gente de populare" upheld the rights of the Canons. The result was a tumult, for which the Priors and Camarlenghi banished the leaders of both factions "con molte populari e con molta gente de grandezza."[2] Apparently, pardon followed close upon the heels of condemnation; Messer

---

law (Lib. iii. Rubric 13); to lay informations before certain officials (Lib. iii. Rubric 144), and to enter the public palaces (Lib. iii. Rubric 143). If a Noble committed any crime to the injury of one of the *popolari*, he and his accomplices were liable to a fourfold penalty, or, in cases of homicide or mayhem to capital punishment (Lib. iii. Rubric 150). Moreover, when accused of any offence, there was no necessity for the production of probable proof before his arrest. The bare fact that he was a Noble sufficed to overbear every presumption of innocence (Lib. iii. Rubric 144). See on the whole subject DEGLI AZZI, *I " Paria" delle Società democratiche medievali, ubi cit.*

[1] Fra Alessandro de' Vincioli, Cavaliere Gerosolimitano, was ambassador to the Pope at Avignon, in 1322. PELLINI, i. 460.

[2] GRAZIANI, i. 104; *Brevi Annali*, 65-66; FABRETTI, *Cronache*, i. 20-21; PELLINI, i. 511-512; BONAZZI, i. 406-407.

Oddo Degli Oddi had served the State in many capacities [1] and was far too valuable a citizen to be allowed to languish long in exile. Unfortunately, however, the Vincioli were not minded to forgive the part he had played in thwarting their scheme for the advancement of Fra Alessandro, and, on the 1st of December, 1331, Messer Oddo Degli Oddi was treacherously slain by Don Uccio di Gualfreduccio de' Baglioni, Priore di Fonte, his brother Filippuccio and Cecchino di Messer Vinciolo, "with certain of their cut-throats and varlets." And thus, says Bonazzi, "miserably perished the man most deserving of his country's gratitude, after having cheated Death in so many glorious battles." His murder aroused the strongest indignation in Perugia, and the assassins would, probably, have been torn in pieces by the populace, if they had not sought refuge in the Convent of S. Domenico.[2] On the 30th of January, 1332, they were outlawed by the Potestà Ottaviano "domini Belfortis de Vulterris," and their banishment lasted full twenty years, since they were only permitted to return to their homes in July, 1352, when the loss of Bettona and the war with the Visconti induced the Magistrates to grant

[1] A few of the services which Messer Oddo Degli Oddi rendered to Perugia may be here recorded. In 1309, he was sent to Bologna to request that " amore et gratia comunis Perusij . . . per comune Bononie detur licentia . . . domino Jacobo Belviso de morando et stando in civitate Perusij ad legendum " (*Annali Decemvirali*, 1308-1310, c. 36t). From 1315 to 1316, he was Potestà in Castel della Pieve, and succeeded in reducing " ad concordiam et unitatem . . . homines ipsius castri ad invicem se odiantes " (*Annali Decemvirali*, cc. 144r-148r). In 1321, he was sent as ambassador to quiet a tumult between the Guelfs and Ghibellines of Chiusi ; and, in 1322, to persuade the Monaldeschi of Orvieto to live at peace among themselves. During the war with Città di Castello, in 1325, he was commissioned to treat on behalf of Perugia with the Bishop of Arezzo and the Marquises of S. Maria del Monte ; while, in 1326, he acted as ambassador " ad regiam maiestatem domini Regis Roberti in servitium comunis Florentie " (*Annali Decemvirali*, cc. 223r, 227t e 228r). He was also a valiant captain, and the Perugian levies fought under his command, in 1315, at the Battle of Montecatini, in 1322, in defence of the fortress upon Monte d' Artone, in 1324, at the siege of Spoleto, in 1325, against Castruccio Castracane at Altopascio, and, in 1327, against the Marquis of the March, who had espoused the Ghibelline cause. Compare *Arch. Stor. It.*, XVI. i. 86, 91 ; FABRETTI, *Cronache*, i. 9, 12, 14, 72, 75, etc. ; and, on the whole subject, see ANSIDEI, *Alcuni appunti*, etc., *op. cit.*, p. 15 n.

[2] GRAZIANI, pp. 105-106 ; FABRETTI, *Cronache*, i. 21-22, 82.

a general amnesty to all exiles.[1]   In a note to the Chronicle
of Graziani, Fabretti publishes a petition which was presented, in that year, by the procurators of the Baglioni to
Bartolomeo " de Mangiatoribus de Sancto Miniate," Captain
of the People, beseeching him to compel Giacomo Degli
Oddi and all his house to *facere pacem veram et bonam*.[2]
The document clearly demonstrates the mortal hatred
which still existed between the two families and the
unalterable determination of the Degli Oddi to take
vengeance for the death of their great kinsman.   In those
days, blood could only be washed out with blood ; and,
from thenceforward, the feud between the Baglioni and the
Degli Oddi never died.

The split in the ranks of the Nobles may have seemed to
the Raspanti too excellent an opportunity to be lost.   At
any rate, as I have said, the *Libro Rosso* made its appearance in 1333.   The result was calamitous in the extreme.
No longer able to present a united front to her enemies,
Perugia's strength was fatally diminished, and her loss of
independence was merely a question of time.   For many
years the internal history of the Commune is simply the
history of the struggle between the Nobles and the *Popolo
grasso*.   As early as 1351 there was a dangerous conspiracy to overthrow the popular government, in which
several of the Vincioli were implicated ;[3] while, in 1353,
there were renewed disorders, which resulted in the whole
body of the Nobles leaving the city.[4]   However, the details
of the conflict between the classes continue to be extremely
meagre until after the disastrous war with Siena had
undermined the prestige of the ruling oligarchy.   Thenceforward the weakened condition of the body politic rendered
it incapable of further resistance to the deadly virus with
which it had been inoculated ; and, reckless of everything

---

[1] GRAZIANI, p. 160 : " Adì 20 de luglio nel dicto millesimo el
comuno de Peroscia fece rebandire tutti li sbanditi della cità e del
contado. . . . "

[2] *Arch. Stor. It.*, XVI. i. 106-107.

[3] *Supplemento secondo al* GRAZIANI, *ubi cit.*, p. 154.

[4] GRAZIANI, p. 169 : " per la qual cosa dicti principali citadini . . .
partirono tutti de la cità. . . . "

THE CHURCH OF S. AGATA

save factional hatred, Perugian fought with Perugian until the Raspanti were annihilated.

In other cities the *Popolo minuto* took advantage of the struggle between the *Magnati* and the *Popolo grasso* to assert its own supremacy. As early as the last decade of the thirteenth century, Florence had seen a sword-cutler, a butcher and a baker seated among her Priors; [1] while, in 1378, all social distinctions were temporarily obliterated by the rebellion of the Ciompi.[2] Siena had her *Monte de' Dodici* her *Monte de' Riformatori* and her *Monte del Popolo* : [3] but Perugia knew none of these. As long as the Commune endured, her citizens were divided into two, and only two, hostile camps. The battle was fought out between the Nobles and the Raspanti. It is true that the inhabitants of Porta S. Angelo often showed themselves turbulent and intractable. Assembled in their Church of S. Agostino they fearlessly criticized the conduct of the Magistrates, and more than once forced them to conform to their wishes : [4] but all they ever demanded was redress of grievances; they never themselves attempted to grasp the reins of government. The only record which I have found of the election of a *Priorato* consisting of members of the *Popolo minuto* belongs to the year 1378 ; and the cause and manner of its creation go far to show how little reason the ruling classes in Perugia had to dread an upheaval from below. A joint government of Nobles and Raspanti had proved unworkable ; accusations of treachery and worse were being freely bandied about, and a commission had been appointed to inquire into the matter. Under these circumstances it was felt that, pending the investigation, the chief magistracy of the Commune should be filled by persons who had no interest in the questions at issue. The Priors for the next two months were therefore chosen *a saputa* from the ranks of the *Popolo minuto*. They

[1] See SALVEMINI, *Magnati e Popolani in Firenze, op. cit.*, p. 196.

[2] NAPIER, *Florentine History*, ii. 421 *et seq.*

[3] See my *Historical Introduction* to Miss L. OLCOTT's *Guide to Siena, op. cit.*

[4] PELLINI, i. 1096, 1312-1313, 1320, etc. etc.

obediently accepted the office assigned to them and as obediently left it when their services were no longer required by their social superiors.[1]   Neither Giano della Bella nor Michele di Lando have any counterpart in Perugian history.

[1] PELLINI, i. 1195, and see Chapter XX. *infra.*

CHAPTER XIII

THE WARS WITH AREZZO AND WITH THE TARLATI

THE death of Bishop Guido, in 1327, had not shaken the power of his house, and, under the leadership of Pier Saccone, the Tarlati of Pietramala not only continued to rule as despots in Arezzo, but extended their dominions as far as Romagna and the March. Masters of Borgo S. Sepolcro, of Città di Castello, of Fabriano, of Massa Trabaria, of Castiglion Aretino, and of the whole of the Casentino, they reached the apogee of their greatness in 1335, when, grown arrogant with good fortune, they attacked the town of Cagli, which was under the protection of Perugia.[1]

The loss of Città di Castello still rankled, and, at this new aggression, the Perugians forthwith prepared for war. Neither did they lack allies; the aggrandisement of the Tarlati had been accompanied by infinite usurpations, and the Ubertini, the Faggiuola, the Counts of Montefeltro and of Montedoglio, together with innumerable petty seigniors, both Guelf and Ghibelline, were only too anxious to take vengeance on their despoilers. A secret agreement was entered into with Ranieri de' Casali, lord of Cortona, and a body of troops under Neri della Faggiuola was sent to surprise Borgo S. Sepolcro. The town itself was betrayed into his hands on the 8th of April, 1335; but the citadel held out until the 20th, when the Aretines, who had marched to its relief, were defeated with considerable slaughter at Anghiari. Many prisoners were taken and three standards. The garrison thereupon capitulated—a heavy blow to the reputation of Piero, and "the beginning of the ruin and abasement of his house."[2]

[1] See *Bollettino* cited, iii. 197-198, Doc. xxxvi.-xxxvii. (28th May, 1259).
[2] G. VILLANI, xi. 25; *Annales Arretini*, in MURATORI, *R. I. S.*, xxiv. 873;

devastation of Aretine territory, every punctilio of vengeance was fully satisfied, and the Perugians, upon whom the expenses of the war were beginning to weigh somewhat heavily, were about to disband their army when a new and unexpected success determined them to press their advantage with all possible vigour. The cause of this revival of martial ardour was no less an event than the taking of Città di Castello, which was betrayed into the hands of the Marquis of Monte S. Maria, on the night of the 30th of September, by three brothers, former vassals of his, who were on guard at one of the gates. The garrison, though completely taken by surprise, barricaded the streets and made a gallant defence, but were unable to withstand the onset of the German men-at-arms. Before sunrise, the town was once more in possession of the Perugians. The Citadel was starved into surrender five days later. Among the prisoners were Messer Rodolfo Tarlati and his three sons.[1] In after years the Castellani observed the 1st of October as a public festival " ad decorem, memoriam et reverentiam propter recuperationem nostri status per expulsionem tyrannicæ pravitatis Petramalensium." [2]

At about the same time an incursion of the Aretines into the Cortonese was repelled with considerable slaughter, the raiders being driven into Montecchio in headlong rout,[3] and a general invasion of the enemies' territory was resolved on. The allied army was increased by levies from Assisi, Spoleto, and other vassal cities ; and, on the 28th of October, the great Standard of the Commune, a Lion Gules upon a field argent,[4] was solemnly consigned to Messer Nicolò degli Armanni.[5] A large body of horse under Neri della Faggiuola

[1] VILLANI, xi. 37 ; GRAZIANI, pp. 110-111 ; PELLINI, i. 530 ; FABRETTI, Cronache, i. 84.

[2] Statuto di Città di Castello, Lib. ii. c. 104 ; MUZI, Memorie Civili, etc., op. cit., i. 147.

[3] GRAZIANI, p. 111 ; PELLINI, i. 531.

[4] " el gonfalone bianco con lo leone vermiglio." The Lion was the emblem of the Guelf party and consequently the Standard of all the Guelf cities. PELLINI (i. 533) tells us that " questo standardo . . . era con molto solennità conservato e per ogni picciola impresa non si traheva fuori."

[5] This was the illustrious house which afterwards took the name of Della

rode northward to Citerna, which had rebelled against the Tarlati and appealed to Perugia for succour,[1] while the main army entered the Aretine *contado* from the southward. Foiano and Gargonza opened their gates at the first summons, and numerous towns and villages in the Val d' Ambra sought refuge from the coming storm in voluntary dedition to Florence, agreeing to present a wax candle yearly at the feast of S. Giovanni in sign of vassalage ; " the which," says Villani, " was a fine acquisition for the Florentines and a great enlargement and gain to their *contado*." [2]

A momentary reverse at Castel di Rondine[3] hardly delayed the Perugian advance, and on the 12th of November the invaders encamped at the Cathedral of Arezzo, which, in those days, stood outside the walls of the city. " And," says an old chronicler, " they gave battle to the city ; also they caused the prostitutes to run the *palio*, before the gate thereof, with their garments raised even to their girdles ;[4] and they coined money in the said Cathedral according to the coinage of Perugia. Divers days they encamped at the said Cathedral, and ever the Standard of the Commune of Perugia stood planted upon the bell-tower thereof . . . also, while they abode there, Messer Boso degli Ubertini, the

Staffa. *Dominus Nicolaus Cieccoli domini Hermanni* is inscribed in the *Libro Rosso* among the *Mangnates et Nobiles de prole militari ex paterna linea de Porta S. Angeli.*

[1] *Arch. Stor. It.*, XVI. i. 112. [2] G. VILLANI, xi. 41.

[3] GRAZIANI, pp. 112-113.

[4] See on the whole subject my *Palio and Ponte, op. cit.*, Book I. chap. i., and especially page 21 n. Throughout the Middle Ages such spectacles continued to be extremely common ; and, over a century later, we find that a race for prostitutes was included among the other pageants which were organized to do honour to the Feast of S. Feliciano at Foligno. The course extended from the Palace of the Governor to that of the Priors. The winner received a handful of hemp, a pound of pepper, and two bundles of leeks. Compare A. FABRETTI, *La Prostituzione in Perugia* (Torino, 1898), where the following extract from the *Annali della Riformazione di Foligno* (an. 1447-1450, fol. 19) is printed :—

Ordo omnium que fieri solent in festo beati et glorioso Feliciano. . . .

. . . .

14. Meretrices currunt ab hostio Gubernatoris usque ad Palatium magnif. d. Priorum, ubi ponitur manipulus unus canapis, libra una piperis, et manipuli duo porrorum, et prima adiungens et citius currens ea omnia reportat.

Bishop-elect of Arezzo, sang mass therein ;[1] and there were done many other despites which are not here set down." Lastly, on the 17th of November, the victors returned to Perugia. " And the prostitutes which had run the *palio* at Arezzo returned ; and they came all clad in rosy-red, both they and their horses ; and they brought with them the said *palio*. Moreover, many marble images were brought, which were found in the said Cathedral, the which were drawn on waggons by oxen ; and the oxen and the waggons were covered with red cloth ; and the said images were set before the Church of S. Lorenzo in Perugia, toward the Piazza ; and in like manner the said *palio* was placed there, *perpetue rei memorie*."[2]

In February, 1336, hostilities recommenced, and, after gaining a bloody victory near Monte S. Savino,[3] the Perugians once more advanced upon Arezzo, which they hoped would be betrayed into their hands by adherents within the walls. The attack failed owing to the vigilance of Pier Saccone,[4] but the peril had been imminent, and repeated reverses had so humbled the pride of the Tarlati that they now professed themselves ready to treat for peace. Their real object, however, was to gain time, and the negotiations which followed led to no result.[5] In April it became known that Messer Piero had entered into an alliance with

---

[1] Boso, who had been appointed to succeed the deposed and excommunicated Guido Tarlati, had as yet been unable to take possession of his See (MANCINI, *op. cit.*, pp. 96-98, and authorities there cited). In August, 1325, Pope John XXII. had requested the Perugians to assist him (*Arch. Stor. It.*, XVI. ii. 495).

[2] It has been conjectured that some of the *inmagine de pietra o volemo dire de marmo*, which were thus brought from Arezzo, may still be seen in the courtyard of the *Canonica* of Perugia, *e.g.* those which are numbered respectively, 69, 88 and 89 (see the article signed " K " in *Il Giornale dell' Umbria* of 13-14 January, 1906) ; while, if we may credit the inscription between the two small columns at the so-called *Arco de' Pucci* in Assisi, the Assisani also, who fought in the Perugian army, carried similar trophies away with them. Compare CRISTOFANI, *op. cit.*, i. 224.

[3] GRAZIANI, p. 114 ; PELLINI, i. 534-535.

[4] *Annales Arretini, ubi cit.*, col. 876 (20th March) : " Tunc Dominus Petrus tractabat cum ipsis proditoribus, ita quod ipsi milites venerunt ad ipsam januam (*i.e.* Porta Buia) dicta die et subter pontem miserunt aliquos famulos, non enim Capitanei ausi sunt intrare quia sagaces fuerunt."

[5] GRAZIANI, pp. 114-115.

Mastino della Scala, and was hourly expecting reinforcements ; while, a little later, news arrived that eight hundred
men-at-arms had actually reached Forlì. Their further
advance was only prevented by the prompt action of the
Florentines, who occupied all the passes into the Romagna.[1]
On the 3rd of July the great Standard of Perugia was once
more brought forth and consigned to Guido, Marquis of
Monte S. Maria. On the same day the Florentines invaded
the Aretine territory by the way of the Val d' Arno, and,
after terribly devastating the *contado*, the allied armies encamped beneath the walls of Arezzo, where, on the 2nd of
August, the festival of S. Donato, the patron saint of the
beleaguered city, the Perugians caused a *palio* to be run on
the *Prato Vecchio*. The prize was a piece of red velvet, or,
as the Aretine chronicler calls it, a *tovaglia*.[2] The race was
run " in the same way as the Aretines were wont to run it
on that day, in despite of the men of the City of Arezzo, and
to their shame and infamy." [3]

Despairing of succour from Verona and alarmed at the
growing discontent among the citizens, Piero was now
ready to treat for peace in earnest ; but he was none the
less determined to make the best terms possible, and while
he openly negotiated with Perugia, his agents were busy in
Florence, where he possessed many friends and kinsmen.[4]
According to the terms of the league between the two
communes, exclusive acquisitions or separate negotiations
were forbidden to either confederate without the express
sanction of the other ; but Florence, now as always, utterly
unscrupulous when honest dealing stood in the way of her
ambition, shamelessly betrayed her ally, and agreed to
purchase the rights of the Tarlati in Arezzo for 25,000
florins of gold, and those in the Val d' Ambra for another

---

[1] VILLANI, xi. 48. On the 22nd of April, 1336, Pope Benedict XII.
wrote to the Perugians informing them that he had forbidden Mastino
della Scala to give help to Pier Saccone. The document is published in
Arch. Stor. It., XVI. ii. 508.

[2] " Et ibi currerunt Palium, videlicet unam Tovagliam."

[3] GRAZIANI, p. 115 ; FABRETTI, *Cronache*, i. 85 ; PELLINI, i. 535 ;
Annales Arretini, ubi cit., col. 876.

[4] His mother was a member of the Frescobaldi family.

14,000 florins. This *grande tradimento*, as Graziani calls it, was completed on the 7th of March, 1337, and, three days later, twelve Florentine Commissaries, at the head of five hundred men-at-arms and more than three thousand foot soldiers, took possession of the city.[1]

Great as was the indignation of Perugia, she was in no condition to break with Florence, and, finding that all her complaints and protests were disregarded, she was fain to content herself with the temporary acquisition of a few inferior towns,[2] and the right of nominating a Judge of Appeals, who should reside in Arezzo for seven years, with the title of "Conservator of the Peace."[3]   On the 29th of April, the syndics of Florence, of Arezzo, and of the Tarlati, came to Perugia, and there, *in gradibus campanilis ecclesie sancti Laurentij*, "they ratified the peace between the Commune of Perugia, the Commune of Arezzo, and the Commune of Florence ; . . . and, in token of peace, they kissed one another upon the mouth, to wit the Syndic of the Commune of Florence and the Syndic of the Commune of Arezzo with the Syndic of the Commune of Perugia . . . and at all these things were present Messer Rodolfo of Pietramala and his three sons, the which were prisoners of the Commune of Perugia : and that same day they were released from prison.   Moreover, when the said

[1] G. VILLANI, xi. 59-61 ; AMMIRATO (edition cited), Vol. II. Lib. viii. pp. 301-307 ; PELLINI, i. 537 ; *Arch. Stor. It.*, XVI. i. 117 ; *Cronica Sanese*, in MURATORI, *R. I. S.*, xv. 96 ; BONAZZI, i. 418-419 ; SISMONDI, *op. cit.*, Vol. II. cap. xxxiii. p. 289.

[2] *Annales Arretini, ubi cit.*, col. 877 ; and compare the document printed in *Arch. Stor. It.*, XVI. ii. 510-514, with DEGLI AZZI, *Le Relazioni*, etc., *op. cit.*, ii. § 301, pp. 75-76 and note.   The Perugians were given Foiano, Lucignano and Monte S. Savino for eight years and a half.   DEGLI AZZI, *op. cit.*, ii. p. 69.   In 1339, according to G. VILLANI (xi. 105), " quietarono i Perugini a' Fiorentini ogni ragione della questione d' Arezzo, rimanendo a' Perugini libero Lucignano d' Arezzo, e il Monte a San Savino, e altre castella d' Arezzo che si teneano."   *Cf.*, however, document in *Arch. Stor. It.*, XVI. ii. 515-521, and especially p. 520.

[3] VILLANI, xi. 61 ; FABRETTI, *Cronache*, i. 86 ; PELLINI, i. 540.   The " Conservator of the Peace " seems to have been a mere figure-head, without influence or authority : " Tunc, die 23 Setembris, Iudex Appellationum de Perusia venit Arretium, qui habebat salarium per sex menses in C Florenis et NIHIL ALIUD LICET EI FACERE IN CIVITATE " (*Annales Arretini, ubi cit.*, col. 878).

peace was made, there were present ambassadors from Gubbio, ambassadors from Città di Castello, ambassadors from Assisi and from Foligno, and from many other towns which are not here set down.[1]   And all the aforesaid persons ate together in the Palace of the Captain of the People, with the Lords Priors of the Arts, at the expense of the Commune of Perugia.   The aforesaid Messer Rodolfo was clad in scarlet silk with two skins of miniver, and each of his sons in a garment of divers colours with French lining, at the cost of the said Commune." [2]   On the 2nd of May, the prisoners who had been taken at the Battle of Carbognana returned to Perugia ; and, on the 3rd, Messer Rodolfo and his sons departed for Arezzo.[3]

Though the war with the Tarlati had been a heavy drain upon the resources of the Commune, it was no sooner over than a considerable reduction in taxation was found to be possible ; and, on the 12th of May, 1337, the Artificers of the Arts, in council assembled, *guastaro tutte le gabelle fatte e ordinate per la guerra de Arezzo*.[4]   Fresh money was coined ;[5] and, during the comparatively peaceful years which followed, large sums were spent upon the embellishment of the city.   In 1338, the Church of S. Elisabetta nella Conca was built ;[6] in 1345, the work on the Cathedral was at last begun,[7] and, six months later, foundations were laid for an extension of the Palazzo del Popolo.[8]   In 1339 "The Council of the Two Hundred and of the People" of Città di Castello resolved to grant to the People of Perugia "rectoria civitatis et comitatus Castelli," or, in other words,

---

[1] According to GRAZIANI (p. 117) and PELLINI (i. 540), the date of this ratification of the peace was the 19th of April.   AMMIRATO (*ubi cit.*, p. 312), states that it occurred on the 29th ; and that this was, in fact, the case is proved by documentary evidence.   See DEGLI AZZI, *op. cit.*, ii. § 281, pp. 68-70, where a full synopsis of the convention is given.

[2] " . . . fu vestito dicto meser Rodolfo de uno scarlatto con doi vaia, e gli figliuoli ciascuno con una veste partita con fodero francesco."

[3] GRAZIANI, p. 118.   [4] *Ibid.*, 118-119 ; PELLINI, i. 540.

[5] PELLINI, i. 545.   [6] PELLINI, i. 544.

[7] " Adì 20 d' agosto si cominciò a fondare la chiesa nuova di S. Lorenzo. . . ."   *Brevi Annali*, ad ann.; GRAZIANI, p. 137.

[8] " Alli 27 de febraio fu comenzato a fondare el palazzo delli signori Priori della cità de Perugia nella piaza grande."   GRAZIANI, p. 141.

the right to elect the Potestà and the Captain, to have the custody of the fortress and of the keys of the city for twenty years.[1] In 1342 the Statutes of Perugia were revised and translated into the vulgar tongue.[2]

In the same year, the disbanding of the German mercenaries in the pay of Pisa resulted in the formation of the *Gran Compagnia della Corona*, under the leadership of the ferocious Werner, or *Guarnieri* as the Italians called him, a descendant of that Conrad of Hurselingen who was invested by Frederick Barbarossa with the Duchy of Spoleto.[3] The numbers of his followers are variously estimated at from 1500 to 4000 *barbute*,[4] besides a considerable body of infantry.[5] According to a Perugian chronicle, when they entered the Cortonese they were about 3000 horse and 950 foot.[6] In the *contado* of Siena, they had robbed and devastated without meeting any resistance ; encamped at Buonconvento, they had wasted the Val' d' Arbia ; Torrenieri and Bagno di Vignone went up in flames ; and, at last, the Magistrates, after vainly summoning the citizens to take up arms,[7] were obliged to purchase the withdrawal of the invaders by a disbursement of over 2800 florins of gold.[8] Followed by a crowd of malefactors, procurers and women

[1] See ANSIDEI e DEGLI AZZI, *Regesto*, etc., *op. cit.*, Doc. cccxix.-cccxx. (*Bollettino* cited, vi. 509).

[2] See DEGLI AZZI, *Sulla questione della data dello Statuto Volgare* in *Bollettino* cited, iv. 177-182.

[3] E. RICOTTI, *op. cit.*, Vol. I. Parte ii. cap. ii. p. 244.

[4] As to the difference between *barbute* and men-at-arms, see RICOTTI, Vol. I. Parte ii. cap. iii. p. 259.

[5] G. VILLANI, xii. 9, and compare MURATORI, *R. I. S.*, xv. col. 105 (*Cronica Sanese*) ; col. 600 (*Chr. Mutin.*) ; col. 900 (*Cron. Riminese*), and col. 1012 (*Cron. di Pisa*).

[6] *Frammento di cronaca perugina inedita*, published by O. SCALVANTI in *Bollettino* cited, xi. (1905), p. 584.

[7] " Molti " (says the chronicler Agnolo di Tura del Grasso) " non volevano andare contro a sì gran gente disperata ; di che il Capitano della guerra di Siena fè porre il ceppo e la mannara a la porta a Camollia per dare timore a chi non voleva ubbidire."

[8] In the *Cronica Sanese* the Sienese are said to have disbursed 2500 florins ; but to this must be added 300 florins " per li cavalli morti e scorticati " (FABRETTI, *Cronache*, i. 88). The precise sum appears to have been 2852 florins. See A. LISINI, *Provvedimenti economici della Rep. di Siena in* 1382 (Siena, Torrini, 1895), p. xviii.

of loose character,[1] drunk with blood and rapine and arrogant with success, the "Great Company" passed into the territory of Cortona by the way of Monte S. Savino and Castiglion Aretino. Thence Duke Werner sent his ultimatum to Perugia demanding six months' pay for three hundred of his men, and free passage through Perugian territory, whensoever he should desire it.[2] It is possible that, if he had asked for free passage alone, his request might have been granted;[3] but the Perugians had no mind to pay blackmail, and, without distinction of class, the citizens, in parliament assembled, resolved to make no terms with the insolent barbarian. Nobles and people alike declared " that, rather than ransom themselves with money or pay such a tax, they would endure that the whole *contado* of Perugia should be ruined and wasted, and that the father for very hunger should devour his own son. Moreover, it was decreed that, if any man should make any pact or accord with the said company, nay, even if he gave them food or forage or free passage, he should lose his head therefor. Then were all the shops and offices closed, and no one attended to any manner of work save that of arms alone and to defence and protection against the aforesaid Great Company, ever proclaiming war against them with trumpets and with bells.[4] Two days later [5] "the troops in the pay of the Commune of Perugia, together with all their allies and a great company of foot-soldiers, issued forth from Perugia for the defence and protection of the City of Perugia against the said Great Company; and they went to Monte Colognola and to Monte Rufiano; and with our folk were the men-at-arms of the Marquis of the March, horse and foot of Camerino and knights of Messer Malatesta of Rimini. The

---

[1] In the *Chronicon Mutinense*, above cited, Joh. de Bazano tells us that with the three thousand five hundred *barbute* of the Great Company were *mille meretrices, ragazii, et rubaldi satìs.*

[2] *Bollettino* cited, xi. 585; PELLINI, i. 554.

[3] MANCINI (*op. cit.*, p. 188) tells us that the Perugians had actually granted a free passage, when Duke Werner raised his demands. He cites Cod. 540, fo. 50, in the *Biblioteca Cortonese.*

[4] GRAZIANI, pp. 125-126.

[5] According to the chronicle attributed to GRAZIANI, this was on the 3rd of October.

Captain of our folk was Count Guido Orsini of Soana, who came to the aid of our Commune with four *bandiere*[1] of horse ; and also there were foot-soldiers from all the Ducato." As the Great Company advanced along the northern end of the Lake, past Passignano, and thence, by the Val di Fiume, to the Pian di Marte, the Perugians closed it round and hemmed it in, "marching on the right hand and on the left so that the said enemy could not offend our *contado*." Thus, guarded by an overwhelming force, the Germans were conducted like prisoners through the territories of Perugia and Città di Castello, only being released from surveillance when they had crossed the frontiers.[2]

In view of this admirable unanimity in the face of a common danger, we might almost be tempted to infer that, at this period, the enmity between the classes had grown less virulent ; but the extraordinary events which took place at Bettona, in the spring of 1343, prove beyond question that any such inference would be entirely fallacious. The whole incident is obscure and the details are tantalizingly meagre ; but enough is told us to show how easily the smouldering fires of civic discord might be fanned into a blaze. I translate from the chronicle attributed to Graziani. There are no prefatory remarks. He begins abruptly as follows :—

"On the 21st day of April in the year aforesaid there was great strife and tumult between the *popolo* and the *Grandi* in the town of Bettona, by reason whereof they all took up arms and fought together. And the said town was divided after this manner, to wit : the faction of the People was called the *Parte di sotto* and that of the Grandi the *Parte di sopra*, and to the aid of the said factions went many Perugians, some to the aid of the Grandi and some to the aid of the People. Finally, on the 22nd day of April, the said factions fought together, the said folk of

---

[1] A *bandiera* was a company composed of forty men.

[2] GRAZIANI, pp. 126-127 ; FABRETTI, *Cronache*, i. 88 ; PELLINI, i. 554-555 ; BONAZZI, i. 422-423 ; MUZI, *Memorie civili*, etc., *op. cit.*, i. 151. It is thus sufficiently clear that Muratori was mistaken when he asserted (an. 1342) that "i Perugini . . . coll' esorcismo d' alcune migliaia di fiorini fecero passare questo mal tempo in Romagna."

Perugia, both of the city and of the *contado* being there also. Moreover, there were present two of the Lords Priors of Perugia who had gone thither to pacify the said factions and the said town. And while yet they fought together and the battle waxed great, the Mareschal of the Duke of the Ducato entered into the said town of Bettona, with much folk on foot and with divers men-at-arms, in favour and aid of the faction of the Grandi. And incontinently they put the faction of the People to the rout and drave forth from the said town all the faction of the People and all the Perugians which were with them. The head of the faction of the People was Messer Crispolto, the son of Messer Pietro of Bettona, and the heads of the faction of the Grandi were the sons of Segnarello and of Ranaldello of Bettona ; and with them was Lodovico, the son of Messer Vinciolo, and Vinciarello, the son of Messer Piero, and many other Perugians both gentlemen and common folk (*popolari*). On the side of the People was Simone di Armanno of Castiglion Ugolino and many of his kin and many other gentlemen and *popolari*. Now, the faction of the Grandi being victorious, they spoiled all the town and burned the houses of the vanquished. The fugitives took refuge in Torgiano and some in Perugia ; and thereafter the sons of Segnarello and the other Grandi bare rule in Bettona."

That is all we know about the matter, except the fact that, some two and a half months afterwards, such of the Perugians as had taken part in the conflict were fined by a decree of the General Council of all the Artificers of the Arts. The justice meted out to the offenders seems to have been impartial enough, except that, the laws being what they were, the Nobles paid twice as much as the *popolari*.[1]

Meanwhile, things were going so ill with Florence that in a superstitious age it might well have been believed that some higher power had interposed to prevent her

---

[1] GRAZIANI, pp. 127-128 ; PELLINI, i. 555-556 ; BONAZZI, i. 423. The modern historian of Bettona, Cav. G. BIANCONI, *Su Bettona, Terra antichissima ed illustre dell' Umbria* (Perugia, Bartelli, 1892), does not even allude to these disturbances.

drawing any profit from her treachery. In March, 1340, a mighty comet blazed in the heavens between the Signs of the Virgin and the Balance, the harbinger of a terrible pestilence which slew more than a sixth part of the inhabitants of Florence. In the wake of the pestilence came famine, and, in May, all the fruit trees were ruined by a hailstorm which lay upon the ground like a deep snow. In July a great fire broke out in S. Brancazio, where the wool-merchants dwelt, and burned forty-four houses and palaces with great damage to the Arts and to Trade. Next came the conspiracy of the Bardi and the Frescobaldi, the disastrous war with Pisa, the loss of Lucca, and, finally, the despotism of the Duke of Athens, which in a few short months destroyed the fruits of many fortunate years. Florence, the rich and powerful, the rival of Venice and of Genoa, lost all her treasure and nearly all her conquests ; and the first of the subject cities to revolt against her was that Arezzo whom she had broken faith to win.

When Arezzo was sold to the Florentines, in March 1337, she had been Ghibelline for more than sixty years ; [1] and the first act of her new masters was to recall the Guelfs. A general amnesty was proclaimed, and the government was remodelled in its old democratic form without distinction of party. But hereditary hatreds cannot be allayed by protocols, and the return of the Guelfs, so far from being productive of peace, immediately plunged the city into internecine strife, which inevitably ended in the expulsion of the Ghibellines. Even had the Florentines desired to hold the scales of justice evenly between the factions, they could hardly have done so ; and there is not the slightest reason to suppose that they did so desire. The struggle began in May, 1337, when the Guelfs rose and attacked the Tarlati ; [2] and, in 1341, we find a conspiracy afoot, hatched by the Florentines and openly supported by Florentine officials, for the reformation of Arezzo to the Parte Guelfa. " Tractatum fuit," writes the Aretine annalist, " per aliquos Florentinos et Rectores Florentiæ reducere dictam civitatem Arretii ad partem

---

[1] G. VILLANI, xi. 60.   [2] *Annales Arretini, ubi cit.*, col. 877.

Guelfam." The first step was to deprive the Ghibellines of their leaders ; and, on the 20th of November, Rosso de' Rossi, the Potestà, and Guglielmo degli Altoviti, the Captain of the Guard, suddenly arrested Messer Pier Saccone and others of the Tarlati clan.[1] At the same time their fellow-conspirators took up arms and scoured the city, shouting, "Live the Florentines and die the traitors!" The next day, two hundred Ghibellines were cited to appear before the Potestà; and, says the chronicler, "they abode in the hall of the Potestà in exceeding great dread, because all the Guelfs of the City of Arezzo desired to burn them ; and, thereafter, they were sent into exile to divers places beyond the borders." A little later, all Ghibellines, from thirteen years old to sixty, were ordered to leave the City.[2] Messer Piero was sent to Florence, where he narrowly escaped being put to death "quia ipsi Florentini volebant occupare castra et tenimenta eidem." [3] The rest of the Tarlati thereupon fled to their castles and broke into open revolt. They were joined by the Ubaldini,[4] and having received reinforcements from the Romagna and a few men-at-arms from Milan, besieged Firenzuola and routed a detachment which was marching to its assistance under one of the Medici. The town was betrayed into their hands and was sacked and burnt; they refortified and garrisoned the strong castle of Montecoloreto, and occupied Tirli.[5] In March, 1342, we find the Florentines writing to Perugia to beseech her to sequestrate all the property of the Ubaldini in Città di Castello [6] and to take steps "ad delendum" the entire clan:[7] but, in the mean-

---

[1] *Annales Arretini, ubi cit.*, col. 880.   Compare *La Cronaca di Ser Gorello, ubi cit.*, col. 832.

[2] *Annales Arretini, ubi cit.*, col. 880.

[3] *Ibid.*, col. 881.   The Florentine chroniclers assert that Pier Saccone was arrested on suspicion of plotting a rebellion in Arezzo.   See VILLANI, xi. 139 ; AMMIRATO, *op. cit.*, Vol. II. Lib. ix. p. 364 ; and compare the *Cronica Sanese* in MURATORI, *R. I. S.*, xv. 96.

[4] As to the Ubaldini the reader may consult an interesting note in DEN-NISTOUN, *Memoirs of the Dukes of Urbino* (edition cited), Vol. I. pp. 49-50.

[5] AMMIRATO, *loc. cit.*, p. 365 ; G. VILLANI, xi. 139.

[6] DEGLI AZZI, *Le Relazioni*, etc., *op. cit.*, i. § 99, p. 30.

[7] DEGLI AZZI, *op. cit.*, i. § 101, p. 31.

while, the Pazzi and the Ubertini of Val d' Arno had taken up arms, and Castiglione,[1] Campogiallo and Treggiaia were wrested from Florence.[2]

In June[3] the Tarlati and their allies attempted to surprise Arezzo itself, but were repulsed with considerable slaughter. Their houses and gardens in the city (*ædificia cum viridariis*) were thereupon destroyed and many Ghibellines were banished—a measure which only served to increase the numbers of the rebels, who, as Villani tells us, thereafter made great war against Arezzo.[4] Hostilities continued until October, when Walter de Brienne, Duke of Athens, who was now despot of Florence, made peace with Pisa and confirmed to her the possession of Lucca for fifteen years. A general pardon was granted to the Florentine exiles in the Pisan service as well as to the Ubaldini, Pazzi, Tarlati and Ubertini clans. Pier Saccone and his kinsmen were set at liberty, and both the Pazzi and Tarlati hastened to acknowledge that they held their fiefs and castles of the Duke.[5]

The alliance with Pisa not unnaturally alarmed the Guelfs; while the unbridled ambition of Walter de Brienne seems early to have given cause for uneasiness to the neighbouring States. According to the *Cronica Sanese*, he openly plotted with the *Gentiluomini* against the Magistracy of the Nine[6]; and Professor Mancini assures us that he aspired to the Signory of both Siena and Perugia.[7] However this may be, we know that, on the 25th of December, 1342, the representatives of the two communes met at Montepulciano

---

[1] ". . . rubellarono Castiglione loro castello," says Villani, alluding, I presume, to Castiglion-Fibocchi in the Val d' Arno Aretino. See REPETTI, *Dizionario* cited, i. 606.

[2] G. VILLANI, xi. 139.

[3] I have followed Villani. According to Ser Gorello, the attack upon Arezzo took place in May.

[4] G. VILLANI, xii. 5 ; *Annales Arretini, ubi cit.* ; *Cronaca di Ser Gorello*, col. 833.

[5] G. VILLANI, xii. 8 ; AMMIRATO, *loc. cit.*, p. 381 ; *Cronica Sanese*, in MURATORI, *R. I. S.*, xv. 105 ; *Cronaca di Ser Gorello, ubi cit.*, col. 833-834.

[6] MURATORI, *R. I. S.*, xv. 107. Compare TOMMASI, *Historie di Siena*, P. ii. pp. 293-294.

[7] MANCINI, *op. cit.*, p. 191.

and entered into a league and confederation for five years for the common defence.[1] In January, 1343, Clement VI. wrote to the Perugians belauding the Duke as one whom *specialis dilectionis et favoris prerogativâ prosequimur*;[2] and on the 1st of the same month Messer Baglione de' Baglioni, who had been appointed *Vicarius d. Ducis Athenarum et Comunis Florentie* (Villani speaks of him as "Potestà"), entered upon the duties of his office.[3] In February, the Duke wrote to the Perugians, addressing them as "Amici karissimi";[4] but honied words cost nothing, and the disturbances in Bettona, in the following April, may well have caused fresh suspicions of a prince who, as the Florentines subsequently declared, was plotting "ut alas sue tirampnidis per orbem extenderet."[5] Fortunately, however, such danger as may have existed vanished with the overthrow of the ducal despotism in July, 1343.[6]

The first to take advantage of this revolution were, as

[1] R. ARCH. DI STATO IN SIENA, *Caleffo Nero*, c[te] 163-165[t]; TOMMASI, *op. cit.*, ii. 291; MALAVOLTI, *op. cit.*, P. ii. Lib. v. c 102[t]; *Arch. Stor. It.*, XVI. ii. 525-527.

[2] *Arch. Stor. It.*, XVI. ii. 532.

[3] DEGLI AZZI, *Le Relazioni*, etc., *op. cit.*, i. 261; G. VILLANI, xii. 8.

[4] *Arch. Stor. It.*, XVI. ii. 532-533.

[5] DEGLI AZZI, *Le Relazioni*, etc., *op. cit.*, i. § 106, p. 33.

[6] The details of this revolution have, of course, nothing to do with Perugian history; but the manner in which Messer Guglielmo of Assisi and his son were done to death is worth recalling as thoroughly typical of what the Italians of the Middle Ages regarded as a *bella vendetta*. The mere death of the enemy was insufficient: all the senses of the slayer must be satisfied. The screams of the victim must be heard, his agony beheld, his hot blood smelt, while, finally, to make the vengeance wholly complete, his quivering flesh must be torn with the teeth and eaten. Let us hear MACHIAVELLI (*Istorie Fiorentini*, Lib. ii.) : " E perchè tutti i sensi si soddisfacessero nella vendetta, avendo prima udito le loro querele, veduto le loro ferite, tocco le loro carne lacere, volevano ancora che il gusto le assaporasse, acciocchè come tutte le parti di fuori ne erano sazie, quelle di dentro ancora se ne saziassero." Such was the philosophy of methods which were common to Florence and Perugia alike. Filippo di Braccio tore out the heart of Astorre Baglioni and bit it on the night of the " Great Betrayal " ; while in the chronicle of Matarazzo we have an account of a man who died from a surfeit of human flesh (*Arch. Stor. It.*, XVI. ii. pp. 118, 150. Compare also my *The " Ensamples " of Fra Filippo, op. cit.*, pp. 201, 289).

12

I have said, the Aretines; and no sooner did the news reach them that Walter de Brienne was besieged in his palace by the citizens of Florence than Guelfs and Ghibellines alike took up arms and attacked the fortresses which had been built to overawe their town.   The resistance of the garrisons was half-hearted at the best.   Indeed, according to Giovanni Villani there was no resistance at all.[1] Scarcely, however, had the common enemy been defeated than the Guelfs once more expelled the Ghibellines;[2] while the Tarlati, aided by reinforcements from Pisa, overran the *contado* and cut off all supplies.   The fate of Arezzo hung in the balance, and the lesser towns of the Aretine State each hastened to seek its own protector. Thus the Guelfs of Montecchio gave themselves to Perugia and accepted a Perugian Potestà;[3] while, a little later, Castiglione Aretino followed their example.   As the Perugian troops approached the town, the inhabitants of all ages and of every rank, men, women and children in their hundreds, poured out of the gates to meet them, piteously imploring succour and protection.   The citadel, however, was occupied by a Florentine garrison and refused to open its gates except on payment of a heavy bribe, the castellan cynically informing the Perugians that they must give him seven thousand florins of gold or he would sell the place to the Tarlati.   Negotiations were still going on when " Messer Piero Saccone rode to Castiglion Aretino with much folk of his alliance and took all the town by battle and drave out the men of the Commune of Perugia." The garrison thereupon received their price and evacuated the Citadel.   "And the said Messer Piero caused all the said town to be sacked, to wit both Guelfs and Ghibellines, and fortified himself therein with much folk."[4]   In spite

---

[1] G. VILLANI, xii. 17.   Compare, however, the *Annales Arretini*, where we are told that " proeliando continue ipsum habuerunt."

[2] *Annales Arretini*, col. 882 : " Guelfi vero, hoc facto, expulserunt Guibellinos de Civitate."

[3] GRAZIANI, p. 134 ; FABRETTI, *Cronache*, i. 91 ; PELLINI, i. 558.

[4] Besides the chronicles, see the *Ambaxiata Perusinorum missa ad Florentinos* and the *Responsio Florentinorum facta Perusinis*, in DEGLI AZZI, *Le Relazioni*, etc., *op. cit.*, i. §§ 105-106, pp. 32-34.   The dates given

of every effort to dislodge him he maintained himself there
for over eighteen months.

> Più d' anno e mezzo tutto sano e'ntero
> Fo assediato da' Guelfi Toscani
> Con grande spesa, a voler dire el vero,

sings Ser Gorello ;[1] but, according to the Perugian
chronicles, which are now our principal authority—the
Annales Arretini end with the year 1343—operations
were not begun in earnest till the following summer.

In March, 1344, Arezzo, Siena and Perugia entered
into a league with Florence " to fortify their state and
to overthrow the Tarlati and every other despotism round
about."[2] On the 22nd of June, "the Commune of Perugia
with its mercenary troops (*con la sua gente soldata*) encamped
against Castiglion Aretino in the Val di Chio, and builded
a *battifolle* over against the said Castiglione, at a place
which is called ' la Pieve de Retene ' ; and they laid waste
the land round about the said Castiglione even unto the
gates thereof, ever holding Messer Piero Saccone besieged
therein." Nevertheless, a few weeks later, while the greater
part of the Perugian army was at Tuoro, Messer Piero
succeeded in stealing through their attenuated lines.

> Per un tragetto
> Uscì quel Cavalier senza lucerna,[3]

and swooped like a hawk—the simile is Ser Gorello's—
upon Citerna. No sooner did the Perugians hear of his
escape than they broke camp and hurried after him ; "and
also there went all Città di Castello and all the vicinage,
friends of the Commune of Perugia." Yet, for all their
hastening, they came too late to save Citerna, which was
betrayed into his hands by certain *Lambardi* who dwelt

by GRAZIANI (p. 134) are obviously wrong. According to Ser Gorello
(*Cronaca* cited, col. 834),

> Quando fu preso Castiglione Artino
> Corrìa quarantatre trecento mille
> Decimo giorno del mese Agustino.

[1] *Ubi cit.*, col. 835.

[2] G. VILLANI, xii. 28 ; PELLINI, i. 561 ; TOMMASI, *Historie di Siena*, ii.
297. See also for a full synopsis of the terms of the confederation, DEGLI
AZZI, *op. cit.*, ii. § 304, pp. 77-78, and compare §§ 303, 305, 306.

[3] *Cronaca di Ser Gorello, ubi cit.*

therein.[1]   According to the chronicle attributed to Graziani, this happened on the 15th of September, 1344; and, in November, Messer Piero seems to have been at the head of so "great a multitude of armed men" as to have caused considerable uneasiness to the Rector of the Ducato, who feared an invasion of the Ecclesiastical State.[2]

Meanwhile, however, the Perugians had returned to Castiglione, where they built another *battifolle*, which, by reason of the continual rain, they called the "Battifolle del mal tempo." Between January and March, 1345, five more *battifolli* were constructed; and, thereafter, "they caused to be made a palisade of timber with two ditches round about the said town, to the end that none might enter therein or depart therefrom; and so was the said town besieged. . . . In the month of April of the said year, the said town of Castiglione being thus shut up, the Commune of Perugia commanded that it should be taken by battle, and assailed in divers places.   Wherefore the said Commune of Perugia sent thither four thousand foot-soldiers, the same being mercenaries who were paid six soldi a day for each man. Also they sent a thousand foot-soldiers of the most valiant citizens of Perugia, the which were constrained to go thither for ten soldi a day for each man.   And unto this adventure were summoned all our vicinage, to wit Assisi, Spello, Foligno, Spoleto, Bettona, Nocera, Camerino, Gualdo, Gubbio, Rocca Contrada, Città di Castello, Borgo S. Sepoloro, and Sassoferrato; and each of them sent men of valour both horse and foot; and so they went all of them to Castiglione, and, round about it in divers places, they set their battle in array. . . . On the 27th day of April, in the said year, the host which had gone up against Castiglione returned to Perugia.   It returned with victory; because

[1] GRAZIANI, p. 135.   As to " gli Lambarde de Citerna, gli quali stavano dentro nel decto castello," compare G. VOLPE, *Lambardi e Romani nelle campagne e nelle città*, etc., in *Studi Storici, op. cit.*, Vol. XIII. fasc. i. *et seq.*

[2] FUMI, *I Registri del Ducato di Spoleto, op. cit.*, xvii. § 12, p. 175: " 1344. Nov. 20— . . . propter quandam magnam multitudinem hominum armatorum de gente d. P. Sacconis et aliquorum aliorum potentium tyrannorum, qui prope fines Perusii et ducatus predicti coadunati erant, propter quod dubitabatur de invasione et occupatione terrarum ducatus eiusdem," etc.   Compare also § 5, p. 174.

they of Castiglione had surrendered to the Commune of Perugia. Wherefore our Commune sent thither a Potestà, the which was Cecchino di Messer Vinciolo of Perugia.[1] And then the Perugians decreed that Castiglion Aretino should be called Castiglion Perugino."[2] Finally, at the beginning of June, peace was concluded between the Tarlati and the Guelfs. The ambassadors met at S. Polo, a village to the north-east of Arezzo; Citerna was restored to Perugia and her dominion over Castiglione recognized.[3]

The war thus happily ended, the Perugians, who had already begun to earn the reputation, which, in the following century, they shared with the Bolognese, the Genoese and the men of Città di Castello, of being " the most armigerent and bellicose " of all the nations of Italy,[4] were at liberty to respond to the exhortations of the Pope to take up arms against the Infidel;[5] " and," says the chronicler, " on the 15th of August, in the said year, very much folk both on horse and foot departed from Perugia to go into Turkey against the Turks. . . . The Captain of the men-at-arms was Vinciarello di Messer Pietro di Messer Vinciolo;[6] and they which were on foot were an infinite multitude with many captains." According to Pellini, there were about 1500 foot-soldiers, while among the captains were " twenty-five nobles, rich citizens and valiant."[7]

In September news arrived that King Andrea of Naples had been murdered.[8]

[1] " Cicchinus filius domini Vencioli Novelli " is mentioned in the *Libro Rosso*, among the *Mangnates et Nobiles de prole militari ex paterna linea de Porta Sancti Petri*. He is the same Cechino di Messer Vinciolo who was implicated in the murder of Messer Oddo Degli Oddi, in 1331.

[2] GRAZIANI, pp. 135-137 ; PELLINI, i. 558-559 ; FABRETTI, *Cronache*, i. 91-93.

[3] G. VILLANI, xii. 45 ; PELLINI, i. 565 ; *Cronaca di Ser Gorello*, col. 835. See also DEGLI AZZI, *Le Relazioni*, etc., *op. cit.*, ii. § 311, p. 80.

[4] MUZI, *Memorie civili*, etc., *op. cit.*, i. 10.

[5] BELFORTI, *Bolle e Diplomi*, *op. cit.*, Sec. XIV. No. 141 ; *Arch. Stor. It.*, XVI. ii. 533. Compare the *Chronicon Estense*, in MURATORI, *R. I. S.*, xv. 418.

[6] " Venciarellus domini Peri domini Vencioli." *Libro Rosso*, *ubi cit.*

[7] GRAZIANI, p. 138 ; PELLINI, i. 564.   [8] GRAZIANI, p. 138.

CHAPTER XIV

GIOVANNI DI VICO, *ALME URBIS PREFECTUS*

PERUGIA was now at the zenith of her power. From Cagli, in the Apennines, to Monte S. Savino, on the road between Arezzo and Siena, from Borgo S. Sepolcro to the confines of Todi, all Umbria acquiesced in her hegemony. Her borders no longer marched with those of the treacherous Florence, for Arezzo was once more a free Commune ; and, for the moment, it seemed as though she were destined to absorb all the lesser Republics which surrounded her and to become the capital of a great State. Unhappily, however, no time was granted her to consolidate her dominion. Hardly had the war with the Tarlati been brought to a fortunate ending than she was threatened with new dangers, not the least of which was the growing power of Giovanni Di Vico, who, after the murder of his illegitimate brother, Faziolo, in 1338, aspired to establish a despotism on the ruins of the Ecclesiastical State.[1] Already master of Viterbo, he began, in 1345, to give concrete form to his vast designs by the acquisition of Vetralla, which he bought from the Orsini for 16,000 florins. The Pope protested, but in vain, and henceforward we shall find Di Vico in open antagonism to the Church.[2]

In January, 1346, a great Diet, or *Parlamento*, was held in Perugia, " whereto came Messer Giordano degli Orsini of Rome, the Count Guido of Sovana, the ambassadors of Spoleto, Foligno, Assisi, Gubbio, Città di Castello and Borgo S. Sepolcro, the Seignior of Cortona, the representatives of the neighbouring towns and the barons of all the land ; the which Parliament (says Graziani) was held for the

---

[1] C. CALISSE, *I Prefetti Di Vico, op. cit.*, pp. 69 *et seq.*
[2] ANTONELLI, *Vicende della dominazione pontificia nel Patrimonio di S. Pietro*, etc., *op. cit.*, pp. 107-108.

defence of all the land, by reason of the coming of the
King of Hungary, who was expected to descend into Italy
to avenge the death of Andrea, his brother."[1]　Others,
however, assert that the principal reason of the assembling
of the Diet was the condition of Orvieto, which, after a long
period of internecine strife, had now fallen under Ghibelline
influence.[2]　In February, troops were sent thither by Perugia
and by the Rector of the Patrimony; the Guelfs were
reinstated in power, and the Ghibellines in their turn were
driven into exile.　Messer Benedetto di Bonconte became
Seignior of Orvieto;[3] and, on the 1st of March, the Florentines wrote to congratulate the Perugians and to urge them
to continue the good work.[4]　Unfortunately, however,
dissensions soon arose among the Guelfs themselves,[5] and,
on the 22nd of May, the walls of the city were scaled at daybreak, and, after "a great battle," Corrado Monaldeschi
della Cervara made himself master of Orvieto.[6]　In this
enterprise he was materially aided by Giovanno Di Vico,
who in return for his services was assisted to annex Bagnorea, Toscanella, and Piansano.[7]　A fierce war followed
which divided the Patrimony and the City of Rome itself
into two hostile camps.　In July, the armies of the Rector
were utterly routed, and the captured standards were borne in
triumph to Viterbo, there to be displayed as trophies on the
roof of the Palace of the Potestà.[8]　To take vengeance for
this reverse the territory of Orvieto was invaded and
devastated in the following October.　At the head of two
hundred men-at-arms and many foot-soldiers, Bernardo
"de Lacu," the Rector, advanced almost to the gates of
the city: "and" (says a contemporary writer) "they
burned Petroio and Sucano, and brake into the Convent of

---

[1] *Arch. Stor. It.*, XVI. i. 138.　Compare FABRETTI, *Cronache*, i. 94-95.

[2] PELLINI, i. 567.

[3] GRAZIANI, p. 140; *Ephemerides Urbevetanæ* (edition FUMI in the new
Rerum Italicarum Scriptores, Città di Castello, 1903), p. 15.　Messer
Benedetto de' Monaldeschi belonged to the Ramo della Vipera.　Compare
the genealogical tables of the Casata Monaldeschi in PARDI, *Dal Comune
alla Signoria in Orvieto*, *op. cit.* (*Bollettino* cited, xiii. pp. 426-428).

[4] DEGLI AZZI, *Le Relazioni*, etc., *op. cit.*, i. p. 43 § 144.

[5] *Eph. Urbev.*, *ubi cit.*, p. 16, ll. 93 *seq.*　　[6] *Ibid.*, p. 17.

[7] CALISSE, *I Prefetti Di Vico*, *op. cit.*, p. 71.　　[8] ANTONELLI, *op. cit.*, p. 109.

S. Trinità and robbed it, and drave out the nuns that were
therein ; and, thereafter, they returned to Bolsena and to
Montefiascone ; and, from that day forward, the war between
Orvieto and the Patrimony increased beyond measure, so
great a war that no Orvietan was able to remember that
ever, in the past, Orvieto hath had so great a war." [1]

Like Achilles, inexorable in his tent while defeat attended
the Greeks, Perugia seems to have taken no part in these
hostilities ; and the reason is, probably, to be found in the
fact that, at this moment, her relations with the Papacy were
strained almost to breaking point.   The news which had
reached her from Avignon, on the 8th of July, had, as we
have seen,[2] provoked the fiercest resentment, and not only
did she turn a deaf ear to the entreaties and exhortations of
Clement that she should assist the Rector against the rebels,[3]
but she actually permitted Cecchino de' Vincioli to assume
the office of Potestà, and afterwards of Captain of the People
in the revolted Orvieto.[4]   Moreover, it is not impossible
that the aid which she gave to Cola di Rienzo, when he
laid siege to Vetralla and ravaged the *contado* of Viterbo, in
July, 1347, may have been rendered the more willingly
because the Rector, acting upon secret orders from Avignon,
now appeared disposed to support the Prefect in his defiance
of the Tribune.[5]   Be this as it may, Di Vico was compelled

[1] *Eph. Urbev., ubi cit.,* pp. 18-20.   [2] See page 97 *supra.*

[3] *Arch. Stor. It.,* XVI. ii. 533 ; BELFORTI, *Bolle e Diplomi,* Sec. xiv.,
No. 143.

[4] *Eph. Urbev., ubi cit.,* p. 18, ll. 25-34 ; PARDI, *Serie de' Supremi Magistrati
e Reggitori di Orvieto,* etc., in *Bollettino* cited, i. 391-392.

[5] CALISSE, *op. cit.,* p. 75.   I do not, of course, overlook the fact that in
April 1347, Perugia entered into a league with Florence and Siena, " ad
fortificationem, augmentationem et statum pacificum totius partis guelfe
Italie que est ymitatrix dicte sancte Romane ecclesie," and " ad confusionem, exterminium, desolationem et mortem perpetuam inimicorum
dicte sancte matris Ecclesie et supradictorum Comunium."   Such expressions had, by long use, become little better than empty formulas,
and the real object of the League was no doubt for the common defence
against Lewis of Bavaria and his namesake of Hungary, who were preparing to invade Italy with a force sufficient to take vengeance on the
Pope, the Guelfs, and the hated house of Anjou.   See SISMONDI, *op. cit.,*
Vol. II. cap. xxxvi. p. 344, and NAPIER, *Florentine History,* Vol. II. p. 117.
A full synopsis of the League referred to will be found in DEGLI AZZI, *Le
Relazioni,* etc., *op. cit.,* ii. pp. 82-83, § 321.

to make submission at the feet of his conqueror and to swear
fealty to the Roman Republic.[1]

On the 1st of September, almost all the communes of
Sabina and the Patrimony voluntarily acknowledged the
signory of Cola, to the end (as he wrote to the Pope) that
they might escape the exactions of the officials of the
Church and the fury of the despots.[2] In November, Clement
commanded the Papal Legate to gather troops for the protection of the Papal State, warning him to put no trust in
the promises of Cola, who, he declared, lied as shamelessly
as a harlot.[3] The peril was averted by the sudden ruin of
the Tribune and his flight from Rome; but preparations
for defence continued to be pushed forward with feverish
activity, since a more dangerous enemy was approaching in
the shape of the Great Company. Anagni was sacked with
horrible slaughter, and the Roman Campagna wasted;[4]
the Registers of the Ducato are full of expenses incurred
"ad resistendum Tribuno et magne societati";[5] and, for
about three months (March-May, 1348) the terror and
distress were great.[6] In May, Orvieto seems to have voluntarily given herself to Perugia for ten years, in return for
the promise of assistance and protection;[7] while, more than

[1] GREGOROVIUS, op. cit., Vol. III. Lib. xi. cap. vi. p. 375.

[2] THEINER, Codex diplomaticus dominii temporalis S. Sedis, ii. Doc. 176;
FUMI, I Registri del Ducato di Spoleto, op. cit., p. 182, xvii. § 58.

[3] ANTONELLI, op. cit., p. 111 n. 5.

[4] Chronicon Estense, ubi cit., col. 449; MURATORI, Annali d' Italia, a. 1348.

[5] FUMI, I Registri, etc., op. cit., xvii. passim. Much material seems to
have been purchased from Perugia. Thus, as early as September, 1347,
we have an entry: " Pro provvisione et guarnimento armorum et aliorum
necessariorum repositorum in fortillitiis plebis et palactii novi E. R. de
Montefalcone, Bertrando de Mantua—pro .viij. paribus cornetiarum de
ferro—pro .viij. elmis de acciario—pro x barbutis munitis de maglia—
pro x cronis pro balistis—pro xx paribus cirotecarum de ferro—pro ijm.
iijc. garroctis pro balistis grossis emptis in Perusio per ipsum—63 fl. 2 lib.,
2 sol." And again: " Pro .ij.m. .v. c. (2500) velectonis . . . emptis in
civitate Perusina—39 lib., 5 sol."   [6] ANTONELLI, op. cit., p. 114.

[7] FUMI, Cod. Dipl., op. cit., p. 524 n.; Eph. Urbev., ubi cit., pp. 24-25,
and p. 22, l. 96 et seq.; GRAZIANI, p. 149; PELLINI, i. 583; MONTEMARTE,
Cronica inedita degli avvenimenti d' Orvieto e d' altre parti d' Italia dall'
anno 1333 all' anno 1400 (Torino, 1846), Vol. I. p. 22. The signoria of
Perugia actually lasted about three years. It appears that they sent
Leggerio degli Andreotti as Captain of the People; PARDI, op. cit., in Bollettino cited, i. 393.

a year later, mutual defence against the Great Company was still the principal object of a league which was entered into at Monte S. Savino, on the 21st of October, 1349, between Giacomo and Giovanni Pepoli of Bologna and the communes of Perugia, Florence, and Siena.[1]

Meanwhile, however, during the summer of 1348, all lesser strifes were hushed in a terrible struggle for existence with a more merciless invader than Duke Werner. On the 8th of April, the Black Death reached Perugia and slew a hundred thousand persons in the city and in the *contado* before the end of August. "And" (says an old chronicler) "none were found to bury the dead. All the folk of the City and of the walled places abode continually in processions and in disciplines and in litanies. . . . It was the greatest sickness whereof any man hath memory; and so terrible was it that neither the cemeteries nor the burial places within the churches sufficed to hold the dead; wherefore for sepulchres were made very deep wells, and they were filled full of corpses; yet on no wise might they suffice."[2]   In September, 1349, ere yet the pestilence was over,[3] a great part of Central and Southern Italy was smitten by a horrible earthquake, the like of which had been seen by no man living. Many of Perugia's seven hundred towers fell ruining into the streets below. In Orvieto, in like manner "there fell many walls and great buildings and towers and palaces." For six days and more no mechanic was able to do any work, and for nearly two weeks the water in the fountain was so turbid that it looked like milk; "and every day, they made procession and scourged themselves." Spoleto, Aquila, and Borgo S. Sepolcro also suffered greatly; the walls of the citadel of Toscanella were left cracked and gaping, while in Rome "the campanile of the great Church of S. Paolo fell, with part of the *loggi* thereof, and part of the noble Torre

[1] A. SORBELLI, *La Signoria di Gio. Visconti*, etc., *op. cit.*, p. 84, citing A. PEPOLI, *Documenti storici del Sec. XIV. estratti dal R. Arch. di Stato fiorentino* (Firenze, Tip. Galletti e Cocci, 1884), Doc. iv. p. 27. See also DEGLI AZZI, *Le Relazioni*, etc., *op. cit.*, ii. §§ 344, 346, 347, pp. 89-91.

[2] GRAZIANI, pp. 148-149. Compare C. MASSARI, *Saggio storico-medico sulle pestilenze di Perugia* (Perugia, Tip. Baduel, 1838), pp. 18-21.

[3] PELLINI, i. 891.

delle Milizie and the Torre del Conte." What marvel if all
men eagerly awaited the approaching Year of Jubilee, in the
hope that it would purge the world of diabolic influences![1]
To prevent the pilgrims being attacked and plundered as
they journeyed towards Rome, Giacomo de' Gabrielli, the
Rector of the Patrimony, gathered troops from Pisa, from
Perugia, and from Foligno to patrol the highways,[2] with
the result that, as Matteo Villani informs us, during the
whole of the year 1350, travel was exceptionally safe.[3] In
September, even in faction-tormented Orvieto, the gates
stood open day and night by reason of the multitude of
pilgrims which passed through them continually, " and," says
the chronicler, " the artisans took great gain of money, and
it seemed not that Orvieto had ever had war, so that all
good men were content." [4]

Nevertheless, even in the year of Jubilee, peace was not
universal. The war with the Tribune had momentarily
weakened Di Vico, and, in his negotiations with the Papal
Legate, he showed himself unexpectedly tractable ; a truce
was agreed upon for a term of three years ; the Rector,
Guiscardo di Comborino,[5] was permitted to occupy Bagnorea
and Toscanella without opposition ; while, in February
1348, the Prefect undertook to relinquish all his rights in
Vetralla, provided that the sixteen thousand florins which
he asserted that he had expended in its purchase were
repaid to him within two months. In the alternative he
offered to hold the place as a feud of the Church, paying
tribute, doing liege homage between the hands of the
Legate, and making oath of fealty in the usual form.[6]　It,

---

[1] FABRETTI, *Cronache*, i. 101 ; GRAZIANI, p. 151 ; PELLINI, i. 891 ;
BONAZZI, i. 430 ; *Eph. Urbev., ubi cit.*, p. 29 ; M. VILLANI, i. 45 ; FUMI,
I Registri del Ducato di Spoleto, op. cit., p. 263, App. vi. § 41 ; ANTONELLI,
op. cit., p. 117 ; MURATORI, *Annali d' Italia*, a. 1349. As to the diabolic
element in such phenomena, compare my *The " Ensamples " of Fra Filippo*,
op. cit., pp. 292-294.　　　　　　　　　　[2] CALISSE, *op. cit.*, p. 81.

[3] M. VILLANI, i. 56.　　　　　　　[4] *Eph. Urbev., ubi cit.*, p. 35.

[5] Guiscardo di Comborino was the last of the French Rectors of the
Patrimony. He died on July 16th, 1348, probably of the plague, and
was succeeded by Giacomo de' Gabrielli of Gubbio.

[6] ANTONELLI, *op. cit.*, pp. 112-113 ; CALISSE, *op. cit.*, Doc. 100ter in
Appendix, pp. 376-378.

however, soon became obvious that these concessions were only dictated by necessity. Di Vico bowed before the storm that he might not be broken, but in his heart he had abandoned none of his ambitious designs. In July, he purchased Castello di Carcari, a fortified place on the sea-coast near Civitavecchia, from the Normanni of Rome ;[1] and his assumption of the title of IOHANNES DEI GRATIA ALME VRBIS PREFECTVS CESARE ABSENTE SVMMI PONTI-FICIS DVCTOR[2] constituted a scarcely veiled claim to the sovereignty over the whole Ecclesiastical State.[3] In November, he re-established his authority in Civitavecchia, which had been taken from him by Cola di Rienzo, and from thenceforward his every movement was watched by the officials of the Patrimony with the utmost anxiety and suspicion. A typical instance of the mistrust with which they regarded him is to be found in the hurried fortifying of the Rocca di Orchia, in the summer of 1351, simply because Di Vico had been seen hunting in the neighbour-hood ;[4] while, when it was reported that he intended to pass through Gallese, the citizens were immediately ordered to close the gates against him.[5] In the early spring of 1350, partly for self-protection and partly for the sake of plunder, he entered into an alliance with the Duke Werner, who unexpectedly invaded the Patrimony. " Behold, now is the viper joined with the basilisk," wrote Clement VI. to the Legate Anibaldo ; and terrible, indeed, were their devastations.[6] Later on, in the same year, Di Vico assisted the Ghibellines of Narni to expel the Guelfs from Terni,

---

[1] CALISSE, op. cit., Doc. ci. in Appendix, p. 270.

[2] This legend will be found on one of the Seals of the Prefect published by BUSSI.

[3] CALISSE, op. cit., pp. 80-81.

[4] " Die .xiv. iul. 1351 solvi [ego thes.] . . . pro reparationibus turris, pontis levatorii, campane, brecthescarum et andaveniorum rocche Orcle devastatorum, cum Prefectus Urbis persepius sub colore venandi ambulabat circa dictam roccham inspiciendo quomodo eam possit invadere, pecunias infrascriptas . . ." (ARCH. VATIC., Introit., et exit. Patrimonii S. Petri in Tuscia, n. 266 c. 43, cited by ANTONELLI, op. cit., p. 119 n.).

[5] ANTONELLI, op. cit., p. 118.

[6] " Ecce iam coluber iunctus est regulo, et ambo insimul per improvisam inmunitamque patriam discurrentes, que possunt occupant, et que occupare nequeunt, inexplicabili feritate foris destruunt et devastant. . . ."

hus establishing himself in the favour of the dominant
party in each of those important communes.[1]

However, it was not until November, 1351, that he
embarked upon that series of successful aggressions which
almost entirely destroyed the papal authority throughout
the Patrimony.   About the middle of the month, he made
himself master of Orchia without striking a blow, in spite of
its newly repaired towers, drawbridge, bell, and portcullises.
It was betrayed into his hands by a certain Guercio da
Meano ; and, in fact, there was hardly a town or fortress in
which he did not possess devoted friends and partisans.
Next, he occupied Abbadia al Ponte and Montalto.
Giacomo de' Gabrielli, who had just finished his term of
office, came hurrying back from Città di Castello to organize
the defence of the places most endangered ; but Fortune
now favoured the Prefect.[2]   The war, being waged as it
was against the officials of a distant and alien Pope,
gradually assumed the character of a struggle between
Italians and foreigners, and thus the *Prefetteschi* were
enabled to pose as the champions of national liberty.
" Hujus tempore fere omnes civitates, terræ et castra
patrimonii b. Petri se rebellaverunt sedi apostolicæ et
ipsius in illis partibus rectoribus et officialibus," says the
annalist.[3]   Even Montefiascone, the seat of the Curia,
showed signs of disaffection.   The inhabitants, perceiving
that the Church was impotent to protect their celebrated
vineyards and fruitful hills from the ravages of the Prefect,
rose in revolt, and, during the night time, changed the
locks of all the gates of the town, including even those of
the citadel.   Thus the Rector, who held the keys, found
himself imprisoned in his own capital, while the malcontents
threatened, from one moment to another, to admit the
enemy.   Montefiascone was saved by the energy of Giacomo

---

[1] ' 'Anno dñi 1350 die xv Augusti.   Gibellini de Interampna cum gente
prefecti quæ venerunt de Narnea expulerunt Guelfos de Interampna et
desolaverunt omnes domos Guelforum. . . ." (See the *Cronaca di* F.
MERLINO in FR. ANGELONI, *Historia di Terni*, a. 1350, p. 109, Roma, 1649 ;
CALISSE, *op. cit.*, p. 81.)

[2] ANTONELLI, *op. cit.*, p. 120 ; CALISSE, *op. cit.*, pp. 82-84.

[3] RAYNALD, *Ann. Eccles.*, a. 1350 ; CALISSE, *op. cit.*, pp. 81-83.

de' Gabrielli, who succeeded in reinforcing the garrison
but Canino fell into the hands of Di Vico at the end o
December, and, almost contemporaneously he occupiec
Marta, first the *borgo* and then the *rocca*, which surrenderec
after a brief siege.[1]   In the spring of 1352, fresh subsidies
arrived from Avignon, and the Treasurer, Tavernini, was
ordered to devote the revenues of the Province for an entire
year to the prosecution of the war.   Perugia, Florence, anc
Siena were earnestly entreated to send assistance, and, ir
June, the armies of the Church laid siege to Viterbo.   Un
fortunately, however, the death of the Rector, La Serra
whose horse fell upon him and crushed him, put an end to
the campaign,[2] and the Prefect was once more enabled to
assume the offensive.   Fortune still smiled upon him, and
in August, the acquisition of Orvieto enormously increasec
his power.   On the 26th of that month, he was acclaimec
Seignior of the Commune and of its territories, assuming
the title of *Civitatis Urbisveteris Liberator, Gubernator a*
Dominus generalis et districtus et comitatus ejusdem ;[3] anc
ere long, as his ambition grew with what it fed on, he
entertained dreams of ruling even in Perugia.   "Gianni D
Vico teneva Terani, Amelia, Nargni. . . . Era magno e
bussava per corrompere Perusia." [4]

[1] CALISSE, p. 85 ; ANTONELLI, p. 122.
[2] M. VILLANI, iii. 18 ; CALISSE, pp. 89-90, and Doc. cv. ; ANTONELLI
pp. 127-128.
[3] M. VILLANI, iii. 32 ; *Eph. Urbev., ubi cit.*, pp. 55 *seq.* ; CALISSE, pp. 93-96
[4] *Vita di Cola di Rienzo*, ii. 5 ; CALISSE, p. 105 ; FILIPPINI, *La Riconquista dello Stato della Chiesa*, etc., *op. cit.*, in *Studi Storici*, Vol. VI. fasc. ii
p. 210.

CHAPTER XV

THE WAR WITH THE VISCONTI

IN October, 1350, the Pepoli, unable any longer to maintain themselves in Bologna, sold that city to Giovanni
Visconti, Archbishop of Milan, for 200,000 florins of gold.
The Florentines, who knew and dreaded the ambition of
that masterful prelate, were seriously alarmed, and hastened
to open negotiations with Perugia and Siena with the object
of forming a league for the common defence.[1]   About the
middle of November the ambassadors of the three communes
met at Arezzo, but separated without taking any definite
action.[2]   It had been hoped that the alliance would be
supported by the Pope, and would receive the adherence
of other communes and seigniors ; [3] but the unsuccessful
issue of the conference seems to have been mainly due to
the lukewarmness of the Perugians and Sienese, who,
apprehending but little danger to themselves, preferred to
leave Florence to bear the brunt of the impending invasion
alone.[4]   Negotiations were resumed in February, 1351, the
Florentine ambassadors, who went to Arezzo on the 1st of
March, being instructed " to *fare lega e compagnia et taglia*
with the ambassadors of our lord Messer the Pope, of the
communes of Rome, Perugia, and Siena, and with every
other commune and seignior who should prove willing to
enter into league and company with the Commune of
Florence." [5]   The Sienese were gradually brought into

---

[1] See page 99 *supra*.

[2] SORBELLI, *La signoria di Giovanni Visconti a Bologna*, etc., *op. cit.*,
pp. 93-97 ; CANESTRINI, *Alcuni documenti*, etc., *op. cit.*, in *Arch. Stor. It.*,
Serie i. Tom. VII. Doc. xxxvi., xxxvii., xxxix. ; DEGLI AZZI, *Le Relazioni*,
etc., *op. cit.*, i. pp. 48-49, §§ 165, 167, 168.

[3] See CANESTRINI, *op. cit.*, Doc. xxxvi., and compare SORBELLI, *op. cit.*,
pp. 44-45.   [4] M. VILLANI, i. 76 ; PELLINI, i. 900.

[5] SORBELLI, *op. cit.*, App., Doc. xxxiii. pp. 374-375.   Compare also

line with the Florentines, but the Perugians still hesitated,[1] and in June, "as it pleased God, news came of the death of Messer Mastino della Scala ; for the which cause the *parlamento* was dissolved without signing the league, and each ambassador returned to his seignior and to his commune." [2] Scarcely, however, had hostilities actually begun than the Perugians perceived that their own safety was endangered by the ambition and machinations of the Archbishop, and on the 26th of September the league was finally concluded at Siena with a *taglia*, according to Ammirato, of 3000 men-at-arms and 1000 cross-bowmen.[3]   The delay, however, had deprived the confederates of the support of the Pope, who was rapidly drifting towards a reconciliation with the Visconti ; and the seigniors of Lombardy, when invited to join the allied communes, put the ambassadors off with empty expressions of good-will.[4]

For a fortunate issue to the war, the Archbishop trusted greatly to the universal discontent of the *Signorotti* of the Florentine State, with some of whom, at any rate, he was already on very friendly terms.[5]   No sooner did he unfurl his banner than almost all the Ghibelline chieftains of Tuscany and the mountains took up arms : the Ubaldini, the sons of Castruccio Interminelli, Francesco Castracani of Lucca, Messer Carlino of Pistoia, the Count Nolfo of Montefeltro, the Aldobrandeschi of S. Fiora, the Count Guglielmo Spadalunga, the Tarlati, the Bishop of Arezzo and the

---

CANESTRINI, Doc. xxviii., xxix., xxx., xxxi., all of which are dated February, 1350, instead of 1351, the error, no doubt, being due to the fact that, according to the Old Style, the Florentine year began on March 25th. As to the various methods of computing the year in the different Tuscan cities, compare R. H. HOBART CUST, *Giovanni Antonio Bazzi, hitherto usually styled " Sodoma." The Man and the Painter* (London: Murray, 1906), p. 227 n. 3.

[1] Compare TOMMASI, *Historie di Siena*, II. x. 318 : " In queste pratiche i Perugini venivano lentamente nella lega, percioche fra loro ed il nemico i Fiorentini ed i Sanesi facevano bastioni."

[2] M. VILLANI, i. 76.   Compare SORBELLI, *op. cit.*, 97-99.

[3] AMMIRATO, *op. cit.*, Vol. II. Lib. x. p. 516.   Compare also DEGLI AZZI, *Le Relazioni*, etc., *op. cit.*, ii. § 360, pp. 93-94.

[4] SORBELLI, *op. cit.*, pp. 102-104.

[5] Compare VELLUTI, *Cronica di Firenze* (Firenze, Manni, 1731), ad ann. 1350, and SORBELLI, pp. 110-111.

Ubertini, the Pazzi of Val d' Arno, and the Count Tano of Monte Cerelli, all of whom were ostensibly friendly to Florence, but all of whom had been secretly gathering weapons and horses for the enterprise of the Archbishop.[1] We, however, are only concerned with this rising in as far as it affected Perugia. The details of the war with Florence may be read elsewhere.

Already, in June, 1350, there had been a Ghibelline movement in Città di Castello, which ended in the banishment of the Ubaldini;[2] while, in August, Giovanni di Cantuccio de' Gabrielli made himself master of Gubbio and expelled the Perugian garrison. He seems to have been assisted by the Ubaldini, and he hastened to throw himself into the arms of the Archbishop, of whom he agreed to hold Gubbio in feud.[3] Even in Perugia itself there was much suspicion and anxiety. The exclusion of the Nobles from the Government and from the general body of the citizens had begun to bear its inevitable fruit; and we read that, in January, 1351, "the People destroyed all the *sacchi dell' offizio*, doubting that the names of the Nobles, whom they held to be enemies of the liberty of the city, had been placed therein; and they *cavarono li priori a saputa*."[4] Nor does it appear that their precautions were excessive, since, a few months later, a widespread conspiracy was discovered for the subversion of the popular government and the betrayal of the city to Giovanni di Cantuccio and the Visconti. For this treason Messer Cecchino de' Vincioli and his brother Lodovico, who had hoped to make themselves despots of Perugia, together with

[1] M. VILLANI, i. 77, ii. 4, iii. 2.

[2] M. VILLANI, i. 74 ; PELLINI, i. 897 ; MUZI, *Memorie Civili, op. cit.*, i. 152.

[3] *Cronaca di Ser Guerriero da Gubbio* (a cura di G. MAZZATINTI, in the new edition of the *Rer. Italic. Script.*, 1902), pp. 7-8 ; M. VILLANI, i. 81-82 ; PELLINI, i. 901-903 ; P. CENCI, *Le Relazioni fra Gubbio e Perugia*, etc., in *Bollettino* cited, xiii. pp. 566 *et seq.* According to Pellini, " Era governata in questi tempi la città di Ogobbio da Perugini, non che vi havessero Governatori e Ministri di Giustizia, percioche questi erano messi dalla città, ma vi erano soldati Perugini alla guardia, e come molte altre città e terre di queste parte, era anch' ella sotto loro protettione."

[4] " *Cavare a saputa* " corresponds with the Florentine "*fare a mano*," *i.e.* when, instead of drawing the names of the Magistrates by chance from the ordinary *borse*, they were elected by a *Balìa* or by *Accoppiatori*.

13

their cousin, the Abbot of S. Pietro in Gubbio, were beheaded, on the 28th of April, "at the head of the Piazza,
at the foot of the stairway of the Palace of the Potestà, over
against the Vescovado." [1]

Meanwhile, Perugia gradually lost her hold on Orvieto,
which had been coquetting with the Prefect since early in
April ; [2] Ghibelline conspiracies were hatched in Assisi and
in Todi ; [3] Spoleto expelled her Guelfs and gave herself to
Giovanni Di Vico,[4] while all through the summer there was
war with Gubbio.   Indeed, the Perugians seem to have
been actually besieging that city when the news that
Giovanni da Oleggio had invaded Florentine territory caused
them to break camp and return to Perugia.[5]   A thousand
German men-at-arms were at once despatched to the assistance of their allies,[6] but were surprised by Pier Saccone at
the village of Olmo, some two miles from Arezzo.   There,
according to the terse statement of the writer of the *Chronicon
Estense*, "conflicti mortui et capti sunt omnes ex parte
Perusij."   Messer Piero and his free riders entered Bibbiena
in triumph with more than three hundred prisoners and
twenty-seven *bandiere cavalleresche*.   The horses and armour
and the rest of the spoil he divided among his followers,
while the captives, having been first stripped of all they
possessed, were released upon giving their parole to fight no
more in that war.[7]

[1] *Arch. Stor. It.*, XVI. i. 154 ; FABRETTI, *Cronache*, i. 102, 159-160 ;
PELLINI, i. 908-910 ; *Cronaca di Ser Guerriero, ubi cit.*, p. 9 ; CENCI, *op.
cit.*, in *Bollettino* cited, xiii. 567-568.   On May 3rd the Florentines wrote
to congratulate the Perugians on the discovery and suppression of the
conspiracy.   DEGLI AZZI, *op. cit.*, i. p. 50, § 174.

[2] *Eph. Urbev., ubi cit.*, p. 36, l. 56, p. 46, ll. 1-5 ; FUMI, *Codice Dipl., op.
cit.*, pp. 529-530.   In July, Orvieto actually appealed to Florence for
assistance against Perugia (DEGLI AZZI, *op. cit.*, p. 50, § 175), while, as we
have seen (page 190 *supra*), she accepted Di Vico as her seignior in the
following year.

[3] *Cronaca di Ser Guerriero, ubi cit.*, p. 9, ll. 6-8.

[4] SANSI, *Storia del C. di Spoleto, op. cit.*, i. 227 ; PELLINI, i. 901.

[5] FABRETTI, *Cronache*, i. 103, 128 ; GRAZIANI, p. 155.

[6] GRAZIANI, p. 156.

[7] M. VILLANI, ii. 22 ; L. ARETINO, *Ist. Fior.*, ad ann. ; AMMIRATO,
op. cit., Vol. II. Lib. x. pp. 506-507 ; *Chronicon Estense, ubi cit.*, col. 467.
Compare also the *Cronaca di Ser Gorello, ubi cit.*, col. 838, and DEGLI AZZI
op. cit., i. p. 51, § 177 (Letter of August 20).   The Perugian chroniclers

In November, Giovanni di Cantuccio, who had received reinforcements from the Archbishop of Milan, twice raided the Perugian *contado*, wasting all the countryside ; Nolfo of Montefeltro made himself master of Cagli, and, on the 26th of the same month, Messer Pier Saccone succeeded in surprising Borgo S. Sepolcro.[1] The story is told at length by Matteo Villani, and should be read by everyone who cares at all to understand how men lived in those troublous times. The employment of Arrighetto of S. Polo, that " great and marvellous robber," who " made great and beautiful thefts of cattle," and was therefore protected by Messer Piero, is alone enough to make the narrative strangely vivid ; while his perilous climb up the gate-tower of Borgo S. Sepolcro in the darkness of a stormy winter night, beaten and buffeted by a mighty wind, what time the *masnadieri*, his companions, crouched below, waiting for a rope-ladder to be sent down to them, is told as only a *trecentista* could tell it.[2] The Tarlati had always treated Borgo S. Sepolcro gently,[3] and now, since the surprise was complete, and the townsfolk made no resistance, " no blow was struck nor any robbery done therein." Only the two fortresses, which were strong and filled with soldiers in the pay of Perugia, held out, hoping for succour ; " but Messer Piero issued forth from the city and encamped outside it, over against the said fortresses, to bar the way to the Perugians ; and round about his camp he digged a ditch and builded a palisade, and sent to all the places where he had soldiers of the Archbishop, commanding them to come

on the other hand, make no mention of this disaster, but assert that " le gente de lo Arcevescovo de Milano se erano partite de la Scarparya et uscite del contado de Fiorenza, subito che gionsero le gente d' arme de Peroscia." GRAZIANI, *ubi cit.* See also FABRETTI, *Cronache*, i. 103, 128.
It is curious to note that the Sienese also had a fable of a similar character, attributing the retreat of Giovanni da Oleggio to Sienese valour. See *Cronica Sanese*, in MURATORI, *R. I. S.*, xv. col. 126-127.

[1] GRAZIANI, pp. 156-157.

[2] M. VILLANI, ii. 42.

[3] According to a manuscript history of the City of S. Sepolcro, quoted by DRAGOMANNI in his edition of the chronicle of G. Villani (Firenze, 1845), Vol. III. p. 399, the Tarlati did much to embellish the town, and, in particular. paved all the principal streets " con mattoni di terra cotta, posti con bellissimo artificio, che si sono poi mantenute fin all' anno 1632."

to his assistance; whereby, in a few days, he had with him eight hundred men-at-arms and foot-soldiers in plenty. And, to hinder the Perugians, Giovanni di Cantuccio of Gubbio made an inroad upon them with the men-at-arms which he had from the Biscione.[1]   Nevertheless, the Perugians, being much disquieted by that loss, sought aid from all their allies for the recovery of the town, while yet the fortresses held out; and presently they had five hundred men-at-arms from the Florentines; and, with fourteen hundred men-at-arms, and with much people, they came to Città di Castello and made ready to succour the fortresses. Yet, so great was the cowardice of them that were on guard therein that they awaited not the succour which was at hand, but surrendered to Messer Piero. Thereupon, they of Castello di Anghiari drove out the Perugian garrison and gave themselves to the Vicar of the Archbishop, who restored the town to Messer Maso de' Tarlati." In those days also Castiglion Perugino and the Pieve di S. Stefano and Caprese rebelled against the Perugians, for they loved them not; while, a little later, Castiglion dell' Abbate was betrayed into the hands of the Ghibellines. The Perugians ravaged the country up to the gates of Borgo S. Sepolcro, and defeated Messer Piero with considerable loss, when he, in return, raided the territory of Città di Castello; they retook Castiglion dell' Abbate in January, and drove the men-at-arms of Giovanni di Cantuccio in headlong rout; but they had lost Borgo S. Sepolcro for ever.[2]

If, in 1351, the brunt of the war with the Archbishop had been borne by Florence, in 1352, Perugia was to learn, to her cost, that she was not, as she had fondly imagined, beyond the reach of his aggressions. In 1351 the spume and surf of the Viscontean invasion had drenched her; but, in 1352, all its waves were to go over her.

As early as the beginning of February, "Bartolommeo di Messer Ranieri, the despot of Cortona, traitor, declared war upon our Commune of Perugia without any cause; and

[1] The *Biscione* or Viper was the device of the Visconti.
[2] M. VILLANI, ii. 42, 43, 45 ; GRAZIANI, p. 157 ; PELLINI, i. 911-914.

with him was Messer Pietro Saccone of Arezzo,[1] and the folk of the Archbishop of Milan, and Count Nolfo of Urbino, and the Ubaldini, and many other Ghibelline chieftains, the which rode through our Chiusi, with two thousand men-at-arms, and wasted it all ; and they gave battle to Castiglion Chiusino and to Montecolognola, where the nephew of Messer Malatesta of Rimini was slain." Fifteen days they besieged it, but they took it not; and, when they had departed thence, they came wellnigh to the walls of Perugia, doing very great damage ; and they wasted all the Piano di Carpena. And because the Perugians were wholly taken by surprise, and had no force to resist them, they returned victorious to Cortona and thence to Borgo S. Sepolcro, where they sold and divided the spoil.[2]

The wrath of the Perugians knew no bounds, and when, early in April, the major part of the troops which had been sent by the Visconti to the assistance of the Seigniors of Cortona were withdrawn, they hastened to take vengeance for the shame and loss which they had endured. The Florentines sent three hundred men-at-arms, and, on the 12th of the month, the allies invaded the Cortonese. Besides the Florentine contingent and the *milites* of Perugia, there were seven hundred *barbute* and a vast number of foot-soldiers. They encamped for eight days at Montanare, for ten at Terontola and Bacialla, for nine at Cignano, for eight at Montecchio del Loto, for six at Tavernelle " overo Carbognana," driving off cattle, cutting down vines, olives, oaks, burning houses, and utterly devastating all the country-side up to the very gates of Cortona. On the 27th of May, they sat down before Vagliano de' Marchesi, which had been taken by Messer Bartolommeo two months earlier. It surrendered on the 17th of June, " per causa che si scavò il

---

[1] On January 4th, a convention was entered into in Cortona between the Tarlati and Bartolommeo and Jacopo de' Casali, whereby they agreed to forgive all past injuries and to accept the arbitration of the Archbishop as to outstanding differences. The instrument was drawn and attested by the notary Giano. See BIBL. PUBBLICA DI CORTONA, codex 415, ii. 70, cited by MANCINI, *op. cit.*, p. 196.

[2] GRAZIANI, pp. 157-158 ; FABRETTI, *Cronache*, i. 104 ; M. VILLANI, ii. 56 ; PELLINI, i. 915. As to the death of the nephew of Messer Malatesta, compare the *Cronaca Riminese*, in MURATORI, *R. I. S.*, xv. 902.

poggio di fuori che riesce alla detta fortezza"; and, for this labour, "there went thither from Perugia a man for each house, to wit from Porta S. Pietro and Porta Borgna." From Vagliano the victors returned to Montecchio, whence, for thirty-five days, they wasted whatever in the *contado* of Cortona had escaped their previous devastations.[1]

Meanwhile, however, matters were going badly elsewhere, since, as Matteo Villani phrases it, "the arrogance of the Archbishop had swollen all the Ghibellines with pride." In February, the Chiaravallesi, assisted by Giovanni Di Vico, attempted to make themselves masters of Todi,[2] an enterprise which, if it had proved successful, would not only have added another link to the chain of hostile cities which ringed Perugia round about, but would also, in all probability, have provoked an insurrection in Assisi. In April, Orvieto welcomed Tanuccio degli Ubaldini della Carda at the head of three hundred men-at-arms in the pay of the Visconti; "and on this wise was the Signoria of Orvieto taken from the Commune of Perugia."[3] On the 17th of June, Roccacontrada opened her gates to Albrighetto, despot of Fabriano;[4] while, a few days later, Messer Bartolommeo de' Casali, who had once more been reinforced by a considerable body of troops in the pay of the Archbishop, suddenly departed from Cortona, and having effected a junction with Gisello degli Ubaldini, invaded the *contado* of Perugia and occupied Bettona. The town was betrayed into his hands by Messer Crispolto de' Crispolti, who is spoken of in the chronicles as the "Seignior of Bettona," and whose father, *dominus Petrus domini Ugolini de Bictonio*, appears in the *Libro Rosso* among the nobles of Porta S. Pietro. With him were "il Bastardo di Mainardo" and "don Verio de' Baglioni, priore di Fonte."[5] According

---

[1] GRAZIANI, p. 158; FABRETTI, *Cronache*, i. 160; PELLINI, i. 915-916; M. VILLANI, ii. 78; MANCINI, *op. cit.*, p. 197.

[2] PELLINI, i. 916; M. VILLANI, ii. 57.

[3] *Eph. Urbev., ubi cit.*, p. 50; CALISSE, *op. cit.*, pp. 93 *et seq.* Compare FUMI, *Cod. Dipl., op. cit.*, pp. 531-532, and DEGLI AZZI, *Le Relazioni*, etc., *op. cit.*, i. p. 55, § 192.

[4] GRAZIANI, p. 160; PELLINI, i. 918-919; FABRETTI, *Cronache*, i. 25.

[5] Elsewhere, he is spoken of as *Don Vecio*, and is called *Priore di Fondi* instead of *di Fonte*. Pellini calls him "Abbate de' Fonti de' Baglioni."

to Matteo Villani, Messer Crispolto was a Guelf, but holding himself to have been " ill-treated by the Perugians, for that reason he admitted Messer Bartolommeo to Bettona."[1]

The blow was a shrewd one, for "the place was strong and on the frontiers of Assisi and other towns of the Perugians which, loving their signory but little, incontinently began to furnish the enemy with provisions." Not only was the army recalled from the Cortonese, but "the Commune of Perugia commanded every household to furnish a man to go and take Bettona ; and they set in order all the soldiers of the said Commune, which were fifteen hundred men-at-arms, and also there was a great multitude of footmen." All the exiles were recalled, and peace was made between the Degli Oddi and the Baglioni, who had been at enmity since the murder of Messer Oddo Degli Oddi, in 1331,[2] as well as between such other noble families as were at feud with one another ; "and they who consented not thereto paid a penalty of a thousand pounds in money."[3] Succours arrived from Florence and from Siena, and, on the 27th of June, the army, which is variously estimated at from 8000 to 18,000 strong, took the field and advanced against Bettona[4] The besiegers were divided into three camps and erected five *battifolli* ; "and on such wise did they encompass the town that no man might come out of it without being taken" ; "neither might any victual or succour enter therein." Moreover, they bethought them to guard all the passes round about, to the end that, if the Archbishop should seek to raise the siege, he might not take them unawares. Now, when they of Assisi and of the other dis-

---

[1] M. VILLANI, iii. 17.

[2] See page 157 *supra*.

[3] *Arch. Stor. It.*, XVI. i. 160. It would almost seem as if the Raspanti adopted the same tactics against the Nobles as Florence adopted in the case of Pistoia (*cf.* MACHIAVELLI, *Il Principe*, cap. xx. § 3). " Divide et impera " was their motto until they needed the services of the class they trampled on. Then, the nobles must make peace at their bidding, and, instead of rending one another, unite against the common enemy.

[4] FABRETTI, *Cronache*, i. 26, 105, 135, 160-161 ; PELLINI, i. 920 ; M. VILLANI, iii. 17 ; *Cronica Sanese*, in MURATORI, *R. I. S.*, xv. col. 136 ; MANCINI, *op. cit.*, 197 ; AMMIRATO, II. x. 533.

affected towns and villages saw this, they were afraid, and
" sent to offer themselves to the Perugians and began to
war against Bettona." Nevertheless, the garrison defended
itself valiantly, and made more than one fortunate sortie.
" And the warriors and captains which were therein were
Campano, and Ciampollo of Pisa, and Speccia of Cortona,
and Nello of the Mountain, and Giovanni of Bettona.
These were paladins, tried soldiers and of renown, men of
prowess ; and there were many other captains, bold and
valiant ; and there was the Bastard of Mainardo, the which
was ever foremost in the sorties ; and there was the Priore di
Fonte, with his three sons ; and from him was Fonte forthwith taken away, to wit his benefice ; and his palace was
wasted and destroyed ; and the stones thereof were taken
to build the new Palace of the Priors of Perugia." Ere long,
however, the besieged began to feel the pangs of hunger and
" were reduced to such straits that they had neither bread nor
wine, nor flesh, nor any other food ; and there was no grain
nor hay for their horses, but only such nettles and weeds as
they could gather beneath the walls of the town ; and the
war-horses, which had been of great price, became exceeding thin, and many of them died ; and those they ate,
without bread or any other thing, either boiled or fried in
oil, for of oil they had abundance " ; and " they grew pale
and wan like ashes, and their faces were very black by
reason of their great abstinence. Yet would they not surrender ; wherefore men praised them much." Only after
Count Nolfo of Urbino, with 2000 *barbute,* had vainly
attempted to raise the siege, did the garrison finally abandon
all hope of succour, and, on the 19th of August, Bettona
capitulated. A few days earlier, the Seignior of Cortona
and Messer Gisello degli Ubaldini had succeeded in stealing
through the Perugian lines at night, " vestiti a modo di
ribaldi," and, as some said, furnished with the password " by
one of the rulers of Perugia," whom they had bribed.
Messer Crispolto, however, was less fortunate, being betrayed
into the hands of his enemies by the very men to whom
he had trusted to secure his escape. He was tied upon a
sorry nag and led prisoner to Perugia, there to be exposed

for the whole of one day, " bound to a window of the Palace
of the Captain of the People, so that all men might look
upon him." Bound to other windows were the bastard of
Mainardo and six of the principal citizens of Bettona.
Thereafter, when they had been " examined " and had
confessed their guilt, they were sentenced to death and
attainder ; and, on the 27th of August, Messer Crispolto
was " brought to the head of the Piazza, to wit between
S. Lorenzo and the Fountain of the said Piazza, and there
was a carpet laid, whereupon his head was smitten off most
honourably as became a gentleman and a knight." His
companions were executed with less ceremony, in the Campo
di Battaglia,[1] " dove se faceva la iustitia ordinaria." [2] As
to the rest of the Bettonesi, which were one hundred and
fifty-three men, they were bound together with great ropes
and were led even to Perugia to the Lords Priors ; " and
the women followed after them weeping, one for her father,
another for her husband, and another for her brother." Yet,
in the end, they were released, " because it was no fault of
theirs that the soldiers of the Visconti had occupied
Bettona : nay, rather were they grieved and sorrowful at
their coming. Wherefore, the city of Perugia was full of
Bettonesi, who knew not whither to go ; and they continued
in the city and laboured every man at his trade, and their
families abode with them, because they might not return to
Bettona to dwell therein, by reason of the proclamation
which the Lords Priors had made that none should approach
the said town within a mile thereof." Moreover, there were
sent thither all the *maestri da pietra e da legname*, " to
destroy the said town of Bettona, to the end that never for
all time to come might it be rebuilt or furnish a shelter or
nest for the enemies of the Commune of Perugia ; and so
was it done, for they brake down all the fortresses and all
the walls thereof ; nor was there left any house or any habita-

---

[1] The *Campo di Battaglia* was a vast open space, extending from S.
Fiorenzo to the Hospital, and bounded on the west by a great wall (*murus
campi prelij*), which appears to have been constructed over the ancient
Etruscan circuit—" sopra il muro della Terra Vecchia volta a Levante."
See PELLINI, i. 286.

[2] Cf. my *Palio and Ponte, op. cit.*, p. 146.

tion which they destroyed not and cast not down to the ground." [1]

One of the earliest results of the fall of Bettona was the submission of Giovanni di Cantuccio; [2] while, on the 2nd of September, the Cortonese was again invaded.[3] The Ghibellines, with the troops of the Archbishop, made a series of futile attempts upon Città di Castello,[4] Arezzo,[5] and Montepulciano,[6] but it soon became evident that the tide of war had now definitely turned. In February, 1353, the Seignior of Cortona made peace with Perugia, and, in the sight of all the city, kneeled him down before the Lords Priors at the foot of the Campanile of S. Lorenzo, and, with head uncovered, besought pardon for his fault.[7] Meanwhile, negotiations were going on at Sarzana between the Tuscan communes and the Archbishop; and, on the 28th of March, a treaty was signed, including all the allies of all the belligerents. The representatives of Perugia were Leggerio Andreotti and Bettolo Pellacani.[8] The news was received with great rejoicing. "For this cause,"

---

[1] In addition to the chroniclers above cited, see especially the *Racconto dell' assedio e della presa del Castello di Bettona*, in FABRETTI, *Cronache*, i 133-143; also M. VILLANI, iii. 17, 24, 26; and BONAZZI, i. 437-439.

[2] GRAZIANI, p. 166; PELLINI, i. 928; M. VILLANI, iii. 27. According to the *Cronaca di Ser Guerriero da Gubbio, ubi cit.*, p. 11, Giovanni di Cantuccio "fecie acordo con Perosini" in 1354, and the same date is given in the *Patti dell' Accordo* (of which a fourteenth century copy is still preserved in the Archivio Armanni in Gubbio): "Anno Domini a nativitate eiusdem millessimo ccc.liiij. ind. v. tempore domini Clementis pp. vi. die xx mensis augusti." The mistake, however, corrects itself when we remember that Clement died in December, 1352.

[3] GRAZIANI, p. 167; FABRETTI, *Cronache*, i. 106; PELLINI, i. 928; M. VILLANI, iii. 29.

[4] M. VILLANI, iii. 34.

[5] M. VILLANI, iii. 36.

[6] M. VILLANI, iii. 39.

[7] GRAZIANI, p. 168; FABRETTI, *Cronache*, i. 107; DEGLI AZZI, *Le Relazioni*, etc., *op. cit.*, i. p. 60, § 209.

[8] The Peace of Sarzana is published in its entirety by UGHELLI, *Italia Sacra* (Venezia, 1719), Vol. IV. col. 222-249. A very full synopsis is given by DEGLI AZZI, *op. cit.*, ii. pp. 99-105, § 381; while for the clauses which particularly affected Perugia the reader may consult PELLINI, i. 934-935. Compare also AMMIRATO, *Ist. Fior.* (edition cited), T. II. Lib. x. pp. 545-548, and SORBELLI, *op. cit.*, 152 *et seq.*

says the chronicler, " was held high festival through all the city, and the Priors and Chancellors danced ; and five hundred pounds in money were given to the churches by our Commune, *amore Dei*." [1]

[1] GRAZIANI, p. 168 ; FABRETTI, *Cronache*, i. 27. Of these dances I shall have occasion to speak more fully hereafter. Suffice it in this place to re-mark that they were probably of a ceremonial and religious character, being, in fact, a continuation and development of the thirteenth century dramatic lauds, which first grew into the *Devozione* and were then gradually secularized and connected with dancing. *Cf.* D'ANCONA, *Origini del Teatro Italiano* (Torino, Loescher, 1891), Vol. I. p. 279.

CHAPTER XVI

ALBORNOZ

ON the 30th of June, 1353, Innocent VI. nominated Cardinal Gil Alvarez Carillo de Albornoz Legate in Italy and Vicar-General of the Ecclesiastical State. His Legation included Lombardy, Tuscany, the Patriarchates of Aquileia and of Grado, the Marca Trevigiana, the Provinces of the Church, the Islands of Sardinia and of Corsica, the Archbishoprics of Milan, Ravenna, Genoa, Pisa, Spoleto, Ragusa, Antibari and Jadra, the dioceses of Pavia, Piacenza, Ferrara, Perugia, Orvieto, Todi, Rieti, Narni, and Città di Castello—in a word, the whole of Italy outside the Kingdom of Sicily.[1] As Legate, Albornoz was invested with absolute authority over the churches, both spiritual and temporal, whether in matters of religion, discipline, and faith, or with regard to ecclesiastical rights and franchises ; but it was as Vicar-General that he exercised his most important functions. By virtue of that office, he became, as no man had been before him, the representative and plenipotentiary of the Pope, governing the Provinces with full jurisdiction for an indeterminate period at the pleasure of the Apostolic See.[2] Unfortunately, however, before he could govern the Ecclesiastical State it was necessary to reconstruct it—I had almost said, to recreate it—since it no longer had any existence except as a geographical expression ; and, therefore, his first duty was to wrest from the grasp of the Despots the towns and cities which they had usurped—a task of such enormous difficulty as to strain to the utmost even his exceptional energy and political ability.

[1] THEINER, ii. 242, 243.
[2] FILIPPINI, op. cit., in Studi Storici, Vol. VI. fasc. ii. p. 190.

It is sufficiently obvious that two offices so ample and
so diverse as those of Legate and Vicar could never be
adequately filled by one and the same individual at one and
the same time.   At first, at any rate, the latter was bound
to absorb all his attention ; but the Pope was, nevertheless,
minded to unite them both in the person of Albornoz,
because he would thus be able to collect the tithes which
were payable to the Legate by all the churches in each
year of his Legation.   With these the Cardinal was expected to maintain himself and his Curia, and with these he
must meet all the expenses of his office.   Nor was this
source of revenue by any means a contemptible one,
when we remember that half of the tithes belonged to the
Camera.   Moreover, Innocent flattered himself that it would
be possible to re-establish the papal authority by diplomatic
means ; the disaffection of Perugia and Florence, which had
been provoked by the policy of Clement,[1] seems to have
ceased with his death ;[2] and, after the Peace of Sarzana, it
was believed that the Papacy might count upon the assistance of the great Guelf communes which had so long been
faithful to the Church, and, above all, on the gold of the Archbishop of Milan.[3]   Albornoz was recommended to the Italians
as a " Zealot of Peace," and set out from Avignon, with a
comparatively meagre following, on the 13th of August.

Meanwhile, in May, 1353, permission had been granted
to Giordano Orsini, Rector of the Patrimony, to take into
his pay the celebrated *condottiere*, Fra Moreale d' Albarno,
who assumed the style and title of Captain and Standard-
Bearer of the Church ;[4] and, on the 1st of June, the truce

---

[1] See page 99 *supra*.

[2] Clement VI. died on the 6th of December, 1352, and in April, 1353,
we find the Perugians bestirring themselves on behalf of the Rector of
the Patrimony ; while, at the same time, the Florentines expressed themselves as eager to help the new Pope against his enemies.   DEGLI AZZI,
Le Relazioni, etc., *op. cit.*, i. p. 62, § 214.

[3] SORBELLI, *op. cit.*, p. 74 ; FILIPPINI, *ubi cit.*, p. 192.

[4] " D. frater Morealis Capitaneus et Vexillifer Ecclesie."   See
GREGOROVIUS, *op. cit.*, Vol. III. Lib. xi. cap. vii. p. 449 n., 63 ; FILIPPINI,
ubi cit.   At about the same time the Pope wrote to Florence, to Perugia,
and to Siena, demanding assistance against Di Vico.   CALISSE, *op. cit.*,
p. 101.

which Ugo Arpaione, the Apostolic Nuntius, had made with Giovanni Di Vico having expired, hostilities recommenced. At first success attended the arms of the Prefect. On the 14th of June he surprised Corneto, in spite of its double circuit of walls and numerous towers,[1] while the magistrates of Perugia, to which commune the inhabitants had given the signory of their town for its better defence, were compelled to save themselves by flight. The conquest of Corneto decided the fate of Toscanella, which offered but slight resistance ; and, after having reoccupied the citadel of Marta, which he had given as a pledge for the faithful observance of the truce, Di Vico returned to Orvieto in triumph, where, says the chronicler, " si fece grande alegrezza e luminaria." [2]

Thereafter the fortune of war changed, and for a time the Prefect was overborne by superior numbers. Reinforcements from Perugia and from the Archbishop of Milan[3] enabled the Rector to reoccupy Marta ; [4] while, a little later, the papal troops stormed Abbadia al Ponte after a vigorous resistance, the Perugian levies taking part in the attack.[5] On the 30th of July the *Prefetteschi* were expelled from Narni,[6] and Nicolò de' Buondelmonti was sent thither from Florence as Potestà.[7] Fra Moreale devastated the country up to the gates of Orvieto, and, from the walls of the beleaguered city, Di Vico could hear the savage cries of his enemies : " Viva la Chiesa di Roma ! Muoia il Prefetto scomunicato ! " [8]   In September it seemed that the victory of the Church was assured,[9] when Fra Moreale, his term of service with the Rector being ended and his pay in arrears,

[1] See CALISSE, *op. cit.*, p. 121 n.

[2] *Eph. Urbev.*, *ubi cit.*, p. 60 ; CALISSE, p. 102 ; ANTONELLI, p. 138.

[3] *Eph. Urbev.*, p. 61, ll. 12-13.   [4] ANTONELLI, p. 139.

[5] " Die .xxiii. augusti solvi comiti Luffo, Lambertino, Sinile, Anechino Rubeo, Caristio, de Brocch, conestabilibus comunis civitatis Perusine, existentibus in provincia Patrimonii in servitium Ecclesie pro provisione eis facta per rectorem quia debellaverunt et per bellum obtinuerunt roccham Abbatie ad Pontem, que detinebatur per Iohannem de Vico, ad rationem 59 flor. pro qualibet bandieria. cclxxxxv. flor." *Intr. et exit. Patrimonii*, ad ann. 1353, n. 266, c. 79 (cited by ANTONELLI, *loc. cit.*, n. 4).

[6] ANTONELLI, p. 140.

[7] DEGLI AZZI, *Le Relazioni*, etc., *op. cit.*, i. p. 63, § 220.

[8] *Eph. Urbev.*, *ubi cit.*, pp. 61-62.   [9] CALISSE, *op. cit.*, p. 299, Doc. cxv.

suddenly changed sides and enlisted under the banners of Di Vico and the Ghibellines of Todi, who hoped, with his assistance., to return in triumph to their homes.[1] Troops were gathered in Perugia and hurried to the assistance of the Guelfs;[2] but, though Todi was saved, the star of the Prefect was now once more in the ascendant.

On the 2nd of October, Albornoz arrived in Florence, where he was received " with great honour and with solemn procession and festival. A rich baldachin of silk and gold was borne over his head by *nobili popolani*, and his bridle was held and his saddle supported by noble knights of Florence, while the bells of the churches and of the Commune rang out the *Te Deum*."[3] On the 11th he departed for Siena,[4] and, a few days later, he reached Perugia.[5] He was welcomed by the citizens with great rejoicing, and, with the major part of his retinue, was lodged in S. Pietro. Jousts and games were celebrated in his honour ; " and the Commune of Perugia gave him a goodly horse, which was bought for the price of 225 florins from Lambertino, the German, *conestabile* of the said Commune.[6] He was further presented with 23 baskets of spelt and 26 *some* of wine, with sweetmeats and wax in plenty, to wit tapers and candles of divers sorts, and 10 great boxes filled with fruit and jujubes and sugared pine seeds, and 11 cakes of marchpane. All these things were taken to S. Pietro, and the Cardinal received them gladly."[7]

[1] GREGOROVIUS, *op. cit.*, Vol. III. Lib. xi. cap. vii. p. 432 ; FILIPPINI, *ubi cit.*, p. 193 ; CALISSE, pp. 104-105 ; ANTONELLI, p. 140.

[2] ANTONELLI, p. 142 ; CALISSE, p. 105 ; M. VILLANI, iii. 81.

[3] M. VILLANI, iii. 84 ; MURATORI (*Annali d' Italia*, ad ann.) says that Albornoz reached Florence on the 11th of October, the day of his departure according to Villani.

[4] FILIPPINI, *ubi cit.*, p. 209 n. 3, citing THEINER, ii. 379. Compare the *Cronica Sanese*, in MURATORI, *R. I. S.*, xv. col. 138, where we read that Albornoz " venne in Siena di Novembre," an obvious error.

[5] FABRETTI, *Cronache*, i. 147, gives the date as October 23rd ; whereas, according to the chronicle attributed to GRAZIANI (p. 170), Albornoz arrived on the 12th.

[6] We have already seen the same Lambertino at the storming of Abbadia al Ponte. See page 206 n. 5 *supra*.

[7] FABRETTI, *Cronache*, i. 147, 169-170 ; PELLINI, i. 939. Compare my *The " Ensamples " of Fra Filippo*, *op. cit.*, p. 50 n.

Albornoz found the Perugians in great discord by reason of recent disorders. About the middle of August, a conspiracy had been discovered for the subversion of the popular government, and, as a consequence, the whole body of the nobles had left the city. A little later, Franceschino Degli Oddi, Potestà of Castel della Pieve, was arrested on the charge of plotting the betrayal of that town to the *fuorusciti*. His guilt was more than doubtful, but, after suffering atrocious torments to compel confession, he was secretly beheaded on the night of the 24th of September "nella stalla del palazzo"—the victim, as many thought, of his loyalty to the Commune.[1] Of these dissensions Di Vico was only too ready to take advantage, and, as he had formerly attempted to make himself master of Rome, so now he "bussava per corrompere Perugia."[2] The Legate succeeded in re-establishing peace among the citizens, and the *fuorusciti* were permitted to return to their homes;[3] while, probably about the same time, he was joined by Cola di Rienzo, who had now become a willing instrument in the hands of the Pope, and who owed his liberation in no small degree to the intercession of the Perugian ambassadors at Avignon.[4]

Not only had the insurrection of the nobles been suppressed without necessitating the recall of the forces which Perugia had sent to the assistance of the Rector of the Patrimony, but, while Albornoz was in the city, fresh troops had been levied and fresh succours sent to Todi.[5] By the end of October, Fra Moreale had abandoned the service of Di Vico and was gathering men to form upon his own account one

[1] GRAZIANI, 169; FABRETTI, *Cronache*, i. 108; PELLINI, i. 936-937.

[2] See page 190 *supra*, and authorities there cited.   [3] GRAZIANI, p. 170

[4] See FILIPINNI, *ubi cit.*, p. 203 and note, where a letter of Innocent VI to the Perugians is quoted. On the authority of the *Vita*, all the historians affirm that Cola set out from Avignon in the suite of Albornoz. The contrary is, however, the case, and FILIPPINI (pp. 199-206) has clearly demonstrated that when the Legate departed the Tribune was still in prison. It is clear that the Pope desired to keep the two men and their duties distinct and separate; but Cola, too weak to act alone, found himself compelled to seek the assistance of Albornoz, not only for the means to reach Rome, but even for his daily bread.

[5] FILIPPINI, *ubi cit.*, pp. 210-211; ANTONELLI, p. 142; CALISSE, p. 105

of those Great Companies whose terrible power Italy had
already experienced.   It was obviously impossible for the
Legate to begin the work of reconquering the Ecclesiastical
State while a great brigand army assembled in the very
centre of his jurisdiction, and it is probably to this cause
that we may attribute his prolonged sojourn in Perugia.
How the negotiations into which he entered were conducted
we do not know, but their success is proved by the fact that
Moreale left the *contado* of Todi without doing any further
damage, and went with 1500 *barbute* and more than 2000
masnadieri to the aid of Gentile da Mogliano against the
Malatesta.[1]   Then, at last, Albornoz felt himself free to
move.   Giordano Orsini was ordered to meet him at Castel
della Pieve *cum tota gente sua armigera*,[2] and, on the 15th
or 16th of November, he left Perugia with a bodyguard of
200 horse, which was furnished by the Commune for his
protection.   He also seems to have been accompanied by
several of the leading citizens, " whom," says Pellini, " he
added to the number of his councillors." [3]   Among the rest
was that Leggerio Andreotti whom Matteo Villani describes
as "senza appello il maggiore cittadino ch' avesse città
d' Italia che si regesse a popolo e libertà," [4] and who has
already been mentioned more than once in these pages.
On the 20th, the Cardinal entered the Patrimony and,
passing beneath the walls of Orvieto, took up his residence
at Montefiascone, a place which, besides being the traditional
seat of the Rector, possessed a certain strategical importance,
standing, as it did, at the southern extremity of the Lake of
Bolsena, between Viterbo and Orvieto.   For the rest, in all
the Province, only Acquapendente, Bolsena, and a few minor
towns of but little importance still held out for the Church.
All the others, Viterbo, Orvieto, Toscanella, Corneto, Civitavecchia, Terni, Amelia, Narni, either openly acknowledged
the suzerainty of Di Vico or were held in his interest by the
Ghibelline faction.   Indeed, the anonymous author of the
Life of Innocent VI. asserts that, when Egidio entered Italy,

---

[1] M. VILLANI, iii. 89 ; GRAZIANI, p. 170 ; RICOTTI (edition cited), i.
261 ; TONINI, *op. cit.*, p. 137.   [2] ANTONELLI, p. 144.
[3] PELLINI, i. 939.   [4] M. VILLANI, xi. 5.

he found, in all the dominions of the Church, nowhere to safely lay his head save only Montefiascone in the Patrimony and Montefalco in the Ducato.[1]

Ever since his arrival in Siena, Albornoz had been treating with Giovanni Di Vico,[2] who, if his professions could be relied upon, was himself also extremely anxious for peace ; while the two ambassadors[3] whom the Archbishop of Milan had sent to Orvieto to induce him to submit to the Church seem to have found him unexpectedly tractable. But Di Vico was a man of great shrewdness and of even greater bad faith, capable of promising everything and performing nothing, of making agreements only to break them, of amusing his adversaries with endless negotiations, and of profiting by peace to carry on war with more advantage. When Albornoz entered the Patrimony, he came out of Orvieto to meet him and did him reverence on the highway below the city, promising to observe the conditions imposed upon him by the ambassadors of the Archbishop, and to restore all the towns and cities which he had usurped. According to the author of the *Life of Cola*, " while they were together, the Legate said : ' I desire that thou render unto the Church all that is hers, and retain that which is thine own.' Said the Prefect : ' Willingly will I do so. I am content ' ; and therewithal he set his seal to the parchment whereupon the terms of the agreement were written."[4] Men thought that peace was assured ; but Di Vico had not the least intention of abandoning any of his conquests. He was willing to acknowledge the suzerainty of the Church ; but that was all. He was determined to remain seignior of every town which he had occupied ; while, with regard to Orvieto, it is clear from the resolutions passed by the General

[1] FILIPPINI, *ubi cit.*, p. 213, citing RAYNALD, a. 1353, iii. Apparently Todi is forgotten in this statement ; while, as we have seen, the *Prefetteschi* were expelled from Narni in July (see page 206 *supra*). I have found no record of their having recaptured it in the interval ; but such may have been the case.

[2] " Et queste pace si cominzaro a trattare quando il legato gionse a Siena." *Eph. Urbev.*, p. 63.

[3] Dominus Guilglielminus de Armondis de Parma, legum doctor, et ser Octinus de Marliano, collateralis domini supradicti.

[4] *Vita*, ii. 5 ; *Eph. Urbev.*, pp. 63-64.

Council on the 16th of November,[1] that that city only
desired peace with the Legate provided that she was asked to
assume no greater obligations than those to which she was
held *de iure vel de consuetudine*, and that the jurisdiction of
the Prefect was not encroached upon. In other words, the
Orvietans would acknowledge no other seignior than him
whom they had proclaimed their Liberator and Defender.[2]
The ambassadors who had been sent by Giovanni Visconti
were entirely on the side of the Commune ;[3] and, indeed, it
is difficult to perceive how, as competent jurisconsults, they
could have taken any other view. Orvieto was not and
never had been immediately subject to the Pope. Thus,
when the war was renewed, Di Vico was enabled to pose as
the defender of popular liberties against the aggressions of
the Church.

Even if, at first, the Prefect had been honestly willing to
make some concessions, he completely changed his mind
when he saw how few soldiers Albornoz had brought with
him.[4] Summoned to Montefiascone, he not only refused to
obey, but, if we may credit Villani,[5] actually profited by the
suspension of hostilities to possess himself of two fortified
places belonging to the Church ; while, on the other hand,
the Legate declined to give audience to the ambassadors
from Orvieto until he had received an explicit declaration
that the Commune was willing to submit itself without any
reservation.[6] Negotiations were broken off ; an attempt on
Orvieto was frustrated by the vigilance of Di Vico, and
Albornoz found himself shut up in Montefiascone without
food for his troops or forage for his horses, while the enemy
ravaged the country up to the very gates of the city.[7] The

[1] FUMI, *Cod. Dipl., op. cit.*, pp. 535-537 ; CALISSE, Doc. cix. 63, pp.
290-295.

[2] FILIPPINI, *op. cit.*, in *Studi Storici*, VI. fasc. iii. p. 345.

[3] SORBELLI, *op. cit.*, pp. 77-78.

[4] He is reported to have said to his companions, " Lo legato ha 50 tra
compagni e cappellani : li miei ragazzi bastano a contrastare a li preti
suoi." *Vita di Cola di Rienzo*, ii. 5.

[5] M. VILLANI, iii. 98.

[6] FUMI, *Cod. Dipl., op. cit.*, p. 537.

[7] See ANTONELLI, p. 149, and the documents published by FILIPPINI
in *Studi Storici*, Vol. V.

violence of its anathemas prove how great was the wrath and terror of the Papacy. "Viper," "scorpion," "cancer," "poison," "a monster issuing from the abyss of rottenness, upon whose horns blasphemies are inscribed." Such were the titles which Innocent showered upon the insolent rebel ;[1] but it was worse than useless to fight such an adversary with spiritual weapons.[2]   In the spring, the Legate received reinforcements from Perugia, Florence, and Siena ; a considerable body of German horse deserted from the Prefect and took service with the Church ; troops were brought from Lombardy, and, at the end of March, Andrea de' Salamocelli of Lucca arrived with a hundred and twenty-five *barbute*.   Henceforward Albornoz proceeded rapidly from conquest to conquest.   In May, his army was further increased by ten thousand Romans under the command of Giovanni Conti di Valmontone, and, in the following month, Di Vico was compelled to sue for peace in real earnest.[3]

On the 9th of June, 1354, Albornoz entered Orvieto, and, on the 10th, the Prefect abdicated the Seigniory of the city, delivering the keys of the gates to his conqueror and swearing upon the Gospels to be faithful to the Church.   A fortnight later the General Council unanimously elected Innocent VI. and Albornoz "et quemlibet ipsorum ad vitam pro toto tempore vite ipsorum" to be "Lords, Rectors, and Governors" of the Commune, the Legate accepting the Seigniory with the title of *Liberator Comunis et Populi Urbevetani et Dominus Generalis*.[4]   On the 23rd the Procurator of Viterbo appeared in Orvieto and made submission in the name of his commune; the Perugian Leggerio Andreotti was sent thither as Potestà[5] and, on the 26th of July, Albornoz entered the city amid

[1] CALISSE, *op. cit.*, p. 111, and Doc. cxx. and cxxii.

[2] " . . . altra medecina bisognava a riducere costui alla via diritta che suono di campane o fummo di candele."

[3] For details of the war, see FILIPPINI, *op. cit.*, cap. iii. pp. 348 *seq.* ; ANTONELLI, *op. cit.*, pp. 146-160.

[4] FUMI, *Cod. Dipl.*, *op. cit.*, Doc. dclxxx.

[5] " Die .ii. iul. solvi ser Antonio de Parma misso apud Perusium per dominum legatum ad portandum electionem potestarie civitatis Viterbii Legerio Andreocti de Perusio, qui stetet. vi. diebus, *iv. flor.*" *Introit. et exit. Patrimonii*, an. 1354, c. 246 (ANTONELLI, p. 164 n.).

the plaudits of the inhabitants, who, utterly weary of the tyrannies of Di Vico, besought him to build a citadel for their protection.[1]

The prosperous issue of the war in the Patrimony was decisive also of the fate of the Ducato ; and the fall of the Prefect was followed by that of other lesser despots, who speedily realized that they could no longer hope to resist the victorious arms of the Church. Moreover, many of the rebellious towns had been weakened by the devastations of Fra Moreale, who, after forcing the Malatesta to purchase a cessation of hostilities for the enormous sum of 60,000 ducats,[2] once more invaded Umbria in the beginning of June.[3] Spello especially suffered from the ravages of the Grand Company, and Albornoz, taking advantage of its exhaustion, ordered the Rector of the Ducato to attack it. On the sixth day the inhabitants surrendered.[4] Meanwhile, the *fuorusciti* of Gubbio besought the aid of the Legate against Giovanni Cantuccio de' Gabrielli, and the Count Carlo di Dovadola was sent against him with six *bandiere* of horse. Hated by the citizens and without hope of succour from without, Gabrielli was obliged to make a virtue of necessity, and, on the 8th of July, the Count took possession of Gubbio in the name of the Church.[5]

The brief episode of Cola di Rienzo's return to Rome and his ignominious death at the hands of the populace did nothing to retard the reconquest and consolidation of the Ecclesiastical State ; while the taking off of Fra Moreale by the ex-tribune not only removed a cause of continual peril to the schemes of Albornoz, but also served to fill the coffers of the Perugian Commune, since, as soon as the news reached them, the Magistrates ordered the confiscation of the vast

[1] FILIPPINI, *ubi cit.*, pp. 370-371.

[2] TONINI, *op. cit.*, p. 138.

[3] GRAZIANI, pp. 171-172 ; PELLINI, i. 945 ; M. VILLANI, iv. 14.

[4] FILIPPINI, *op. cit.*, cap. iv. p. 481 (*Studi Storici*, Vol. VII. fasc. iv.). *Cf.* Doc. viii. in Vol. V. pp. 81 *seq.*

[5] M. VILLANI, iv. 13 ; *Cronaca di Ser Guerriero da Gubbio, ubi cit.*, pp. 11-12 ; FILIPPINI, *ubi cit.*, pp. 482-484 ; P. CENCI, *op. cit.*, in *Bollettino* cited, xiii. p. 569. See also G. MAZZATINTI, *Il Cardinale Albornoz nelle Marche e nell' Umbria* (*Appunti*), Doc. i., in *Arch. Stor. per la Toscana, per le Marche e per l' Umbria*, Vol. IV. fasc. xv.-xvi., pp. 467 *et seq.*

sums which the great *condottiere* had deposited with the bankers of their city.[1]

Towards the end of September a *Parlamento* of the Patrimony assembled at Montefiascone, and thither came all the Bishops and Prelates, the Nobles and the representatives of the communes.   Through lapse of time and the incapacity and neglect of the Rectors, many of the rights of the Church had fallen into abeyance, and Albornoz was determined to establish the dominion which he had recovered by force of arms on a solid legal basis.   To this end a new Register of the Curia was compiled from the ancient documents ; fresh constitutions were promulgated, and the numerous petty seigniors of the Province were required to prove the legitimacy of their titles, under pain of being treated as usurpers.   The communes were still permitted to govern themselves by their own laws, and, for the most part, the old democratic régime was restored, as in Orvieto and Gubbio ; but the power of making new laws was declared to appertain " ad dominum," and, in each subject town, the authority of the Church was represented by a Vicar, who was appointed by and directly dependent on the Legate. The duties and prerogatives of these officials somewhat resembled those of the thirteenth century Potestà, and it was the special care of Albornoz to select upright and honest men, over whose actions he exercised the strictest supervision.[2]   His justice and moderation, in marked contrast with the violence and partiality of the French Rectors, soon gained him unlimited confidence.   Many powerful cities besought his good offices as reformer and peacemaker, and voluntarily accepted his seigniory.   Among the rest may be mentioned the communes of Amelia, Narni, Terni, and Rieti.[3]

The papal authority having been re-established in the Patrimony, Albornoz prepared for war with the Malatesta.

[1] FILIPPINI, *ubi cit.*, p. 493.

[2] FILIPPINI, *ubi cit.*, pp. 496 *et seq.*   Compare also GREGOROVIUS, *op. cit.*, Vol. III. Lib. xi. cap. vii. p. 435, and Lib. xii. cap. i. p. 463.

[3] ANTONELLI, *op. cit.*, pp. 172-174.   The Act of Submission of Rieti is published by A. BELLUCCI, *Sulla storia dell' antico Comune di Rieti*, in *Bollettino* cited, vii. 423.

On the 7th of January, 1355, he left Orvieto for Foligno, whence he proposed to direct the operations in the March, while, at the same time, he completed the pacification of the Ducato. And here the difficulties which beset him were redoubled, since he could hardly move without antagonizing Perugia, who, although she had been willing enough to assist him against the Prefect, was by no means willing to abdicate the hegemony of Umbria. The submissions of Spello and Gubbio, which had been followed by those of Foligno and of Norcia, already caused her serious misgivings,[1] and when, in February, the syndics of Spoleto and of the Spoletine *fuorusciti* appealed to the Legate to heal their discords,[2] she was compelled to realize that an united and homogeneous Ecclesiastical State might well prove a greater menace to her power than ever Di Vico had been. According to Parruccio Zampolini, it was at this time that "the Church of Rome . . . took Spoleto and drew it out of the hands of the Commune of Perugia;"[3] but the statement appears to be an exaggeration, since, though the government of that city was reformed and many of the exiles were allowed to return to their homes, the right of nominating the Potestà was still left to the Perugians.[4] Less moderation was shown in the matter of Gualdo and Bettona, which were declared to be immediately subject to the Holy See;[5] and albeit, for the present, no attempt was made to deprive Perugia of her jurisdiction in Assisi, it is probable that her resentment would have taken an active form had not the hands of Albornoz been strengthened by the presence in Italy of an Emperor who was not only on terms of amity with the Church, but who had recently despatched a considerable body of German horse to his assistance.[6]

---

[1] See FILIPPINI, *ubi cit.*, p. 511, and authorities there cited.

[2] SANSI, *Storia del C. di Spoleto, op. cit.*, i. 232.

[3] SANSI, *Documenti storici inediti*, etc., *op. cit.*, i. 113: " . . . et poi la Chiesa de Roma fece la pace, et remise li usciti Gibellini, pigliò Spuliti et trasselo delle mani del commune de Peroscia."

[4] FILIPPINI, *ubi cit.*, pp. 511-512.

[5] *Ibid.*, p. 513.

[6] GRAZIANI, pp. 175-176; M. VILLANI, iv. 67. They passed through Perugia on the 7th of March, " con la bandiera imperiale spiegata, nella quale era dipinta l' arme del dicto Imperatore, cioè una aquila nera con

Elected Emperor in 1346, Charles of Luxemburg had long delayed his descent into Italy, and it was not until the autumn of 1354 that he finally crossed the Alps. On the 6th of January, 1355, he received the iron crown at the hands of the Archbishop of Milan, and, on the 18th of the same month, he reached Pisa. Thither came the representatives of all the Tuscan communes, and, among the rest, a "fair and great embassy" from Perugia.[1] The Florentine and Sienese ambassadors entered the presence-chamber together, but the Perugians refused to join them, believing that "they could deliver themselves from subjection to the Empire on the pretext that they were vassals of the Church." [2] This plea, however, was not allowed to serve them, for, when Charles and Albornoz met in Siena, some three months later, it was agreed that "without offending Holy Church, the Emperor might deal with Perugia as with the other cities of Italy." [3] The persistent rumours which attributed to Charles a readiness to assist the Pope in re-establishing the dominion of the Holy See over all its ancient State, including Ferrara and Perugia, cast a sinister light upon this agreement; [4] but the danger was soon averted. The rebellion of Pisa (20th May) so terrified the degenerate descendant of Dante's "alto Arrigo" [5] that he abandoned all further hopes of Italian conquest and hurried northward, *die et nocte equitans ut in fuga.*[6] Before he left Pisa, the Perugian ambassadors, profiting by the changed condition of affairs, obtained ample privileges, sealed with the golden seal, confirming the Commune in all its possessions, howso-

doi teste nel campo giallo ; et questi passando fuoro molto onorati dal nostro Comuno, et alcuni, di quelli principali andarono a mangiare con li Priori."

[1] GRAZIANI, p. 175. Of the demeanour of the Emperor while giving audience to the ambassadors, M. VILLANI (iv. 74) gives us some curious details : " Suo costume era ezandio stando a udienza di tenere verghette di salcio in mano e uno coltellino, e tagliare a suo diletto minutamente. . . ." The American habit of whittling would seem to have Imperial precedent.

[2] M. VILLANI, iv. 49, 53.   [3] M. VILLANI, v. 15.

[4] FILIPPINI, *op. cit.*, cap. v. p. 519 (*Studi Storici*, Vol. VII. fasc. iv.) and cap. vi. p. 299 (*Studi Storici*, Vol. VIII. fasc. iii.).

[5] *Paradiso*, xvii. 82, xxx. 137.

[6] GREGOROVIUS, *op. cit.*, Vol. III. Lib. xii. cap. i. § 1, pp. 460-461.

THE PRINCIPAL DOORWAY OF THE PALAZZO PUBBLICO

ever acquired. Thus did Perugia gain a legitimate title to all her conquests in Tuscany : Montecchio, Castiglion Aretino, Lucignano, Foiano, and generally to "every other thing which the City possessed which appertained to the Empire." The Bishop was created one of the Counts Palatine, and the University—*lo Studio Generale*—was confirmed for ever. For the better preservation of these documents they were bricked into a cavity which was made in the wall of the Palazzo Pubblico, above the principal doorway, and covered with a stone inscribed with the following legend :—

> CAROLVS IMPERATOR PERVSINI STATVS AMATOR
> HAS GRATIAS DONO EGIT QVAS LAPIS ISTE TEGIT.[1]

Thus did the means used by Albornoz to tame Perugia turn to her advantage. In the weak and cowardly Charles no help was to be found either material or moral, and, all too late, the Pope perceived how great had been his error in too openly allying himself with the Empire. The Tuscan communes hastened to renew their ancient defensive league, which, directed in the first instance against the Visconti and afterwards against every ultramontane prince, including even the Emperor, was now revived for the mutual protection of the allies against every one, not excluding the Pope himself, who should attempt anything to their prejudice.[2] The heads of the confederation were Florence and Perugia, both smarting from recent indignities and both wavering in their allegiance to the Church.

The peace made by Albornoz, in February, 1355, between

---

[1] GRAZIANI, p. 180 ; FABRETTI, *Cronache*, i. 113 ; PELLINI, i. 953. *Cf.* SCALVANTI, *Considerazioni*, etc., *op. cit.*, pp. 40-42.

[2] See FILIPPINI, *op. cit.*, cap. vi. pp. 300-301 (*Studi Storici*, Vol. VIII. fasc. iii.) and FABRETTI, *Cronache*, i. 30, where the action of the Pope and the Legate in seeking to *render le terre della Chiesa* is mentioned as one of the reasons of the League. A full synopsis of its provisions is given by DEGLI AZZI, *Le Relazioni*, etc., *op. cit.*, ii. pp. 114-116, § 419. It is true that one of the clauses definitely states that it was not directed either against the Church or the Empire, but there is no indication that the allies intended thereby to hold themselves absolved from their mutual obligations if the Pope or the Emperor assailed their liberties. M. VILLANI (vi. 4) states that it was made against the Great Company of Count Lando. Siena refused to join, for reasons which we shall see hereafter ; and the members of the League (which was concluded on the 18th of February, 1356) were Florence, Pisa, Perugia, Volterra, Pistoia, and S. Miniato.

the hostile factions of Spoleto, was, from the nature of the case, not likely to prove durable. For years that Commune had been torn by civic disorders ; blood had flowed like water ; there were infinite wrongs to be avenged, and life was full of suspicion and uncertainty. It was, therefore, hardly to be wondered at if, after a few months, the Guelfs, discontented at having been forced to share the government with their enemies, once more took up arms and expelled the Ghibellines with horrible slaughter.[1] They filled the offices of the Republic with their own partisans, and then, allying themselves with the numerous outlaws of the Province, attacked and devastated the towns and villages which remained faithful to the Church. From Fermo, on the 19th of September, Albornoz promulgated an edict against the rebels, which he caused to be published in the churches of Trevi, Foligno, and Montefalco, declaring that if the revolted city failed to return to obedience within twenty days, it would forthwith be sentenced to deprivation of all its benefices and all its rights.[2] The Guelfs, however, were not minded to yield and hastened to seek the protection of Perugia, offering to submit themselves to her, and to permit the completion of the citadel which had been begun thirty years earlier, close to the *porta fuga*, on the height which dominates the Borgo S. Gregorio.[3] The Perugians, whom long experience had made contemptuous of papal anathemas, had no hesitation in accepting their overtures, and began to construct a fortress not only in Spoleto but also in Gualdo ;[4] they once more sacked the luckless Bettona, and prevented the Potestà who had been sent thither by the Rector of the Ducato from exercising his office.[5] The Pope was naturally greatly incensed, but he was at least as much alarmed as

---

[1] MINERVIO, *ubi cit.*, cap. ix. p. 40 : " Anno postea dñi MCCCLV, Gibellini expulsi fuerunt, magnaque eorum clades fuit." See also *Gli Annali di* PARRUCCIO ZAMPOLINI, *ubi cit.*, p. 113.

[2] FILIPPINI, *ubi cit.*, p. 302, citing G. SALVI, *Il card. Egidio Albornoz e gli archivi di S. Ginesio*, Doc. iv. The names of the persons cited to appear before the Legate fill fifty-two lines of the parchment.

[3] See SANSI, *Storia del C. di Spoleto, op. cit.*, i. 201.

[4] THEINER, ii. cap. 313, pp. 315-316.

[5] It would seem that the destruction of Bettona in 1352 had not been as complete as the chroniclers would lead us to suppose (*cf.* pages 201-2 *supra*).

angered, and while he administered a severe rebuke to the
Perugians, exhorting them to refuse all unlawful dominion
and to destroy the fortresses under pain of grievous spiritual
censures, he, at the same time, warned Albornoz to act with
prudence, lest, by undue rigour, the powerful Commune
which had so long upheld the papal authority in Umbria
should be hopelessly alienated.[1] His moderation seems to
have been crowned with success, for, a little later, we find
the Perugians besieging Spoleto on behalf of the Church and
compelling the rebels to implore pardon of the Legate.[2] An
oath of allegiance, whereby each and every citizen declared
himself "subjectus et peculiaris sanctæ Romanæ Ecclesiæ," was
exacted from all persons over fourteen years of age, whether
male or female. They further swore that from henceforward
the city would never, under any pretext, submit itself to any
seignior or commune.[3] The sum to be paid in composition

for the document published by THEINER (*ubi cit.*) speaks of *domorum Terre
Bictonii . . . que remanserant post ipsius Terre depopulationem*, which
were now demolished. The hatred of Perugia for Bettona lasted as long
as the Commune endured. Her inhabitants are discriminated against in
the Statute of 1523 (see Vol. III. Rubric 56, c. 27) ; Lorenzo Spirito
speaks of her with contempt : " Bettona saggio poco ; " and it is alleged
that, when the Perugians desired to test the virtue of their celebrated
" acquetta," the charcoal-burners of Bettona were their favourite victims.
See Z. ZANETTI, *L'acquetta*, Article in *Augusta Perusia*, Anno i. pp. 113-
115, and compare G. BIANCONI, *Su Bettona, Terra antichissima ed illustre
dell' Umbria, op. cit.*, p. 48 n. 11.

[1] FILIPPINI, *ubi cit.*, p. 302.

[2] *Ibid.*, p. 303 n. 1, citing ARCH. VAT., Reg. n. 238, fol. 21 retro (Letter
of Innocent VI. to the Commune of Perugia). " Sed illud ex omnibus in
pubblicum proferre sufficiat, quod hactenus Spoletanis illis in manibus tunc
ecclesie prefate rebellibus, arta obsidione constrictis et ad dedicionem
compulsis, eidem ecclesie iura sua et pacem patriæ reddidistis." As far as
I am aware no reference to this siege is to be found in any of the
chronicles.

[3] ARCH. COM. DI SPOLETO, *Pergamene*, Cass. iv. n. 181. Letter of
Albornoz ordering Filippo, Bishop of Ferrara, to go to Spoleto with two
notaries and to absolve the citizens. Given in Ancona, 9th February, 1356.
This document is cited by SANSI (*ubi cit.*, p. 234) under the date of February,
1355, thus referring it to the first submission of the Spoletini to Albornoz.
Moreover, on the authority of CAMPELLO, who quotes the *Libro di Riformagioni* of 1355, he relates several facts which tend to prove the perfect devotion of the city to the Church, to which it looked for deliverance from
the yoke of Perugia. This, however, is in direct contradiction with the

for the crime of rebellion was fixed at 8000 florins. The *fuorusciti* were not readmitted, Albornoz having learned by bitter experience that such a policy must inevitably result in fresh disturbances.

The Pope had soon further reason to congratulate himself on his moderation towards the Perugians, for Di Vico was once more plotting against the Church, and, in February, 1356, he attempted, with the connivance of the Chiaravallesi, to make himself master of Todi.[1] It is noticeable that, in his appeal to Perugia, the Pope demands assistance not only, as of old, *pro nostra et apostolice sedis reverentia*, but also *pro publici utilitatis intuitu*.[2] That same summer, the whole chivalry of France was shattered by a handful of Englishmen at the Battle of Poitiers, and Innocent, fearing to be expelled from Avignon, "wrote to the Lords Priors of Perugia that, if he were compelled to depart out of France, he would come straight to Perugia."[3] Thus was the breach between the Papacy and the great Guelf commune wholly healed, though the Perugians had not yet entirely abandoned their claim to the suzerainty of Bettona and other places in the Ecclesiastical State.[4] They were still far too useful to the Church to be needlessly offended, and the Papacy, though now, as always, utterly unmoved by gratitude and wholly careless of its plighted word, was never lacking in astuteness.

In the autumn of 1357, Albornoz returned to Avignon, having recovered for the Church the whole of the Ecclesiastical State with the exception of Forlì. In a fine passage Mr Hutton likens him to "a thunderstorm sweeping the

---

evidence of the other documents, and it appears reasonably certain that Campello wrote the date 1355 by mistake for 1356. Such is the opinion of FILIPPINI (*ubi cit.*, p. 303 n. 2), who, after searching in vain for the aforesaid *Libro di Riformagioni* among the Archives of Spoleto, has come to the conclusion that thus alone can the apparent contradiction of the documents be explained.

[1] M. VILLANI, vi. 10.

[2] CALISSE, *op. cit.*, Doc. cxlii. p. 310. Letter of Innocent VI. to the Perugians, 28th March, 1356.

[3] PELLINI, i. 963. Compare FABRETTI, *Cronache*, i. 176.

[4] FILIPPINI, *op. cit.*, cap. vii. p. 488 (*Studi Storici*, Vol. VIII. fasc. iv.).

world ; " [1] but he was at least as great a diplomatist as he
was a warrior ; he conquered his enemies as much by conciliation as by repression, and his triumphs were rather
those of a statesman than of a general. [2]

[1] E. HUTTON, *Sigismondo Pandolfo Malatesta, Lord of Rimini* (London, 1906), p. 12.

[2] FILIPPINI, *ubi cit.*, p. 491.

CHAPTER XVII

THE WAR WITH SIENA

THE power of Perugia in Umbria had been seriously curtailed by the conquests of Albornoz, and it was obvious that, unless she were willing to break with all her old traditions and to take up a position of open antagonism to the Church, any future extension of her dominion must lie to the westward. Such a policy must necessarily entail a rupture with Siena; but, in her present circumstances, it was believed that Siena was in no condition to offer any very effectual resistance to Perugian aggressions.

For many years the two communes had lived on terms of perfect amity. They were both Guelf, and their interests and form of government were in many respects identical. The merchant oligarchy of the *Raspanti* found its natural counterpart and ally in the merchant oligarchy of the *Nove*.

Under the rule of the *Nove*, Siena had consolidated and enlarged her dominion until it embraced almost all the modern provinces of Siena and Grosseto; trade flourished, and the city was embellished with splendid edifices. Unfortunately, however, unlimited and irresponsible power gradually sapped the energy and virtue of the ruling class, and the end came in March, 1355. The insurgents were aided by the Emperor, and the place of the *Nove* was taken by the *Dodici*, a magistracy of retail tradesmen (*negotiatores abjecti*), vulgar, incapable, and turbulent, who lived and governed in an atmosphere of continual strife.[1] Many of

[1] See my Historical Introduction to Miss L. OLCOTT's *Guide to Siena* (Siena, Torrini, 1903), pp. 54-67; LANGTON DOUGLAS, *A History of Siena* (London: Murray, 1902), chap. ix. pp. 132-152. Compare also G. LUCHAIRE, *Documenti per la storia de' rivolgimenti politici del C. di Siena dal 1354 al 1369 pubblicati con introduzione ed indici.* Lyon, A. Rey, 1906. This is the latest work on the subject.

the subject towns revolted, Grosseto, Massa, Montalcino, Casole ;[1] while in July, the men of Montepulciano flung off their allegiance to Siena and offered " to give themselves freely to the Perugians."[2]   When the delegates from Montepulciano reached Perugia, the ambassadors of Siena and Florence were already in that city, having been sent thither to discuss the renewal of the Tuscan League.[3]   For a moment the Perugians hesitated ; but the offer of the Montepulcianesi was too tempting to be refused, and greed of dominion triumphed over loyalty.   The Sienese ambassador departed in high dudgeon, refusing to have anything further to do with the proposed alliance.[4]

In the same month, if we may credit the chronicle attributed to Graziani, Sarteano submitted to Perugia,[5] while the annexation of Chiusi followed in November.[6]

These acquisitions may well have led the Perugians to believe that the overthrow of the *Nove* presaged a general disintegration of the Sienese State, and it is, probably, to this impression that we owe their change of policy with regard to Spoleto.[7]   If they could reasonably hope to carve out for themselves a new dominion to the westward of the Chiana, it was clearly unwise to insist upon doubtful rights

[1] MALAVOLTI, *Historia de' fatti e guerre de' Sanesi*, P. II. c. 113t.

[2] According to the chronicle of Neri di Donato (MURATORI, *R. I. S.*, xv. col. 153) Montepulciano submitted to Perugia in June, while GRAZIANI (*ubi cit.*, p. 181) gives the date as the 23rd of August. See, however, DEGLI AZZI, *Le Relazioni*, etc., *op. cit.*, i. p. 75, § 259, where we have a document of July 31st, which proves that only a day or two earlier the ambassadors of Montepulciano had come to Perugia " per volersi dare liberamente a' Perugini." According to GRAZIANI, the Perugians did not send a Potestà thither until the 2nd of November. The *Memorie di Perugia dall' anno, 1351 al 1438* (FABRETTI, *Cronache*, i. 174) give the date of the formal submission as the 23rd of October ; while the document published in the *Arch. Stor. It.*, XVI. i. 181 n., bears date the 15th of December, 1355.

[3] DEGLI AZZI, *Le Relazioni*, etc., *ubi cit.* See also page 217 *supra* and n. 2.

[4] GRAZIANI, p. 183 : " . . . et li Senese non volsero lega con Peroscini nè con quilli altri ; però che li dicti Senese ebbero a schifo e a sdegno che li Peroscini aceptassoro Monte Pulciano." See also M. VILLANI, v. 83.

[5] GRAZIANI, p. 180.

[6] PELLINI, i. 957-960. He bases his statement on certain " istrumenti publici," of the contents of which he gives an elaborate synopsis.

[7] See pages 218-219 *supra*.

in the Ducato, the enforcement of which must necessarily involve them in a war with the Church. The aim of the mediæval communes was to surround themselves with subject territories from which the necessities of life could be drawn. The unit was the town and not the nation ; the *contado* was simply the storehouse, the preserve of the city.[1] Without it the life of the citizen was impossible ; but its existence was all that mattered ; North, South, East, or West, if its extension was large enough to supply the wants of the Commune, its geographical position was relatively unimportant. The Pope had manifested a disposition to check the expansion of Perugia in Umbria, while the Emperor, on the contrary, had shown himself only too willing to legalize her conquests in Tuscany. To Tuscany she would go.

The natural boundary between the territories of Perugia and Siena was the Chiana, a vast pestiferous swamp,[2] which spread over the whole valley, extending from Carnaiola in the district of Orvieto to the Pieve al Toppo, near Arezzo, and from Foiano almost to Castiglion Aretino.[3]   As far as I

---

[1] Compare R. CAGGESE, *La Rep. di Siena e il suo Contado nel secolo decimoterzo*, in the *Bullettino Senese di Storia Patria*, xiii. 40.

[2] Thus, when Dante wished to describe the tortures of the damned in the last cloister of Malebolge, he could find no better parallel than the hospitals of Valdichiana. *Inferno*, xxix. 46-51. Compare also FAZIO DEGLI UBERTI, *Il Dittamondo*, iii. 10 :

> Quivi son volti pallidi e confusi
> Perchè l' aere e la Chiana è lor nemica
> Sicchè si fanno idropici e rinfusi.

Later on the evil reputation of the district caused the name Chiana to be used as a generic term for a marsh. See, for example, L. PULCI, *Morgante Maggiore*, Canto xxiii. stanza 41 :

> Tutto quel giorno cavalcato avieno
> Per bosche, per burron, per mille chiane.

Of the changed conditions nothing, perhaps, gives us a more vivid idea than the fact that, during the Middle Ages, the Magistrates of Chiusi were wont to imitate the splendid espousals of the Adriatic by the Doge of Venice, traversing the marsh in skiffs, on Whitsunday, until they reached the confines of Montepulciano, where they solemnly cast a ring into the water, *desponsare Clanas ut consuetum est.* See REPETTI, *Dizionario* cited, i. 719 ; F. PETRUCCI, *I confini Senesi di Val di Chiana*, in the *Bullettino Senese* (cited *supra*), ii. 289.

[3] The reader should consult the old map of the Valdichiana reproduced by NAPIER, *Florentine History*, vi. 398.

can discover, there were, at this period, only two bridges : one at the foot of the hill of Chiusi,[1] and the other to the south of Castel della Pieve.[2] The Ponte di Valiano was not built until 1359.[3] There were, however, certain fords (*passi*), more or less impracticable according to the season and the amount of rainfall, as well as numerous little harbours (*porti*) whence the passage could be made in boats ; as, for example, those of Pulciano, Torrita, Valiano, Foiano and Omomorto.[4]

The Perugians, as we have seen, had already occupied Foiano and Lucignano on the western side of the Chiana, while their approach from the eastward was secured by the possession of Castiglion Aretino. As yet the Sienese had no outpost on the Perugian side of the swamp, and, unless they could obtain one, it was more than likely that in the impending struggle they would be forced to fight on the defensive, and in their own territories. To avoid this danger they entered into negotiations with Bartolommeo de' Casali, Seignior of Cortona.[5] The injuries inflicted by the Perugians in the late war were not forgotten by the Cortonesi, and now that the deaths of Giovanni Visconti (Oct. 1354) and Pier Saccone (Feb. 1356) had deprived them of their most powerful allies, they were only too eager to accept the overtures of the Sienese. The negotiations consequently proceeded with unusual smoothness, and, on the 4th of December, 1357, at the request of Casali, it was resolved that a *bandiera* of horse and a body of fifty or a hundred foot should be despatched from Siena to the

---

[1] This bridge is mentioned in a Bull of Celestine III., and by G. VILLANI (vii. 136) in 1289. In a document of 1416 it is referred to as *Pontem et Passum dictarum Clanarum cum Palatio et Fortilitio posita super dictis Clanis*, etc. REPETTI, *Dizionario* cited, i. 685.

[2] M. VILLANI, viii. 34 : " Ponte Cavaliere in sulle Chiane di là dal Castello della Pieve."

[3] M. VILLANI, ix. 8 ; *Cronica Sanese*, in MURATORI, *R. I. S.*, xv. col. 164.

[4] F. PETRUCCI, *ubi cit.*, p. 284 *et seq.* In Valiano, Perugia had acquired rights as early as 1288, " . . . de tertia parte pro indiviso Navium, pedagii et portus Clanorum de Valiana." Compare PELLINI, i. 306. It is said that certain country lanes (*viottole campestre*) in the neighbourhood of Foiano, Bettole and Torrita still preserve the names of " via del porto," " via del porticciolo " and the like.

[5] MALAVOLTI, P. ii. c^ta 116t.

15

defence of Cortona.[1]   The Perugians thereupon attempted
to surprise the town.   Not only was there no declaration of
war, but the commencement of hostilities was an absolutely
unprovoked outrage, an "insolence" of the strong against
the weak,[2] for which the whole responsibility lay with
Leggerio Andreotti.[3]   The moment was critical, and he
clearly perceived that Perugia must either abandon her
dream of expansion to the westward or strike at once.
With so much at stake, he resolved to be hampered by no
scruples; he used his enormous influence to override all
opposition, and thereby involved his native city in a war
which indirectly brought about her ruin.   On the night of
the 10th of December the expedition started.[4]   There were
apparently good grounds to believe that the gates might be
opened by malcontents within the walls; but the Perugian
advance was delayed by torrential rains, and when they
reached Cortona, on the morning of the 11th, they found
that the plot had been discovered, and the citizens were
under arms.   So far, however, from abandoning their enterprise, they encamped at Ossaia, and prepared to blockade
the town; "and there they drave into the ground an iron
post, being minded to signify thereby that only when that
post should have rotted away would they depart thence,
unless they should first have the city of Cortona at their
commandment."[5]   The *contado* was ruthlessly devastated;
fresh troops were hurried to the front; divers *battifolli* were

[1] MANCINI, *Cortona nel Medio Evo, op. cit.*, p. 201; R. ARCH. DI STATO
IN SIENA, *Delib. del Concistoro*, x. 37.

[2] FABRETTI, *Cronache* cited, i. 30: "Nacque discordia fra il signor di
Cortona e Perugini per l' insolenza." Compare M. VILLANI, viii. 14, and
SISMONDI, *Rep. Italiane, op. cit.*, Vol. III. c. xlv. p. 21.

[3] M. VILLANI (viii. 35) calls Leggerio Andreotti "motore di questa guerra."

[4] According to the Perugian chronicles the date was either the 12th or
13th of December; but MANCINI (*ubi cit.*) tells us that the expedition
started between the evening of the 10th and the morning of the 11th—
a statement which seems to be borne out by documentary evidence, since
we read in the *Delib. del Concistoro* that "il capitano senese di Torrita
avvisò subito Siena dell' invasione e dei bruciamenti fatti dai Perugini
nel contado di Cortona all' aurora del giorno 11."

[5] "Et ine ficcarono il palo del ferro, significando che allora si parti-
rebbano da Cortona, quando quel palo infradiciasse, et in prima non
havessero la città di Cortona a loro comandamento." *Codice Cortonese*,
578, fo. 5, cited by MANCINI, *ubi cit*,

constructed,[1] and a great military arsenal was established at Ossaia.[2]

For a time the vigilance of the besiegers frustrated every effort of the Sienese to introduce reinforcements into the beleaguered town, and an attempt to create a diversion by threatening first Chiusi and then Sarteano grievously miscarried.[3] Finally, however, a body of two hundred cavalry, under Mainetto of Jesi, crossed the Chiana on the night of the 10th of February, and, stealing through the Perugian lines, entered Cortona before dawn. "Incontinently they set the banner of the Commune of Siena above the tower of the principal gate, and thereafter they began to sally forth at their good pleasure, and to harass the camp of the enemy."[4]

In March the Sienese hired Anechino Baumgarten (whom the Italians called Bongardo or Mongardo) as their Captain of War, with 800 cavalry and 400 infantry; they further took into their pay a large body of Hungarians;[5] "and, when they had set in order all their army, many citizens, both on horse and foot, issued out of Siena, and also the cross-bowmen of the city; and they went into Valdichiana. And, when they were at Torrita, the Perugians hearing that the Sienese had come to Torrita to succour Cortona, sent to guard all the passes and fords of the Chiana so that they might not be able to cross over." According to Matteo Villani, Anechino thereupon advanced towards Olmo di S. Fiora in the Aretino, as though with the intention of

[1] M. VILLANI, viii. 22; FABRETTI, Cronache, i. 177; GRAZIANI, p. 184.

[2] See the document published in the Giornale d' erudizione artistica dell' Umbria (Perugia, Tip. Boncompagni, 1873), Vol. II. pp. 191-207. It contains an invaluable list of the weapons, etc., distributed to the Perugian army.

[3] M. VILLANI, viii. 27. There seems to have been an attempt to take Chiusi by storm. See the Cronica Sanese, in MURATORI, R. I. S., xv. col. 160: "la Città di Chiuci fu scalata per lo Comuno di Siena, e non potero pigliare la terra e tutti quelli che saliro sulle mura furono pagati dal Comuno di Siena."

[4] M. VILLANI, viii. 28.

[5] "The Hungarian horse, so much employed during this century in consequence of the connection between that kingdom and Naples, were principally archers of almost Parthian celebrity, and kept the head unarmed to insure a greater command of their weapon, especially in retreat; they were the Cossacks of that day with all the ferocity of their Hunnish ancestors." NAPIER, Florentine History, ii. 595.

skirting the northern end of the swamp, and then, turning suddenly southward, entered the *contado* of Orvieto and crossed the Chiana at Ponte Cavaliere, below Castel della Pieve.[1]   The more probable account,[2] however, is that of the Sienese chronicler Neri di Donato, who tells us that "when the Commissaries of Siena and the Captain saw that all the passes were taken by the Perugians, an old man of Torrita spake unto the Commissaries and said, ' What will ye give me if I make a ford whereby ye may all pass safely, on such wise that at daybreak to-morrow ye shall all have crossed over without let or hindrance ? '   The Commissaries said, ' Ask what thou wilt.'   The old man said, ' Give me fifty florins of gold,' and, when they had agreed thereto, he took unto him certain of his companions, and, with timber and trunks of trees and brushwood and earth, they filled a very great ford and pass, so that all the folk of Siena, having recommended themselves to God, passed over safely without let or hindrance.   Or ever the sun had risen they all passed over ; and they signalled unto them that were in Cortona, and they rejoiced exceedingly." [3]

Now, when the Perugians heard thereof they were afraid, and they abandoned their camp and burned their *battifolli* ; and on the 30th day of March, 1358, the Sienese came to Ossaia and encamped there.   Thereafter they furnished Cortona with men and with provisions, and returned to Torrita safe and sound without striking a blow.   "And on this wise was Cortona delivered from the arrogance of the Perugians by the hand of the Sienese." [4]

[1] M. VILLANI, viii. 28.

[2] I say "the more probable account" because, as a Sienese, Neri di Donato was more likely to be correctly informed on a matter of this kind than the Florentine Villani.   Indeed, he may well have heard the details of the conversation between *il detto homo vecchio di Torrita* and the Sienese commissaries from one of the latter.

[3] *Cronica Sanese, ubi cit.*, col. 158-159.

[4] M. VILLANI, viii. 34.   The accounts of the Sienese and Perugian chroniclers are hopelessly discordant.   According to Neri di Donato there was a great battle under the walls of Cortona.   Graziani, on the other hand, while admitting that the Perugians retreated when the Sienese had crossed the Chiana, speaks of two subsequent skirmishes in which the former had the advantage.   However, the account most unfavourable to the Perugians is to be found in the one Perugian chronicle which has any claim to be

When the shameful news reached Perugia, so great was the indignation of the populace that Leggerio Andreotti ran considerable danger of being torn in pieces by the mob. His eloquence saved him ; but, although he persuaded the Raspanti to continue the war, Smeduccio da Sanseverino was appointed captain-general in his stead.[1]

From the first commencement of hostilities, Florence had strained every nerve to induce the belligerents to submit their differences to arbitration. As surety to Cortona for the loyal observance by the Perugians of the peace of 1353, she had a direct interest in the questions at issue ; [2] while the fact that, at this time, almost all her transmarine traffic passed through Talamone made her extremely anxious to maintain friendly relations with Siena.[3] The Sienese were not unaturally perfectly willing to accept her mediation ; [4] but the Perugians proved obdurate and suspicious, not only attempting to justify their unprovoked attack upon Cortona,[5] but adding insult to injury by compelling the Florentine merchants resident in Perugia to furnish large sums of money for the prosecution of the war.[6] Their mistrust was further increased when, early in March, the Florentines, with the full consent of the Sienese,

contemporaneous, and which Fabretti declares in so many words to be "dettata da autori contemporanei " (see FABRETTI, *Cronache*, i. 177). It may be remarked that, owing to the loss of the *Annali Decemvirali* from 1352 to 1374, we have no trustworthy evidence with regard to this war from Perugian sources.

[1] M. VILLANI, viii. 35 ; PELLINI, i. 973-974.

[2] DEGLI AZZI, *op. cit.*, p. 60, § 209.

[3] See herein L. BANCHI, *I Porti della Maremma Senese durante la Repubblica* (Firenze, Tip. Galileiana, 1871), pp. 48-55.

[4] " Da' nostri ambasciatori che sono in Siena questo dì (7 Aprile, 1358) a terza ricevemmo lettera come ieri ebbono risposta da' Senesi che liberamente erano disposti di remettere nel comune nostro la questione di Montepulciano e di Cortona e ciò che da essa dependesse." *Signoria fiorentina. Missive*, xii. 12t, published by DEGLI AZZI, *op. cit.*, i. p. 79, § 270. *Cf.* M. VILLANI, viii. 39.

[5] M. VILLANI, viii. 17 ; AMMIRATO, *Ist. Fior.* (edition cited), Vol. III. Lib. xi. p. 53. It would seem that the Perugians, relying on the terms of the League of February, 1356, actually expected the Florentines to openly espouse their cause. See GRAZIANI, p. 184.

[6] See the letters of the Florentine Signoria of 5th March and 1st April, in DEGLI AZZI, *op. cit.*, i. pp. 76-79, §§ 266, 267, 269.

sent a body of troops into the Maremma for the protection
of merchandise which they expected shortly to arrive at
Talamone ;[1] and there can be but little doubt that, whatever its object, the result of such action was to free the
hands of the Sienese for the relief of Cortona. A little
later, the Florentine ambassadors were openly insulted in
Perugia, and their arguments rendered inaudible by the
interruptions of the populace, who whistled and beat upon
the benches when they rose to speak.[2]

The continuance of the war was thus inevitable, and,
early in April, the Perugians took the field with an
army of at least 2000 *barbute*, 6000 foot-soldiers and 400
light Hungarian horse.[3] Having once more invested Cortona,
they crossed the Chiana and encamped at Gracciano in
the *contado* of Montepulciano.[4] The Sienese, who had
been entreated by the Florentines not to destroy such
faint hopes of an accommodation as might still exist by
remaining on Perugian territory,[5] were strongly posted
at Torrita, with 1600 *barbute* and a considerable body
of infantry ; "and in the town and in its suburbs they
were sufficiently secure, if lack of foresight and mad
rashness had not destroyed them."[6]   On the 10th of
April, the Florentines wrote to their ambassadors in Siena,
bidding them go to the camp of the Sienese to dissuade
them from fighting,[7] it being evidently taken for granted
that they could not be forced to an engagement against
their will. Unfortunately, however, the instructions came
too late ; before the letter reached Siena the Battle of
Torrita had been fought and lost.

The Perugians perceived that any attempt to dislodge
the enemy must inevitably prove disastrous ; but they
also felt that their honour was involved ; the memory of

---

[1] DEGLI AZZI, *op. cit.*, i. p. 77, § 268.   [2] M. VILLANI, viii. 39.

[3] FABRETTI, *Cronache*, i. 177.

[4] M. VILLANI, viii. 39 ; PELLINI, i. 974 ; MANCINI, *op. cit.*, p. 203.

[5] DEGLI AZZI, *op. cit.*, i., § 269.   [6] M. VILLANI, viii. 39.

[7] In the same letter they were ordered to cause the Florentine troops
which were returning from Grosseto to halt at Poggibonsi, to the end that
they might be ready to go to the assistance of the Sienese if they were
defeated by the Perugians. DEGLI AZZI, *op. cit.*, i. p. 80, § 272.

their flight from Cortona still rankled, and something must be done to purge the shame of it. Accordingly, on the 9th, they sent a formal challenge to the Sienese camp, and, on the 10th, they marched out of Gracciano, advancing to the foot of the hill upon which Torrita stands, where "they began to blow upon their trumpets and to defy the enemy to battle." It was a mere bluff. Neither the Sienese nor the Perugians really wanted to risk a general engagement; but, owing to a series of blunders, what was only meant to be a demonstration in force ended in actual hostilities. The total number of the slain scarcely reached a hundred, but the capture of Anechino in the mêlée left the Sienese without a general, and they retreated into the *castello*. The victors thereupon "sacked and burned the *borgo*, and returned with the prisoners and with the spoil and with the unlooked-for victory to Gracciano."[1] The Perugian chroniclers further tell us that " in the said discomfiture they took forty-nine banners, among which was the banner of the Commune of Siena, which they (the Sienese) had from the Emperor; and there upon the field of battle were made many knights in honour of that victory."[2]

The defeated army seems to have been utterly demoralized; there was suspicion of treachery, and, during the night, the vast majority of the troops abandoned Torrita and scattered in all directions,[3] so that the Commissaries were compelled to write to Siena, "that, if they did not at once receive reinforcements, the *contado* would be wasted and burned by the Perugians."[4]

[1] The only adequate account of the Battle of Torrita is that given by M. VILLANI, viii. 40-41.

[2] GRAZIANI, p. 186; FABRETTI, *Cronache*, i. 31, 177-179. On the other hand, M. VILLANI (viii. 41) informs us that these banners were not taken in the battle, but " trovate negli alberghi " when the *borgo* was sacked and burned.

[3] Possibly, it was after this reverse that the *Alberto da Siena* of FRANCO SACCHETTI (Nov. 13), having lost his horse, fled away on foot " e cogliendolo la notte in certe vie tra boschi, e traendo vento, che facea sonare le foglie, gli pareva avere mille cavalieri dietro; e come un pruno il pigliava, dicea: Oime! io mi t' arrendo, non mi uccidere; credendo che fossono nemici che 'l pigliassono; e così con gran paura e con grande affanno consumò tutta quella notte."

[4] M. VILLANI, viii. 41.

No sooner did the news reach Florence than a considerable force was despatched to Siena, " a defesa et conservatione dello stato di Siena popolare, libero et guelfo " ;
while, on the 12th of April, the Florentine Signoria wrote
to their ambassadors in that city, announcing the departure
of a hundred *barbute* over and above the troops already
sent, and offering five hundred cross-bowmen who were
ready to march at a moment's notice in case of any disturbance in Siena.   At the same time the Perugians were
informed that the only object of these succours was " per
fugire che lo stato di Siena non riceva turbatione nociva a
loro et a Noi."[1]   Whether they believed these assurances
may well be doubted, and the more so that they did not
immediately follow up their victory.   Indeed, if we may
credit Malavolti, before invading the Senese, they returned
to Perugia.[2]   Their delay may, however, be equally well
accounted for by the fact that they had secretly leagued
themselves with the Tarlati of Pietramala, hoping with their
assistance to acquire the signory of Arezzo.[3]   Only when
their schemes had been discovered by the Florentines (who,
albeit they studiously abstained from taking offence, none
the less took immediate steps to thwart them) did they
finally resolve to " cavalcare i Sanesi."   They advanced by
the way of Chianciano and the Val d' Orcia to Buonconvento,[4] whence they pushed their ravages up to the very
gates of Siena, encamping at the Forche di Pecorile, outside

---

[1] DEGLI AZZI, *op. cit.*, i. p. 81, § 274.

[2] MALAVOLTI, ii. 117t.   Possibly, also, we may draw the same inference
from the only contemporary Perugian chronicle, since we are there told
that some nine days after the Battle of Torrita, " rivennero in Perugia
con gran festa e allegrezza i cavalieri novelli quali si fecero cavalieri alla
sconfitta della gente di Siena a Turrita, e arrecarono tutte le loro bandiere, che la gente del comune di Perugia guadagnò e tolse alla gente di
Siena. . . . " (FABRETTI, *Cronache*, i. 178-179).

[3] The terms of the treaty between Perugia and the Tarlati will be found
in the document published by DEGLI AZZI, *op. cit.*, i. p. 89, § 291.   From
this alliance Messer Luzzimborgo da Pietramala was expressly excluded,
he being leagued with the Sienese, *ad mortem detrimentum desolationem
perpetuum et extirminium Comunis et hominum Civitatis Perusij*.   R. ARCH.
DI STATO IN SIENA, *Caleffo Nero*, c. 361-362t.

[4] The approximate dates of several of the steps in this invasion may be
learned from the documents published by DEGLI AZZI, *op. cit.*, i., §§ 282, 285.

the Porta Nuova,[1] on the 28th or 29th of April. There they created more knights, and, after hanging an Hungarian prisoner in full sight of the town—"on the walls of Siena," according to Graziani—they returned to Perugia carrying with them the chains of the gallows as a trophy.[2]

The Sienese chronicler, Neri di Donato, tells us that this incursion was made with the consent of the Florentines, who hoped that the Perugians would be willing to make peace if they were first allowed to "fare le lor vendette." It had, however, been stipulated that the invaders should not pass beyond Buonconvento; and, when the enemy appeared beneath the walls of Siena, the whole population rushed to arms. Wherefore "the Perugians, hearing all the bells of Siena sound to arms, and beholding much folk continually issuing forth from the gates, were afraid, and beat a retreat and departed and fled away and awaited not the fury of the people of Siena. And verily, had they stayed but a little while, scarce one of them had escaped alive; for the Sienese had ordered that all the passes should be occupied. Thus the Perugians departed and gat them hence as if in rout." It is more than likely that the writer was actually present at the scene which he describes; and, when all due allowance has been made for bias and prejudice, there is nothing improbable in the facts which he relates. Besides the Florentine succours in Siena, the great majority of the mercenaries who had fled from Torrita had by this time, no doubt, found their way back to the city; and the Perugians may well have felt uneasy at the prospect of a battle so far from their own territories and under the very walls of a hostile town, the whole population of which was swarming like a hive of angry bees. Nor does our chronicler endeavour to minimize the loss and shame of the Sienese. The Perugians, he tells us, "took with them thirty-six prisoners, citizens of Siena, and some few they slew. Also

---

[1] The Porta Nuova is, of course, identical with the Porta Romana. As to the *Forche* (gallows) *di Pecorile*, see the *Miscellanea storica Senese*, iii. 92.

[2] M. Villani, viii. 48; *Cronica Sanese*, in Muratori, *R. I. S.*, xv. col. 160; Graziani, pp. 186-187; Fabretti, *Cronache*, i. 61, 115, 130-131; Pellini, i. 980.

they carried away the said chains . . . and therewith they entered Perugia in triumph . . . *et parve loro aver fatto le lor vendette*." [1]

The damage inflicted had, probably, not been very great,[2] but it sufficed to stiffen the backs of the Sienese, who were now obstinately determined to continue the war. Whatever its results, the Battle of Torrita had, in fact, been a mere skirmish which had done nothing to permanently cripple their resources, and with a little energy they might still hope to fully retrieve all that they had lost. To the alarm of the Florentines, ambassadors were sent to Milan to beseech the aid of the Visconti ; [3] while, early in June, negotiations were entered into with the Great Company of the Count Lando, who was offered a large sum of money to devastate the territories of Perugia ; [4] Giovanni Di Vico was elected Captain of War ; Monte S. Savino was invested (21st June),[5] and, but for the practical annihilation of the Great Company while attempting to pass Le Scalelle (25th July),[6] Perugia must have paid dearly for her aggressive policy in Tuscany. "But know ye," says Neri di Donato, "that, if the Company of the Count Lando had been able to pass, the Sienese had resolved to rebuild the gallows of Pecorile with the stones of the walls of Perugia." [7] Even as it was

---

[1] *Cronica Sanese*, in MURATORI, *R. I. S.*, xv. 160-161. As to the chains which the Perugians carried away with them, see Note at the end of the chapter.

[2] M. VILLANI, viii. 41.

[3] M. VILLANI, viii. 62 ; DEGLI AZZI, *op. cit.*, i. p. 83, § 280.

[4] A. PROFESSIONE, *Siena e le Compagnie di Ventura nella seconda metà del Sec. XIV.* (Civitanova-Marche, casa editrice " Domenico Natalucci," 1898), p. 25.

[5] M. VILLANI, viii. 64. Nothing definite is to be learned concerning the siege of Monte S. Savino either from the confused account of Neri di Donato, or from that of Malavolti, who seems to have followed him ; but it is tolerably clear that the Perugians more than held their own. See ARCH. VATIC., *Introit. et exit. Patrimonii S. Petri in Tuscia*, an. 1358, c. 313, cited by ANTONELLI, *op. cit.*, p. 179.

[6] M. VILLANI, viii. 74. Commenting on this disaster the Sienese chronicler says : " La Compagnia del Conte Lando non potea passare, bontà de' Fiorentini e loro malizia che aiutavano sotto mantello a' Perugini ; e questo fanno i Fiorentini per amore che non portano nè portaranno mai a' Sanesi."

[7] MURATORI, *R. I. S.*, xv. 162.

the Perugians suffered severely ; their territories were repeatedly raided by the Cortonesi,[1] while it appears that the
Sienese also, upon at least one occasion, made an incursion
almost up to their very gates, burning and plundering " per
tutto il viaggio." [2]   The financial side of the war had been
grossly mismanaged ; [3] and the already wellnigh exhausted
coffers of the Commune were still further depleted by the
outrageous conduct of the German mercenaries, who not only
declined to renew their term of service, but united with their
fellow-countrymen in the pay of Siena to form a new
Company which quartered itself upon the Perugian *contado*
until it should be bought off with 4000 golden florins.[4]
Their ultimate departure for the March of Ancona put an
end to regular military operations, and the sieges, both of
Monte S. Savino and of Cortona, were perforce abandoned ;
but from thenceforward the raids of the Cortonesi grew daily
more and more daring, until " at last the time came when fifty
horsemen and a mere handful of foot were able to make the
entire circuit of the Lake and to return to Cortona, loaded
with booty, without encountering any resistance ; . . . to
such straits was Perugia reduced by the continual drain of
the war." [5]   Florence redoubled her efforts to bring about a
cessation of hostilities, offering to each Commune that which
it most desired : liberty to Montepulciano, protection to
Cortona, and ample satisfaction to Siena and Perugia.
What mattered it to her that her promises were incompatible and contradictory ?   She never meant to keep them.
Enough if they served her immediate purpose, and induced
the belligerents to lay down their arms.   Thereafter she
would betray them all to her own profit.[6]

[1] M. VILLANI, viii. 48, 86.
[2] MALAVOLTI, P. ii. c. 117t.   *Cf.* PELLINI, i. 980.
[3] See the next chapter.
[4] M. VILLANI, viii. 85.
[5] M. VILLANI, viii. 86.
[6] This is the view taken both by MANCINI (*op. cit.*, p. 204) and DEGLI
AZZI (*op. cit.*, p. xv), and it seems to me to be fully borne out by the documents published by the latter : q.v.   There is, of course, no doubt that
Tuscan liberties were seriously imperilled by the war and that Florence
was serving the best interests of both parties in trying to put an end to it ;
but it is equally indisputable that her patriotic efforts were sullied by the

Something of her double dealing was known to the Perugians and more suspected ; yet, in the end, exhaustion compelled them to come to terms. Nevertheless, neither they nor the Sienese were willing wholly to trust the Florentines ;[1] and when at last they submitted their differences to arbitration, the Rector of Romagna sat with the appointees of Florence.[2] The award, which was published in Arezzo, on the 31st of October, 1358, destroyed for ever Perugia's dream of expansion to the westward.[3] For many months she declined to accept it. In January, 1359, we find the Florentines remonstrating with her because she was seeking to hire the Great Company " per rivoltarla poi in Toscana," a thing, as they declared, " extrana da ogni fratellanza."[4] Albornoz, who had now returned to Italy, joined in exhorting her to peace, but without result,[5] and, early in April, she once more garrisoned the *battifolli* which she had in the Cortonese.[6] In the same month the Legate published a new award ;[7] but, as late as the 17th of June, we find her still recalcitrant.[8] Finally, however, on the 15th of July, when, in the picturesque phrase of Matteo

basest duplicity and self-seeking. She certainly coveted Cortona and probably Montepulciano. No doubt, at first, she loyally endeavoured to do her best for the Sienese ; but when, in June, 1358, the Pisans abandoned their attempts to destroy the commerce of Talamone (M. VILLANI, viii. 63) the bonds of material interest which united the two Communes must have been considerably weakened. Thereafter the Florentines returned to their time-honoured policy of *recare* all that was possible *al loro molino.*

[1] The chronicle of Neri di Donato clearly indicates the rapid growth of suspicion on the part of the Sienese, and we have documentary evidence that, in August, 1358, troops were sent from Florence to the assistance of Perugia. DEGLI AZZI, *op. cit.*, i. p. 91, § 298.

[2] The arbitrators were *dominus Petrocinus Torcellanus Episcopus, provincie Romandiole pro sancta romana Ecclesia rector, et dominus Andrea de Bardis miles et Uguccio de Ricciis, florentini cives.*

[3] R. ARCH. DI STATO IN SIENA, *Caleffo Rosso*, cta 29 ; *Arch. Stor. It.*, XVI. ii. 539-543 ; GRAZIANI, p. 187 ; M. VILLANI, viii. 102 ; PELLINI, i. 981 ; MALAVOLTI, ii. 118-118t ; MANCINI, *op. cit.*, pp. 205-206.

[4] DEGLI AZZI, *op. cit.*, i., § 302.

[5] DEGLI AZZI, *op. cit.*, i., §§ 307, 309.

[6] DEGLI AZZI, *op. cit.*, i., § 317.

[7] R. ARCH. DI STATO IN SIENA, *Caleffo Rosso*, cta 45t 48 ; MALAVOLTI, ii. 119t.

[8] DEGLI AZZI, *op. cit.*, i. 339.

Villani, "on squeezing their purses they could find therein nothing save darkness and wind," the Perugians renounced their rights over Montepulciano,[1] and, a little later, " created eight ambassadors of their most valued and renowned citizens, and clad them in scarlet, and their attendants in liveries of scarlet and black, and sent them to Siena with great pomp, where they were welcomed as befitted their rank according to the Sienese usance"; and on this wise was made " a perpetual, free and honourable peace." [2] In the following year Cortona voluntarily accepted the suzerainty of Siena.[3]

Thus, for the second time, Perugia's designs of Tuscan conquest were frustrated by the Florentines. It is not impossible that, had she been left to fight out the war with Siena single-handed, she might have been victorious. Entirely apart from the fall of the *Nove* and the consequent revolt of so many subject towns, Siena was the weaker of the two communes,[4] and probably, at this period, the less warlike;[5] but the intervention of Florence more than neutralized all Perugia's advantages, and the only result of the war was to leave her shorn of half her strength, at the very moment when she was compelled to face a new and terrible danger in the reawakened ambition of the Papacy.

[1] R. ARCH. DI STATO IN SIENA, *Caleffo Nero*, c. 345 ; *Arch. Stor. It.*, XVI. ii. 343-344.

[2] M. VILLANI, ix. 44 ; MALAVOLTI, ii. 121t ; PELLINI, i. 989.

[3] R. ARCH. DI STATO IN SIENA, *Caleffo Nero*, c. 297-404 ; MALAVOLTI, ii. 121 ; MANCINI, *op. cit.*, 208-209.

[4] The comparative weakness of Siena is proved by the fact that at each renewal of the Tuscan League, her *taglia* was considerably less than that of Perugia. See, for example, DEGLI AZZI, ii. p. 82, § 321, and p. 109, § 398.

[5] The events already recorded, in Chapter XIII. of the present work, appear to me sufficient evidence of this. While the Perugians rose as one man to resist the *Gran Compagnia della Corona*, the citizens of Siena could hardly be forced to take the field by the threat of capital punishment. (See page 170 and n. 7 *supra*). The difference lay, I suspect, not in any natural inferiority of the Sienese in this regard, but in their earlier persecution of the nobles. Compare what MACHIAVELLI (*Istorie Fiorentine*, Lib. iii.) says of his fellow-citizens : " . . . quella virtù d' armi e generosità d' animo che era nella nobiltà si spegneva, e nel popolo dove la non era, non si poteva raccendere, talchè Firenze sempre più umile e più abietta ne divenne."

NOTE

(See pages 232 and 233 *supra*)

Of late years an absurd fable has gained currency with regard to the chains which the Perugians carried away from Siena as a trophy in 1358, and it is possible that a re-statement of the actual facts of the case may prove useful.

There is, of course, no manner of doubt what these chains really were, *i.e.* the chains of the gallows which stood outside the Porta Nuova. The only authorities which we have upon the question are the chronicles of Perugia and Siena, and they are all in absolute agreement : " *Le catene de la iustitia di Siena*" (GRAZIANI, p. 187). "*Quelle catene che fur levate dal luogo della giustizia di Siena*" (FABRETTI, *Cronache*, i. 63). "*Le catene delle Forche di Pecorile . . . le quali catene erano a traverso su le more delle Forche in luogo di pertiche et ine s' appicavano i malfattori* (*Cronica Sanese*, in MURATORI, *Rer. Italic. Script.*, xv. 160, 161). There is not a discordant voice among them all, and no statement could well be more definite. Yet modern writers have gone out of their way to invent the ridiculous story that the chains in question were "the chains of the Palace of Justice of Siena"! The originator of the fable is the always inaccurate BONAZZI, who, on page 447 of his *Storia di Perugia*, informs us that " si portavano in trionfo le catene del palazzo di giustizia di Siena." The assertion itself is one which might well have given pause to any serious student. What was the *palazzo di giustizia di Siena*? Was there ever such a palace, and, if so, where was it situated? Outside the walls, apparently, or the Perugians, who never passed the gates of the city, could not have carried away its chains. Nevertheless, in spite of all these difficulties, Miss SYMONDS and Miss DUFF GORDON, misled by their blind faith in Bonazzi, unhesitatingly assure us (*Story of Perugia*, p. 22) that the chains in question were the chains of the Palace of Justice of Siena. The passage is worth quoting in its entirety :

" Perugia's culminating success seems to have been at Torrita in 1358, when the Sienese were defeated, and forty-nine banners brought back tied to the horses' tails, and the chains of the Palace of Justice torn away and hung in triumph at the feet of the Perugian griffin."

So far, perhaps, but little harm had been done. The untrustworthiness of Bonazzi's history is too well known for his unsupported testimony to carry any weight, and no serious student would be likely to accept as fact so inherently improbable a statement on the uncorroborated evidence of a Guide Book written by two young ladies. Unfortunately, however, they return to the subject on page 118, and, after converting the chains into keys, quote Professor ADAMO ROSSI as the authority for their preposterous assertion about the Justice Hall of Siena. What Professor Rossi really wrote is this :

" A piedi di questi animali (*i.e.* the bronze griffin and lion over the doorway of the Palazzo del Popolo in Perugia) si appesero come glorioso trofeo, nel 1321 i ferramenti e chiavi delle porte di Assisi, e nel 1358 le catene della giustizia di Siena."

THE PERUGIAN GRIFFIN AND THE GUELF LION AT WHOSE FEET
WERE HUNG THE CHAINS OF THE *FORCHE DI PECORILE*, IN 1358

The general reader, however, does not as a rule verify quotations, and the introduction of the honoured name of Professor Rossi may well have appeared to give credibility to an otherwise incredible story. Certainly very few would suspect that he was quoted as saying precisely what he did not say.

The consequences have been sufficiently deplorable, and the fable has acquired a new lease of life in the Count DE LA DUFFERIE'S monograph on the Baglioni (*Histoire de la Maison de Baglion*, etc., *op. cit.*), where, on page 15, he writes :

" Pérouse connut cependant de beaux succès ; celui de 1358 marque un point culminant dans sa gloire. Les Siennois sont écrasés à Torrita, 42 de leurs bannières, prises en trophées, sont traînées à la queue des chevaux dans la capitale ombrienne, alors que sous les pattes du griffon communal les vainqueurs accrochent les chaînes du Palais de Justice de Sienne."

The passage is obviously borrowed from *The Story of Perugia*, but the result is the same, and the next equally careless historian of the city may make the same ridiculous statement and cite as his authority quite a respectable list of names. I imagine a footnote running as follows :

"See BONAZZI, *Storia di Perugia*, i. 447 ; Comte DE LA DUFFERIE, *Histoire de la Maison de Baglion*, p. 15 ; SYMONDS and DUFF GORDON, *The Story of Perugia*, pp. 22 and 118, and A. ROSSI, *Il Palazzo del Popolo di Perugia*, there quoted."

And yet, as I have said, the whole story is a pure invention, unsupported by a single shred of evidence. The only writer of any standing who even hints at these chains having been taken from any place other than the Gallows of Pecorile, is JOHN ADDINGTON SYMONDS, in his *Sketches in Italy* (page 62 of the Tauchnitz edition), where he speaks of them as " chains wrested in old warfare from some barricaded gateway of Siena." This is obviously a mere slip of the pen, and, in any case, lends no support to the Bonazzi fable.[1] Compare, on the whole subject, my *La Guerra con Perugia* (1357-1358) in the *Bullettino Senese di Storia Patria* Anno xiv. fasc. iii., and a review of Comte de La Dufferie's book which appeared in *The Nation* (New York) under the date of April 30th, 1908.

---

[1] It is, perhaps, just possible that Symonds may have been misled by the manuscript *Diario* of Bandini, which, when relating how these chains were brought back to Siena by Muzio Malavolti, in 1799, refers to them as " alcuni catenacci pesti ed altri serrami che dai Perugini erano stati tolti da alcune porte di Siena nell' anno 1358." It is, however, obvious that Bandini was simply reporting the current gossip of the day, and his statement can have no possible weight as against the concordant evidence of the Sienese and Perugian chroniclers above quoted. See MENGOZZI, *Note Storiche* (Siena, Lazzeri, 1909), Vol. VII. p. 368.

CHAPTER XVIII

THE BEGINNING OF THE END

I HAVE dealt thus fully with the war with Siena because it seems to me to mark the first downward step of Perugia—a step so long and so irrevocable that, from henceforward, she no longer possesses a history in the proper meaning of the term. She continues to have a biography, if one could by pains get at it, which is the sum of her character and environment;[1] but the history of Italy, in its wider sense, knows her no more. In a few short years the Papacy will lay its grasp upon her, and the free Commune will cease to exist for ever. She may continue to be a mother of warriors, a breeder of *condottieri*; under able chieftains, like the great Braccio Fortebracci, she may once more defy the Church and become the capital of wide territories; but the *stato popolare libero e guelfo* is doomed to speedy destruction. We may follow its death agony with some particularity of detail; but, once we have buried it, the barest synopsis will suffice.

For years the ruling oligarchy had been growing narrower and more intolerant, until, at this period, the vast majority even of the bourgeois class were excluded from any share in the government, all real authority being concentrated in the hands of a mere clique under the direction of Leggerio Andreotti and the Michelotti.[2] The Machiavellian cycle was fulfilling itself,[3] and the yoke which had been unwill-

[1] I borrow this definition from Mr Maurice Hewlett's article, "Siena," in the *Quarterly Review* of July, 1903.

[2] "Erano nella città di Perugia in questi tempi molti e molti cittadini, e gentili uomini e popolani di buone e antiche famiglie d' animo guelfo, li quali quasi del tutto erano schiusi dagli ufici e governo della città, regendosi la terra per popolani mezzani e minuti sotto la guida e consiglio della famiglia de' Michelotti e di Leggieri d' Andreotto." M. VILLANI, x. 75.

[3] "E questo è il cerchio, nel quale girando tutte le repubbliche si sono governate e si governano," etc. MACHIAVELLI, *Discorsi*, Lib. i. cap. ii.

ingly borne while the Commune was great and prosperous, was now felt to be unendurable. The award of October 1358 had excited intense indignation ; and ere long the insistent demands of the citizens forced the Raspanti to consent to an enquiry into the conduct of the war. In January, 1359, Messer Gerio de' Pazzi came from Florence to fill the office of Maggior Sindaco,[1] and a rigid investigation began. It soon became manifest that there had been gross malversation, and Leggerio Andreotti and his colleagues were summoned to give an account of their stewardship. Process was actually commenced against them ; no one doubted their guilt, and, as confession would have been forced from them by torture, they would most certainly have been condemned had not the too openly displayed hostility of the Nobles caused a reaction in their favour. It was perceived that the overthrow of the Raspanti might result in the establishment of an aristocratic government, and, thenceforward, the very men who had previously urged on the prosecution laboured day and night to save the accused. An old statute was resuscitated, whereby it was provided that, if any citizen should be chosen to serve as ambassador for the Commune, all processes which had been commenced against him should be suspended during his embassy.[2] Leggerio Andreotti was forthwith sent as Ambassador to Albornoz. We have documentary evidence of his arrival at Cesena in that capacity early in April, together with a certain Fidanzio " Jannis," [3] whom we may doubtless identify with the *Fidanzino* of Graziani's chronicle.[4] Messer

---

[1] It was provided by law that the office of *Maggior Sindaco* should be filled by a noble " grande e di schiacta de cavaliere de paterna linea," etc. (*Statuto di Perugia*, 1342, Lib. i. Rubric. 20). According to BONAINI(*Prefazione* cit., p. lvii) Messer Gerio was a *Sindaco speciale* and not the *Maggior Sindaco* of the Commune. This, however, appears to be a mistake. See DEGLI AZZI, *op. cit.*, ii. p. 121, § 444, where he is described as " maggior sindaco, sindacatore degli officiali ed utile conservatore del C. di P."

[2] M. VILLANI, ix. 15 : " . . . si dierono a cercare de' rimedi, e trovarono uno statuto," etc. The language used seems to imply that it had fallen into abeyance.

[3] DEGLI AZZI, *op. cit.*, i. p. 96, § 314.

[4] GRAZIANI, p. 188. Elsewhere he is spoken of as " Fidanzio di Giovanni di Gnagne del Marescalco." See FABRETTI, *Cronache*, i. 176.

16

Gerio, rather than remain in Perugia "cum verecundia et dedecore," thereupon resigned his office and returned to Florence in high dudgeon.[1]   His successor, "finding the process pending, acquitted the great citizens, and, to show himself energetic in the performance of his duties, condemned the weak and uninfluential. Wherefore the people were moved to fury, and, or ever his term was ended, laid hands upon him and cast him into prison, where he finished his days in ignominy." [2]

The prestige of the Raspanti was still further impaired by their refusal to join with Florence in opposing the advance of the Great Company,[3] and the consequent devastation of Perugian territory.[4]   Their efforts to prevent the complete supersession of their authority in Spoleto hopelessly failed ; the ambassadors whom they sent to remonstrate with Albornoz returned "with little honour," and the building of the great citadel which was destined to hold that city faithful to the Church went on apace.[5]   Disaffection was rife among all classes of the community, and when, in the summer of 1361, a conspiracy was formed with the object of making Messer Alessandro de' Vincioli despot, it was joined not only by all the gentlemen of Perugia, but also by more than a thousand *popolari*. The plot was betrayed to Andreotti on the 24th of August, but, though six of the leaders were taken and brought to justice, the vast majority of the malcontents made good their escape and fortified themselves in the towns and castles of the *contado*.[6]   The war which

---

[1] See DEGLI AZZI, *op. cit.*, i. 97, § 319, and ii. 121, § 444.

[2] M. VILLANI, ix. 15. If we may credit PELLINI (i. 992) it was about this time that the name of " *Raspanti*," which had apparently fallen into disuse, was revived and, as we may imagine, with a new and sinister significance. See page 44 n. 1 *supra*.

[3] M. VILLANI, ix. 20.

[4] GRAZIANI, p. 188.

[5] GRAZIANI, p. 189 ; FABRETTI, *Cronache*, i. 116-117 ; SANSI, *Storia del C. di Spoleto, op. cit.*, i. 236-237. See also FILIPPINI, *La seconda legazione del Card. Albornoz in Italia* (1358-1367), in *Studi Storici, op. cit.*, Vol. XII. p. 327 Doc. xxii.

[6] *Arch. Stor. It.*, XVI. i. 191-192 ; M. VILLANI, x. 75 ; PELLINI, i. 992-993 ; BONAZZI, i. 449-451. Villani concludes his account of the punishment of the rebels with the words " e così furono dipinti quelli che doveano esser dipinti." The painting of the effigies of traitors, either with a mitre

followed lasted many months, and the difficulties of the Raspanti were increased by the attitude of Albornoz. In March, 1360, Giovanni da Oleggio had surrendered Bologna to the Church, and, in the following summer, the armies of the Visconti were completely routed at S. Ruffillo on the Savena. Thus was the work of recovering the Ecclesiastical State practically completed ; and henceforward Perugia was regarded by the Legate with an unfriendly eye, since only through her abasement could Assisi and Città di Castello become subject to the immediate dominion of the Holy See. It was feared that he might espouse the cause of the *fuorusciti*, but, in February, 1362, he was prevailed upon to enter into a definite undertaking that neither directly nor indirectly, openly nor secretly, personally nor by his agents, would he do anything to subvert the existing form of government.[1] This concession was probably obtained through the influence of Andreotti, and if so, it was well-nigh the last service which he was able to render to his party. Among the nobles who had been beheaded in the previous August was Messer Ceccherello de' Boccoli, and, in June, 1362, his execution was avenged by his bastard son Donato de' Boccoli, who cast a great stone out of a window upon the head of Andreotti as he stood reading a letter in the street below. " And," says the chronicler, " it smote him to earth dead and never more spake he word." [2] Thus perished the greatest Perugian citizen of his day, and, if we may credit Villani, " the greatest citizen of all the free cities of Italy." [3] For full a quarter of a century he had been the guiding spirit of Perugian statecraft, and wherever there was difficulty or danger he was sent to face it. He was Potestà in Spoleto in 1327, when the Spoletini refused to present the *palio* with due words of subjection,[4] and in Anghiari, in 1349, while that town was seething with rebellion and when his predecessor had just been punished

on their heads or suspended by the leg, was a usual part of the penalty inflicted. It is useless to cite examples. Every chronicle is full of them.

[1] FILIPPINI, *ubi cit.*, pp. 323-325, Doc. xix., xx.
[2] M. VILLANI, xi. 403 ; FABRETTI, *Cronache*, i. 119, 181.
[3] See page 209 *supra.*
[4] PELLINI, i. 491; FABRETTI, *Cronache*, i. 15, 77. See also page 138 *supra.*

for timidity and incompetence.[1]   When all Italy sent
ambassadors to Cola di Rienzo, he was one of the ten who
represented Perugia.[2]   Caressed and trusted by Albornoz,
he was charged with the government of Viterbo in the
critical first days of its subjection to the Church,[3] and, in
1355, we find him among the envoys to Charles IV., who
brought back from Pisa the eight imperial privileges, " four
with seals of wax and four with golden *bullae*." [4]   His
obvious prototype in the history of Central Italy is
Provenzano Salvani, the last great Ghibelline of Siena,
with whom, as with Andreotti, " Toscana sonò tutta."   Each
of them died a violent death at the moment when his
services were most needed by his native city, and each
of them was soon forgotten.   " Ed ora a pena . . . sen
pispiglia." [5]

The Raspanti honoured their murdered chieftain with
splendid obsequies, even setting at defiance their own
statutes to gird him dead with the girdle of knighthood.[6]
The house whence the fatal stone was hurled was levelled
to the ground and all the Boccoli were outlawed.[7]   Henceforward the *fuorusciti* received no quarter.   At Tuoro, in
August, 1363, and at Monte Fontegiano del Lago, in
November, all the nobles who fell into the hands of the
Perugians were decapitated ;   among the rest Messer
Alessandro de' Vincioli who had been knighted on the
field of battle at Torrita five years earlier ; " only that
Donato who slew Leggerio, as God willed it, they found
not, neither alive nor dead ; and it was reported that he
swam out into the Lake ; and no man saw him more." [8]

The years which followed were years of ever-increasing
suspicion and difficulty.   In 1362 Guillaume de Grimoard

[1] FABRETTI, *Cronache*, i. 100.
[2] GRAZIANI, p. 144 ; PELLINI, i. 879, and page 97 *supra*.
[3] See page 212 *supra*.
[4] FABRETTI, i. 148 ; PELLINI, i. 953, and page 216 *supra*.
[5] *Purgatorio*, xi. 110, 111.
[6] *Statuto di Perugia* (1342), Lib. iii. Rubric 229 : " De l acegnente overc
acegnere facente alcuno morto de centura de cavaliere."
[7] FABRETTI, *Cronache*, i. 181.
[8] FABRETTI, *Cronache*, i. 182-185 ; GRAZIANI, pp. 192-194 ; M. VILLANI
xi. 66 ; PELLINI, i. 999-1002.

had been elevated to the Papacy, under the title of Urban V., and a general league had been organized against Bernabò Visconti. It, however, effected little, and, in 1364, peace was signed in Milan, whereby it was agreed that Albornoz should be transferred to the Southern legation. His absence, unfortunately, was not sufficiently protracted to afford Perugia any opportunity of recovering the ground which she had lost, and, after his return, his attitude towards her was even more unfriendly than heretofore. The Florentines ordered their ambassadors to intercede on behalf of their old ally, and to remind him of the many services which she had rendered to the Church and the Guelf cause, seeking to "levare ogni salvatichezza nata fra lui et perugini";[1] but they pleaded to deaf ears. In spite of all his solemn promises, he showed himself ever more and more favourably disposed towards the *fuorusciti*, who, for their part, offered to submit Perugia itself to the absolute dominion of the Holy See, if, through his assistance, they should be enabled to triumph over their enemies.[2] Meanwhile, the *contado* was repeatedly invaded by Companies of Adventure, which, whether they came as friends or foes, equally burned and sacked and devastated.[3] Of these, the "White Company," as the most openly hostile to Perugia, was so unblushingly favoured by the Church, that a contemporary chronicler does not hesitate to declare that *in tota Italia in solemnitatibus missarum post orationem dominicam fiebant orationes pro mala compagnia alba.*[4] At S. Mariano the Perugians were victorious, and we possess a curious letter from the despairing and beleaguered English (the White Company was Hawkwood's Company) begging for mercy in the most abject terms.[5] But by that imprudent magna-

[1] DEGLI AZZI, *op. cit.*, i. p. 113, § 372. Compare also AMMIRATO, *Ist. Fior.* (edition cited), Vol. III. Lib. xii. p. 175.

[2] PELLINI, i. 1015, 1019.   [3] FABRETTI, *Cronache*, i. 186.

[4] *Arch. Stor. It.*, XVI. i. 199 n. 1.

[5] GRAZIANI, pp. 198-200 ; BONAZZI, i. 456-457. See also, for a fuller account of this matter than I have space to give, SYMONDS and DUFF GORDON, *op. cit.*, p. 119. Here too, however, the enormous inaccuracy of these writers must be guarded against and allowed for. They state that the prisoners were captured "at the great fight down by the Tiber," and that the letter referred to in the text was written "as they lay in their

nimity which gave to their Council Chamber its ill-omened title of the *Sala di mal consiglio*, the Perugians threw away every advantage which they had gained;[1] and, "in the accursed month of March, 1367," they were utterly routed in the valley of the Tiber, between Colle Strada and Bruffa. The slain are said to have numbered fifteen hundred, and as many more were taken prisoners. During the battle "the Legate abode at Foligno with full five thousand cavalry and with many foot-soldiers; and he was passing glad of our discomfiture, the which the English inflicted upon us by his consent and with his aid."[2] Assisi, Gualdo and Nocera at once threw off the Perugian yoke and submitted to the Church, while, by the orders of Albornoz, the walls of Bettona were rebuilt.[3] To the lamentations and complaints of the Raspanti the Pope returned no other answer than this: *De morte hominum dolemus, sed de recuperatione Terrarum nostrarum gaudemus.*[4] Help there was none. Siena had already done all she could; there had been a Sienese contingent in the defeated army;[5] and, although the Florentines hastened to send troops for the defence of the city and its *contado*, they stipulated that these should not be used to prevent the Legate from taking possession of any town to which he laid claim as belonging to the Church.[6]

On the 4th of June Urban landed at Corneto, and, on the 9th, he reached Viterbo, where he took up his residence in

cells." They have evidently been misled by the phrase *Vestri pauperes carcerati servitores Anglici*. The document itself disproves their assertion, since its date of place is *in castro S. Mariani de Perusio*. Nevertheless, while it is necessary, in the interest of historical truth, to notice such inexcusable blunders as this, I would not have the reader imagine that I have anything to say against *The Story of Perugia* as a guide-book. Regarded from that point of view, it has, no doubt, an excellent *raison d' être*. It has been translated into Italian; and, after the lapse of more than a decade, is still the best guide-book Perugia possesses.

[1] PELLINI, i. 1017; BONAZZI, i. 460.

[2] FABRETTI, *Cronache*, i. 35, 188-191; PELLINI, i. 1021-1023.

[3] FABRETTI, *Cronache*, i. 131, 191; *Eph. Urbev., op. cit.*, p. 90; CRISTOFANI, *Storia della Città d' Assisi, op. cit.*, i. 231; MONTEMARTE, *Cronaca* cit., p. 35.

[4] PELLINI, i. 1024.

[5] *Cronica Sanese*, in MURATORI, *R. I. S.*, xv. 191; MALAVOLTI, ii. 128t.

[6] DEGLI AZZI, *op. cit.*, i. 115, § 381; AMMIRATO, *Ist. Fior.* (edition cited), Vol. III. Lib. xiii. p. 181.

the great fortress which Albornoz had built.[1]   Though a man
of sincere and earnest piety who looked with disgust upon
the pomp and luxury of the Avignonese Court, he was none
the less determined to assert the temporal rights of the
Apostolic See.   Dante's lofty conception of a priesthood
wholly dedicated to spiritual things[2] was altogether beyond
his comprehension.   He sincerely deplored the vices of the
age, but he felt that the reconquest of the Church's earthly
heritage was every whit as much his duty as was the reformation of the morals of his Curia, and his earliest efforts were
devoted to completing the work which Albornoz had begun.
In spite of the expostulations of Florence,[3] the revolted Todi
was subdued by force of arms,[4] while an anti-French tumult
in Viterbo was bloodily suppressed.[5]   The Perugian ambassadors were coldly received,[6] and, ere long, the Raspanti
were informed that they were expected to assist the Church
against the Visconti.   Like the Florentines,[7] they pleaded
their obligations under the Peace of Sarzana, but weaker
than the Florentines, they were terrorized into at least a
semblance of obedience.[8]   Their subservience, however,
availed them nothing ; for the Pope, Perugia was a veritable
Naboth's vineyard, and he was determined to possess it by

[1] The best account of the coming of Urban with which I am acquainted
is to be found in Mr E. G. GARDNER's *Saint Catherine of Siena* (London :
Dent, 1907), pp. 61 *et seq.*

[2] *Purgatorio*, xvi.

[3] AMMIRATO, *op. cit.*, Vol. III. Lib. xiii. pp. 182, 183.

[4] PELLINI, i. 1028. Operations against Todi had been commenced
before the arrival of Urban. See MONTEMARTE, pp. 35-36.

[5] GRAZIANI, pp. 205-206 ; MONTEMARTE, i. 36.

[6] BONAZZI, i. 461. Compare GRAZIANI, pp. 203-204.

[7] AMMIRATO, *op. cit.*, Vol. III. Lib. xiii. p. 185.

[8] I have followed PELLINI, i. 1029-1030. On the 31st of July, 1367,
a League was concluded between Urban V., the Gonzaga, Francesco da
Carrara and the Marchesi d' Este. Such of the Tuscan communes as joined
it joined it later. Apparently, in October the Perugians still hesitated.
See the letter from Francesco de' Casali, Seignior of Cortona, to the Sienese
magistrates, published by G. SANESI, *Siena nella Lega contro il Visconti*,
in *Bullettino Senese di Storia Patria*, i. 242-243. Compare also *Ibid.*, p.
246 and note, from which it seems that as late as May, 1368, Perugia
continued neutral. The fact that the *Annali Decemvirali* are lacking
from 1352 to 1374 deprives us of any trustworthy information on the
subject from Perugian sources.

fair means or foul. Even Albornoz would hardly have
counselled a policy of open aggression such as Urban
adopted ; but Albornoz had died of the Plague on the 24th
of August,[1] and the Perugians were left at the mercy of a
narrow-minded French monk, who chose to regard the
fuorusciti as the only lawful representatives of the Commune.[2]   At his instigation, Città di Castello revolted in
July, 1368,[3] and, in September, we find him intriguing with
the Baglioni and other malcontents for the surrender of
Perugia itself ; soldiers were to be introduced by night into
the monastery of S. Pietro, and the Raspanti and their
adherents to be put to the sword.   When the plot was
discovered, the Duke of Spoleto had already advanced as
far as the plain below Bettona.   Most of those implicated,
and among them the Abbot of S. Pietro, succeeded in
making good their escape, but four of the conspirators were
captured and paid for their treason with their lives.[4]

"Ye have done to death the servants of the holy Church
of God," wrote the indignant Pope.[5]   All Perugians found
in the Papal States were seized and imprisoned, and the city
itself was laid under an interdict.[6]   War followed, and for
wellnigh two years the little Umbrian republic defied the
whole power of the Apostolic See.   The direction of the
papal armies was entrusted to Pierre d'Estaing, Archbishop
of Bourges ;[7] while the Perugians were assisted by Bernabò

[1] GRAZIANI, p. 204.

[2] The Pope's mental attitude was, no doubt, the natural one for a French-
man in the fourteenth century ; and it is curious to note how quickly
feudalism revived in the Ecclesiastical State after the restoration of the
papal sovereignty.   See ANTONELLI, *Di alcune infeudazioni nell' Umbria
nella seconda metà del Secolo XIV.*, in *Bollettino* cited, Vol. XIII. (1907),
p. 219.

[3] PELLINI, i. 1037 ; MUZI, *Memorie civili*, etc., *op. cit.*, i. 166 ; *Arch.
Stor. It.*, XVI. i. 208.

[4] PELLINI, i. 1041-1042 ; FABRETTI, *Cronache*, i. 36 ; L. BRUNAMONTE
TARULLI, *Appunti storici*, etc., *op. cit.*, in *Bollettino* cited, xii. 460.

[5] "*Fecistis cædem de devotis Ecclesiæ sanctæ Dei.*"

[6] PELLINI, i. 1043, 1045 ; BONAZZI, i. 462.   A hundred years later, we
find Pope Sixtus IV. taking up a very similar attitude with regard to the
Florentines when the conspiracy for the murder of Lorenzo de' Medici
was frustrated. (See CREIGHTON, *op. cit.*, iv. 90.)   Thus does history
repeat itself.

[7] MONTEMARTE, i. 38 ; GARDNER, *op. cit.*, p. 74.

Visconti, Francesco, the son of Giovanni Di Vico,[1] and Hawkwood's English mercenaries. At first they more than held their own; in the summer of 1369 they besieged the Pope in Montefiascone, and, after wasting all the country round, "encamped before the gates thereof and shot arrows into the town, and used evil words concerning the Pope."[2] Also they sent for the prostitutes of Perugia that they might run a *palio* beneath the walls of Montefiascone, as they had done beneath those of Arezzo over thirty years before. That his Holiness was spared this crowning insult was due to the timely interposition of the Hungarian ambassador,[3] but for the moment it seemed as if the Church were destined to be worsted in the conflict which it had so unjustly provoked.[4] Little by little, however, the fortunes of war changed. Monte Sansavino was seized by the Aretines,[5] and Castiglion Aretino by the papal troops,[6] while Lucignano and Foiano gave themselves to Siena,[7] thus depriving Perugia of almost her last precarious foothold in Tuscany. One after another vassal towns and seigniors revolted; the city itself was seething with sedition, and the *fuorusciti* and their allies dominated the *contado*. During the spring and summer of 1370 disaster followed disaster,[8] and when, on the 12th of November, Bernabò made his peace with the Pope,[9] it became obvious that further resistance was worse than useless.

At this time Urban was no longer in Italy,[10] and the Perugian syndics and procurators—among whom was the

---

[1] Giovanni Di Vico died in 1366. CALISSE, *op. cit.*, p. 137.

[2] MONTEMARTE, i. 38; *Arch. Stor. It.*, XVI. i. 209 n. 3.

[3] PELLINI, i. 1059; BONAZZI, i. 465-466.

[4] "Et andava le cose de' Peroscini nel principio molto prospere, et fece dubitare dello stato della Chiesa." MONTEMARTE, *ubi cit.*

[5] FABRETTI, *Cronache*, i. 37; PELLINI, i. 1045; *Arch. Stor. It.*, XVI. i. 209.

[6] PELLINI, i. 1056-7; FABRETTI, *Cronache*, i. 131.

[7] PELLINI, i. 1067; *Cronica Sanese*, in MURATORI, *R. I. S.*, xv. 218-219; MALAVOLTI, ii. 138; R. ARCH. DI STATO IN SIENA, *Caleffo Nero*, c. 527-530.

[8] PELLINI, i. 1061-1080.

[9] *Chronicon Estense*, in MURATORI, *R. I. S.*, xv. 493.

[10] Urban sailed from Corneto on the 5th of September, 1370. Ambassadors from Perugia had been sent thither to treat for peace, but without result. PELLINI, i. 1077.

celebrated Baldo, *utriusque Iuris professor*—betook themselves to Bologna to make their submission to the Pope's brother the "Cardinal of Avignon," Anglico de Grimoard. As a condition precedent to all negotiations, they were required to confess that, "from a time whereof there is no memory of man to the contrary *et in ante*," Perugia had always been subject to the Holy See, and that the suzerainty which she had exercised over Spoleto, Assisi, Gubbio, Borgo S. Sepolcro, Castel della Pieve, and other towns and fortresses of the Ecclesiastical State, was a direct usurpation of the rights of the Church. The *justum et verum dominium* of the Papacy having been thus explicitly admitted, it was agreed that the keys of the city should be formally delivered to the commissaries of the Cardinal Legate in sign of subjection, and that the Priors of the Commune should thereupon be created vicars of the Pope during his lifetime. Three thousand florins were to be paid annually by way of tribute (*census*), and the *fuorusciti* were to return to their homes and to be reinstated in their possessions.[1]

At first sight these conditions seem far more favourable to the Perugians than could have been reasonably expected. Their claim to independence was no doubt abandoned ; but, of itself, the acknowledgment of the suzerainty of the Church by no means destroyed or even curtailed the liberties of the Commune. In theory of law, every Italian Republic, however powerful, held either mediately or immediately of Pope or Emperor—a fact which the great Bartolo himself admitted when he adduced Perugia as the one exception.[2] The real question, therefore, was the character of that suzerainty, and in this connection the interpretation of the clause touching the creation of vicars became a matter of paramount importance. The death of Urban would certainly not affect the Church's dominion over Perugia. Would it affect the

[1] GRAZIANI, pp. 210-214; PELLINI, i. 1081-1083. The original document from which Graziani made his synopsis still exists in the *Archivio Decemvirale* (*Contratti B. B. n.* 159 *bis.*).

[2] " Et si dicas quicquid non subest imperio est sub Ecclesia, concedo : nisi Civitas aliqua non subsit Ecclesiæ ex privilegio concesso, sed Perusina est hujusmodi, nam Imperator donavit eam Ecclesiam seu permutavit cum ea, et ex privilegio Ecclesia liberavit eam." See pages 100, 149 *supra.*

vicariate of the Priors? The Florentine ambassadors, who had been present in Bologna and had taken part in the negotiations, promised to obtain a definite pronouncement from the Cardinal;[1] but the question was still undecided when, on the 19th of December, Urban died at Avignon, and was succeeded by Cardinal Pierre Roger de Beaufort, who took the title of Gregory XI.

The news of the peace and of the consequent suspension of the interdict was received in Perugia with the wildest delight. Bonfires blazed to heaven; bells rang out from every tower, and laity and clergy alike danced through all the streets and squares of the city. Men laid aside their armour and clothed themselves once more in civic attire; and on Christmas Eve, for the first time after full twenty months, divine offices were celebrated in the churches.[2] Only the Raspanti were ill at ease, for their day of reckoning was at hand. Their prestige was hopelessly ruined; the public treasury was empty, and the war had brought famine in its wake. During the preceding summer the rich corn lands of Il Chiugi had lain fallow; sufficient wheat to feed the populace could not be imported, and, rendered desperate by their sufferings, the proletariat were ripe for any mischief.[3]

In February, 1371, the *fuorusciti* began to return; and "they came with so much arrogance and pride" that the Magistrates, fearing a tumult, ordered "that they should not return all together but separately"; and "those of them who had received injury by the death of members of their families who had been beheaded (and there were many such) returned clad in mourning and lamenting, yea even though their kinsfolk had been dead six or seven years; and this

---

[1] PELLINI, i. 1081.

[2] *Arch. Stor. It.*, XVI. i. 215; PELLINI, i. 1083-1085.

[3] To raise the money necessary for the payment of the mercenary troops which had been employed during the war, the Raspanti had not only borrowed from the Florentines (DEGLI AZZI, *op. cit.*, ii. 141, § 548), but had been compelled to mortgage *redditum Lacus pro xxxviiii milibus florenorum ad tempus quatuor annorum*. See A. GHERARDI, *La guerra dei Fiorentini con papa Gregorio XI. detta la Guerra degli Otto Santi*. Doc. 130, in *Arch. Stor. Ital.*, Sierie III. Vol. VII. Parte i. p. 220. As to the causes of the unpopularity of the Raspanti generally, see PELLINI, i. 1094-1095.

they did to the end that the *Popolari* might perceive that they had not forgotten the injuries which they had suffered." [1]

Meanwhile the new Pope absolutely declined to confirm the Priors in the vicariate, and ordered Pierre d'Estaing, Cardinal of Bourges, who was then at Todi, to assume the government of the city. [2] In vain the Raspanti hurried off ambassadors to Florence to beseech assistance ; the Florentines promised to send both troops and money ; [3] but their plans were frustrated by the prompt action of the Cardinal. His nephew, Messer Aronne, was despatched to Perugia with the papal briefs, and, in spite all the efforts of the magistrates, a general council was convened in the Palace of the Priors on the 16th of May. " Si fece," says the chronicler, " una grande addunanza, la maggiore e la più generale che mai si facesse." All classes of the community were represented, and " with one accord and with one voice, the whole assembly shouted that the People of Perugia willed that Monseigneur de Bourges should come and take the seignory of the city ; to the end that the people might not die of hunger and might be delivered out of the hands of the Raspanti." Thereupon, Messer Aronne took horse for Todi ; and, as night fell, the city rose in tumult behind him. " Every man ran to arm himself, and in every *Porta* the mob swept through the streets shouting, ' Live the People ! Live the Church of Rome ! Death to the Raspanti ! ' " And, " anon all the houses of the Raspanti were set on fire and robbed and burned by the people, so that not one of them was left in all the *Porte*." The prisons were broken open and the prisoners set at liberty, and till day dawned anarchy reigned supreme. Yet the revolution was almost a bloodless one, and before morning the fury of the populace seems to have spent itself. Three citizens were chosen to fill the places of such of the Priors as had fled ; the laws which forbade the Nobles to hold office were repealed, and

[1] PELLINI, i. 1088-1089 ; *Arch. Stor. It.*, XVI. i. p. 215 ; FABRETTI, *Cronache*, i. 39, 194.

[2] PELLINI, i. 1096 ; AMMIRATO, *Ist. Fior.* (edition cited), Vol. III. Lib. xiii. p. 216.   [3] PELLINI, i. 1099.

the Captain of the People and the soldiers of the civic guard took oath of allegiance to the Church.[1]

On the 18th the rest of the *fuorusciti* returned, and, finding no living enemies to oppose them, wreaked a belated vengeance on the dead.   The splendid marble tomb which had been set up in the Duomo to the honour of Leggerio Andreotti was broken open and destroyed, and the remains of the great *popolano* were cast into the Piazza, where they were subjected to the ribald insults of the mob.[2]   The following day Cardinal d'Estaing entered Perugia with " grandissima festa," and " the Priors and all the citizens went forth to meet him, on horseback and on foot, even unto Ponte S. Giovanni, carrying olive branches in their hands and shouting, ' Live the Church !   Live the Seignior !   Death to the Raspanti ! ' "   He was accompanied by full a thousand horse and four hundred foot-soldiers.[3]

[1] FABRETTI, *Cronache*, i. 40, 195 ; PELLINI, i. 1096-1102. According to Pellini, in all that night only three persons were slain and two of them by private enemies (p. 1101), On the other hand, we read in the *Cronica Sanese* (*ubi cit.*, col. 223) that " fuvi morti 14 di nome, e robate e arse case, e cacciati tutti li Raspanti ; e fuvi gran male di morti e di robati."

[2] PELLINI, i. 1102 ; BONAZZI, i. 476.

[3] FABRETTI, *Cronache*, i. 64, 195. On the 17th the Cardinal had gone from Todi to Foligno, " non volendo così all' improviso entrare nella Città così piena di rapine e d' incendii, dove egli doveva essere come Legato Apostolico ricevuto."   The night of the 18th he spent at S. Crispolto di Bettona. See PELLINI, i. 1103.

CHAPTER XIX

THE PAPAL FORTRESS IN PORTA SOLE

FOR four years and a half Perugia lay supine beneath the heel of the Church, her liberties destroyed, her national diversions prohibited,[1] and her magistrates mere puppets in the hands of the foreign representatives of a foreign Pope.[2]

In December, 1371, Cardinal d'Estaing was transferred to the Legation of Bologna and his place at Perugia was taken by Philippe de Cabassole, Petrarch's friend,[3] the Cardinal of Jerusalem, a just and amiable old man, who won golden opinions from the citizens during the few months of his government.[4] He died in August, 1372, and was succeeded by Gérard du Puy, Abbot of Marmoutier, a nephew of Pope Gregory, who is known in Perugian annals as " the Abbot of Mommaggiore." [5] Under his rule, the building of the great Citadel, begun by Cardinal d'Estaing, was pushed forward with unremitting energy and finally completed in 1374.[6] To obtain a suitable site the greater part of the houses on the Monte di Porta Sole were pulled down, and upon their ruins was constructed a *castello* which a contemporary writer informs us was " the fairest fortress in all

[1] PELLINI, i. 1121. In the graphic phrase of the Perugian chroniclers, " i ministri del Papa havevano tolto loro ogni diletto." Compare my *Palio and Ponte, op. cit.*, p. 153.

[2] According to SISMONDI, *op. cit.*, Vol. III. cap. xlix. p. 92, the Perugians were not " despoiled of all their privileges and constrained to recognize the absolute power of the Pope " until 1372. This, however, is obviously a mistake. See MONTEMARTE, i. 39 and ii. 190, n. 46.

[3] E. G. GARDNER, *op. cit.*, p. 106.

[4] A contemporary chronicler informs us that, at his death, " li cittadini di Perugia ne furono assai dolenti perchè esso era uomo buono e manteneva la città e contado in ragione e buono stato." FABRETTI, *Cronache*, i. 196.

[5] See MARIOTTI, *Saggio*, etc., *op. cit.*, pp. 292-293.

[6] For all that concerns the " *La Fortezza di Porta Sole* " see the article of Ing. G. BACILE DI CASTIGLIONE, in *Augusta Perusia*, Anno i. pp. 111-113.

Italy." Therein were many towers and many lordly palaces, and, among the rest, a " Papal Residence," so sumptuous and so commodious, that "it seemed a very paradise." So certain did it appear that the Papal Curia was about to be transferred to Perugia that foreign merchants began to negotiate for the hire of shops and warehouses in the city.[1] A second fortress was built at the northern extremity of the Borgo di S. Antonio, above the Convent of S. Maria di Monteluce, and was connected with the Citadel by a lofty *ala*, or covered way supported upon arches, wide enough to permit the passage of four men-at-arms riding abreast ; while a second *ala* led from the Citadel to S. Lorenzo, and hence to the Palaces of the Potestà and of the Priors. Each of these *ale* was furnished with parapets and with overhanging battlements, through the apertures of which the garrison might pour boiling water or hurl missiles upon the heads of assailants attempting to destroy the pillars of the arches. The *ala* leading to the Palace of the Priors, which was the narrower of the two, is said to have been over six feet wide and fifty feet high ; and, because the Church of S. Lorenzo stood in the line of its construction, " more than half of S. Lorenzo was pulled down." [2] A third fortress was erected in Porta S. Angelo, which, if the Abbot had been allowed time to carry out his plans, would, in its turn, have been connected with the Citadel by a third *ala*. Thus, as a modern writer justly remarks, " Mommaggiore may be said to have run over half the city of Perugia." [3] Outside the Citadel was a barbican and a deep moat, which was filled with water at a cost of no less than thirty thousand florins, and all the gates were furnished with drawbridges " bene inchio- ate e incatenate." Not only were the cross-bows and other implements of warfare belonging to the Communes removed

---

[1] Thus, for example, we learn that certain Florentine merchants rented apothecas, domos et hospicia " in Perugia, paying therefor an enormous price. See DEGLI AZZI, *Le Relazioni*, etc., *op. cit.*, i. 130, § 449.

[2] Compare *Annali Decemvirali*, a. 1376 (13 gennaio) : " In primis cum pro honore civitatis Perusie et civium Perusinorum eiusdem civitatis sit necesse providere quod Major ecclesia et domus S. Laurentii de Perusia, que per inimicos italice regionis incepta fuit discarchari durante regimine ecclesie romane, solepniter reactetur," etc.

[3] *The Story of Perugia*, *op. cit.*, p. 184.

from the public arsenal in the Piazza and stored in the Citadel, but artillery of every kind was specially constructed for its defence : *un trabocco e sette manganelle ; molte balestre a telaro e a staffa, e molto saettame e molte bombarde e spingarde e mazzi e frombole.*   Finally, it was victualled " with more than four thousand measures of grain and flour with wine in proportion, and generally with all manner of necessary supplies on such wise that, if it had been besieged for ten years, the garrison would have lacked nothing." The architect was the celebrated Gattapone of Gubbio, and in all, the Holy See is said to have expended upon its construction the enormous sum of two million four hundred thousand florins of gold.[1]   In 1373, the chains were removed from the streets and piazze, so that, in case of insurrection, the papal cavalry might charge through the city without impediment.[2]

Henceforward Perugia was governed with the most detestable tyranny.   Not only were the Raspanti ruthlessly persecuted and the people ground down with taxes, but the Priors, though no longer *popolani*, were ignominiously expelled from their Palace.   Even the haughtiest nobles were excluded from the Councils of the Legate, and men whispered that the sudden death of Abbot Vibi of S. Pietro was due to that prelate's determination to take the same part in public affairs as his predecessors had done before him. The Province was governed through the agency of corrupt notaries and foreign captains ; and the most outrageous licence on the part of the officials of the Church was openly connived at.   Of these the worst offender was a kinsman of Marmoutier's.   To escape violation at his hands a gentle

---

[1] FABRETTI, *Cronache*, i. 41, 65, 131, 149-151, 197-198 ; PELLINI, i. 1111-1112. See also, for important particulars, AMMIRATO, *1st. Fior.* (edition cited), Vol. III. Lib. xiii. p. 243.   PIETRO BONINSEGNI (*Storia Fiorentina* Lib. iv. p. 160, Firenze, presso Giorgio Marescotti, 1580) relates tha " circa il 1373 i preti che governavano lo Stato della Chiesa mandaron segretamente un Matteo Gattapone d' Agobbio, grande maestro di fa casseri, ed altri maestri a desegnare ed avvisare dove ponessero le fortezz per poterle tenere." He had already been employed by Albornoz on th citadel of Spoleto.   See FILIPPINI, *op. cit.*, in *Studi Storici*, Vol. XII p. 327, Doc. xxii.

[2] PELLINI, i. 1131.   [3] PELLINI, i. 1135.

woman threw herself out of the window of her house and was dashed to pieces on the pavement beneath. Complaint was made to the Abbot, who dismissed the subject with a brutal gibe : *Vos Italici credetis quod omnes Galli sunt eunuchi.* On a subsequent occasion, when the same offender abducted the wife of one of the citizens, he was ordered, on pain of death, to return her to her husband within fifty days ! [1] Such were the men whom the pastors of Avignon sent to govern their Italian flocks, and for such services as these Gérard du Puy was made Cardinal on December 21st, 1375.[2]

Meanwhile, however, the conduct of the Apostolic Legates had aroused the suspicions of Florence, and, fearful for her own liberties, she entered into a league with Bernabò Visconti (July 1375), which resulted in the celebrated war known as *La Guerra degli Otto Santi.*[3] Envoys were sent to stir up a general rebellion in the Ecclesiastical State, and the response was immediate and well-nigh unanimous. Within ten days more than eighty cities

---

[1] MONTEMARTE, i. 41 ; *Chronicon Regiense* in MURATORI, *R. I. S.*, xviii. 85 ; BONAZZI, i. 479-481. In a letter of the 7th of December, 1375, the Florentine Signoria, after congratulating the Perugians on the recovery of their liberty, demands emphatically, " Erat ne apud vos aliquis qui de filijs, de re familiari, de coniugali thoro aut de se ipso aliquid tutum vel certum posset habere ? Omnia exposita erant occitane avaricie, crudelitati atque cupidini."

[2] It is startling to find such a man—*illud monstrum abominabile*, as he is called in a contemporary document—selected by the Pope to act as his intermediary when communicating with St Catherine of Siena. (See GARDNER, *op. cit.*, p. 110.) According to FRANCO SACCHETTI (*Nov.* 41), Messer Ridolfo da Camerino congratulated him upon his preferment in the following terms : " Avendoci fatto male, se' fatto Cardinale ; se ci avessi fatto peggio, saresti fatto Papa." In this connection another witty saying of the same worthy gentleman deserves to be recorded, if only because it must have appealed so strongly to the Perugians : " Dicea che de' Papi si facea come del porco ; quando il porco muore, tutta la casa e ciascuno ne fa festa ; e così per la morte de' Papi tutto il mondo e tutti i cristiani ne fanno festa." It is, perhaps, fortunate that he did not push the parallel any further.

[3] See GHERARDI, *La guerra dei Fiorentini con Papa Gregorio XI.*, in the *Arch. Stor. It.*, Serie iii. Vols. V.-VIII. The clearest and best English account of the causes and origin of this war is probably that of E. G. GARDNER, *op. cit.*, pp. 141 *et seq.* NAPIER'S *Florentine History* may also be consulted with profit.

and walled towns had broken the yoke of the Church from off their necks and achieved their freedom.[1] The first to revolt was Viterbo, the second Città di Castello.[2] The Abbot of Marmoutier promptly sent a part of his English mercenaries against the rebels, and then Perugia rose. The story shall be told, as far as may be, in the words of a contemporary chronicler, who probably shared the dangers and the glories of those twenty-four days of struggle and of conquest.[3]

"In the name of God and His holy mother Mary, of the blessed Sant' Ercolano, San Lorenzo and San Costanzo, who set free the people of Perugia and delivered them from bondage and out of the hands of the accursed pastors of the Church.

"In the said year [1375], on the 7th day of the victorious month of December,[4] through power and miracle divine, the holy people of Perugia, on Friday morning, of common consent, little and great, nobles and *popolari*, forgetful of every injury and discord, in perfect peace and amity, each man kissing his enemy, gat them all together into the Piazza,

[1] *Chronicon Estense*, in MURATORI, *R. I. S.*, xv. 499.

[2] According to AMMIRATO (*op. cit.*, Vol. III. Lib. xiii. pp. 242-243), "La prima ribellione che si sentì fu quella di Città di Castello. . . . Dietro a Città di Castello e a Perugia seguì la rebellione di Viterbo"; but we have documentary evidence "che 'l Prefetto da Vico a dì xviii di questo mese (novembre) à preso Viterbo e còrsolo per sè; e sono cacciati gli uficiali della Chiesa." (See GHERARDI, *op. cit.*, Doc. xcvi., xcvii., and compare CALISSE, *I Prefetti Di Vico, op. cit.*, p. 145.) Città di Castello did not rise till December 3rd. GHERARDI, *op. cit.*, Doc. ciii.; DEGLI AZZI, *op. cit.*, i. p. 121, § 409. See also the *Cronica Sanese*, in MURATORI, *R. I. S.*, xv. 246-247.

[3] FABRETTI, *Cronache*, i. 151-156, 199-204. The two accounts are almost identical. The second is printed in the *Arch. Stor. It.*, XVI. i. 220-224, as "Supplemento Terzo al Graziani." A few minor details may be gleaned from FABRETTI, *Cronache*, i. 41, 65, 122. See also AMMIRATO, *ubi cit.*, and, of course, PELLINI, i. 1143-1149. Compare GHERARDI, *op. cit.*, Doc. cvii., cix., cx., cxi., cxxi., cxxviii., cxxx., cxxxiv., cxxxvi., cxxxviii., and DEGLI AZZI, *op. cit.*, i., §§ 410, 412, 413, 416, 419, 420, 421, 422, 423, 429.

[4] This date would at first sight appear to be open to question, though there is too much evidence in its favour to be lightly rejected. "La battaglia," we are told, "durò dalla mattina fino a nona"; so that it was already afternoon when the victory of the Perugians became assured. Yet we have a letter from the Florentine Signoria, of the 7th December, congratulating them on their recovered liberties (DEGLI AZZI, *op. cit.*, i. 121, § 410).

THE PALACE OF THE PRIORS
FROM THE AFFRESCO OF BONFIGLI

crying with one voice, 'Live the people and die the Abbot and the pastors of the Church!' And all the people, being in the Piazza of Perugia armed, went up against the Palace of the Priors, where was Messer Gomez[1] and his company; and he, when he heard the uproar, forthwith commanded that the doors of the Palace should be made fast, and sent folk into the towers thereof to defend the same, and bade them cast great stones; and on this wise the battle lasted from morning even unto the ninth hour, and slackened not; yet, by the mercy of God, no man suffered any harm, nor was smitten by any stone to do him hurt. Wherefore Messer Gomez, wotting well that he might not withstand the fury of the people, and because in the said Palace there was naught to eat, fled away and abandoned the Palace of the Priors and that of the Captain and that of the Potestà, and came through S. Lorenzo to the Citadel. And with him there went the Bishop of Bologna, who was lately come to Perugia to examine the accounts of the Abbot,[2] Messer Ugo della Recchia, a kinsman of the Pope, Messer Grazino, official of the Church, and Messer Lodovico of the March, Vicar of the City of Perugia for the Church,[3] Messer Bernardo da Sala also, with all the English, all the soldiers on foot and on horseback, and all the French and Burgundians, which were without the Citadel and stood on guard at the head of the Piazza, to the number of fifteen hundred men. Likewise there fled Messer Borgaro da Marsciano and Messer Francesco of Santa Fiora,[4] who, a

[1] Gomez Albornoz, the warlike nephew of the Cardinal. He had been in Perugia since 1372, and, on the death of Philippe de Cabassole, had assumed the government of the city until the appointment of Marmoutier. See PELLINI, i. 1117, 1126.

[2] " per udire le ragioni dell' abbate insieme con messer Gomese." According to PELLINI (i. 1144), he was sent by the Pope " per rivedere i conti all' Abbate di Mommaggiore dell' aministrate Provincie."

[3] PELLINI (loc. cit.) calls him " Luogotenente dell' Abbate in Perugia."

[4] This is the same Francesco Aldobrandeschi, Count of S. Fiora in M. Amiata, who is mentioned in the statute of the Castello della Triana of 1351. See P. PICCOLOMINI, Lo Statuto del Castello della Triana (Siena, Tip. Lazzeri, 1905), p. 7. Several letters of his to the Signoria of Siena are preserved in the Archives of that city, and he is referred to by Fra Filippo in one of his " ensamples." See Gli Assempri di Fra Filippo da Siena (edition CARPELLINI), cap. xxxv. p. 120.

few days before, had come to have speech with the Abbot, and also Messer Ranieri with all his household,[1] for fear of the people.   All these were driven into the Citadel on such wise that none of them remained in the city who escaped not into the Citadel.   Then went all the people to the gates of the Citadel, and there befel a great battle ; and the bridge without the gates was burned so that no man might come forth into the Piazza.   And incontinently they made a barrier of great stones and of *grelli* [2] from S. Lorenzo even to the house of Leggieri ; [3] and afterward they builded another wall higher up, over against the bridge which they had burned, so that the enemy could not issue forth.   Moreover, there were made many *gatti* and *grelli* [4] to breach the walls of the Citadel.   Then too was the bridge of the fortress of S. Antonio set on fire, so that the garrison might not be able to receive succour [from without].   This done, the Priors of Perugia made proclamation that all the masons and carpenters which were in the city should go and break down and cast to the ground that *ala* which led from the Citadel to the fortress of S. Antonio, on such wise that no succour might be sent thereby : [5] and the said *ala* was cast down and ruined and burned for more than fifty paces ; and, a few days thereafter, the like was done to that other *ala* which led from S. Lorenzo to the Citadel, so that it fell for more than fifty paces.   And all the people stood ready for battle, both day and night, keeping watch and ward continually ; and ever the people remained under arms in the Piazza and round about the walls of the Citadel.   The said Abbot, being thus besieged, he and Messer Gomez and

[1] This Messer Ranieri was one of the very few Perugians who refused to join the rebellion.   PELLINI, i. 1143.

[2] *Grelli* for *grilli*.   The *grillo* was a military engine of the nature of the *Testudo*.   See *Arch. Stor. It.*, XVI. i. 221 n. 1.

[3] PELLINI (i. 1144) has " infino alle case de' Ranieri."

[4] *Gatti* were battering-rams, so that it is presumable that the *grelli* here mentioned were *testudines arietariæ*.

[5] The object of the insurgents was the isolation of the citadel.   The first step, therefore, was to burn *il ponte del cassero di S. Antonio*, that no reinforcements might be introduced into the city ; and then to separate the fortress of S. Antonio from the citadel by the destruction of the *ala*.   To make this clearer I have added the words " from without " in square brackets.   They have no equivalent in the original.

the other adherents of the Church who were therein, sent to beseech the company of the English, which was without the walls of the city, to wit at Ponte S. Giovanni, to give them succour; but Giovanni Aguto and the other captains who were with him were wise men and did naught, for our lord Priors and Chancellors sent ambassadors unto the camp to the said Messer Giovanni and to his companions, praying them not to aid the French against the people of Perugia; and because of their importunity and of a certain sum of money which the said English had from the Commune of Perugia, they gave no help to them which were in the Citadel. Now our ambassadors were Gualfreduccio di Messer Giapeco [Degli Oddi][1] and Messer Giapeco d' Agnolello; and wellnigh every day they rode to the camp to speak with Messer Giovanni Aguto.[2] Meantime a *trabocco* was constructed between the Vescovado and the Fountain of the Piazza, the largest and most beautiful which ever was seen. The beam thereof was fifty feet long, and it cast stones fifteen hundred pounds in weight.[3] This *trabocco* did great hurt to them which were in the Citadel, and thereby was slain Messer Francesco of S. Fiora, what time he stood with Messer Gomez on the tower before the Piazza. . . ." Indeed, so effective was this instrument, and such terror did it cause the garrison, that the Perugians christened it *Cacciapreti* or "priest-hunter."[4] "Also

[1] See PELLINI, i. 1145. "Dominus Gualfredutius domini Iacopi de Oddonibus" is registered in the *Libro Rosso* among the Mangnates et Nobiles, etc., de Porta S. Susanne.

[2] Giovanni Aguto is, of course, Sir John Hawkwood. The Florentines seem to have entertained considerable doubts of his good faith; and, in their letters of the 22nd and 29th of December, exhort the Perugians not to trust him too implicitly, but to prevent any chance of reinforcements being introduced into the city by completing the "bastitam quam extra civitatem contra casserum sancti Anthonij prudentissime munivistis." See DEGLI AZZI, *op. cit.*, i. pp. 123-125, §§ 419, 422.

[3] Compare MURATORI, *Dissertazione*, xxvi., and NAPIER, *Florentine History*, i. 630-631. In his article on *La Fortezza di Porta Sole* (*ubi cit.*), G. BACILE DI CASTIGLIONE asserts positively that this *trabocco* must have been a cannon (*una grossa bombarda*). His position, however, appears to me wholly untenable in view of the details given by the chronicler both with regard to its construction and the nature of the projectiles which it discharged.

[4] See PARRUCCIO ZAMPOLINI, *Annali di Spoleto, ubi cit.*, p. 114.

a mangonel was set up in the cloister of S. Lorenzo, which cast stones of fifty pounds weight all the day long, and did, passing, great damage to the enemy ; for the which cause they which were within the Citadel sought to make peace with our commune ; wherefore our ambassadors spake with Messer Giovanni, and agreed with him after this manner, namely, that the Abbot and all they who were with him should depart safely, they and all their goods ; and for greater security two trusty and indifferent men were chosen to hold the Citadel until such time as they should have reached a safe place ; to wit, on their behalf, Messer Trinci of Foligno, and, on ours, Messer Raniere, Marquis of Monte S. Maria.   But, or ever the said peace was made, on the next day after our rebellion, to wit on Saturday, an ambassador was sent to Florence, praying that commune to send us instant aid against the said pastors of the Church ;[1] and anon, as soon as the Florentines had received our embassy, without any delay they sent to Perugia five hundred lances of the folk of the League, and therewithal a fair company of foot-soldiers, which stood on guard in our Piazza every night ; and three hundred lances abode in the Palace of the Captain. . . . With them came the Ambassadors of Florence, of Siena, and of Arezzo, cities of the League.[2] And to the end that the Church might not be able to succour our enemies, the people of Perugia forthwith began to build a *battifolle* before the gate of the fortress of S. Antonio, outside the walls of the city hard by the kiln, which is above S. Maria di Monte Luce ; . . . and so close was it to the fortress that every little cross-bow might shoot thereunto.[3]

"In 1376, on the 1st of January of the new year, on a Thursday morning, all the folk of the Church came out of

[1] Compare GHERARDI, *op. cit.*, Doc. cix.

[2] In token of gratitude the Perugian citizenship was granted to the Otto di Balìa of Florence. See GHERARDI, *op. cit.*, Doc. ccclxxxvi., and DEGLI AZZI, i. pp. 143-144, § 502. Compare also PELLINI, i. 1203 ; BONAZZI, i. 491. Apparently Siena and Arezzo, as well as Florence, sent troops to the succour of the Perugians. See FABRETTI, *Cronache*, i. 65, 122. According to the *Cronica Sanese* (*ubi cit.*, col. 247), "Sanesi vi mandaro e rimaservi 500 fanti al servizio del Popolo di Perugia."

[3] See page 261 n. 2 *supra*.

the Citadel and down through the *ala* of S. Antonio,[1] and
entered into the fortress and departed thence by the way
which goeth to S. Giorgio. They brought with them all
their gear, as much as they and their horses might carry ;
but the grain and the wine and the things belonging to the
Commune which had been taken into the Citadel they
carried not away ;[2] and so they gat them thence at the
hour of terce. . . . The first to come forth was Messer Bernardo della Sala, an Englishman, a great captain who had
been castellan of the fortress, and after him Cucco, another
great captain. Then came Messer Ugo, the Pope's kinsman, then Grazino, a soldier of the Church, then the Bishop
of Bologna, then Messer Gomez, and then the Abbot which
was our seignior, to whom may God do ill ! all of them
unarmed, some on foot and some on horseback. Thereafter
followed all the other folk, both cavalry and infantry, to the
number of more than fifteen hundred, the greater part
whereof were fighting men ; and for their escort Messer
Giovanni Aguto and Messer Giovanni Breccia came even
unto the fortress with three hundred lances of their English
company."

The departure of Marmoutier seems to have been ignominious enough even to satisfy his worst enemies. The
ground was muddy with recent rain, and, clad in heavy
armour, he could scarcely drag one foot after another.
From the Porta S. Antonio the slope is still a steep one,
and, in those days, was probably far more so. Terrified by
the jeers and execrations of the populace, the Abbot slipped
and fell more than once. Clutching wildly at the soldiers
for protection and support, he finally reached the high road
and was set upon a horse, but not before he and his companions had been despoiled of all their goods. Indeed,
according to Pellini, the fugitives were pursued as far as the

---

[1] According to PELLINI (i. 1148) a wooden bridge had been constructed
during the night to enable Marmoutier and his attendants to cross over
that part of the *ala* which had been destroyed by the insurgents.

[2] Among other things which were left behind in the Citadel were " 650
balestre grosse, 230 cassette di verrettoni, 18 spingarde, 5 manganelle
picciole e 500 verrettoni grossi," all of which were transferred by the
Perugians to the public armoury. See PELLINI, i. 1150.

Tiber, and some of them were killed.[1] The substantial truth of his narrative appears to be confirmed by documentary evidence, since, in an inventory of the stolen property which was restored to its owners a few days later, by the command of the magistrates of Perugia, we find not only armour, clothing, and other personal effects, but also " *equi, ronzoni et muli, in totum numero xxxvij.*" [2] At first sight the thing appears incomprehensible. Even if, as one chronicler asserts, the escort consisted of only a hundred lances instead of three hundred, such a force of regular troops should surely have experienced but little difficulty in repelling the attacks of an undisciplined mob. Probably, however, the explanation may be found in the statement of Montemarte, who informs us that Hawkwood awaited the Abbot and his companions at some distance from the walls, and that they took the wrong road and so failed to find him.[3]

Of the fortress of S. Antonio a good part still remains to us, but that of Porta Sole has wholly disappeared. Hardly had the French left the city than the work of demolition began ; the *ale*, walls, and towers were forthwith razed to the ground ; and, in 1389, the spot which had been occupied by the moat in front of the principal gateway, was levelled to form the Piazza della Paglia.[4] A good many of the houses and palaces which had been built within the Citadel, were, however, left standing, to be inhabited in after years by Biordo Michelotti, by Braccio, and by Piccinino ; but, in the end, these too were destroyed in the conflagration of 1463 ;[5] and, to-day, scarcely a vestige remains to mark the site of what was once " la più bella fortezza che fosse in Italia."

The Perugians celebrated their recovered freedom with

---

[1] PELLINI, i. 1148-1149.

[2] *Arch. Stor. It.*, XVI. ii. pp. 547-553.

[3] MONTEMARTE, i. 42 : " Era poco lontano messer Giovanni Acuti che li doveva ricevere, ma si perdiro di strada."

[4] PELLINI, i. 1371. The ancient name of *Piazza della Paglia* was changed for that of *Piazza del Papa* in 1816, when the bronze statue of Pope Julius III. was removed thither from its original site, " su a la porta de Santo Lorenzo, cioè sotto la volta." FABRETTI, *Cronache*, ii. 219.

[5] PELLINI, ii. 671.

the wildest rejoicings; and, for a perpetual memorial of
their great deliverance, it was ordered that the 7th of
December, the day of St Ambrose, should be observed for
ever as a solemn festival of thanksgiving.[1]   For the moment,
the old rancours were entirely forgotten. Nobles and people
had fought side by side against the common enemy, and
were content to share the fruits of victory.   Even before the
capitulation of the Citadel, steps had been taken which
practically removed all the disabilities under which the
former had laboured for the last four decades;[2] and, on the
13th of January, 1376, the General Council "civium
perusinorum artificium nobilium et popularium" decreed
that the Nobles might freely inscribe themselves in the
Colleges of the Arts and be admitted to the public offices.[3]
Among the Priors, elected on the 4th of March, were Filippo
di Oddo Degli Oddi and Pellino di Cucco Baglioni;[4] while,
on the 16th of the same month, it was resolved that the
number of the Priors should be increased to twelve, three of
whom should be nobles.[5]   On the 29th, a *balìa* of ten
citizens, among whom was Simone di Filippuccio Baglioni,
was appointed to revise the statutes, and to expunge the
enactments contrary to the nobles.[6]

The Feast of S. Ercolano, which had ceased to be commem-
orated during the papal tyranny, was once more solemnized
with more than all its ancient pomp. The festivities lasted
for nearly a week, and not only the Companies of the Gates,

---

[1] PELLINI, i. 1163.

[2] See ANSIDEI, *Alcuni appunti per la storia delle famiglie perugine
Baglioni e Degli Oddi.*   Per le nozze Manzoni-Degli Oddi (Perugia, Unione
Tip. Cooperativa, 1901), p. 21.   On the 15th of December, three of the
Priors being dead, their successors were chosen by a *balìa* of which Oddo
Baglioni and Oddo Degli Oddi were members.   Among those who were
elected was " dominus Bartholomeus domini Felcini miles."   According to
MONTEMARTE (i. 42) the insurrection was mainly due to the " Baglioni
et altri gentilhomini," and we find that, on the 14th of January, 1376, the
General Council granted to Oddo Baglioni, " in ejus vita dumtaxat fortili-
tium hospitalis de Colle cum omnibus juribus, emolumentis, pertinentiis,"
on the ground that " pro honore et statu comunis Perusij cum omnibus
de domo sua posuerunt vitam et opes pro recuperatione presentis liberi
status civitatis."   (*Ann. Decemv.*, c. 18.)

[3] ANSIDEI, *ubi cit.*; *Ann. Decemv.*, c. 18.   [4] *Ann. Decemv.*, c. 39.

[5] PELLINI, i. 1154; *Ann. Decemv.*, cc. 41t, 42r.

[6] *Ann. Decemv.*, cc. 45t e 54r.

but Nobles and *popolari*, staid jurists and learned professors,
nay, even the very Priors and Camarlenghi danced publicly
through the piazze.[1]   It is true that there were no longer
any subject cities to present their offerings of tribute, *palii*
and *cere* ; but the almost daily news of fresh papal reverses
no doubt did much to compensate for their absence.
Indeed, the temporal dominion of the Church might have
been swept away for ever, if Florence could have brought
about the Italian League which she desired.   But Rome
hung back.   In vain the *Otto Santi* adjured her, with
burning words, to take up the proud position to which her
ancient glories entitled her, to expel so foul an abomination
(*tantam abominationem*) from the Ausonian coasts, and to
live free among the free.[2]   It has been well said that, "from
a commercial point of view, the Pope was to Rome what
Diana was to Ephesus," and, unhappily, she was too eager
for the material prosperity and wealth which the residence of
the Papal Curia would bring her to listen patiently to the
remonstrances of the Florentines.   Her self-seeking deprived
Italy of her last real chance of freedom for wellnigh . five
centuries.   " There is," says Bonazzi, " no Italian city which
does not deserve well of Italy for some great deed ; but
neither is there any which does not owe atonement for some
grievous crime committed against her." [3]

In March, 1376, to the cry of *Viva la Chiesa*, Faenza
was horribly sacked by Hawkwood and his English ; all
the inhabitants were expelled except such women as the
soldiers kept for their own lusts ; even the sacred character of the nunneries could not protect their inmates
from outrage ; and, if the frightful story of the doings
of those ruffians told by Fra Filippo of Siena be even
approximately true, we can hardly quarrel with the assertion that, at least in those days, an Italianized Englishman was the devil incarnate.[4]   In May, a company of

---

[1] PELLINI, i. 1152.

[2] GREGOROVIUS, *op. cit.*, Vol. III. Lib. xii. cap. ii. pp. 506-507.   Compare also GHERARDI, *op. cit.*, Doc. cxl.   [3] BONAZZI, i. 487.

[4] See *Gli Assempri di Fra Filippo*, etc., *op. cit.*, cap. lviii. ; *Cronica
Riminese*, in MURATORI, *R. I. S.*, xv. 914, and AMMIRATO (edition cited),
Vol. III. Lib. xiii. p. 246.

Bretons left Avignon under Cardinal Robert of Geneva, boasting that if the sun's rays could find their way into Florence they could do the like ;[1] and, in September, Gregory XI. himself set out for Rome, which he entered on the 17th of January, 1377, not as St Catherine would have had him enter it, "with crucifix in hand, like a gentle dove," but surrounded by the ferocious mercenaries of Raymond de Turenne.[2] Little more than two weeks later the terrible massacre of Cesena thrilled all Italy with horror.[3] Masses were said for the souls of the victims in Perugia and in the other cities of the League ;[4] the Florentine ambassadors, who had arrived in Rome on the 26th of January, departed full of grief and indignation, and the war against " the accursed pastors of the Church " was continued with renewed vigour.[5] Fortunately, however, the death of Gregory, in March, 1378, was followed by the election of two rival Popes,[6] each of whom was naturally anxious to gain every possible ally ; and, before many months were over, the

[1] AMMIRATO, *ubi cit.*, p. 243.

[2] GREGOROVIUS, *op. cit.*, Vol. III. Lib. xii. cap. ii. p. 515, and p. 522 n. 66. *Cf.* GARDNER, *op. cit.*, p. 201.

[3] AMMIRATO (*ubi cit.*, p. 257) tells us that, by comparison, the sack of Faenza " parve una specie di mansuetudine e di cortesia." In addition to the chronicles, see G. GORI, *L' eccidio di Cesena del 1377 di anonimo scrittore coetaneo*, in the *Arch. Stor. It.*, N.S., T. viii., P. II. p. 1.

[4] According to the *Cronica Sanese, ubi cit.*, col. 253, the example seems to have been set by Perugia : " Li Perugini subito, e quasi tutta la Lega ne fero fare Vigilie e dire Messe, serrare buttighe, tutti li Rettori e tutti li Cittadini con molta cera in tutte le chiese, e spezialmente nelle maggiori se ne fe' pietosi e divoti e lagrimosi ossequj."

[5] Meanwhile, however, the negotiations for peace continued. On the 3rd of June, 1377, ambassadors were elected to treat with the Pope, but nothing was accomplished, and, in September, 160 florins of gold were voted by the Priors and Camarlenghi to do honour to Sir John Hawkwood, who was expected in Perugia " cum mangna hominum comitiva ad defensam perusine civitatis et aliorum colligatorum, ad extirpandum sevissimam rabiem clericorum." (ANSIDEI, *op. cit.*, p. 22 n. ; *Ann. Decemv.*, cc. 122ʳ, 197 e 217ᵗ.) After the manner of his kind the great English *condottiere* had not hesitated to change sides as soon as it proved to his interest to do so. As to the details of the war, see PELLINI, ad annos 1377-1378.

[6] With regard to the origin of the schism, consult E. G. GARDNER, *op. cit.*, chap. xii. His account of this extraordinary event is based upon original documents in the *Archivio Segreto* of the Vatican, which had not been made accessible when CREIGHTON wrote his *History of the Papacy*.

revolted communes easily made their peace with an enfeebled and divided Papacy.

On the 1st of November, Urban VI. addressed a most conciliatory brief to "our well-beloved sons the people of our Perugian Commune," wherein he expressed himself as so confident in their sense of justice and reverence for the Church that he was willing to leave the manner and form of their reconciliation with her entirely to their own discretion.[1] The advancement of Andrea Bontempi, Bishop of Perugia, to the Cardinalate, in the previous September, had flattered the pride of his fellow-citizens ;[2] and, thanks in a measure to his good offices, negotiations proceeded with so much smoothness that articles of peace were signed on the 4th of January, 1379.[3] By the terms of this instrument, of which an elaborate synopsis is given us by Pellini, the suzerainty of the Holy See was duly acknowledged, and the Perugians agreed to pay an indemnity and an annual tribute ; but the Commune was confirmed in all its ancient privileges and immunities, while the Priors and their successors were created Vicars of the Church for a hundred years.[4]

Hardly had Perugia made her peace with Urban than, on the 17th of April, the Antipope, Clement VII., issued his famous Bull creating the Kingdom of Adria, including Ferrara, Bologna, Ravenna, all Romagna, the March of Ancona, Perugia, Todi, and Spoleto—the greater part, in fact, of the Papal States—and conferred it on Louis of Anjou. "The Avignonese pretender was resolved to show how little he cared for Italy or for the old traditions of the Italian greatness of his office."[5]

[1] The document is published by PELLINI, i. 1237, and BONAZZI, i. 494.
[2] PELLINI, i. 1220-1221, 1231.
[3] MARIOTTI, *Saggio*, etc., *op. cit.*, p. 85.
[4] PELLINI, i. 1238-1242. Compare also SCALVANTI, *Considerazioni*, etc., *op. cit.*, p. 84.
[5] CREIGHTON, *op. cit.*, i. 81 ; GARDNER, *op. cit.*, p. 307 ; GREGOROVIUS, *op. cit.*, Vol. III. Lib. xii. cap. iii. p. 542.

CHAPTER XX

THE RASPANTI AND THE NOBLES

FOR a time it seemed as if the days when Perugia was the acknowledged head of Umbria had returned once more. Every year saw some fresh *palio* waving beneath the Campanile of S. Lorenzo ;[1] and even if the number of subject towns never reached that of 1351, the number of those which were *raccomandate* was possibly greater.[2] Had she known how to use her opportunities all might yet have been well. Her only real danger was the Papacy ; and, during the thirty-eight years of the Great Schism, time was given her to set her house in order and to prepare for the inevitable struggle. Internal union might still have made her one of the most powerful communes of Italy. Good and evil were within her grasp, but she chose the latter, and her strength was wasted by internal strife. The harmony between the People and the Nobles hardly outlived the occasion which had given it birth, and no sooner was she well rid of her oppressors than the old jealousies broke forth anew.

Already, in the summer of 1376, the lawless behaviour of certain *Beccarini*[3] had given cause for uneasiness ;[4] but it was not until eighteen months later that the peril became palpable and urgent. The year 1377 closed amid general

[1] In 1377 there were only five *palii* ; in 1380 there were fifteen ; in 1381, nineteen, and in 1382, twenty-three. See PELLINI, i. 1169, 1259, 1281.
[2] BONAZZI, i. 495. *Cf.* SCALVANTI, *Considerazioni*, etc., *op. cit.*, pp. 35-86.
[3] See pages 44-45 *supra*.
[4] MAROTTI, *Saggio*, etc., *op. cit.*, p. 511 ; *Ann. Decemv.*, ad ann. c. 121. On the 2nd July it was resolved that the Maggior Sindaco should keep an increased number *famulorum et biruariorum*, because *multi dissoluti et celeribus dediti, qui Beccarini et malœ aviati vulgo appellantur, multa mala et enormia, die noctuque perpetravit* (sic) *et faciunt, arma quoque offenibilia portando.*

suspicion ; no man ventured forth unarmed,[1] and there were persistent rumours of impending tumult. Some said that the Raspanti were preparing to attack the Nobles, others that the Nobles were intriguing with the Pope ; and, on the 4th of January, 1378, to the end that the Commune of Perugia might be preserved "in sua sancta libertate," the Council of the Priors and the Chancellors of the Arts appointed a special commission to inquire into the matter.[2] On the 19th it was resolved that, pending these investigations, both Nobles and Raspanti should be excluded from the Signoria ; and, instead of drawing the names of the Priors who were to hold office during the next two months from the election-purses in the usual way, they were chosen "a saputa" and from the ranks of the *popolo minuto*.[3] Meanwhile the Commissioners were busy, and, after examining numerous witnesses, came to the conclusion that a widespread conspiracy was on foot " pro subvertendo et destruendo statum popularem liberum pacificum et tranquillum civitatis Perusij."[4] Early in February a General Council was assembled, and, "in the presence of much people," the Nobles were openly accused of plotting with Ugolino Montemarte, Count of Corbara,[5] and other partisans of the Church, to massacre the Raspanti. To the cry of "Live the People and die the traitors!" the populace rushed to arms. Several of the nobles were slain, and many fled the city ;[6] and, although the accusation was probably a slander,[7] the majority of the fugitives were condemned to banishment, and ordered to take up their residence in places assigned to them by the Magistrates. A few were given the option of a fine,[8] but

---

[1] *Ann. Decemv.*, c. 18t, 2 gennaio, 1378 : " . . . cum per cives perusinos et alios in civitate burgis et suburgis Perusij ultra modum consuetum . . . arma portantur et differuntur."

[2] *Ann. Decemv.*, c. 21 ; Ansidei, *op. cit.*, p. 23.   [3] Pellini, i. 1193-1197.

[4] *Ann. Decemv.*, c. 43r, 3 febbraio, 1378.

[5] The brother of Francesco Montemarte, the chronicler.

[6] Pellini, i. 1197-1198 ; Fabretti, *Cronache*, i. 123 ; *Arch. Stor. It.* XVI. i. 226.

[7] See Pellini, i. 1199. Bonazzi (i. 490-491) has, of course, no doubt about the matter. For him, the bare fact that the accused were nobles is sufficient to raise an irrebuttable presumption of their guilt.

[8] For the names of the proscribed, see Pellini, i. 1200-1201, and Ansidei *op. cit.*, p. 24 n.

all, without exception, were absolutely debarred from holding office, and the election-purses were filled, as of old, with the names of "good and loyal men, lovers of liberty and the *stato popolare*."[1]

The narrow oligarchy of the Raspanti once more ruled supreme; but the times were difficult; Italy was overrun by Companies of Adventure;[2] the public treasury was wellnigh empty,[3] and the multitude of exiles were an ever present source of anxiety.[4]   The bare name of *fuoruscito* seems to have driven the Magistrates half crazy with terror; and when peace was made with the Pope, and the public rejoicings were at their height, a certain Francesco d' Agnoluccio was beheaded merely for saying, " So peace is made, is it?   Let the *fuorusciti* return and we shall see."[5]   Fresh laws were enacted against the Nobles,[6] and such of them as ventured to depart from the towns to which they had been banished, or were reported to be plotting against the State, were punished by the destruction of their palaces and estates.[7]   These severities, however, only served to exasperate the victims, and ere long we find the exiles grown so bold that they frequently rode to the very gates of the city for the purpose of communicating with their friends and adherents within the walls.[8]   The Priors and the other Magistrates went in hourly peril of their lives, and a special ordinance was passed permitting them to carry arms of every descrip-

---

[1] PELLINI, i. 1208.

[2] See the contemporary documents edited by DEGLI AZZI, *op. cit.*, i. p. 146-169 *passim*.   PELLINI (i. 1279) speaks of the " grande inondatione i genti barbare per lo Territorio perugino."

[3] Perugia was already largely in debt to Bernabò Visconti, to Venice, and to Florence ; and Florence, at any rate, was pressing for payment. See DEGLI AZZI, *op. cit.*, i. §§ 515, 520, 524, 531, etc. etc.

[4] ANSIDEI, *op. cit.*, p. 25.

[5] PELLINI, i. 1246 ; BONAZZI, i. 497.   [6] PELLINI, i. 1232.

[7] In the cities to which they were banished the exiles were ordered " se representare coram majori offitiali et rectore ter vel quater in edomada et mictere instrumentum representationis de mense in mense " (*Ann. Decemv.*, cc. 116 *et seq.*, 15 aprile, 1378).

[8] PELLINI, i. 1244.   By a printer's error there are, in the *Historia* of Pellini, Vol. I., two sets of pages, both of which are numbered from 1236 to 1255.   The passage referred to is in the second series.

tion, whether prohibited by the statute or not.[1]   In August, 1380, the Florentines wrote to warn their allies that there were numerous *fuorusciti* with the army of Charles of Durazzo, and that they would probably attempt a *coup de main* when they reached Perugian territory;[2] Gubbio was full of them,[3] and the *contado* was harried from one end to the other.[4]   They even attempted to surprise Assisi;[5] while, in the autumn of 1381, they took advantage of the difficulties in which the Commune found itself by reason of the war with Città di Castello,[6] to seize and occupy many subject towns and villages.[7]   The centre of their operations was Castel d' Arno, which they had taken at the end of September, or beginning of October, 1381, and held until January, 1382, when the Perugians succeeded in recovering it, not by force of arms, but by the treachery of the mercenaries who formed the garrison.[8]

This reverse did little to check the activity of the exiles and, in the following September, an insurrection broke out in Perugia itself.   It was headed by Giacomo d' Oddo of Porta S. Angelo, and was only suppressed after much hard fighting;[9] the leaders were proclaimed as rebels and traitors of the Commune, but the Magistrates were afraid to take any steps to punish the majority of those implicated on the ground of their great numbers.[10]   Thus matters

[1] PELLINI, i. 1245.

[2] DEGLI AZZI, *op. cit.*, i. p. 158, § 562.   *Cf.* PELLINI, i. 1253.

[3] *Cronaca di Ser Guerriero da Gubbio, ubi cit.*, p. 19, ll. 12-14 : " . . vennero a stare in Ugobio molti usciti de Peroscia de Fabriano, de Assisi de Todi e de la Cetà de Castello, che fo facto conto ci erano più de doimilia forastieri."

[4] *Ann. Decemv.*, c. 161r, settembre, 1381 ; ANSIDEI, *op. cit.*, p. 26 n. PELLINI, i. 1275.

[5] DEGLI AZZI, *op. cit.*, i. p. 160, § 570.

[6] MUZI, *Memorie Civili*, etc., *op. cit.*, i. 187.   See also ANSIDEI e DEGL AZZI, *Regesto di Documenti del Sec. XIV. relativi a Città di Castello*, etc. in *Bollettino* cited, vii. pp. 349 *et seq.*

[7] *Ann. Decemv.*, 167t.

[8] ANSIDEI, *Alcuni appunti*, etc., *op. cit.*, p. 26 ; PELLINI, i. 1278 FABRETTI, *Cronache*, i. 66.

[9] PELLINI, i. 1290 ; *Arch. Stor. It.*, XVI. i. 228.

[10] " cum in proxima novitate attentata et facta in civitate Perusij pe quosdam robbatores et proditores comunis Perusij . . . multi et mult et in maximo numero fuerint culpabiles."

continued to go from bad to worse, until, in the autumn of 1383, a terrible rumour began to spread that even the ranks of the Raspanti were not free from taint. At first the thing appeared incredible, but ere long it was proved beyond any question of doubt that two of the Michelotti were intriguing with the Antipope and the Duke of Anjou. Every effort was made to induce them to return to their allegiance; they were promised a free pardon, and when they fled to their fortress of Castelnuovo, repeated embassies were sent thither to beseech them to reconsider their action. They, however, repaid the leniency of the Priors by raiding Il Chiugi with the mercenary bands of Bartolomeo da Pietramala and Boldrino da Panicale, by sacking Isola Maggiore and Isola Polvese,[1] and by leaguing themselves with Messer Guglielmo of Assisi; who, in his turn, surprised Coldimancio, and after ravaging the country up to Ponte S. Giovanni and Ponte Valle Ceppi, returned home loaded with booty.[2]

The result of this rebellion was to fling the city into hopeless confusion. Several of the kinsfolk and adherents of the Michelotti were roughly handled by the mob; one at least was slain and more than one sought safety in flight; while lawless and violent men who had private grudges to revenge took advantage of the turmoil to assassinate their enemies. To strike terror into evil doers the gallows and the headsman's block were set up in the Piazza, but apparently without effect, since we are informed that, in March, 1384, albeit the *palii* were presented as usual, there were no festivities nor any dancing of the Companies " by reason of the murders which were committed every day." [3]

To the Magistrates the treason of the Michelotti seemed all the more heinous in direct proportion to the value of the services which they had heretofore rendered to the Raspanti and to the Commune. Their guilt was, in fact, held to be analogous to that of a parricide who plants a dagger in the heart of his own flesh and blood; and for such iniquity

[1] PELLINI, i. 1307-1310; FABRETTI, *Biografie dei Capitani Venturieri dell' Umbria* (Montepulciano, Fumi, 1842), Vol. I. pp. 67-69.

[2] PELLINI, i. 1312; CRISTOFANI, *op. cit.*, i. 260.

[3] PELLINI, i. 1314.

18

what punishment could be excessive? In the pages of the *Annali Decemvirali* we find ample testimony of the indignation aroused by that "pestiferous conspiracy" hatched "per impios illos cives Nicolaum et Michelozum Ceccholini et quosdam alios in finale excidium populi et Comunis Civitatis Perusij et ejus desiderabilis libertatis"; we read how the Priors and Camarlenghi, to brand with indelible infamy the authors of so great a crime, resolved "quod domus dictorum Nicolai et Michelozi discarcari et demoliri debeant et quod ipsi debeant depingi pro proditoribus comunis Perusij in pariete Ecclesie Sancti Laurentij versus plateam in loco apparente et manifesto," and offered a reward of a thousand florins of gold to whomsoever should take or slay either of the traitors.[1]

Whether it was that their hatred of the Michelotti induced the Raspanti to forget the faults of the Nobles, or that it was recognized as hopeless to resist at one and the same time the assaults of both the old and the new rebels, this much is certain, that the exemplary punishment of the latter was almost immediately followed by the pardon and recall of the former. Welcomed to the city, "tamquam boni et fideles cives," they were not only reinstated in all their possessions, but were permitted to inscribe themselves in the Colleges of the Arts, thus acquiring the right to participate in the government of the Commune.[2]

According to the chronicle of Montemarte the return of the Nobles was followed by the immediate expulsion of the Raspanti,[3] and the same view seems to be taken by the author of the *Supplemento terzo alla Cronaca del Graziani*,

[1] ANSIDEI, *op. cit.*, p. 29; *Ann. Decemv.*, cc. 22t, 23r e 31t (1 e 6 marzo, 1384). The *Atti degli offiziali della guerra contro i rebelli* (14 Aprile al 15 Ottobre, 1384) commence with the statement that the said officials were elected "ad prosternandam et debellandam tirannicam pravitatem Guilielmini de Assisio et ad exterminandas machinationes filiorum Ceccholini et aliorum suis iniquitatibus adherentium, in quorum cordibus diabolus insignitus laborat eorum animas justis muneribus amplexando." Among the five officials were Pellino di Cucco Baglioni (*Arch. Decemv., Misc. N.* 110).

[2] ANSIDEI, *op. cit.*, pp. 29-30.

[3] MONTEMARTE, *Cronica* cited, pp. 53-54: "I Raspanti . . . rimisero dentro i gentilhomeni; i quali come furo dentro fecero novità, et cacciaro fuori i Raspanti, che l' havevano rimessi."

who informs us that the rule of the *Gentiluomini* lasted for nine years and three months, namely from the 1st of April, 1384, to July, 1393.[1] This, however, is certainly an exaggeration ; the complete supersession of the authority of the Raspanti was a gradual process; though it is quite possible that, almost from the very first, the Nobles acquired a preponderant influence in the councils of the State.[2] Their return, it is true, was inaugurated by a dangerous insurrection, in which, to the cry of " Live the People and die the Raspanti ! " more than thirty persons were slain ;[3] but this, if we may credit Pellini, was no fault of theirs, the rioters consisting almost entirely of *banditi,* or criminal outlaws, who, though not included in the general amnesty, which was applicable only to political offenders, had re-entered the city with the other *fuorusciti.* Indeed, it was largely owing to the efforts of the Nobles that the tumult was ultimately suppressed ;[4] and it was probably not until 1389 that they acquired an undisputed predominance in the State.[5]

Nevertheless, even from the first, their behaviour was hardly such as to inspire confidence ; and the chroniclers tell a horrible story of a certain Bettolo d' Andrucciolo di

[1] *Arch. Stor. It.*, XVI. i. 259 : " Il reggimento de i gentiluomini era durato anni nove e mesi tre, cioè dal 1384 el primo d'aprile fino al 1393, sempre gridando : Muoiano i Raspanti."

[2] On August 19th, 1384, the Florentines wrote to dissuade the Perugians from carrying out their resolution to change the government of the Commune (DEGLI AZZI, *Le Relazioni*, etc., *op. cit.*, i. 173, § 629)—an obviously useless step if the Raspanti were already expelled and the Nobles the sole rulers.

[3] *Arch. Stor. It.*, XVI. i. 229 (1st April, 1384).

[4] PELLINI, i. 1318-1319. Pellini is, in fact, our only authority. The chroniclers, with their accustomed brevity, give us no information concerning the cause of the tumult ; while, possibly owing to the disturbed condition of the city, there are no entries in the *Annali Decemvirali* between the 31st of March (the date of the decree admitting the Nobles to the Arts) and the 5th of April.

[5] GRAZIANI, p. 235 *et seq.* It was in this year that the Magistracy of the *Cinque di Arbitrio* was created, which practically superseded that of the Priors. (See PELLINI, ii. i.) In after years the number of its members was doubled ; but, whether the *Batìa* in question consisted of five or of ten, it was equally a dictatorship. See *Arch. Stor. It.*, XVI. ii. p. 635, in *Tavola alfabetica delle materie*, s.v. *Arbitrio*.

Barciglione, of what family I know not, who, having fled
from the city, was overtaken by some of the Montesperelli
not far from Colle Strada ; "and there, after cutting off
both his hands, his nose and his lips, they gouged out his
eyes and left him, marred beyond all human semblance, half
dead upon the high road ; and this those gentlemen did
because, a few years earlier, he had slain Monaldo di
Agabito, their kinsman."[1]   Such were the men whom the
Raspanti had recalled from banishment and reinstated in
the public offices.

The most lawless and violent section of the Nobles were
headed by that Pandolfo Baglioni whom Bonazzi calls "the
Perugian Satan" ;[2] and it was probably mainly due to his
example that the annalist is able to declare that, during the
years which followed, "there reigned in this poor city treasons,
rapes, homicides, assassinations, thefts, adulteries, violences,
sacrileges, and every manner of ill licence."[3]   One after
another all the Raspanti were driven into exile, thus increasing the number of the *fuorusciti* and rebels who continually
waged war against the Commune, while finally profound
dissensions arose in the breast of the dominant party itself ;
and in May, 1391, the Ranieri and Arcipreti, on the one side,
and the Baglioni, with Pandolfo at their head, on the other,
actually came to blows on Colle Landone ; so that it seemed
as if to the ever-present danger from without were to be added
the horrors of civil war within the very walls of the city.[4]
Under such circumstances, what wonder if the Perugians were
willing to accept the arbitrament even of the Papacy ?

Three years earlier, to the undisguised alarm of the
Florentines,[5] Urban VI. had visited Perugia, but then all the
Raspanti had not been banished ; and though the citizens
received him gladly and welcomed him royally, they had
still known how to protect their liberties from papal aggression.[6]   Now, on the contrary, when Boniface IX. entered

---

[1] PELLINI, i. 1319.   [2] BONAZZI, i. 512.
[3] FABRETTI, *Cronache*, i. 52 ; *Arch. Stor. It.*, XVI. i. 259.
[4] GRAZIANI, p. 253 ; PELLINI, ii. 19.
[5] DEGLI AZZI, *op. cit.*, i. p. xx. and p. 180, § 655.
[6] See MARIOTTI, *Saggio*, etc., *op. cit.*, pp. 476 *et seq.* DIETRICH VON
NIECHEIM (T. de Nyem, *De Schismate*, i. 67, ed. Erler, Lipsiæ, 1890,

Perugia on the 17th of October, 1392, he entered it as a sovereign, with absolute dominion over the city and *contado* for as long as he should choose to remain there ; the towns and fortresses of Castiglione del Lago, Fratta, Montone, and the Bastìa d' Assisi were delivered into his hands, and the Priors abandoned their palace in his favour. The only limitation to his authority consisted in a proviso that, in the event of his departure *animo non redeundi*, then and in such case the vicariate granted to the Commune by Pope Urban VI. of holy memory should, *ipso facto*, be revived.[1]

His first care was to bring about a peace between the contending factions and to persuade the Nobles to consent to the recall of the exiles. The magistrates were profuse in their expressions of loyalty and devotion, replying to his exhortations to unity in the words of the Lord's Prayer : *Fiat voluntas tua sicut in Cœlo et in Terra*. Yet barely a month had passed from the day of his arrival when the condemnation of a partisan of the Nobles by a papal official raised all the city in tumult. To the cry of " Live the Church and die the Raspanti ! " the proletariat flew to arms, and, led by Pandolfo Baglioni, massacred six persons ; one of the Priors who joined in the mêlée was wounded on the head by a stone, and Boniface became so much alarmed for his own safety that he abandoned the Communal Palace and took refuge in the Monastery of S. Pietro, which he ordered to be fortified and surrounded with moats and bastions. Fearing lest the punishment of the guilty should only tend to embitter factional hatred, he gave instructions that no process, whether civil or criminal, should be issued against

p. 117) informs us, in this connection, that, when Urban came from Lucca to Perugia, in 1388, " ubi pene per annum postea stetit, accidit tamen ibidem dicto Francisco seu Butillo magna contumelia, qui, more suo quandam nobilem dominam Perusinam adamavit, quod quosdam dicte domine fratres non latuit. Unde quadam vice, dum noctis sub silencio penes domum dicte domine habitu dissimulato idem Franciscus incederet, per dictos fratres in ipsum impetuose irruentes fuit fortiter baculatus. Quod dum sentiret dictus dominus Urbanus de hoc vehementer dolens extunc disposuit quod ab eadem civitate Perusina quantocicius recedere vellet." Butillo was the Pope's nephew. *Cf.* CREIGHTON, *op. cit.*, i. 101.

[1] See MARIOTTI, *Saggio*, etc., *op. cit.*, p. 498 *et seq.* ; *Annali Decemvirali*, ann. 1392-1393, c. 104-105 ; *Arch. Stor. It.*, XVI. ii. pp. 558-562.

those implicated in the recent disturbances, and finally prevailed upon the Priors and the principal citizens to grant him full powers to make peace with the *fuorusciti*.[1]

The difficult negotiations, in which the Commune of Florence also intervened,[2] dragged on for several months, and it was not until the 19th of May, 1393, that articles of agreement were signed at Deruta, whereby over two thousand Perugians were permitted to return to their homes. The *fuorusciti* re-entered the city on the 1st of July, and " a few days thereafter the Priors were published and made *a saputa*, and five of them were Gentlemen and five Raspanti ; and each of them entered upon his office honourably, in the house of Simone dell' Abbate, because the Palazzo de' Signori was adorned for the Pope." [3]   On the 25th of the month the Priors and the principal citizens made oath of fealty to Boniface in the Monastery of S. Pietro, and swore to maintain the peace which he had made ; [4] yet, only five days later, Perugia was once more in insurrection. The sanguinary conflict which broke out on the 30th of July proved that the hostile factions had, in fact, made peace with hatred in their hearts, and Pellini and Bonazzi hint at an agreement between the Baglioni and the Pope to the prejudice of the Raspanti.[5]   After a stubborn resistance the

---

[1] PELLINI, ii. 37 *et seq.* ; *Arch. Stor. It.*, XVI. i. 255-257 ; BONAZZI, i. 515-516 ; ANSIDEI, *op. cit.*, pp. 32-33.

[2] According to PELLINI (ii. 41) the Pope sent the Bishop of Fermo to Florence to beseech her intervention with the Perugians because " senza l' autorità di quella Republica, confidando essi più in ogni minimo Fiorentino che in lui, non era per riuscirli cosa alcuna." In response to this appeal, the Florentines wrote advising the Perugians to trust absolutely in the Pope " sicut optimo medico, verique et immortalis medici vero vicario," who would heal all their diseases (DEGLI AZZI, *Le Relazioni*, etc., *op. cit.*, i. 207, § 770. See also § 772.   [3] FABRETTI, *Cronache*, ii. 73.

[4] ANSIDEI, *op. cit.*, p. 34. They swore never to contribute " ad suscitandum tumultum aliquem vel rumorem," and to co-operate " ad conservandam et manutenendam et pro viribus augendam pacem . . . civitatis perusini per eundem Dominum nostrum celebratam."

[5] PELLINI, ii. 44 ; BONAZZI, i. 517 ; ANSIDEI, *op. cit.*, pp. 34-35. There is a lacuna in the *Annali Decemvirali* from July 12th to August 20th, which is only partially filled by a volume of *Riformanze*. But, when the record is resumed it certainly breathes no spirit of regret for the recent conflict. The 30th of July is spoken of as " dies salutis populi perusini." (*Ann. Decemv.*, c. 26, 20 Agosto, 1393.)

Nobles were worsted, and the chronicler asserts that " all the gentlemen of Perugia were driven into exile, so that there remained not one of them "[1]—a far more sweeping assertion than that of Graziani with regard to the insurrection of 1353.[2] Among the slain were Pandolfo and Pellino Baglioni and Oddo d' Agnoluccio Degli Oddi, the brother of the famous Miccia. Many were hurled from the windows of their palaces and towers to fall ruining on the stones below. Pellini tells us that the butchery continued for four days, for in their hour of victory the Raspanti showed no mercy.[3] On the evening of the 30th the Pope and his cardinals fled to Assisi, and on the 3rd of August Biordo Michelotti entered Perugia at the head of five hundred horse. The enthusiastic welcome which the valiant *condottiero* received at the hands of his fellow-citizens, and the extraordinary honours which were heaped upon him, lead us to suspect that he, albeit from a distance, had been the moving spirit of the rising which reconquered the city for the Raspanti. In confirmation of this view, we may cite the decree of the Priors and Camarlenghi of the 6th and 8th of September, which invested Biordo with the most absolute and unlimited authority to indicate, in conjunction with Bishop Pileo, Legate of the Apostolic See, and the Florentine ambassadors, Andrea de' Minerbetti and Guido di Tommaso, those who for political reasons ought to be exiled or otherwise punished ; while to Biordo alone was entrusted the naming of such citizens as deserved to be rewarded for their services, " pro recuperatione presentis popularis status."[4] He was appointed Captain-General of all the Perugian armies, with an allowance from the public treasury of a thousand florins a month ; a palace

---

[1] FABRETTI, *Cronache*, i. 204 : " . . . furono cacciati tutti i gentiluo-mini di Perugia, che non ci rimase niumo."

[2] GRAZIANI, p. 169 : " . . . dicti principali citadini così bellamenti se absentarono e partirono tutti da la cità." *Cf.* p. 208 *supra*.

[3] FABRETTI, *Cronache*, i. 51, 204, ii. 73-74 ; *Arch. Stor. It.*, XVI. i. 257-258 ; PELLINI, ii. 45-47. Compare also DEGLI AZZI, *op. cit.*, i. p. 209, §§ 779, 780. The Florentines, while deploring the tumult, declared that they had learned with rejoicing " inde stetisse factionem nobilium, hinc bonorum civium congregationem, illisque contigisse victoriam, qui pro iustitia resistebant."

[4] ANSIDEI, *op. cit.*, p. 35.

was purchased and furnished for his residence, and a bronze statue was erected to his honour on the southern side of the Cathedral, overlooking the Piazza.[1]

The list of the proscribed was diligently compiled, and scarcely one of the partisans of the defeated faction can have escaped the vigilance of the victors ; nor was it until nearly a year later that the sentences inflicted began to appear excessive.   Then, indeed, some of the penalties were diminished and some remitted ; but for the majority of the Baglioni, at any rate, there was no thought of mercy.   Of the revengeful sentiments which the popular party still cherished against this family we have evidence in a resolution of the 9th of September, 1394, whereby it was decreed that their houses should be demolished and the bricks thereof used to repair the streets of the city.   Among those included in the edict was that same Oddo Baglioni who had been rewarded by the Commune for his services against the Abbot of Mommaggiore ;[2] but the fury of the Raspanti was most violent against Pandolfo, whose very memory they would fain have destroyed and blotted out even as they destroyed the palace in which he had lived and lorded it so arrogantly.[3] Such enactments were inspired by a hatred, of which, in this less virile age, we can hardly form an adequate conception ; but it is only fair to remember that the old sores were never allowed time to heal, and that the machinations of the *fuorusciti* were an ever-present source of irritation and of peril.

For the twenty-three years which elapsed between the 30th of July, 1393, and the 19th of July, 1416 (the day on which, after the Battle of S. Egidio, the Nobles once more returned to their homes), the history of Perugia is little more than a narrative of the contest between the Commune and its

[1] PELLINI, ii. 48 ; FABRETTI, *Biografie*, etc., *op. cit.*, i. 38.

[2] See page 265 n. 2 *supra*.

[3] PELLINI, ii. 62 ; ANSIDEI, *op. cit.*, pp. 36-37 ; *Ann. Decemv.*, c. 157t. It was known (so runs the resolution) that " Pandolfum de Balionibus cum omnibus de domo sua fuisse semper rebellem et inimicum popularis status civitatis Perusij atque insudasse quantum in eo erat ad desolationem et destructionem popularis status et civitatis Perusij " ; wherefore it was fitting " non tantum ejus abolere memoriam sed etiam funditus eius domos et alias aliorum de domo discarcare et radicitus ruinare ne unquam possit in dictis domibus habitare."

exiles. The latter continually increased in strength, through the more or less open support of the Pope, through the discords which sprung up among the Raspanti themselves, and led to the miserable death of Biordo Michelotti, and, last but not least, through the wisdom and valour of Braccio Fortebracci. Of the tragedy of the 10th of March, 1398, it is unnecessary to speak at any length. Suffice it to recall the fact that, bribed by the promise of a Cardinal's hat and envious of the greatness of his victim, Francesco Guidalotti, Abbot of S. Pietro, with his brothers Anibaldo and Giovanni, assassinated Biordo in the cloister of his own house on the Monte di Porta Sole, under circumstances of the basest treachery. As the news of the crime spread through the city the whole population flew to arms, and the murderers, fleeing to Casalina, saw behind them the smoke of their burning palaces. They were condemned *in here et persona*, and their effigies were painted *ad portas et ad postribulum* ; [1] but the dagger which had ended the life of Biordo had also destroyed Perugian liberty.[2] The rebels were not slow to perceive all the advantages which they derived from his murder, and, led by Braccio,[3] they devoted themselves to the accomplishment of their end with ever-increasing energy and tenacity. The *deliberazioni* of the Priors and Camarlenghi, in the late summer and early autumn of 1398, indicate only too clearly the terrible condition of the body politic owing to the incessant attacks of the *fuorusciti* ; [4] while the deso-

[1] GRAZIANI, pp. 263-266 ; FABRETTI, *Cronache*, i. 56-60, 205-206, ii. 74-75 ; PELLINI, ii. 95-98. As to the complicity of the Pope, it has been urged that there is no documentary evidence which inculpates him. That is perfectly true, but in such a case we should hardly expect to find any. Neither in the character of Boniface nor in his subsequent conduct is there anything to render the statement of the chroniclers improbable. His one acknowledged virtue is his freedom from sexual vice, and that virtue he shared with Ezzelino da Romano !

[2] ANSIDEI, *op. cit.*, p. 39. Compare GRAZIANI, p. 273 : " Onde che, per farte de questo conclusione, la morte de Biordo tolse la grandezza e la reputazione a questa città de Peroscia."

[3] As soon as Biordo was dead Braccio seems to have come to an understanding with Miccia Degli Oddi and the other Nobles. PELLINI, ii. 98 ; BONAZZI, i. 619 ; FABRETTI, *Biografie*, etc. *Schiaramenti alla vita di Braccio*, p. 78.

[4] ANSIDEI, *ubi cit.*; *Ann. Decemv.*, cc. 123 e 161t (3 settembre e 2 novembre, 1398).

lated *contado* was overrun by great packs of wolves, which became so bold that they even ventured into the city itself.[1]

On the other hand, the Raspanti, rather than come to terms with the Nobles, did not hesitate to sacrifice the independence of the Commune. A few months after Biordo's death, Onofrio Bartolini was sent as ambassador to Milan,[2] and thus were begun those negotiations which ended in the submission of Perugia to Gian-Galeazzo Visconti. If it was necessary to submit to a despot at all, the choice was, perhaps, a prudent one. The citizens had already suffered too much from ecclesiastical tyranny to lend a willing ear to papal blandishments,[3] and even if the partiality of the Pope for the *fuorusciti* had been less marked than it was, his insincerity and duplicity would have rendered it sheer folly to trust him. As Bonazzi justly remarks, of the half-dozen conventions which the Raspanti had concluded with Boni-

---

[1] See PELLINI, i. 1335 and ii. 19. The following passage from the chronicle of Fra Salimbene of Parma is worth comparing. That he was writing of events which took place some century and a half earlier is immaterial. The conditions were the same : —" For in the days of Frederick, and especially from the time when he was deposed from the Empire, and when Parma lifted up her head against him, ' the paths rested, and they that went by them walked through by-ways.' And evils were multiplied on the earth ; and the wild beasts and fowls multiplied and increased beyond all measure—pheasants and partridges and quails, hares and roebucks, fallow deer and buffaloes, and wild swine and ravening wolves. For they found no beasts in the villages to devour according to their wont : neither sheep nor lambs, for the villages were burned with fire. Wherefore the wolves gathered together in mighty multitudes round the city moats, howling dismally for exceeding anguish of hunger ; and they crept into the cities by night and devoured men and women and children who slept under the porticoes or in waggons. Nay, at times they would even break through the house walls and strangle the children in their cradles.'" (COULTON, *From St Francis to Dante, op. cit.*, p. 60. *Cf.* also pp. 39, 171, 249.) Names of places, such as *Montelupo, Montelupone, Lupara, Lupaiolo,* etc., etc., tell their own tale as to the condition of mediæval Italy; while the Perugian chroniclers of a much later period show how quickly a devastating war caused the countryside in the immediate neighbourhood of the cities to be " overrun with wolves and deer and wild goats and every kind of beast of the field, in great multitudes and innumerable." MATARAZZO, *Cronica*, in *Arch. Stor. It.*, T. XVI. P. II. p. 15.

[2] *Ann. Decemv.*, c. 135[t] (1398). He was invested " cum arbitrio et potestate plenissima faciendi, perpetrandi et concludendi omnia et singula que ad statum, unionem et preservantiam utilia seu necessaria fore cognoverit quovis modo."   [3] PELLINI, ii. 99.

face, " not one had been observed for a single day." [1]   Moreover, they wisely preferred a new and distant master to an
old and near one.   In vain the Florentines exhorted them
not to trust a prince whose one desire was " to swallow up
their liberty and that of all Italy," [2] whose " preludes and
beginnings are bland and honied and sweet, but the end
thereof harsh and bitter and full of poison." [3]   In vain they
sought to bring about an accommodation with the Pope ;
his unconcealed determination to assert his dominion over
Perugia,[4] and the favour which he showed to the Guidalotti
and the other rebels,[5] rendered all their efforts abortive.   It
is true that peace was actually concluded in 1399 ; [6] but the
good understanding with the Visconti continued unimpaired,
and "on the 19th day of January, 1400, a General Council
assembled in Perugia, in the which all the Raspanti and the
people with one accord gave themselves freely, with all the
City of Perugia and all the *contado*, to the Duke of Milan," [7]
who, for his part, promised that neither he nor his officials
would ever readmit the exiles, and that he would always
hold the Abbot of S. Pietro and his brethren for mortal
enemies.[8]

[1] BONAZZI, i. 523 ; ANSIDEI, *op. cit.*, p. 40.

[2] DEGLI AZZI, *op. cit.*, i., § 894.

[3] DEGLI AZZI, *op. cit.*, i., § 906.   *Cf.* the documents published in *Arch. Stor. It.*, XVI. ii. pp. 566-570.

[4] See ANSIDEI, *op. cit.*, p. 40, and documents cited in note 1.

[5] On the 20th of June, 1399, he lamented that the goods of the Guidalotti were not yet restored to them, and that their effigies still remained painted in infamous places ; while, on the 8th of December, he even more energetically commanded the magistrates to make peace with the Guidalotti and the other *fuorusciti*, by the mediation of Marino Tomacelli, castellan of the fortress of Spoleto (*Bolle e Diplomi*, B. n. 272 e 274 ; *Arch. Stor. It.*, XVI. ii. 565).

[6] PELLINI, ii. 107.   *Cf.* DEGLI AZZI, *op. cit.*, ii. p. 200, § 800.

[7] *Arch. Stor. It.*, XVI. i. 274-275.   See also MINERBETTI, *Cronica* (in MANNI, *S. R. I.*, ii. 414-415) there cited.   It is asserted by Miss C. M. ADY (*A History of Milan under the Sforza*, London, Methuen & Co., 1907, p. 6) that " Perugia made a desperate attempt to escape the fate of her sister republics (*i.e.* subjection to the Duke of Milan) by taking Sforza into her service. . . . " I have in vain endeavoured to find any authority for this statement.   She cites none, and no data which I can gather from Perugian chronicles or documents lend it the slightest support.

[8] Among the *capitoli* of the submission to Gian-Galeazzo, executed on the 20th of January, 1400, is the following clause : " Item al facto degli

Henceforward, Boniface openly sustained the cause of the exiles, and finally, in October, 1402, after the death of Gian-Galeazzo,[1] sent his brother Gianello Tomacelli, against Perugia, " with three hundred lances and a thousand lances of the Commune of Florence, and all the force of our *fuorusciti* with three hundred horse ; and they besieged the city round about so that no man was able to issue therefrom, and they took many of our walled places." [2]   Long and fierce was the resistance which the Perugians opposed to the papal arms ; but the death of the Duke had deprived them of all hope of effectual succour, and when, in October, 1403, the Duchess Caterina Visconti professed herself helpless to protect them any longer, and counselled them to make their peace with the Pope,[3] they abandoned the useless struggle.   Nevertheless, they would not even now consent to the return of the exiles, and among their *capitoli* of submission to the Church was one which provided for the continued banishment of the *fuorusciti*, and particularly of the Guidalotti.[4]   On the 20th of November, Gianello

oscite de Peroscia . . . promecte el dicto Piero [Scrovigno] en vece et en nome del dicto Signore maie per veruno tempo non remettere veruno nè fare remettere de quegnunche conditione se fosse per sè nè per suo offitiagli, cioè quilgli che sonno de fuore de Peroscia per cagione de Stato," who must always remain " da vinte milgla en fuore del contado de Peroscia. E quisto non s' entenda per verun modo de l' Abate de Santo Pietro e dei fratelgli o altre sue consorte e amice condannate per lo Comuno, ei quagli deggano remanere principagli nemici del Signore mesere lo Duca, commo sonno al presente del Comuno " (*Ann. Decemv.*, c. 13t).

[1] Gian-Galeazzo died on the 3rd of September, 1402, and, on the 26th, the Ducal Lieutenant, the Priors and the Officiali di Arbitrio sent ambassadors to the Duchess and to the youthful Gio. Maria, " ad condolendum et lamentum faciendum cum illustrissima domina Duchessa de obitu condam sancte et per comunitatem perusinam recolende memorie domini nostri domini Ducis Mediolani et ad recommendandum comunitatem predictam perusinam dicto domino nostro novello." *Ann. Decemv.*, c. 110r.

[2] *Arch. Stor. It.*, XVI. i. 276 ; FABRETTI, *Cronache*, i. 208, ii. 76.

[3] The letter of the Duchess is registered in the *Annali Decemv.*, c. 156t. See also PELLINI, ii. 137.   It was written in answer to a letter of 17th September from the Perugian magistrates.   The documents clearly demonstrate that, as soon as Gian-Galeazzo was dead, the Visconti began to take less interest in Perugia.   See ANSIDEI, *op. cit.*, p. 41.

[4] A synopsis of the peace with the Pope, which was concluded at Todi on the 25th of October, 1403, will be found in PELLINI, ii. 138-140.   See also ANSIDEI, *op. cit.*, p. 42 n., and *Ann. Decemv.*, c. 173t.

Tomacelli entered the city, and Perugia cheerfully submitted to his rule and to the loss of the last remnant of her ancient liberties;[1] but though she might bow her neck beneath the ecclesiastical yoke, she refused to bear it any longer when she found herself insufficiently supported in her struggle with her mortal enemies; and, in 1408, she acclaimed Ladislaus of Naples her seignior, with the object of depriving Braccio, the dreaded leader of the *fuorusciti*, of the countenance and assistance of that powerful prince.

In April, 1408, Braccio had taken service under Ladislaus, and abandoning the March, invaded Umbria, where he defeated Ceccolino Michelotti and Rosso di Aquila, and occupied Coldimezzo and Deruta.[2] Terrified by the rapid progress of so formidable an adversary, the Raspanti hastened to seek an accommodation with Ladislaus, and, on the 28th of May, it was resolved to send ambassadors to Rome with full authority "to give, grant and assign to the said Royal Majesty full, free and complete dominion over the Commune and *contado* of Perugia *cum mero et mixto imperio*." On the 19th of June, Ser Angelo "Canginecti," Procurator of the Commune, presented to Ladislaus, in the Apostolic Palace, the *capitoli* of the submission, among which was included a solemn undertaking on the part of the King to defend the city and its dominions against all its enemies in general and the *fuorusciti* in particular; to treat the rebels of the Commune as rebels against himself, and never to permit the return of any citizen who had been banished for political reasons and whose name was registered in the Chancery of the Commune of Perugia.[3]

[1] *Arch. Stor. It.*, XVI. i. 277-278. How completely the Priors were deprived of all initiative may be inferred from the following entry in the *Annali Decemv.*, c. 40t (23 settembre, 1404): " Illustris et excelsa domina domina Agnesella Gaytana consors et locumtenens illustris et excelsi domini nostri domini Iohannis Tomacelli . . . commisit et voluit quod domini Priores cum plenissima auctoritate eligere possint custodes portarum civitatis Perusij."

[2] *Vite di Braccio Fortebraccio e di Nicolò Picinino, Perugini. Descritte da Monsig. Gio. Antonio Campano, Vescovo di Cotrone, e da Gio. Battista Poggio, Fiorentino.* Tradotte da POMPEO PELLINI (In Perugia, nella stampa Augusta, Appresso Pietro Tomassi, 1636), pp. 42 *et seq.* See also FABRETTI, *Biografie*, etc., *op. cit.*, Vol. I. pp. 122-124, and BONAZZI, i. 621.

[3] PELLINI, ii. 167-169; FABRETTI, *Schiarimenti alla Vita di Braccio,*

Menaced by the Council of Pisa, and with an ever-dwindling obedience, Gregory XII. was far too weak to have any hope of successfully opposing the defection of Perugia. It does not seem that he even protested ; and, a little later, he actually legalized the usurpations of Ladislaus by selling him the States of the Church and even Rome itself for the ridiculous sum of 25,000 florins.[1]

Perugia was twice visited by her new master, in June 1409 and July 1414 ;[2] but his death, on the 6th of the following month, filled the Raspanti with the utmost alarm, since they perceived only too clearly that they were no longer in a position to oppose an effective resistance to Braccio.[3]   The numerous abortive attempts of the *fuorusciti*[4] had, however, taught him patience and prudence, and he was resolved not to strike until he could strike a decisive blow.   Only in 1416, after his war-chest had been filled by the 100,000 florins which he had exacted as the price of Bolognese liberty, did he deem it safe to leave the Romagna and advance upon Perugia.   The Raspanti summoned Carlo Malatesta of Rimini to their assistance ; but after his defeat and capture in the sanguinary Battle of S. Egidio, on the 12th of July,[5] they were forced to come to terms with the

p. 87 ; ANSIDEI, *op. cit.*, p. 43 ; *Annali Decemv.*, 28 maggio, 1408, cc. 71 e 72 ; *Contratti*, CC. n. 15.

[1] SOZOMEN, *Specimen*, in MURATORI, *R. I. S.*, xvi. 1193 : " Concessit dicto regi Romam et Marchiam, Bononiam, Forlivium, Perusiam et omnes Terras Ecclesiæ. . . . "   Compare BONINCONTRIUS, *Annales* (in MURATORI, *R. I. S.*, xxi. 100), and CREIGHTON, *op. cit.*, i. 233.

[2] PELLINI, ii. 172, 202-203.   Compare also *La Cronaca di Bindo da Travale. Edita a cura di* V. LUSINI (Siena, Tip. S. Bernardiono, 1900), p. 54, cap. lxviii.

[3] That they did not altogether lack assistance is proved by two letters from Giovanna, Queen of Naples, published by FABRETTI, *ubi cit.*, pp. 91-93.

[4] For example, that of Giacomo di Francesco degli Arcipreti, in May, 1404, and that of Braccio himself, in 1410. See FABRETTI, *Cronache*, i. 210-211, ii. 77 ; PELLINI, ii. 177.

[5] A sufficient account of the Battle of S. Egidio will be found in SYMONDS and DUFF GORDON, *op. cit.*, p. 43.   See also E. HUTTON, *Sigismondo Malatesta, op. cit.*, pp. 17-18.   For full details the reader should consult *La Vita di Braccio, op. cit.*, pp. 130-150.   According to that work the engagement took place on the 15th of July.   See, however, FABRETTI, *Biografie*, etc., *op. cit.*, p. 164 ; PELLINI, ii. 231, and the *Cronica Riminese*, in MURATORI, *R. I. S.*, xv. 927.

victor, and, by the peace of Monte Morcino (16th July), they agreed to accept Braccio as Seignior of Perugia.[1] To him was granted *plenum et omne dominium dicte civitatis, fortie ac districtus, cum mero et mixto imperio et omnimodo gladij potestate,* and by him it was decreed, on the 28th of July, that all processes which had been instituted from the 30th of July, 1393, up to the 19th of July, 1416, should be burned ;[2] while, on the 3rd of August, the names of the rebels, inscribed in the *Annali Decemvirali* in 1403, were utterly erased.[3]

Thus ended the régime of the Raspanti, and with it the *Stato Popolare libero e guelfo.*

[1] FABRETTI, *Cronache*, ii. 79 ; PELLINI, ii. 225.

[2] " Statuimus quod omnes processus in causis criminalibus facti et sententie inde secute et late ac etiam banna et condemnationes quecumque criminales late et facte a millesimo trecentesimo nonagesimo tertio a die trigesima mensis Julij usque ad diem xviiij presentis mensis Julij qua feliciter intravimus ipsam civitatem comburantur . . . ita quod totaliter in cinerem convertantur."

[3] ANSIDEI, *op. cit.*, p. 41 n. 3.

CHAPTER XXI

FROM THE BATTLE OF S. EGIDIO TO THE EXPULSION OF THE DEGLI ODDI IN 1488

IT would hardly be more inappropriate to include an account of the wars and conquests of Alexander the Great in a history of Pella, or of those of Napoleon in a history of Ajaccio, than to deal in these pages with the efforts of Braccio Fortebracci to establish a powerful Italian principality. For us Braccio is simply the Seignior of Perugia ; and he exercised his authority over Perugia almost entirely through the agency of his lieutenants.[1]

By a decree of the 31st of July, 1416, given "in felice campo . . . juxta Bictonium prope Clasium," he nominated Pietro "de Mutiliana," of the Counts Guidi di Bagno, his Lieutenant in Perugia, and albeit, on the 20th of the same month, he had solemnly promised to observe the statutes of the Commune, he invested him with full powers to abrogate, suspend, or amend them. The Lieutenant was assisted by a Council of eighteen citizens selected from those who were the most faithful and obsequious to their new master, and the authority of the Priors and Camarlenghi was reduced almost to nothing.[2] It is true that many of the Nobles

---

[1] The principal source from which I have drawn my account of Perugia under the dominion of Braccio is Count V. ANSIDEI's *Nuovi appunti per la storia delle famiglie perugini Baglioni e Degli Oddi*, pubblicati per le nozze del Conte Giuseppe Manzoni Ansidei colla signorina Beatrice de' Conti Manzoni, Perugia, Unione, Tip. Coop., ottobre, 1902. This work, which is based upon an accurate study of contemporary documents, is, in fact, the only book which deals at all adequately with the period under consideration.

[2] ANSIDEI, *op. cit.*, pp. 14-15. For the decree nominating Piero "de Mutiliana," see ARCH. DECEMVIRALE DEL C. DI P. . . , *Decreta Brachij de Fortebrachiis*, iii. 21, c. 12r. On March 31st, 1417, Pietro was succeeded in the Lieutenancy by Bindaccio, "Granelli de Fibindacciis, alias Ricasolis de Florentia," who appears to have continued in that office until after the

took advantage of the decree which readmitted them to the
Colleges of the Arts, and that, from henceforward, their
names are often to be found among the members of the
Signoria,[1] but they possessed no real power.   From the
latter half of July, 1416, the volumes in which are registered
the proceedings of the civic magistrates record no events
of political importance ; the achievements of the famous
Seignior of Perugia find no place in their pages ; they have
dwindled to mere minutes of a municipal council, whose
principal business was the granting of exemptions and
immunities to artisans and peasants who returned to the
city and *contado*, impoverished and depopulated by nearly
half a century of desolating warfare.[2]   That the *Annali
Decemvirali* should be silent concerning Braccio's conquest
of Bologna for the Holy See, in 1420, and his glorious but
fatal achievements in the realm of Naples, need not surprise
us ; the Braccian Eagle was flying too far afield.   But how
shall we account for the absence of any reference to the
splendid festivities which were celebrated in Perugia on the
occasion of the marriage of her Seignior with Nicola Varani
da Camerino, and subsequently for the birth of an heir to the
house of Fortebracci ?[3]   Why is there no word as to the
great public works which Braccio completed in the city and
in its territory,[4] no mention of Città di Castello's submission
to him in 1422,[5] nor of his solemn coronation as Prince of
Capua in 1423 ?   This constant silence proves, if proof be
needed, that the life of the Commune was indeed ended.
Only one inglorious victory of Braccio's is recorded in the

death of Braccio. *Cf.* GRAZIANI, p. 296: " Adi 4 de agosto [1424] partì da
Peroscia Bindaccio, lo quale era stato per lo passato luocotenente del
signor Braccio. . . . "

[1] ANSIDEI, *op. cit.*, pp. 15-16 and notes.

[2] ANSIDEI, *op. cit.*, p. 17 n. 1, and the codices there cited.

[3] Braccio's first wife was Elisabetta degli Armanni or della Staffa. She
died in 1419. He married Nicola Varani in the following year, and his
son Carlo Fortebraccio was born on the 1st of September, 1421.

[4] The principal public works completed by Braccio in Perugia and its
territory were the Loggia in the Piazza di S. Lorenzo, begun in March,
1323 (see *Arch. Stor. It.*, XVI. i. 284) ; the gigantic arches for the support
of the Piazza di Sopramuro, and the *cava . . . pro diminutione ac evacua-
tione superfluitatis aque lacus perusini.* ANSIDEI, *op. cit.*, p. 21 n. 3.

[5] MUZI, *Memorie civili*, etc., *op. cit.*, i. 244-249.

19

Annali, and that record is, alas, itself but fresh evidence of servitude.   Scarcely had he conquered Perugia than he turned his thoughts to the neighbouring Assisi, then in the possession of Guidantonio of Urbino.[1]   For the moment, Guidantonio escaped the threatened danger by the cession of Sigillo and Spello ; but in March, 1419, Assisi was occupied by Malatesta Baglioni in the name of the Seignior of Perugia, only to be recaptured on the 15th of October of the same year.   Braccio thereupon swooped upon the luckless city and retook it after five hours' furious conflict. His success was sullied by abominable cruelty ;[2] yet when, by his orders, the news of this pitiable victory was sent to Perugia, the servile Priors hastened to offer him their most fulsome congratulations, and so low were they fallen that they feared to perform even this act of respect and loyalty without the express permission of Braccio's Lieutenant ![3] In the following May they were brusquely ordered to send the splendid *argenteria* of the Commune to be used for the honourable entertainment of Donna Violante, the Pope's niece, who was expected to pass through the city, and were menaced with a fine of a thousand ducats in case of disobedience.[4]   From the rulers of a free state they had

---

[1] Guidantonio di Montefeltro became Seignior of Assisi in 1409.   See CRISTOFANI, *op. cit.*, ii. 8.

[2] PELLINI, ii. 240-241 ; FABRETTI, *Biografie*, etc., *op. cit.*, i. 211-212 ; UGOLINI, *op. cit.*, i. 209-210.   Among the prisoners was a certain Gragnuola of Porta S. Pietro, who had been present at the death of Pandolfo Baglioni in 1393 ; and for this cause, twenty-six years afterwards, Malatesta Baglioni caused him to be tied to the tail of a horse and dragged from the *Due Porte* to the Piazza Maggiore of Perugia.   He died before he reached S. Domenico, " et per tutto dove era corso (says Pellini) haveva lasciato piena la via di sangue ; spettacolo veramente horribile e spaventosa."

[3] In the resolution taken by the Priors we read that the congratulatory letter must not be sent to Braccio, " nisi ad mandatum domini locumtenentis quando et prout domino locumtenenti videretur."   *Annali Decemv.*, 23 Ottobre, 1419, c. 118t.

[4] ANSIDEI, *op. cit.*, pp. 24-25 ; *Decreta Brachij* cit., cc. 16t e 17r ; *Annali Decemv.*, c. 134r.   Of the diligence which the civic magistrates used in adding to the splendour of their *argenteria* we have evidence in a " contractus super constructione Crucis fiende pro capella Palatij," which constitutes one of the few notable entries in the *Annali Decemvirali* of this period.   The Priors entrusted the work to the Perugian goldsmith, Raffaello, son of " condam Antonij Francischini " of Porta S. Angelo and

become the menials of the Lieutenant of their Despot!
Yet, in Perugia as elsewhere, "the *tyrannis* was simply
imposed upon the municipal constitution;"[1] there was no
attempt to destroy it. The Magistracy of the Priors outlived the Braccian despotism, but it never recovered its
pristine vigour.

If the loss of communal freedom had resulted in the
extinction of factional hate, the benefits of Braccio's rule
would, perhaps, have outweighed its disadvantages; but this
was far from being the case. It is true that the Consiglio
Generale of the 18th of July, 1416, showed the utmost
eagerness in passing resolutions directed "ad unionem
civium perusinorum et ad deponendum et abolendum odia
inter ipsos quomodolibet, vigentia";[2] that Braccio's decree
of the 25th began with the expression of an unquestionably
sincere aspiration for "peace, unity, tranquillity and the
maintenance of justice,"[3] and that the records of the proceedings of the Priors and Camarlenghi in their session of
the 10th of August are little less than a hymn of praise for
the peace which her new Seignior had bestowed upon
Perugia;[4] but ere many months had passed, the Perugians
were once more in insurrection, and all the Michelotti were
banished.[5] The harsh decree of March 2nd, 1418, which
deprived the wives of the rebels of the enjoyment of their

of the parish of S. Martino del Verzaro. The Cross in question was to be
made of fine silver, and among the ornaments was "a piei d' essa Sancto
Arcolano con una bandiera en mano collo grifone," while "da piei del
Crocifisso al capo de Sancto Arcolano" was "l'arme del nostro Synore
Braccio esmaltata" (*Annali Decemv.*, cc. 171 e 172t). Such importance
did the Priors attach to their plate that, in the *Capitoli* of 18th July, 1424,
entered into with Martin V., a special section was introduced providing
"quod argentaria in palatio Priorum conservetur et augeatur de tempore
in tempus de salario Priorum, juxta formam statutorum et ordinamen-
torum de dicta argentaria loquentium, et prout et sicut est actenus consuetum." According to Marcantonio Maltempi, this *argenteria* was
"stimata di chi fu vista per una delle più belle e pregiate cose dell' Italia,"
while Girolamo di Frolliere devotes almost an entire chapter to the description of it. (See *Arch. Stor. It.*, XVI. ii. p. xli, n. 2, and pp. 446-449.)

[1] C. M. ADY, *op. cit.*, p. 31.

[2] ANSIDEI, *op. cit.*, p. 17; *Annali Decemv.*, cc. 82t e 83r.

[3] Published by FABRETTI, *Schiarimenti alla Vita di Braccio*, pp. 114-116.

[4] ANSIDEI, *op. cit.*, p. 18; *Annali Decemv.*, c. 87.

[5] PELLINI, ii. 228: "Erano fatti fuorusciti tutti li Michilotti."

dowries during the lives of their husbands,[1] seems to point to the continued uneasiness caused by the machinations of the exiles ; while after the recapture of Assisi, in the following year, forty of the *fuorusciti*, who were taken prisoners, were brought to Perugia and decapitated.[2]   Thenceforward the Raspanti and their adherents were gradually excluded from all the more important offices of the State, until at last, as Fabretti declares, " the government of Perugia became wholly aristocratic.[3]   Yet not for that did peace come, and, in June, 1420, a decree was promulgated " contra portantes divisam," because it was found that the use of colours, uniforms and liveries which marked the wearers as members of particular parties and associations, or as the retainers of some great family, was a source of constant rivalries and dissensions.[4]   On at least one occasion, Braccio himself had to intervene to make peace between contending nobles.[5]

On the death of Braccio beneath the walls of Aquila (5th June, 1424), Martin V. resolved forthwith to re-establish the authority of the Church in Perugia, and hardly had the Perugians proclaimed Braccio's bastard son Oddo their seignior[6] than steps were taken in Rome to depose him. In Malatesta Baglioni, who had been wounded and taken prisoner at the Battle of Aquila, the Pope found an agent ready to his hand ; for that nobleman quickly realized that the best chance of maintaining the ascendancy of an aristocratic oligarchy lay in accord with the Church, and on his undertaking to do all in his power to persuade his fellow-citizens to submit to the papal authority, he obtained his

[1] ANSIDEI, *op. cit.*, p. 20 ; *Decreta Brachij*, cc. 19t e 20r.   See also *Misc., Atti diversi*, n. 8 bis c. 89t.

[2] PELLINI, ii. 241.

[3] FABRETTI, *Biografie*, etc., *op. cit.*, i. p. 174: " e così una perfetta aristocrazia soggiogava Perugia."

[4] ANSIDEI, *op. cit.*, p. 26 ; *Decreta Brachij*, cc. 17r *et seq.*

[5] Thus, for example, on the 6th of April, 1418, by Braccio's orders, the Priors concluded a peace between Giliotto, " Subalzi de Acerbis," and Bernardo, " Corgnoli de Corgnis."   From the document in question we learn that " jam venerunt in armis," and that they were compelled to promise observance of the terms imposed not only for themselves, but also for " eorum complices et sequaces vel aliquem suorum consanguineorum." *Annali Decemv.*, c. 78t.

[6] GRAZIANI, p. 287 ; FABRETTI, *Cronache*, i. 219, ii. 4 ; PELLINI, ii. 280.

liberty and a promise of honours and power.   On the 8th of June he reached Perugia with letters from the Pope, and "for this cause a great council was assembled wherein the said Malatesta set forth his embassy and commission and the letters were read."   The city was divided and there was great fear of tumult, inasmuch as "those of the *parte di sotto* desired the Church and peace and those *di sopra* desired them not."[1]   Finally, however, the influence of Malatesta, the example set by not a few of the cities and towns formerly subject to Braccio which now hastened to recognize the papal authority, and the approach of three thousand horse in the pay of the Church, convinced the Count Oddo and his adherents that resistance would be worse than futile.   On the 1st of July he restored to the Commune the keys of the gates and of the fortresses, and, on the same day, the Priors and Camarlenghi resolved to send ambassadors to Rome to make submission to the Pope.[2] Once the fatal step was taken, their eagerness knew no bounds ; they tripled and quadrupled their embassies, and even before the conditions of the peace were determined Martin found himself seignior of Perugia.   Thanks, however, to the sagacity of the envoys and the moderation of the Pope, the terms imposed were far from being burdensome ; many of the ancient privileges of the Commune were preserved, and from henceforward in all their disputes with the Papal Legates and Governors, we shall find the Perugians appealing to the *Capitoli* of Martin V. as the *Magna Charta* of their remaining liberties.   They bear date the 18th of July, 1424, and were approved by a Bull of the 29th of the same month.[3]

The absolute sovereignty of the Church was no longer disputed, and henceforward *la libertà sotto il papa* was Perugia's highest ideal ; but though she had lightly surrendered her independence, she was still minded to cherish

[1] GRAZIANI, p. 290 ; FABRETTI, *Cronache*, ii. 4 ; FABRETTI, *Biografie*, etc., *op. cit.*, i. 286.

[2] *Annali Decemvirali*, cc. 9ᵗ e 10ʳ.

[3] These documents are published by FUMI, *Inventario e spoglio dei Registri della Tesoreria Apostolica di Perugia e Umbria* (Perugia, Unione Tip. Coop., 1901), p. xxx *et seq.*

and perpetuate her ancient hates, and the Pope was compelled to promise that he would never seek to recall the political exiles. As a consequence the city continued to be harassed by the plots and machinations of the men she persecuted, and we have record of embassies despatched to Rome, to Siena, to Cortona and to Montepulciano with no other object than to request that the rebels of Perugia should not receive harbourage or assistance.[1] Nor were the fears of the Magistrates without foundation. On the 16th of July, 1425, news arrived of the attempt of the *fuorusciti* to surprise Assisi;[2] while, on the 4th of August, it was known that Lodovico Michelotti was on the march from the Realm of Naples, accompanied by Jacopo Caldora, Lodovico Colonna and Antoniuccio dell' Aquila.[3] To provide for the defence of the city and *contado*, a special *balìa* of five citizens was appointed, called the " Cinque della Guerra."[4] They proceeded to raise money by forced loans and to take into their pay Giovanni da Camerino and Tartaglia. Their exactions and violences soon became intolerable, and, under the date of the 23rd of August, the chronicler relates that they " demanded weapons from such citizens as they chose and returned them not ; and this they did for suspicion of State, they said. Also, in those days, to have money, the said Five of War imposed *prestanza* upon whom they would, and also they caused whom they would to be arrested upon suspicion." On the 27th we learn that " certain citizens departed and gat them away for fear."[5]

Such was the condition of Perugia when Fra Bernardino of Siena came thither from Assisi and began to preach and to say mass in the Piazza.[6] He made many converts ; not only was the Battle of Stones abolished, but the Companies danced no more on holidays, and the whole city was sunk in puritanic gloom ; the churches were filled to overflowing,

[1] ANSIDEI, *op. cit.*, pp. 32-34.

[2] GRAZIANI, pp. 309-310. So great was the alarm that " per ditta cagione e sospetto fu levato via el sonare dei tocche la sera, ed ancho lo oriolo, et la mattina el sonare della campana del dì."

[3] GRAZIANI, p. 311 ; PELLINI, ii. 291.

[4] ANSIDEI, *op. cit.*, p. 35 n. 2.

[5] GRAZIANI, p. 312.

[6] GRAZIANI, p. 313. *Cf.* my *Palio and Ponte, op. cit.*, pp. 154-160.

THE BURNING OF VANITIES

DETAIL FROM THE FAÇADE OF THE ORATORY OF S. BERNARDINO

and he boasted, in Siena, two years later, that of all the
cities of Italy, Perugia, which had been the worst, was now
" la più netta." [1]   Indeed, so great was his influence that
the rigid rules of life which he advocated received a legal
sanction in the *Statuta Sancti Bernardini*, which are still
preserved among the communal archives.[2]   Yet all such
religious revivals have been short-lived in direct proportion
to the suddenness of their origin, and the effect of his
preaching was of necessity extremely transitory ; [3] while,
even for the moment, it can hardly have been other than
superficial, since his eloquence was wholly ineffectual to
eradicate factional hatred from the hearts of the citizens.
It is true that in Perugia itself he healed many ancient
quarrels, so that the injured sought out their enemies to
pardon them,[4] but there was no thought of forgiveness for
the *fuorusciti*.   He was still in the city when, on the 29th
of September, 1425, a proclamation was made which added
many fresh names to the already long list of the proscribed ; [5]
and on the 17th of October, while his terrified auditors were
bringing their " vanities " to the Convent of S. Francisco for
the great "burning" of the 30th,[6] the General Council approved
the League with the Count of Urbino, on the distinct understanding that all Perugian *fuorusciti* should be expelled
from the towns subject to Montefeltro.[7]   Moreover, at the

[1] *Le prediche volgari di S. Bernardino da Siena dette nella Piazza del Campo
l' anno,* MCCCCXXVII., edite da L. BANCHI (Siena, 1880-1888), i. 97, 350.

[2] *Archivio Decemv.,* cod. 3 F. de' primi anni del Sec. XV. In the printed
Statutes, the *Statutes of S. Bernardino* are to be found in Vol. III., beginning
with fol. lxii.

[3] *Cf.* my *Palio and Ponte, op. cit.,* p. 156, and COULTON, *From St Francis
to Dante, op. cit.,* p. 39. Compare also for similar results in the case of a
subsequent revival, GRAZIANI, p. 599.

[4] *Prediche volgari, op. cit.,* iii. 497.

[5] GRAZIANI, p. 314: " . . . fuoro banditi per ribelli nuovamente fatti
. . molti . . . cittadini e contadini."

[6] GRAZIANI, p. 314. According to Mr HUTTON (*The Cities of Umbria,*
p. 20) it was " from the little pulpit on the wall of S. Lorenzo " that Fra
Bernardino "watched Perugia at his bidding burn her books, the false
hair of the women, the beautiful pictures, full of desire and life, of the
great lords." But I think that this is a mistake. Apparently the pulpit
in question was not built until fourteen years later ; and Fra Bernardino
did not preach in it until August 1441 (see GRAZIANI, pp. 442, 470).

[7] ANSIDEI, *op. cit.,* p. 37. The *Capitola inter Comune Perusij et Comitem*

same session at which the Priors and Camarlenghi confirmed the Statutes of Fra Bernardino " pro veris, legitimis, sanctis et justis legibus," it was resolved (strange contrast) to send to Rome for a copy of a Bull against the *fuorusciti*, " ad confusionem extirminium et dissipationem exititiorum et rebellium."[1] Nor does this resolution stand alone ; the chronicles and contemporary documents afford ample proof of the fury with which the unhappy exiles continued to be persecuted,[2] and, as late as 1445, we read of a certain " Ser Batiste de la Andrea," who was beheaded in Sopramuro " because he was a Raspante." There is no comment ; the reason was all-sufficient.[3] *Lo Stato popolare libero e guelfo* had been superseded by *Lo Stato felice de' Gentiluomini.*

Though such of the decrees of Braccio as were derogatory to the honour and dignity of the Priors, Camarlenghi, and other officials of the Commune, were abrogated by the *Capitoli* of Martin V.,[4] the custom which prevailed of seeking the advice of the Nobles on all matters of importance, and the frequent presence of the Papal Governor at the sessions of the civic magistrates, would seem to indicate that the Priors scarcely possessed more real authority than they had done under the despotism of Braccio. Their

Urbini are registered in the *Annali Decemvirali*, cc. 72t e 73, while the letter of the 23rd of November to Guidantonio di Montefeltro, which contained the names of the rebels, is published by FABRETTI, *Documenti di Storia Perugina*, Vol. I. pp. 189-197. *Cf.* also *Arch. Stor. It.*, XVI. i. 315-317 n.

[1] ANSIDEI, *op. cit.*, p. 37 ; *Annali Decemv.*, 4 Novembre, 1425, cc. 82t e 83r.

[2] *Cf.*, for example, GRAZIANI, p. 331 and pp. 359-360. The last passage, in particular, is worthy of more than passing notice, since it proves that the ruling faction were so absolutely without scruple in their persecution of the Raspanti that they did not hesitate to request the Commune of Florence to become their hired assassin. *Cf.* PELLINI, ii. 338.

[3] GRAZIANI, p. 574. Further examples of the perdurable character of these enmities will be found at a far later period. See, for instance, the *Cronica perugina inedita* under the 21st of August, 1486. This chronicle, which contains much new and valuable information, is annotated by Prof. O. Scalvanti and published in *Bollettino* cited, Vols. IV. and IX.

[4] Article XVIII. provided " quod omnia decreta et mandata facta per Brachium vel Oddonem, vel eorum locumtenentes, serventur et sint rata . . . salvo quatenus essent diminutiva honoris et commodi Priorum et Camerariorum et aliorum officialium Civitatis Perusij. . . . "

position was, no doubt, improved, and they probably enjoyed a certain limited autonomy,[1] but their pretensions to independent action vanished into thin air when they ventured to set themselves in oppositon to " li citadini grossi che mantenevano lo stato." [2]   Alas for Perugia, her only remaining bulwark against that worst of all tyrannies, an ecclesiastical tyranny, now lay in the power of her Nobles.   From thenceforward, though the foreign policy of the Commune was often dictated by the reigning Pontiff, the internal government of the city was almost entirely in the hands of an aristocratic oligarchy.

A worse government it would be difficult to conceive of. There were, it is true, one or two members of the great houses who deserved well of their fellow-citizens,[3] but they formed a very small minority of the ruling class, and it almost seemed as if the worst days of feudal violence had returned.   The responsibility of the individual was once more merged in that of the *consorteria* or district, and we read of wholesale punishments which must have included many innocent persons.   In two cases, at any rate, entire villages were destroyed for the fault of a fraction of the inhabitants.[4]   Meanwhile the civic magistrates were coerced and thwarted in the execution of their duties, and even the Legates of the Church were unable to exert any effectual control over the turbulent city.   Not only were the democracy deprived of all political power, but they were compelled to bear more than their just share of the public burdens, having become, as one of their own number bitterly declares, " the asses of the others " and " the men of our Nobles." [5]   For many years the *contado* was the chosen

---

[1] ANSIDEI, p. 39.   [2] Read, for example, GRAZIANI, pp. 356-357.

[3] Of these was Braccio Baglioni, justly belauded by FABRETTI in his *Biografie*, etc., Vol. III. p. 18.   Among the other benefits which he conferred upon Perugia was the introduction of the art of printing.   See ANSIDEI, *Ricordi nuziali di Casa Baglioni*, in *Bollettino* cited, xiv. p. 111 n. 2.

[4] For example, Casacastalda in February, 1433, and S. Martino in Colle on the 15th of August in the same year.   See *Annali Decemv.*, 31 Gennaio, 433, c. 187 t, and GRAZIANI, p. 369.

[5] *Cronica perugina inedita*, in *Bollettino* cited, iv. 369, 373.   Surely the words " omeni deli nostri nobili " have a feudal ring, reminding us irresistibly of the *Jeo deveigne vostre home* in the service of homage.

battle-ground on which Niccolò Fortebraccio della Stella
fought out his quarrel with Guidantonio of Montefeltro, and
Francesco Sforza his with Niccolò Piccinino.[1] The phrase
" e fu bandito lo sgombro " occurs in the chronicles with
almost wearisome iteration,[2] and the atrocities committed
by the companies of adventure upon the defenceless
peasantry are wellnigh incredible.[3] Nor was the condition
of the city less deplorable than that of the country ; the
palaces of the aristocracy were filled with *beccarini* and
spadaccini, who were practically little better than highway
robbers,[4] murders and outrages were matters of almost daily
occurrence,[5] and peaceable citizens went in continual danger
of their lives ; trade diminished ; the shops were closed,
and many once flourishing *arti* almost disappeared.[6] The
occasional spasmodic attempts of the Potestà or Captain of
the People to strike terror into evil-doers by the infliction
of atrocious penalties [7] proved worse than useless. The
chance of escape was too great and the punishment too

---

[1] See ANSIDEI, *Ricordi nuziali di Casa Baglioni, ubi cit.*, p. 107.

[2] GRAZIANI, pp. 309, 376, 377, 379, 465 *et passim*.

[3] For a horrible instance see GRAZIANI, pp. 529-530.

[4] In 1443 the Patriarch was robbed near Collestrada by some of the
retainers of Braccio Baglioni ; while a few pages earlier we read of the
discontent of " otto famiglie de Pandolfo de Nello dei Baglioni, li quali se
ne fuggiero da lui ; però che ditto Pandolfo non li usava mai cortesia
alcuna delle cose che essi guadagniavano e che portavano a casa ; et
dicevano che Pandolfo voleva ogni cosa per lui "—a passage which speaks
volumes as to the complicity of the nobles in the crimes of their adherents
(GRAZIANI, pp. 505, 519). Among the gang of housebreakers to which
Don Angelo di Marino belonged, there were, we are told, " più citadini dei
grossi, li quali se taceno per lo meglio " (GRAZIANI, p. 504). The miserable
priest was hung in the cage in the *Via della gabbia*, where he froze to death
on the night of the 31st of January, 1443 (FABRETTI, *Cronache*, ii. 27) ;
but the " citadini dei grossi " seem to have escaped scot-free.

[5] It would be idle to quote specific instances. See the chronicles, *passim*.

[6] *Cronica perugina inedita*, in *Bollettino* cited, ix. 218 n., 292 n.

[7] See *Cronica perugina inedita*, in *Bollettino* cited, iv. 105 and 106 n. 1.
Apparently a terrible abuse of power and the hideous death of an innocent
man were regarded as dust in the balance when the official implicated
had also dealt severely with real criminals. " Egli ha fatto un bell' officio
e ha castigato molti malfattori e ribaldi e à auto grande onore," writes the
chronicler. Nor is his verdict altogether incomprehensible when we recall
the fact that, under the régime of less savage officials, " se amazavano
li homini, e in capo de pochi dì andavano per piazza."

OUR LADY OF PITY PROTECTING PERUGIA IN TIME OF PESTILENCE
(BONFIGLI)

uncertain to act as a deterrent, and the commonest thief went to the gallows fully expecting to be rescued at the last moment.[1] Meanwhile the unhappy city was repeatedly visited by the Pestilence, which, between 1424 and 1486, returned no fewer than eight times, while, from 1460 to 1468, it raged without intermission.[2]

Yet the cup of Perugia's misery was not yet full. To the horrors of tyranny and disease were added those of intestine discord, and in the third quarter of the fifteenth century her nobles were continually at open warfare among themselves. During the long struggle with the Raspanti the necessity of showing a united front to the common enemy had served to obliterate the memory of private hates ; but when once the victory was won, and the strong hand of Braccio had been removed, the ancient enmities blazed out afresh, and year by year became more bitter. Indeed, with the exception of Niccolò Piccinino's five days' sojourn in Perugia (10th June to 15th June, 1440) with the consequent temporary sub-version of the papal authority, the hideous sack of Assisi, in 1442, and the protracted disputes with Siena concerning the possession of the *Sagro Anello*, there is little in the political history of the Commune during *Lo Stato de' Gen-tiluomini* which need claim our attention outside the san-guinary quarrels of the ruling faction.

Of the great houses of Perugia the most powerful were the Baglioni, the Degli Oddi, the Ranieri, the Arcipreti (or Della Penna), and the Armanni (or Della Staffa) ; but, from the second quarter of the fifteenth century, the Baglioni overtopped them all. According to Pellini, " the first founda-tion of their pre-eminence " was the grant of the Signory of Spello to Malatesta Baglioni, in 1425, by Pope Martin V., as a reward for his services in prevailing upon his fellow-

---

[1] Probably we may take the execution of Mariotto da Montone, in 1451, as typical. We are told that " mentre fo letta la condenagione . . . facea un gran guardare in là e in qua ale gente e dice che cie era stato dato ad intendere che esso saria stato artolto." See *Bollettino* cited, iv. 74-76.

[2] In addition to the chronicles, see MASSARI, *Saggio-storico-medico sulle pestilenze di Perugia, op. cit.*, pp. 39-59. It was to those evil days that we owe Bonfigli's banner in the chapel of the Gonfalone, which represents Our Lady of Pity protecting her servants from an angry Christ.

citizens to submit to the authority of the Church.[1]   During
the next few years the dominion of Bastia [2] and of Cannaia [3]
was added to that of Spello, while, in 1433, Eugenius IV.
confirmed the Baglioni in the possession of all their fiefs to
the third generation.[4]   On the death of Malatesta, in 1437,
his vassals hastened to acknowledge his son Braccio as their
seignior,[5] and, in after years, his descendants gradually
extended their suzerainty over Bettona, Bevagna, Col di
Mancio, Castelbuono, Limigiano, and other places,[6] with the
result that their retainers considerably outnumbered those
of their rivals ; and when, at last,

> Azzur nel campo d' oro un leon fero

joined battle with

> . . . una sbarra d' oro degna d' impero
> Nel campo azzur [7]

the final result of the struggle was hardly doubtful.

The enmity of the Baglioni and the Degli Oddi may, as
we have seen, be traced back at least as far as 1331 [8] ; and
when, in 1456, the Degli Oddi and the Della Corgna came
to blows in the streets of Perugia, we find the Baglioni and
their adherents supporting the cause of the latter against
their ancient foes.[9]   This, as far as I am able to discover,

[1] PELLINI, ii. 296 ; GRAZIANI, p. 317.

[2] GRAZIANI, p. 350 and p. 353 n. 5.

[3] In 1437 the inhabitants of Cannaia appeared at the funeral of their
seignior with the standard of that Commune. GRAZIANI, pp. 413-414.
There is a passage in the same chronicle (p. 292) from which we might,
perhaps, infer that Malatesta Baglioni was seignior of Cannaia as early as
1424, but PELLINI (loc. cit.) distinctly speaks of the acquisition of Cannaia
as subsequent to that of Spello : " fu anco poi in diversi altri tempi donato
loro Bastia, Cannaia," etc.

[4] GRAZIANI, p. 368.   [5] GRAZIANI, p. 412.

[6] PELLINI, ii. 296 ; BONAZZI, i. 652.

[7] See MATARAZZO, Cronaca della Città di Perugia, in Arch. Stor. It., XVI.
ii. 100.   The allusion is, of course, to the arms of the Degli Oddi and the
Baglioni.   The former bore a Lion azure on a shield gules, the latter a
shield azure with a bend or.

[8] See p. 157 supra.

[9] Cronica perugina inedita, in Bollettino cited, iv. 310-311 : " Anco
venne su Ridolfo e Guido e Giovagnie dei Baglione con tutti loro amici
de P. S. P. e de P. Borgna, li quali stetteno sempre in piè de la piazza in
favore de quelli da corgne."   Compare also FABRETTI, Cronache, ii. 33-34,
and PELLINI, ii. 632.

was the first occasion on which the great houses openly
warred with one another; but from thenceforward Perugia
was simply the battle-ground of contending factions.   The
slightest provocation, a word, a gesture, the repetition of a
piece of ill-natured gossip, a question of precedence or of
patronage, anything or nothing, afforded sufficient pretext
for the nobles to take up arms and slaughter one another
through all the streets and squares of the city.   No oath,
nor any peace, however solemn, could long restrain their
insatiable lust for blood and for revenge; while, because
their contests were the outcome of purely personal ambitions,
house was often divided against house and kinsman against
kinsman.   The Governors and Legates of the Pope were
utterly helpless, and, again and again, we find them treating
with the heads of belligerent families as if they were treating
with independent potentates or the captains of regular
armies.[1]   In 1482 the Baglioni and Degli Oddi fought a
pitched battle in the Piazza which lasted for the space of
two hours; and so great was their fury that the chronicler
likens them to " mad dogs."   They were finally separated
by the friars *del Monte*, who thrust themselves between the
combatants, bearing a great cross and crying, *Misericordia!
Misericordia! Pace! Pace!*   After almost three weeks'
continual negotiation a temporary peace was patched up
by the Papal Commissary[2]; and in the official records we
read that, in March, 1485, " fuerunt celebrate certe paces et
concordie inter Balleonos et filios Iacobi Tome They ex
una parte et Oddones et Marcum Antonium de Bontempis
ex altera ";[3]   while to strengthen the bonds of amity
Camilla, daughter of Ridolfo Baglioni, was solemnly
affianced to Pompeo Degli Oddi.   The marriage, however,
never took place; the rival houses hated one another too
bitterly for the same city to hold them both, and three years
later the Degli Oddi were driven into exile, on the 30th of

[1] ANSIDEI, *La pace del luglio 1498 fra Guidobaldo I., Duca d'Urbino, e
il C. di Perugia,* in *Bollettino* cited, v. 743.

[2] *Cronica perugina inedita,* in *Bollettino* cited, ix. 195-199; PELLINI, ii.
796-798.

[3] *Libro dei Contratti,* ad ann. 1485 c. 25ᵗ; ANSIDEI, *Ricordi nuziali di
Casa Baglioni,* in *Bollettino* cited, xiv. 131.

October, 1488.[1]   Henceforward, Perugia was ruled by a
section only of her Nobles, and *Lo Stato de' Gentiluomini*
made way for *Lo Stato Baglionesco.*

The great body of the citizens seem to have looked
on at these scenes of bloodshed, inert and helpless ; and
almost the only instance which has come down to us of
any attempt on the part of the down-trodden democracy to
assert its rights is to be found in a rising of the men of
Porta S. Angelo in 1472, to prevent the exportation of
grain in a time of scarcity.[2]   When the Nobles were not
fighting one another, they were either hunting the deer
and wild-boar which frequented the tangled thickets of
the desolated *contado,*[3] or organizing tournaments " per
dare festa al popolo "[4]—the only panacea which they
provided for the infinite miseries which their violence and
lawlessness inflicted upon their weaker neighbours.   Even
their very sports all too often led to brutal outrages on
peaceable folk, as was the case in January 1459, when the
Rector of the Sapienza offered twelve yards of green velvet
as a prize for a jousting, and, in accordance with the
decision of the judges, divided the same between a certain
Gio Matteo and one Casamatta, a retainer of Sforza Degli
Oddi.   On the following Wednesday, Casamatta, who
believed himself to have been justly entitled to the entire
prize, set upon the Rector in the Piazza, and not only
" gave him divers wounds in the head," but added insult
to injury by snatching away his hood.   " A great to-do
was made by the Governor, but nothing followed thereupon,
save to him that had received the injury his damage." [5]   Of
the almost incredible ferocity of the Nobles a well-known
example exists in the terrible punishment which was meted

[1] GRAZIANI, pp. 682-687 ; FABRETTI, *Cronache,* ii. 57-59, 108-109 ;
PELLINI, ii. 846-852.   See also the account of Giacomo di Cristoforo, a
contemporary and probably an eye-witness of the events which he describes,
published by Count V. ANSIDEI in *Bollettino* cited, xiv. 132-133.

[2] *Cronica perugina inedita,* in *Bollettino* cited, ix. 79.

[3] *Ibid.,* 191, 192.

[4] GRAZIANI, p. 380, and see the chronicles *passim.*

[5] *Cronica perugina inedita,* in *Bollettino* cited, iv. 355-356.   The " togliere
il capuccio " was an intolerable insult.   See the Statute of 1528, Lib. iii.
Rubric xiv.

out to Bracciamonte del Miccia by her brother Lionello ;[1]
while wellnigh the only indication which the chroniclers
afford us that the men of those days were ever stirred
by gentler emotions than lust of blood and of revenge
are to be found in the all too meagre references to the
splendid entertainments given by Braccio Baglioni in his
garden in Porta S. Pietro, for love of "the most gentle,
sweet and beauteous lady" Margherita Montesperelli, "than
whom Perugia hath no fairer, nor ever hath had. Neither
do I deem that the World itself hath ever seen her
equal. Certes, she seemeth the goddess Venus, and of
her perfections there is no end."[2]   As I turn from the
study of the chronicles, besides the luckless Bracciamonte
and "Margherita bella," the only women of whom any
definite memory remains to me are a wretched *contadina*,
clamouring outside the Palazzo Pubblico for the life of
her husband, a cruelly-beaten slave-girl, and a certain
Donna Innocentia, wife of Cesare degli Arcipreti, a typical
strong-minded lady of the Renaissance.[3]

[1] *Cronica perugina inedita, in Bollettino* cited, iv. 117 ; FABRETTI,
Cronache, ii. 33 ; *Arch. Stor. It.*, XVI. i. 629. I speak of the incident
as " well-known " because it is recorded by BURCKHARDT in his *Renaissance
in Italy*, a work which is, of course, familiar to every reader. I have not
the English version by me, but the passage in question will be found in
the Italian of VALBUSA (edition of 1900) on p. 208 of Vol. II.

[2] *Bollettino* cited, iv. 374, 390. See also O. SCALVANTI, *Un " Garden-
party " in Perugia nel 1459* in *L'Umbria, op. cit.*, Anno I. Fasc. ii.

[3] *Cronica perugina inedita*, in *Bollettino* cited, ix. 184-185.

GENEALOGICAL TABLE

SHOWING THE RELATIONSHIP BETWEEN THE MORE IMPORTANT MEMBERS OF THE

BAGLIONI FAMILY

DURING THE XVTH AND XVITH CENTURIES

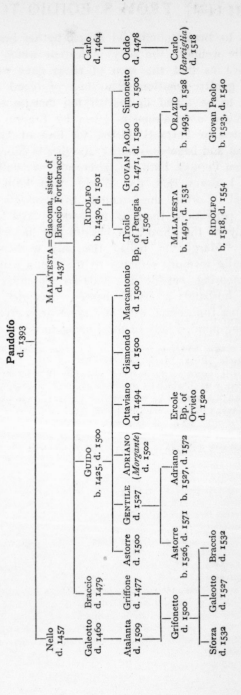

Pandolfo
d. 1393

MALATESTA = Giacoma, sister of
d. 1437   Braccio Fortebracci

Nello
d. 1457

Carlo
d. 1464

RIDOLFO
b. 1430, d. 1501

Oddo
d. 1478

Galeotto
d. 1460

Braccio
d. 1479

GUIDO
b. 1425, d. 1500

Troilo
Bp. of Perugia
d. 1506

GIOVAN PAOLO
b. 1471, d. 1520

Simonetto
d. 1500

Carlo
(*Bariglia*)
d. 1518

Atalanta
d. 1509

Griffone
d. 1477

Astorre
d. 1500

GENTILE
d. 1527

ADRIANO
(*Morgante*)
d. 1502

Ottaviano
d. 1494

Gismondo
d. 1500

Marcantonio
d. 1500

MALATESTA
b. 1491, d. 1531

ORAZIO
b. 1493, d. 1528

Grifonetto
d. 1500

Astorre
b. 1526, d. 1571

Adriano
b. 1527, d. 1572

Ercole
Bp. of
Orvieto
d. 1520

RIDOLFO
b. 1518, d. 1554

Giovan Paolo
b. 1523, d. 1540

Sforza
d. 1532

Galeotto
d. 1527

Braccio
d. 1532

CHAPTER XXII

THE RULE OF THE BAGLIONI

THANKS to Mr Edward Strachan Morgan's masterly translation, the Chronicle of Matarazzo is now accessible to English readers,[1] and it would, therefore, obviously be mere waste of time to treat of the history of Perugia during the next few years with any particularity of detail.[2] Suffice it then to say that on the 3rd of November, 1488, a *Dieci dell' Arbitrio* was appointed, and such unlimited authority conferred upon it that it constituted for all practical purposes a dictatorship of ten, in whose hands were concentrated all the powers of the State.[3] In its original form, two of its members were Baglioni and the remainder adherents of that house,[4] while, later on, we find that the Baglioni themselves

[1] E. STRACHAN MORGAN, *Chronicles of the City of Perugia.* London: Dent, 1905.

[2] I do not, of course, intend to state that Matarazzo's chronicle is exhaustive, but it is, beyond question, the most important document which we possess concerning that period of Perugian history with which it deals. The history of the Baglioni still remains to be written, and the most valuable printed sources for such a work are to be found in the various articles of Count VINCENZO ANSIDEI which I have so frequently quoted in these pages. As we have already seen, the enormous book of Count de Baglion de La Dufferie, though undoubtedly useful to consult, cannot always be implicitly relied upon.

[3] *Annali Decemv.*, ad ann. c. 89. To the Dieci was granted " plenum arbitrium providendi, statuendi circa omnia et singula que necessaria noverint et eis visa fuerint utilia et oportuna pro et super conservatione et amplificatione presentis tranquilli status civitatis ad honorem sancte Romane Ecclesie et presentis status ita quod dictum arbitrium sit generale et generalissimum et spetiale et spetialissimum."

[4] GRAZIANI, p. 689 ; PELLINI, ii. 854. The members of the *Dieci dell' Arbitrio* were :—

Porta Bornia—Guido Baglioni and Ridolfo Signorelli.
Porta S. Pietro—Ridolfo Baglioni and Vincenzio of Monte Vibiano.
Porta Sole—Bernardino de' Ranieri and Francesco de' Montemelini.
Porta S. Angelo—Girolamo della Penna and Bartolomeo della Staffa.
Porta S. Susanna—Pietro Filippo della Corgna and Count Giacomo Piccinini.

formed an actual majority of the Council, occupying no fewer than six out of the ten seats.[1] In 1489, this extraordinary magistracy was confirmed for a year, and again, in 1490, for an unlimited period "ad beneplacitum Camerariorum." [2] The Priors were excluded from its sessions,[3] and it existed simply to carry out the commands of those who had called it into being. The first care of the *Dieci* was to secure the consent of the Pope to the new order of things, and ambassadors were sent to Rome to justify the "expulsionem pestifere familie nefande De Oddis." [4] The cause of the Baglioni was espoused by Lorenzo de' Medici, and, largely through his influence, Innocent VIII. consented to the outlawry of the *fuorusciti*,[5] who, after their second disastrous attempt to re-enter Perugia by force of arms, in September, 1495, were too much weakened to cause the ruling oligarchy any great uneasiness.[6] In the previous year

[1] MATARAZZO, *ubi cit.*, p. 139 ; MORGAN, *op. cit.*, p. 144. By the "Decemviri of Sovereignty," Mr Morgan, of course, means the *Dieci dell' Arbitrio* ; but I venture to think that the paraphrase is an unhappy one, since the *Decemviri* were, in fact, the Priors whom the *Dieci dell' Arbitrio* for all practical purposes superseded. Indeed, almost the only reasonable exception which can be taken to Mr Morgan's work is to be found in the wholly unnecessary and sometimes misleading translation of proper names. It may make the book more readable, but it certainly makes it less intelligible. Thus, for example, in his pages the village of *Olmo* becomes "the place which is called the Elm Tree," and the *Porta delle Voltole* the gate of "the Little Arches," while the identity of *la Mascione del Pian di Carpene* with the modern *Magione* is hopelessly obscured by entitling it "the great House at the Plains of the Alders." As well might an Italian translator of an English book convert "Oxford" into *guado de' buoi* !

[2] See ANSIDEI, *La pace del 6 luglio 1498*, etc., *op. cit.*, in *Bollettino* cited, v. 746 n.   [3] GRAZIANI, pp. 723, 728-729 ; BONAZZI, i. 706.

[4] *Annali Decemv.*, 4 Novembre, 1488, c. 99t.

[5] DEGLI AZZI, *Il Tumulto del 1488 in Perugia e la politica di Lorenzo il Magnifico*, in *Bollettino* cited, xi. 407 *et seq.*

[6] The first attempt of the Degli Oddi was made in 1491 (see GRAZIANI, p. 742 *et seq.* ; FABRETTI, *Cronache*, ii. 64 *et seq.* ; *Cronica perugina inedita*, in *Bollettino* cited, ix. 359 *et seq.*, and a contemporary narrative published by ANSIDEI in *Bollettino* cited, xiv. 134-135). The second attempt is fully described by Matarazzo, and forms one of the most picturesque passages even in his pre-eminently picturesque chronicle. See MORGAN, *op. cit.*, pp. 40-59, and compare, for further details which explain the flight of the *fuorusciti* when the victory was practically within their grasp, FABRETTI, *Cronache*, ii. 114 ; MACHIAVELLI, *Discorsi*, iii. 14, and GUICCIARDINI, *Storia d' Italia*, Lib. iii. cap. i.

forty-eight families, devoted to the Baglioni, had been designated as those from among whose members alone the *Capitani del Contado* could be selected,[1] and *Lo Stato Baglionesco* seemed to be firmly established.   At this period Guido, the eldest of the family, whom Matarazzo speaks of as "subtle and wise beyond all men of his time," [2] appears to have exercised a predominant influence in the direction of public affairs—he is referred to, in a contemporary document, as *primarius civis civitatis Perusij*—but he undoubtedly shared the cares of government with his brother Ridolfo, who, in the opinion of Count Vincenzo Ansidei, was equally reputed *primarius civis* by his fellow-citizens.[3]   Over seventy years of servitude had rendered the democracy incapable of any organised resistance to the dominant class, and if the Baglioni had been able to live at peace among themselves, they might, perhaps, have become true Seigniors of Perugia, owing only such nominal allegiance to the Church as Florence owed to the Empire under the government of the Medicean Grand Dukes.   Unfortunately, however, every member of that family deemed himself as fit to bear rule as his fellows, and the "great betrayal" destroyed more than half of them.[4]   Thus ended what Matarazzo calls "el secondo stato de Peroscia"[5] on the 14th of July, 1500, after twelve years of such terrible misrule that all the ills which men had suffered under *Lo Stato de' Gentiluomini* seemed as nothing in comparison.[6]   Neither womanhood, nor the religious

---

[1] ANSIDEI, *Ricordi nuziali di Casa Baglioni*, in *Bollettino* cited, xiv. 130. As to the *Capitani del Contado*, see DEGLI AZZI, *I Capitani del Contado nel Comune di Perugia*, Perugia, Unione Tip. Coop., 1897 ; BRIGANTI, *Città Dominanti e Comuni Minori*, *op. cit.*, cap. v., and authorities there cited.

[2] MATARAZZO, p. 39 ;   MORGAN, p. 33.

[3] ANSIDEI, *op. cit.*, in *Bollettino* cited, xiv. 130.

[4] An inimitable and perhaps immortal chapter in J. A. SYMONDS' *Sketches in Italy* has made the story of *el gran tradimento* familiar to every English reader.

[5] MATARAZZO, pp. 138-139 ;   MORGAN, 144-145.

[6] MATARAZZO, p. 101 ;   MORGAN, p. 91 : ". . . but not to depart from the very truth, since the day when the Oddi and their followers were banished from our city, matters ever went from bad to worse."   That the chronicler is not exaggerating is proved by contemporary documents. See, for example, the *deliberazione* of 30th March, 1496, printed by ANSIDEI, *La pace del 6 luglio, 1498*, etc., in *Bollettino* cited, v. 749 n.

orders, nor any ties of blood or friendship were sacred to that terrible brood,[1] whose only virtue was their exceeding valour.   Even the panegyrist of the "Magnificent House" reluctantly admits that, as a result of their lawlessness and violence, "everything was undone which had been fairly ordered, on such wise that the city could no longer be spoken of as *Perusia augusta* but *Perusia angusta*, and, *quod peius esset, Perusia combusta*."[2]

Of the Baglioni who survived "the great betrayal," Troilo, Protonotary of S. Lorenzo, and afterwards Bishop of Perugia, was sick of a fever, Ridolfo was dying of the results of his debaucheries,[3] and Marcantonio was a confirmed invalid; Gentile "abode alway in Spello"; and thus the government of Perugia devolved upon Giovan Paolo and Morgante.[4] From thenceforward the edicts and proclamations no longer ran in the name of the *Dieci dell' Arbitrio*, but in that of the *Men of the Ecclesiastical State of Perugia*; and "this was done because the Magnificent House of Baglioni had not men enough left to provide for each Porta, nor would they suffer others, lesser men than they, to have a share in that to win which they had spilled their noble blood."[5]

For a time Perugia was better governed.   Giovan Paolo, who was above all else a warrior, preferred to lead the life of a *condottiero*, taking service with the Florentines, with the Pope and with the Sienese; and, in his absence, Morgante, who, as Matarazzo tells us, was "full of justice and equity, and was firmly purposed, as far as in him lay, to reform the manner of men's lives in Perugia," ruled alone.[6]   His premature death, in the summer of 1502,[7] left Giovan Paolo the sole seignior; but his complicity with the "dieta di

---

[1] See, for example, FABRETTI, *Cronache*, ii. 119.

[2] MATARAZZO, p. 144; MORGAN, p. 152.

[3] As to the terrible sufferings caused by the *male francioso*, compare MATARAZZO, pp. 32-36, a passage which it is much to be regretted that Mr Morgan has omitted from his translation.

[4] MATARAZZO, p. 148.

[5] MATARAZZO, p. 139; MORGAN, p. 148; BONAZZI, ii. 30.

[6] MATARAZZO, p. 154; MORGAN, pp. 166, 219-222.

[7] ALFANI, *Memorie perugine* in *Arch. Stor. It.*, XVI. ii. 247. BONAZZI (ii. 39) hints that Morgante was poisoned by Giovan Paolo. He, however, adduces no evidence in support of his theory.

falliti " at Magione, earned him the hatred of Cesare Borgia, and, after the massacre of Sinigaglia, the Baglioni were compelled to flee for their lives (5th January, 1503).[1]

> Sentì Perugia e Siena ancor la vampa
> Dell' Idra e ciaschedun di quei tiranni,
> Fuggendo innanzi alla sua furia, scampa.[2]

The Degli Oddi and the other exiles thereupon returned to their homes, and for a few months "almost we submitted to be ruled by the light of reason ; nor were the officers of justice any longer stoned like martyrs."[3] Scarcely, however, had Alexander VI. breathed his last than Giovan Paolo and Gentile re-entered the city after four hours' sharp fighting (9th September, 1503).[4] The majority of the populace seems to have rejoiced at their success, for if Perugia had been more law-abiding in their absence, she had also been shorn of all her ancient splendour, and men recalled regretfully " the sumptuous expenditure" of the Magnificent House and the vast sums of money which the soldiers of Giovan Paolo had been wont to squander there.[5] Wherefore "all that day the bells rang merrily, and in the evening bonfires were lighted for joy and gladness at the return of the Magnificent Captain and for the victory which he had won over his enemies." Nor does he seem to have disappointed the high hopes of the citizens. Not only did he restrain his soldiers from plundering the ward of Porta S. Angelo, which had always shown itself hostile to his house, and which they " were minded to sack as they had done at other times " ;[6] but Perugia appears to have enjoyed exceptional prosperity under his rule, so that Giulio di Costantino, who was born in 1503, and whose chronicle begins with the year 1517, was able to look back upon the days of his boyhood as a golden age of peace and plenty.[7]

---

[1] ALFANI, *ubi cit.* Compare *Lettere di Piero Ardinghelli, Commissario fiorentino*, pubblicate da C. GUASTI, *Arch. Stor. It.*, Serie III. Tom. xix. p. 21 *et seq.* Lettera del 19 gennaio, 1503. [2] MACHIAVELLI, *Decennale primo.*
[3] MATARAZZO, pp. 215, 222 ; MORGAN, pp. 239, 245.
[4] In addition to the chronicles, see FABRETTI, *Biografie*, etc., *op. cit.*, iii. 163-172.
[5] MATARAZZO, pp. 215-216 ; MORGAN, p. 240.
[6] MATARAZZO, pp. 242-243 ; MORGAN, p. 275.
[7] G. DI COSTANTINO, *Memorie di Perugia*, in FABRETTI, *Cronache*,

Giovan Paolo was strong enough to ignore the querulous complaints of the aged and decrepit Pius III.;[1] but in Julius II. he found his master ; and, on that Pope's advance towards Perugia, in August, 1506, he hastened to make submission.   At Orvieto, on the 8th of September, he agreed to put all the fortresses of the territory of Perugia and the gates of the city itself into the hands of the Pope, and also to aid him in his expedition against Bologna.[2]   On the 13th of September Julius entered Perugia, attended only by a small guard, and Machiavelli, who was in his train, marvelled at his rashness, since, in his opinion, Giovan Paolo, had he dared to be "honourably base," might not only have rid himself of his enemy at one blow, but might have gained thereby eternal renown.[3]   The policy which he actually pursued was, however, the wiser ; any violence offered to the Pope must have surely brought upon him a terrible retribution, and notwithstanding the recall of the Degli Oddi and other exiles, he still remained the principal citizen of Perugia ; while, after the death of Julius, he soon re-established his seignory,[4] being welcomed by the populace, on his return from Venice, in March, 1513, "almost as

iv. 145 : " In prima dirò che da poie che io conobbe el male dal biene (quale io naque nell' anno 1503 o circa) e poi insino a l' anno 1517, fu un vivere tanto bono e abundante de tutte e' biene, che non se poderia aquiperare ; non mortalità, non carestia, non guerra, ne altre cose a noi nocive, maxime in queste nostre paese de Peroscia, e un pezo atorno."

[1] *Arch. Stor. It.*, XVI. ii. 595.

[2] MACHIAVELLI, *Legazione seconda alla Corte di Roma*, Lettera x.

[3] MACHIAVELLI, *ubi cit.*, Lettera xii. ; *Discorsi*, i. c. 27 ; GUICCIARDINI, *Storia* cit., Lib. vii. c. i. The *Annali Decemvirali* (ad ann. c^ta 32) state that the Pope entered Perugia " cum maximo gentium armorum et aliorum numero " ; but apparently this may be taken as a mere flourish of the notary. See MARIOTTI, *Saggio*, etc., *op. cit.*, p. 556 *et seq.*, and FABRETTI, *Biografie*, etc., *op. cit.*, iii. 194-199, where the subject is fully discussed. Compare also CREIGHTON, *op. cit.*, v. 100-101. It is, perhaps, worthy of note that the annalist Teseo Alfani corroborates the account given in the *Annali Decemv.* : " Papa Giulio II. entrò in Perugia, . . . con molti reverendissimi cardinali, e vescovi et arcivescovi, e molti altri prelati, e con molta gente d' arme a piedi et a cavallo " (*Arch. Stor. It.*, XVI. ii. 249).

[4] At the head of the page of the *Annali Decemvirali* upon which are registered the names of the Priors for May and June, 1505, we see the arms of the Baglioni, flanked with the initials of Giovan Paolo. The fact is the more suggestive inasmuch as none of the Priors were Baglioni. Compare ANSIDEI, *Ricordi nuziali*, etc., *ubi cit.*, p. 136.

though he had been divine." Scarcely could he make his way through the jubilant crowd ; " all the bells of the Commune rang for joy, and all the people showed themselves delighted at his coming."[1] In the magistracy of the *Dodici del buon governo*, instituted in 1516, we find that Giovan Paolo and Gentile were appointed *indifferenter pro omnibus Portis*,[2] while Teseo Alfani tells us that, in the *Dieci dell' Arbitrio*, published on the 15th of June of the same year, Giovan Paolo and Gentile were "above all the others and possessed "l'autorità da tutti gli altri."[3] But, if legally equal, the stronger man was the actual ruler, and Fabretti does not hesitate to speak of "la signoria di Giampaolo."[4] Yet neither his valour nor his popularity long sufficed to save him from his fate ; and his end came in 1520, when he allowed himself to be lured to Rome by the lying promises of Leo X., and paid for his credulity with his life. Men whispered that his cousin Gentile had helped to bring about his ruin " for envy because he was a greater man than he," and he certainly profited by his death.[5]

On the 18th of March the news of Giovan Paolo's capture reached Perugia : on the 23rd his sons Malatesta and Orazio fled away by night, and Gentile remained " lord and master, in the grace of the said Pope."[6] He was, however, little better than a tool in the hands of the priests. The government was carried on by a council called the *Undecim Procuratores libertatis Status Ecclesiastici*, consisting of two members for each Porta, with Gentile himself as its permanent head. Finding it eminently adapted to serve his purpose, the Cardinal Legate invested it with extraordinary powers,[7] and the unfortunate citizens experienced all the horrors of ecclesi-

---

[1] ALFANI, *ubi cit.*, pp. 264-265.

[2] *Arch. Stor. It.*, XVI. ii. 599.

[3] ALFANI, *ubi cit.*, p. 275.

[4] FABRETTI, *Biografie*, etc., *op. cit.*, iii. 213.

[5] G. DI COSTANTINO, *ubi cit.*, p. 147. *Cf.* FABRETTI, *Biografie*, etc., *op. cit.*, iii. 222-232.

[6] FABRETTI, *Cronache*, ii. 137, iii. 81, iv. 147-148 ; *Arch. Stor. It.*, XVI. ii. 288-289.

[7] BONAZZI, ii. 81-82 ; and see the document published in *Arch. Stor. It.*, XVI. ii. 615-616.

astical rule.[1]   However, on the death of Leo, "those twin thunderbolts of war," Orazio and Malatesta, took up arms, and, with the help of the Duke of Urbino, expelled Gentile and his adherents, among whom were Braccio, Galeotto and Sforza, the sons of Grifonetto (4th January, 1522).[2]

Their achievement was of more than merely local importance. With Gentile were the Florentine levies and Vitello Vitelli ; and the victory of the sons of Giovan Paolo was, in fact, a victory of the French party, and in some slight measure tended to remove the disheartenment caused by the expulsion of Lautrec from Milan.

Hardly had Perugia capitulated than Orazio took part in an invasion of the Senese ; but the advance of Giovanni de' Medici with his celebrated *bande nere* compelled a hasty retreat,[3] and Perugia was threatened with a second siege.[4]   A peace was, however, patched up between the Baglioni ; and, in October, Gentile returned to the city.[5] In the events which followed Malatesta took no part, having accepted service with the Venetians ; but apparently Orazio and Gentile soon came to blows, and, on the 24th of January, 1523, the Papal Legate ordered the former to leave Perugia, "perchè stavano in arme lui et il signor Gentile"; while two days later, Gentile followed him into exile.[6] Both of them were subsequently summoned to Rome [7] and

---

[1] G. DI COSTANTINO, *ubi cit.*, p. 148 : " E de li a pocho tempo vine in questa terra a tenere ragione el cardenale de Cortona. . . . E mentre ce ste fe molte pregione in la prima sala del palazo, e impille in pocho tempo ; e faciva pigliare li omene a torto e diritto, e li faceva morire con diverse martorie, e in su la fune, e in to le pregione e faciva paghare molte denare, tal che in pocho tempo acumolò un gran denaio, per tanto che fe un palazzo for de Cortona, e puseli nome la Peroscina." TESEO ALFANI (*ubi cit.*, p. 290) tells us that " fu temuto più che nessun cardinale che fusse stato per legato nella nostra città " ; while Sciro Sciri, in his *Memorie di Perugia* (FABRETTI, *Cronache*, iii. 81) says that " a molti delli buoni cittadini fe mozzare il capo."

[2] In addition to the chronicles, see FUMI, *Relazione della presa di Perugia*, in *Bollettino* cited, vi. 69-97.

[3] ALFANI, *ubi cit.*, p. 295 ; PECCI, *Memorie storico-critiche della Città di Siena*, Parte II. pp. 80-84 ; MALAVOLTI, Parte III. Lib. vii. cta 121 ; GUICCIARDINI, *Storia* cited, Lib. xiv. cap. v.

[4] *Arch. Stor. It.*, XVI. ii. 295-296.   [5] FABRETTI, *Cronache*, ii. 144.

[6] ALFANI, *ubi cit.*, pp. 301-302 ; FABRETTI, *Cronache*, ii. 145, iii. 83.

[7] FABRETTI, *Cronache*, iii. 83 : " Adì 26 marzo [1523] detto Papa mandò

imprisoned in Castel S. Angelo.[1]   Gentile was soon released, but Orazio only recovered his liberty in January, 1527, when Clement VII. required his services in the field.   The lanzknechts of Frundsberg had already reached Piacenza.   His release was hailed with rejoicing by his fellow-citizens,[2] and he took part in the defence of Rome. Repeated references to his actions during those disastrous days will be found in the *Vita* of Benvenuto Cellini, who professes to have been greatly beloved by him : "mi voleva molto bene."[3]   We can well believe it.   They must have suited one another perfectly.   It would be difficult to say which was the greater ruffian.

In July, 1524, Gentile returned to Perugia,[4] where he appears to have once more proved himself a willing tool of the ecclesiastical government ; while so anxious was he to show his devotion to the Pope who had imprisoned him that, in 1526, we find him taking part in the disastrous attack upon Siena.[5]   Among the trophies of the battle of Camollia were five pieces of Perugian artillery.[6]   In the following year the Duke of Urbino encamped at Deruta with the army of the League, and refused to continue his march until Gentile and all his adherents had left Perugia.[7]

per detto signore Gentile e detto signore Orazio che andassero a Roma, e ambidue vi andarono a ribenedirsi, e il medesimo Papa un mese dopo si morì."   This was Pope Adrian VI.   The news of the election of Clement VII. was sent to Perugia from Rome by Gentile.   See ALFANI, *ubi cit.*, p. 303.

[1] ALFANI, *ubi cit.* ; FABRETTI, *Cronache*, ii. 146, iii. 84, iv. 151.

[2] *Annali Decemv.*, ad ann. c. 7 : " Agetis gratias Beatitudini sue nomine totius civitatis, quod magnum virum Oratium Baglionum precipuum inter optimates nostros ex vinculis exemerit ac in gratiam suam benignissime receperit pristineque libertatis restituerit."   Such were the instructions given by the Priors, in February, 1527, to Riccardo Bartolini, ambassador to the Pope.   They declared that the house of Baglioni " semper huic civitati precipuum decus ac ornamentum accessit et sedie apostolice semper fidelissima fuit," etc.   Compare FABRETTI, *Biografie*, etc., iv. 45.

[3] *Vita di Benvenuto Cellini* (edizione BACCI), pp. 75-76.   Compare also pp. 72, 82.

[4] FABRETTI, *Cronache*, iii. 84.

[5] GUICCIARDINI, *Storia* cited, Lib. xvii. cap. iii.

[6] ALFANI, *ubi cit.*, pp. 307-308.   *Cf.* L. DOUGLAS, *A History of Siena, op. cit.*, pp. 217-218, and my *Palio and Ponte*, pp. 44-47.   See also my *A Pictorial Chronicle of Siena* (Siena, Torrini, 1902), pp. 83-86.

[7] *Arch. Stor. It.*, XVI. ii. 316 and n. : " . . . questa opera che fece detto

Malatesta was still in Lombardy, and for the moment the citizens were rid of the Baglioni ; and the helplessness of Clement, shut up in Castel S. Angelo, emboldened them to establish once more a democratic form of government.   On the 21st of May, 1527, four hundred *popolani* presented themselves in the Palace of the Magnificent Priors and demanded the institution of a Council of Five-hundred, consisting of a hundred citizens from each *Porta*, "the which council was to be perpetual and to bear rule and governance over the city."[1]   Their demands were acceded to ; but, on the 12th of June, Orazio returned, to be followed four days later by Gentile.   The Priors and the Council compelled them to make peace in the most solemn and binding form, "and they kissed one another, and bells were rung for joy, and bonfires lighted."[2]   The temporal power of the Papacy seemed a thing of the past ; Clement was still a prisoner, and it was hoped that he would only return to his office as mass priest at St John Lateran.[3]   If her nobles could be induced to live together in unity, Perugia felt that there was yet a fair future before her.   Unfortunately, however, even had her dreams with regard to the Papacy been fulfilled, she was building on sand when she trusted the Baglioni.   Little more than six weeks from the day of their reconciliation, Gentile was assassinated at the instigation of Orazio, while two days later Galeotto shared the same fate.[4]   The death

---

duca d' Urbino, la fece per sodisfare i figlioli di Giovan Paolo Baglioni, i quali non erano nella terra, ma v' erano gli altri loro seguaci che operavano per loro."   Compare DENNISTOUN, *Memoirs of the Dukes of Urbino* (edition cited), iii. 19.   This is one of the very few places where Mr Hutton has neglected to supply us with the necessary data to correct the misleading statements of his author.   The Duke did not " substitute his friend Orazio for Gentile."   Orazio was still in Rome.   The rest of the narrative will, however, prove useful to the reader who is interested in following the " amazing route " of the army of the League.

[1] *Arch. Stor. It.*, XVI. ii. 317 ; BONAZZI, ii. 103.

[2] ALFANI, *ubi cit.*, p. 318 ; FABRETTI, *Cronache*, ii. 151, iii. 86, iv. 158.

[3] VARCHI, *Storia Fiorentina*, v. 15.   Compare CREIGHTON, *op. cit.*, vi. 348 *et seq.* ; ARMSTRONG, *The Emperor Charles V.* (London : Macmillan & Co., 1902), Vol. I. p. 178, and G. DE LEVA, *Storia documentata di Carlo V.*, Vol. II. p. 439.

[4] In addition to the chronicles, see FABRETTI, *Biografie*, etc., iv. 62-67, and VARCHI, *Storia Fiorentina*, iv. 28.

of their murderer, in the following year at the siege of Naples,[1] left Malatesta to rule alone.

Meanwhile Clement had been reconciled with the Emperor, and was devoting all his energies to the restoration of the Medici. In 1529 Malatesta took service with Florence, and conducted the defence of that city against the papal armies. After its surrender he re-entered Perugia in triumph —" con grandissimo trionfo et allegrezza." All the populace, both gentlemen and common folk, poured forth from the gates to meet and welcome him ; the public festivities continued for three successive evenings, and he seems to have been acclaimed as the saviour of Florence. " E salvolla che non fo sacchegiata nè usurpata," writes Zuccone ;[2] while Bontempi tells the same story : " All his soldiers, and especially his captains, returned stuffed with ducats and with gold chains about their necks. The Signoria of Florence, to wit the new government, hath given the aforesaid Seignior Malatesta ten very beautiful pieces of artillery and two lion cubs and many yards of silken stuffs. His Holiness, our Seignior, hath not only pardoned him and all his folk which have been in Florence, but hath given him Bevagna, Castellabono, Limigiana, and half of all the Chiusi, which the Apostolic Camera had, unto the third generation. Moreover, it hath been granted him that the Vice-Legate may recall from exile such homicides as he shall name who have been in Florence,[3] and that he and all his family may carry weapons wheresoever they go. All the which things have been conceded unto him by his Holiness because he hath given him Florence and hath saved her from pillage, contrary to the expectation of all men."[4] Frolliere is even more enthusiastic, declaring that " herein was shown his supreme glory and valour and greatness of mind and prudence in the things of war."[5]

---

[1] *Arch. Stor. It.*, XVI. ii. 328 ; SEGNI, *Istorie fiorentine* (edition of 1857), Lib. ii. p. 62.   [2] FABRETTI, *Cronache*, ii. 159.

[3] See FABRETTI, *Documenti di Storia Perugina*, Vol. II. Doc. xxxix. p. 261 *et seq.*   [4] *Arch, Stor. It.*, XVI. ii. 342-343.

[5] FROLLIERE, *La Guerra del Sale*, in *Arch. Stor. It.*, XVI. ii. 442-443. Malatesta's conduct of the defence of Florence has been stigmatized as " one of the greatest of public crimes " ; but his detractors have, in the

During the preceding year Perugia had been emptied of a large part of her population. Over a thousand Perugians were with Malatesta in Florence, and others with Braccio and Sforza Baglioni in the ranks of the besieging army. Under these circumstances the *Mosceschi,* as the adherents of Gentile were called from the taciturnity of their late chief,[1] had experienced no great difficulty in re-establishing their authority in Perugia "with the favour of the priests," and the government of the city had become almost wholly ecclesiastical. However, on the return of Malatesta, *Peroscia,* to adopt the telling phrase of the annalist, *se nettò de moscesche e birra.*[2] " And," he continues, " the name and fame of the Seignior Malatesta was spread abroad not only in Italy but beyond the borders of Italy, and principally because he had had honour against the Spaniards and the Pope and the Emperor ; and the Pope went in fear of him, so that, as long as he was in Perugia, he dared not command or make other disposition in the city, but let the horse run according to the will of the Seignior Malatesta."[3]

Unfortunately Malatesta's health had been hopelessly impaired by his debaucheries ;[4] and, on the 24th of December, 1531, he passed away at Bettona. Men said that his end was presaged and accompanied by strange portents, and that " there were signs in the heavens as at the death of Cæsar." For many nights a great meteor blazed over Monte Malbe, while, later on, a terrible wind " shattered the roofs and houses which stood in its path, and principally the house of the Seignior Malatesta. . . . Moreover, the night whereon he died, there came rain and hail and thunder and

---

main, judged him almost exclusively from a Florentine standpoint. That his behaviour was blameworthy need not be denied, but there is much to be said in mitigation. The case for the defence is well stated by BONAZZI (ii. 120-129), and his conclusions are the more worthy of serious consideration from the fact that he is by no means an admirer of the Baglioni.

[1] " qual ditta parte era ditta moscesche, perchè el signor Gentile era omo freddo e di poche parole, talchè si uno li andava a parlare li rispondiva pocho o niente."

[2] G. DI COSTANTINO, *Memorie,* etc., *ubi cit.,* p. 164.

[3] *Ibid.,* p. 167.

[4] " Nota ch'el signor Malatesta era como un coccio de bagino per el mal francioso che avia auto per lungo tempo."

many other tokens." [1]   Also it was reported that, in his last hours, he was dowered with prophetic vision, and "spake to them which stood by, saying, ' Aid me, if ye may, for after my death ye will be forced to bear the yoke and to draw the cart like buffalo.' The which thing," says Frolliere, "followed in very sooth ; and not only have we borne the yoke, but also the goad and the whip." [2]

At this time Ridolfo, the son of Malatesta, was only thirteen years old, and his cousin, Giovan Paolo, even younger. The Pope hastened to proclaim them rebels and to despoil them of all their possessions.[3]   In the following July, Braccio Baglioni returned to Perugia, and a period of violence and lawlessness ensued which recalls the worst days of *Lo Stato Baglionesco*.[4]   After the death of Clement, Ridolfo entered the city with his adherents (1st November, 1534), and the *Mosceschi* fled without striking a blow ; the Vice-Legate, Cinzio Filonardi, his auditor Andrea, the Prior Giovanni di Stefano, and Marco, the brother of the Vice-Legate, were brutally murdered ; Porta S. Angelo was sacked and the Palace of the Governor burned to the ground.[5] For a few short weeks Ridolfo was Seignior of Perugia, but the new Pope was resolved to make an end of the Baglioni, and to destroy, once and for all, the last remnants of Perugian liberty. Nor is it probable that, if the government imposed upon them had been even tolerably just and merciful, the Perugians would have offered much resistance to the establishment of a papal absolutism. They were too utterly weary of the Baglioni and all their ways not to believe that any change which would rid them of their old tyrants must be a change for the better ; and, on the 22nd of December, Ridolfo, finding that he could look for no support from the citizens, departed in obedience to the papal orders.

[1] G. DI COSTANTINO, *ubi cit.*, p. 167.   [2] FROLLIERE, *ubi cit.*, p. 443.
[3] FABRETTI, *Cronache*, iv. 172 ; *Arch. Stor. It.*, XVI. ii. 343.
[4] See BONAZZI, ii. 136-138.
[5] *Arch. Stor. It.*, XVI. ii. 356-357 ; FABRETTI, *Cronache*, ii. 123, 173, iii. 94, iv. 204-205. As to Cinzio Filonardi and his government of Perugia, see FUMI, *La legazione del Card. Ippolito de' Medici nell' Umbria*, in *Bollettino* cited, v. 477 *et seq*.

At the same time Braccio was banished with all his house, and the good Bontempi expresses a pious hope that " God may confound both the one party and the other, for they are the ruin of this poor city." [1]

Unfortunately Paul III.'s choice of a governor was not a wise one, and, owing to his tyrannies and indiscretions, the smouldering embers of Perugia's ancient desire for communal liberty were fanned into a fierce expiring blaze. Cesare Trivulzi, the new Vice-Legate and Governor, entered the city on the 1st of January, 1535, and after dispossessing the Priors of their Palace, on the ground that the usual residence of the Governor had been burned by Ridolfo, set up a pulley over the northern doorway, " beside the Griffin," *per dare la fune.* By his orders many of the windows were walled up, and the building was converted into a fortress, [2] while he added insult to injury by scornfully declaring that the Perugians were no better than mongrel curs, who might bark but dared not bite. [3] He was soon undeceived. On the 10th of February the people assembled and demanded that the statutes should be observed and the Council of Five Hundred revived. Trivulzi endeavoured to gain time ; he pleaded that he must first communicate with the Pope, and finally promised an answer on the morrow. Thereupon " every man ran to take up arms : and they returned armed to the Piazza, so that the Piazza seemed a cane-brake." [4] The terrified Governor at once yielded; but on the following day, when the citizens convened to fill the vacancies which had been caused by the death of the members of the Council since its last session eight years earlier, he " abode shut up in the Palace with his guard," and, on the 12th, fled from Perugia " to his little honour." [5]

A new Governor was sent, but new tumults followed, and

---

[1] BONTEMPI, *Ricordi della Città di Perugia*, in *Arch. Stor. It.*, XVI. ii. 359.

[2] BONTEMPI, *ubi cit.*, p. 359 ; FABRETTI, *Cronache*, ii. 176, iv. 207-208.

[3] " al popolo diciva che eravamo can da pagliaio che abaiavamo e non morsichavamo."

[4] " talchè la piaza pariva un canneto." G. DI COSTANTINO, *ubi cit.*, p. 209.

[5] *Arch. Stor. It.*, XVI. ii. 361 ; FABRETTI, *Cronache*, ii. 177-178, iii. 95, iv. 209.

he too departed, " insalutato hospite," as says Bontempi, on the 13th of July.[1] The *contado* was devastated by papal troops,[2] and the citizens were divided against themselves : Guelfs, Ghibellines, and *Preteschi*.[3] Yet the Perugians still hoped against hope, and when Paul himself visited the city, on the 9th of September, he was welcomed with undiminished loyalty.[4] Only in 1540 did the populace finally rise in furious revolt to resist a last intolerable injustice which united all classes against the oppressor. Their cause was righteous, but they were hopelessly overmatched, and the last faint spark of Perugian liberty was all too easily trodden out. The end of Pisa was not unworthy of her ancient greatness ; Siena's sun set in such a blaze of splendour that perhaps the world shall never see the like again ; even the unwarlike Florentines fought, at the last, as fiercely as rats in a trap ; but Perugia's death agony was as the writhing of the worm beneath the plough-share. She has splendid memories and to spare ; but the siege of 1540 is not of them.

In July, 1538, there had been a terrible hail-storm which destroyed and ruined the *contado* " for three or four miles round Perugia." One chronicler tells us that the hailstones were as big as walnuts ; another that the damage was estimated at 30,000 *scudi*, and a third that no grapes were gathered that year and scarcely any olives. " Nor is there any man living who remembers so great a tempest." [5] Thereafter, from the 26th of December, there were continual snowstorms which " did much damage to the olive trees and brake many of them." The cold was intense, and the snow froze on the ground, as hard and slippery as glass, so that the streets of the city and the roads of the *contado* were well-

---

[1] BONTEMPI, *ubi cit.*, p. 364 ; G. DI COSTANTINO, *ubi cit.*, p. 218.

[2] G. DI COSTANTINO, *ubi cit.*, pp. 218, 220 ; BONTEMPI, *ubi cit.*, p. 364.

[3] FABRETTI, *Cronache*, iv. 223. The chronicler adds that " per onne uno de li altre erano vinte ghelfe o più." As to the Guelfs and Ghibellines at this period, compare BURCKHARDT (edition VALBUSA), Vol. I. P. i. cap. vi. pp. 62-63, which corresponds to pages 76-77 of the English translation of S. G. C. MIDDLEMORE. London, 1878. The Guelfs of Perugia were the partisans of Ridolfo.

[4] See MARIOTTI, *Saggio*, etc., *op. cit.*, pp. 591-629.

[5] FABRETTI, *Cronache*, ii. 124, iii. 100, 131, iv. 235.

nigh impassable ; while from the 1st of March to the 12th of April, 1539, there was a perpetual downfall of rain.   As a consequence, every kind of crop suffered, and there was a terrible scarcity of food.[1]

Such was the condition of things in Perugia when, early in 1540, Paul III. published his bull increasing the price of salt by three *quattrini* a pound throughout the states of the Church, *sub pœna rebellionis, interdicti, confiscationis bonorum, privationis privilegiorum et Comitatus.*[2]   At first sight the matter might seem a small one.   In the Italian-English dictionaries the word " farthing " is ordinarily given as the equivalent of *quattrino*, and three farthings in the pound would not appear a very ruinous advance in price. This translation is, however, misleading.   It is true that a *quattrino* was only the sixtieth part of the Tuscan *lira*, containing four *danari* or *piccioli*, and that three *quattrini* went to the *soldo* ; but we must also bear in mind the purchasing power of money at that period.   Even in 1539, when everything was at famine prices, three *quattrini* would buy a measure (*foglietta*) of wine, and five or six *quattrini* a pound of meat.[3]   Moreover, there can, I think, be little doubt that the purchase of a certain definite quantity of salt was compulsory,[4] and a contemporary chronicler informs us that this increase in price constituted a tax of no less than 20,000 or 24,000 *scudi*,[5] which, in the existing condition of affairs, meant absolute ruin to the city and its *contado*.[6]

That the imposition was flagrantly illegal there can be no manner of doubt ; not only was it contrary to the *Capitoli*

---

[1] G. DI COSTANTINO, *ubi cit.*, pp. 236, 238.   See also BONAZZI, ii. 157-159.

[2] BONTEMPI, *ubi cit.*, p. 376 ; FROLLIERE, *ubi cit.*, p. 405 ; FABRETTI, *Cronache*, ii. 87, iv. 241.   Compare also *Compendio degli Annali del* P. TIMOTEO BOTTONIO, in *Arch. Stor. It.*, IX. 115.

[3] G. DI COSTANTINO, *ubi cit.*, p. 240.   On the subject in general, compare my *Palio and Ponte, op. cit.*, p. 87.

[4] Such was the case in almost all the Mediæval Communes.   Compare, for example, C. FALLETTI-FOSSATI, *Costumi Senesi nella seconda metà del Secolo XIV.* (Siena, Tip. dell' Ancora, 1881), pp. 61-62, and CANESTRINI, *La Scienza e l' Arte di Stato* (Firenze, Le Monnier, 1862), P. I. cap. i, § vii., there cited.

[5] G. DI COSTANTINO, *ubi cit.*, p. 242.

[6] BONTEMPI, *ubi cit.*, p. 377.

of Martin V.,[1] but it contravened the plain words of the
Capitoli of Eugenius IV. ;[2] and the Perugians felt all the
more indignant because they were thoroughly convinced
that the Pope's plea that the money was needed to combat
the Lutheran heresy and to provide for the defence of
Christendom against the Turks was a mere pretext, and
that it would, in fact, be used for the expenses of his Court
and the advancement of his bastards.[3] Ambassadors were
sent to Rome beseeching him to respect the rights of the
Commune ; and when the news was brought that he was
immovable in his resolution to enforce the tax, the citizens,
regardless of the hopelessness of the struggle, determined to
resist to the uttermost. " Neither did they attend any more
to business, trade or merchandise, but every manner of folk
gat them ready to battle. . . . And the young men cared
for naught, nor took thought for anything save only to
prepare weapons of every sort, even as if they desired war,
it seeming to every one that, by reason of the righteous-
ness of their quarrel, they must assuredly be victorious.
Wherefore, trusting in Christ, the great Redeemer and
Defender of Justice and Truth, they made ready for the
defence of their native city with glad and courageous hearts.
And if any there was of another opinion, who would have
spoken his mind, incontinently the multitude fell upon him
even as though he had been an enemy of their city and of
its citizens, on such wise that every man kept silence and
opened not his lips for fear." [4]

A commission or *balìa* of twenty-five citizens was elected,
which soon acquired dictatorial powers. Not only did it
override the authority of the Priors and the other Magistrates, but even that of the Vice-Legate himself. His
position soon became intolerable, and, on the 29th of March
according to Frolliere,[5] on the 3rd of April according to
Bontempi,[6] he departed in high dudgeon, " wotting well

---

[1] *Capitula Martini V.*, Art. xxx., *ubi cit.*, pp. xli-xlii.

[2] See FROLLIERE, *ubi cit.*, p. 410 n., and the *Memoriale* of the Perugians
to Cosimo, Duke of Florence, published in *Arch. Stor. It.*, XVI. ii. 626-628.

[3] FROLLIERE, *ubi cit.*, p. 406.   [4] FROLLIERE, *ubi cit.*, pp. 414-415.

[5] FROLLIERE, *ubi cit.*, p. 423.

[6] BONTEMPI, *ubi cit.*, p. 378. Under this date he writes : " God help

21

that the Perugian people was minded to live according to its own good pleasure, licentiously and without the rule of superiors." Ambassadors were sent to the Emperor and to Cosimo de' Medici ; while, if we may credit a contemporary writer, the Perugians were willing to run to any lengths and even to renounce their ancient faith, if so be they might hope to profit by a Lutheran alliance.[1]

Some two weeks earlier the Pope had declared Perugia rebel and excommunicate ; and now that the departure of the Vice-Legate had made an open rupture inevitable, the citizens resolved to appeal to a higher tribunal. The religious orders refused the sanction of their presence ; but, on the 5th of April, all the lay fraternities, the magistrates, and the people gathered at the Church of S. Domenico and marched in procession to the Piazza, where, above the door of the cathedral, hung the image of a Crucified Christ, and below it, a S. Ercolano clad in episcopal robes.[2] To the Saviour of mankind and to Perugia's patron saint the keys of all the gates were offered, being laid at the feet of the crucifix, while the crowd fell upon their knees in the dust, beseeching the Divine Lord to take their city into His most holy keeping, crying with one voice, *Misericordia, Misericordia, Misericordia*. As the papal armies gathered and concentrated upon the town, the confidence of the citizens turned to terror, and the Piazza saw strange sights. The old wild rites of the thirteenth century flagellants were

us, in that we stand in very grievous peril, and the ruin of the city draweth nigh." Evidently he was one of those who would have spoken, but " per timore stava quieto e rimesso, e non ardiva parlare." G. DI COSTANTINO (*ubi cit.*, p. 246) agrees with Bontempi that the Vice-Legate left Perugia on the 3rd of April.

[1] FUMI, *Ragguaglio della Rebellione di Perugia*, in *Bollettino* cited, xiv. 81 : " Nei primi tumulti loro fu pensato se valer si potessero de' luterani che anchor in questo intendevano ; et mentre si stette in quei frangenti, diedero fuora molte opre di tali heresie, et si vedevano ben litterati huomini tra[rre ?] negli avversi grandemente." The words quoted form the concluding sentence of an evidently contemporary narrative existing in the ARCH. DI STATO IN MILANO, *Potenze Estere (Perugia)*, and of which it appears extremely probable that the author was no other than the Vice-Legate himself.

[2] See SCALVANTI, *Il Crocifisso della Porta di S. Lorenzo a Perugia*, in *Bollettino* cited, viii. 185-211.

revived, and, day and night, vast multitudes of people scourged themselves before the dumb, passionless, inexorable Christ whose aid they had so unavailingly invoked.[1]

Only once did their hopes revive for a moment, when Ridolfo Baglioni, whom they had called to their assistance and whose coming they had wellnigh ceased to expect, entered Porta S. Susanna, " like a thunderbolt, with many horsemen and soldiers, and was in the Piazza ere any man knew it." [2]   That was on the 16th of May.   Little more than a fortnight later all was over and Perugia had capitulated.   Before the end of June the houses of the Baglioni were being levelled with the ground to make room for the great fortress which was destined to hold the city in subjection to the Papacy.

---

[1] BONTEMPI, *ubi cit.*, p. 378 ; FROLLIERE, *ubi cit.*, p. 456 ; FABRETTI, *Cronache*, ii. 88, 124, 189, iii. 13, iv. 246.

[2] FROLLIERE, *ubi cit.*, p. 459.   SCIRO SCIRI, in his *Memorie di Perugia* (FABRETTI, *Cronache*, iii. 102), tells us that Ridolfo " venne con cento cavalli incirca e con fanti non già suoi tutti da Firenze " ; NICOLÒ ZUCCONE (*ubi cit.*, p. 190) speaks of " 50 cavalli o circha," while G. DI COSTANTINO (*ubi cit.*, p. 248) writes that " avia con luie da 25 o 30 cavaglie."   They were all eye-witnesses.   The reader may take his choice.

CHAPTER XXIII

THE PAPAL TYRANNY

THE great painters of the Quattrocento never sought to avoid anachronisms, and even when they depicted the scenes and events of a far earlier period, almost invariably filled their canvases with men and women of their own generation and with the objects and places which they saw daily before their eyes. These they represented with marvellous accuracy; and therefore it is that, if we would gain an adequate idea of Colle Landone before the Baglioni palaces were demolished to make way for the Papal Fortress, we can hardly do better than begin our inquiries with a careful examination of the affreschi of Bonfigli, and in particular of that one of them which depicts Perugia besieged by Totila. There we see the Church of S. Ercolano, the street leading to the Porta Marzia, the gate itself, and a considerable part of the ancient walls. Above these are the roofs of the houses, rising like steps on the side of the hill, and surmounted by a veritable forest of lofty towers, the greater part of which must have belonged to the Baglioni.

Already, in the Trecento, the Baglioni were settled in Colle Landone. There, in 1393, Pandolfo "restò morto a' piedi del suo uffizio"; [1] there, in 1436, his son Malatesta demolished the houses of the Guidalotti, to build himself a towered palace; [2] while, before the end of the century, that

---

[1] FABRETTI, *Cronache*, i. 51; *Arch. Stor. It.*, XVI. i. 258; PELLINI, ii. 46.

[2] GRAZIANI, p. 410: "A questi dì fuor fornite de spianare le case dei Guidalotte, cioè le fè spianare e spazzare Malatesta de Pandolfo dei Baglione, che erano casaline lì nel colle di Landone, per farce fare li casamente per sè et anche la torre. Se disse che quando fo murata la dicta torre, ce fu fatto uno prellato che pigliava uno nel petto e davali con uno coltello et amazavalo, sì como advenne quando lo Abbate dei ditti Guidalotti amazzò Biordo dei Michelotti. . . ."

part of the city had been almost entirely monopolized by his descendants. Of the topography of this district anterior to the construction of the Rocca Paolina much may be learned from the sketches of Sangallo, preserved in the Galleria degli Uffizi at Florence, a careful study of which has recently been made by Ing. G. Bacile di Castiglione,[1] with the result that we are now able to speak with tolerable certainty regarding the approximate position of the more important buildings which, in 1540, surrounded the "*due piazze*, where were the houses of the Signori Baglioni."[2]

From the *Piazza Grande*, the *platea comunis* (which then occupied the whole of the space between the *Duomo* and the modern *Piazza Umberto I.*), there were three streets leading to the houses of the Baglioni. Of these, the central one (which, though narrower, corresponded with the present *Corso Vannucci*) led to the *Sapienza Nuova*, where it divided into two branches, one of which led to the *Piazza de' Servi*, and the other, turning almost at right angles, to the *Piazzetta de' Baglioni*. The second street, to the left of the first and central one, would seem to have corresponded with the narrow *Via del Forte*, which now separates the *Palazzo Donini* from the *Palace Hotel*, and led straight to the *Piazzetta de' Baglioni*; while the third street, to the right of the central one, corresponded with the modern *Via Bonazzi*, and led to the *Piazza de' Servi*, skirting the church of the same name. This I believe to be the street which is referred to in the chronicles as the *strada di S. Maria de' Servi*.[3]

The *Piazza de' Servi* was bounded on the north by the *Sapienza Nuova*; on the east by the houses of Ridolfo and of Braccio; on the west by the Church of *S. Maria de' Servi*,

[1] G. BACILE DI CASTIGLIONE, *Dal Corso a S. Giuliana*, in *Augusta Perusia. Rivista di Topografia, Arte e Costumi dell' Umbria* (Perugia, L'Unione Tipografia Cooperativa, 1906), Vol. I. pp. 1-4, 18-21. Compare also *La Rocca Paolina di Perugia* by the same author, published in *L'Arte*, Anno vi., fascicoli xi., xii.

[2] FROLLIERE, *ubi cit.*, p. 473. The Fortress was built "*ai piedi delle due piazze*," and therefore on the southern slope of the hill.

[3] See, for example, FABRETTI, *Cronache*, ii. 182.

and on the south by the ancient Etruscan walls, looking out over the same fair landscape upon which the twentieth century tourist gazes from the modern *Giardinetto*. This was the spot where the Baglioni supped together at the home-coming of the bride of Messer Astorre, on the evening of the 28th of June, in the year 1500, when all the piazza was "covered with cloth broidered with their cognizance and set about with tables and sideboards sumptuous and great." [1]

Up to the second quarter of the fifteenth century, the northern end of the *Piazza de' Servi* had been occupied by an inn, called the *Albergo del Leone*, which was purchased by Benedetto de' Guidalotti, in 1426, and converted into a college for the use of the students of the University. [2] The work was begun on the 7th of June, 1427, [3] but it does not appear to have been finished until 1443. At any rate, we read that, on the 8th of October in that year, "the students began to dwell and reside in the *Sapienza Nuova*." [4]

The Church of *S. Maria de' Servi* seems to have been built between 1432 and 1437, on the site of an earlier church of the same name, by that numerous band of Lombard *maestri* who laboured contemporaneously upon *S. Lorenzo*, *S. Domenico*, *S. Francesco*, and the *Palazzo nuovo de' Priori*. [5] Enlarged and embellished by Braccio Baglioni, the grandfather of Grifonetto, [6] it became a very beautiful church ; and, at the time of its destruction, contained, as Giulio di Costantino tells us, no fewer than "twenty-two altars besides the great altar ; and it was a place convenient for the friars and for the city, remote and apt for devotion and delightful to betake oneself thereunto for the divine offices. . . . And there were many banners of dead Baglioni there. . . ." [7]

On the opposite side of the Piazza, "adjoining the *Sapienza Nuova*," [8] stood the Palace of Braccio, the son of

---

[1] MATARAZZO, p. 108 ; MORGAN, p. 101.
[2] FABRETTI, *Cronache*, ii. 6 ; GRAZIANI, p. 320.
[3] GRAZIANI, p. 324.   [4] GRAZIANI, p. 539.
[5] GRAZIANI, pp. 359, 418.   [6] MATARAZZO, p. 7 ; MORGAN, p. 6.
[7] FABRETTI, *Cronache*, iv. 279-280. Compare also ii. 52, 105.
[8] " e stava appicciato *cum* la Sapienzia Nova."

Grifonetto, the most lordly house in all the city. "In it was a room wherein were painted all the Captains which ever Perugia had even unto that day, and also all the famous jurisconsults, each one after his own likeness. The whole house was painted within and without, from the top thereof even unto the ground, and it had two towers." [1]   In one of these there was a clock, while there seems also to have been a courtyard, surrounded by a portico or peristyle —the *chiostro de casa de Grifone*, into which Giovan Paolo, fleeing across the roofs, on the night of "the great betrayal," was minded to leap down. [2]   To the southward stood the palace of Ridolfo, and it would appear from the drawings of Sangallo that, together with the *Sapienza Nuova*, the houses of Ridolfo and of Braccio formed a single block of buildings.

To the eastward of the *Piazza de' Servi* lay the *Piazzetta de' Baglioni*; and, if I am not mistaken, these two squares were only separated by the houses of Ridolfo and of Braccio, which thus formed the eastern boundary of the one and the western boundary of the other.   From the *piazzetta* a narrow street descended to the Etruscan walls and divided the palace of Ridolfo from that of Gentile. [3]   The latter was a magnificent dwelling-place, richly decorated and surmounted by two lofty towers.   The remains of one of them are said still to exist in the subterranean passages below the *Giardinetto*, though now no longer accessible.   According to one of the drawings of Sangallo, the "*Osteria di S^{to} Marcho*," the most fashionable inn of the city, was situated in the

---

[1] MATARAZZO, p. 104 ; MORGAN, p. 96.   Compare also FABRETTI, *Biografie*, etc., iii. 20-21, and *Schiarimenti alla vita di Boldrino da Panicale*, pp. 43 *et seq.*

[2] MATARAZZO, p. 120 ; MORGAN, p. 119.

[3] According to Ing. G. BACILE DI CASTIGLIONE (*ubi cit.*, p. 3) the Palace of Braccio stood to the south of the Palace of Ridolfo, and he consequently tells us (p. 4) that the street in question separated the houses not of Ridolfo and Gentile but of Gentile and Braccio.   He however admits that, in the drawings of Sangallo, there is no indication of the relative position of the two houses ; and to me it seems obvious that, since the Palace of Braccio "stava appicciato *cum* la Sapienzia Nova," it must have stood to the northward.   Moreover, if we accept this view, the story of the flight of Giovan Paolo "su li tette" becomes more intelligible.

in such devilish sort, that the wretches, who had dared to question the deeds of Christ's Vicar on earth, once introduced into the cavity through the apertures barely sufficient to admit a crawling figure, could neither stand nor sit in them." And albeit, from an æsthetic standpoint, the disappearance of the Papal Fortress is, no doubt, to be regretted, we can hardly wonder at the delight of the citizens whom Thomas Adolphus Trollope (perhaps the last Englishman to see the *Rocca Paolina* before its demolition, in 1862) beheld "gloating over the progressing destruction of the detested walls." [1]

And verily the days of its construction were as sorrowful as those of its destruction were merry ; for the building of it was attended by much cruelty and oppression. All the towns and villages of the *contado* were ordered to provide labourers at their own expense ; [2] while peasants who came to the city on market-days, to sell the produce of their farms or to buy a little bread for their families, were forcibly detained and their beasts of burden taken from them. " Thus," says Giulio di Costantino, " was Perugia reduced to the likeness of hell, in that the entering in was free, but there was no going out again." [3] Nor was this the worst. Not only were the wretched *contadini* forced to labour without remuneration, and, at first at any rate, without either food or drink, [4] but their very lives were imperilled by the brutality of their taskmasters. Monsignor della Barba entrusted the superintendence of the work to one of his grooms, a certain Girolamo Gambaro, who "was of his nature more cruel than any other man of that time ; . . . and ever he carried a great cudgel, wherewith, if by ill fortune any man stayed to draw breath, he smote him so sorely that some died at his hands and many were crippled." [5]

[1] T. A. TROLLOPE, *A Lenten Journey in Umbria and the Marches* (London : Chapman & Hall, 1862), pp. 110-111. This being a good book is, of course, never read by the tourist.

[2] FABRETTI, *Cronache*, iv. 261.   [3] FABRETTI, *Cronache*, iv. 262.

[4] Only in July, 1541, " se ottenne dal Papa che tutte le opere da queste in poi devessero havere pane e vino, che per prima non havevano." FABRETTI, *Cronache*, iii. 22.

[5] MARCANTONIO MALTEMPI, *Trattato*, etc., cited in *Arch. Stor. It.*, XVI. ii. p. xlii. The testimony of Maltempi is confirmed by Giulio di Costantino

AFFRESCO OF BONFIGLI SHEWING THE CHURCHES OF S. PIETRO,
S. DOMENICO AND S. ERCOLANO

Later on, the citizens were forced to take their share in the hateful labour.[1]   The whole of *Borgo di S. Giuliana* was swept away, and it was feared that the monastery itself might have to be demolished.[2]   Nothing was sacred to those priestly tyrants, and, as church after church fell beneath the blows of crowbar and pickaxe, the tombs were violated and the remains of the dead flung out and scattered abroad, so that "one saw in the streets skulls and shin-bones in quantities."[3]   What wonder if, as men believed, the Madonna of the Porta Marzia closed her eyes in horror![4] In October, 1543, *Santa Maria de' Servi* was pulled down "because it was too near the citadel";[5] and, in June, 1545, the tower of *S. Domenico* was condemned to a like fate, because it overlooked the Papal Fortress.   The Pope was finally prevailed upon to spare it; but the work of destruction had already begun, and "el campanile . . . restò sensa cima."[6]   In those evil days the long black robes of the *Conservatori dell' Ecclesiastica Obbedienza*, who had taken the place of the Priors of the Arts,[7] must have seemed to every good citizen horribly typical of their fallen estate. It was as though their magistrates had put on mourning for their loss of liberty and subjection to ecclesiastical hypocrites.[8]

A priestly despotism is, at its best, a terrible and an evil thing; for even the mildest and holiest priest, if called upon to wield the sword of temporal power, is all too prone to confound infractions of the moral law with crimes against the body politic; and the men into whose hands Perugia

---

(FABRETTI, *Cronache*, iv. 261) :   "Vero è che le bastonate ciaschuno ne avia abundante."

[1] FABRETTI, *Cronache*, iii. 22, 23, iv. 266-267.

[2] BONTEMPI, *ubi cit.*, p. 385.

[3] FABRETTI, *Cronache*, iv. 272 : "E quando cavaveno le ditte chiese, li ossa de li morte che erano in esse, li buttavano insieme con el terraccio, e vidivense per le strade caciopole e stinche in quantità."

[4] FABRETTI, *Cronache*, ii. 197, iv. 273.

[5] FABRETTI, *Cronache*, iii. 28, iv. 279.

[6] FABRETTI, *Cronache*, ii, 202, iii. 32.

[7] FROLLIERE, *ubi cit.*, pp. 473-474 ;   FABRETTI, *Cronache*, iii. 25.

[8] Compare J. A. SYMONDS, *Renaissance in Italy.   The Catholic Reaction* (London, 1898), Part II. pp. 33-34.

rounded the *Fonte Maggiore* was continually garnished with rotting heads, till men became connoisseurs in such matters.[1] Those who resisted arrest were dragged to prison by the *sbirri* with a cord tied to the tenderest portion of the human frame, shrieking aloud in intolerable anguish,[2] while a tumult of the populace, starving for lack of bread, was punished with diabolical cruelty, in spite of the entreaties of the Bishop of Perugia, who fruitlessly interceded with the Governor on behalf of his miserable flock.[3]   The chronicles read like one long hideous nightmare, and albeit, from time to time, some papal representative, less iniquitous than his fellows, sought to alleviate the deplorable condition of the citizens, the Inquisition and the Jesuits were always with them.   The supremacy of "that strange third sex, which the Roman Church creates by training up men from boyhood in a world that is not the world of men," poisoned all the land.   No one could say where the temporal power ended or the spiritual began, and the confessional itself became an important branch of that complicated system of espionage which formed the basis of the papal government. Not only was education frowned upon as a design to revolutionize the State, but as late as the second quarter of the last century, Gregory XVI. actually prohibited the intrusion of railways and telegraphs into his dominion.   All progress, whether material or intellectual, became impossible; and "any one supposed to belong to the dangerous class of 'thinkers' was shadowed by the police, even if he had nothing to do with politics."[4]   "It was under the 'orderly' rule of the cassock that the nation reached the perfection

[1] FABRETTI, *Cronache*, v. 49 : "Adì detto [20 settembre, 1584] ad ore 24 dopo l' ave maria è venuta una testa alla fonte in un canestro dentro un sacco, quale è di un bandito da Gualdo : è una bella testa. . . ."

[2] FABRETTI, *Cronache*, v. 98 : "Adì 20 detto [luglio, 1587] è stato preso Belardino rotatore per il gioco, e lui non ci voleva andare, e li hanno legati li testicoli, e lo alzavano da terra, e in questa maniera lo conducevano prigione, che era una bruta cosa a vedere . . . si stima che per questo non se ne morrà. . . ."

[3] FABRETTI, *Cronache*, v. 67-73.

[4] For an excellent account of the government of the Papal States during the first half of the last century, see G. M. TREVELYAN, *Garibaldi's Defence of the Roman Republic* (London : Longmans, Green & Co., 1907), chap. iv.

described by the celebrated formula of the Company of Jesus, and became '*utpote cadaver.*'" [1]   What wonder, then, that the Temporal Power still stinks in the nostrils of the great majority of the Perugians?   What wonder that the priesthood is regarded by so many of the people with an almost physical loathing, or that religion itself is all too often looked upon as the badge and accompaniment of servitude? [2]   An ecclesiastical writer of the sixteenth century speaks of Perugia as "nemica naturalmente di Preti," [3] and it would indeed be marvellous had she changed her nature in this regard. [4]

[1] T. A. TROLLOPE, *op. cit.*, p. 23.

[2] Compare *What we Want. An open letter to Pius X. from a group of priests.* Translated from the Italian by A. LESLIE LILLEY.   London : John Murray, 1907.   The whole volume is worthy of careful study.   See, however, especially pp. 9-10.   The writers, be it remembered, are Roman Catholic priests, and if what they say be true of Italy in general, it is doubly true of Perugia.   I know no other city where the attitude of the lower classes is so universally hostile to the Church and to the priesthood.

[3] FUMI, *ubi cit.*, in *Bollettino* cited, xiv. 74.

[4] Even as I write, a column commemorative of the gallant deeds of June 20th, 1859, is being reared in the Frontone.   Upon its pedestal is carved the Perugian Griffin trampling under foot the triple tiara of the Papacy, while in one of its claws it grasps a writhing serpent, emblematic of superstition.   Thus the latest of Perugia's civic monuments fitly symbolizes the sentiments of the populace.   In many other towns the Italian government would have intervened to prevent so flagrant an insult to what, after all, is still the Italian National Church, but only on the ground that it might lead to a breach of the peace.   In Perugia no such results are to be apprehended.   The unveiling of the monument will be hailed with acclaim.

CHAPTER XXIV

THE MEDIÆVAL CITY

I

TO obtain even an approximate idea of the appearance of Perugia at the dawn of the Communal Era we must carry our thoughts back through the centuries to the year 40 B.C., when, rather than see his native city sacked by the legionaries of Octavian, Caius Cestius Macedonicus set fire to his house, and stabbing himself to the heart, perished in the flames. The conflagration spread until the whole town was consumed, with the exception of the Temple of Vulcan, and the massive Etruscan walls enclosed nothing but ashes. Later on, however, the hand which had smitten knew how to salve the wounds which it had inflicted for the victor of Actium was no longer the avenger of Philippi. A new Perugia rose within the ancient boundaries and bore with pride the title of *Augusta*; but of the Roman Colony nothing remains to us. From the tenth century to the fifteenth, the strong Italian Commune transformed its dwelling-place to its own likeness, and Perugia became a mediæval city girt about by Etruscan walls. It is therefore these same walls which form the natural starting-point of our present inquiry.

Fortunately, a considerable part of them are still standing ; and especially on the western side of the city, they may be traced for a long distance, falling back from the perpendicular, and banded near the top with a projecting *fascia*. The masonry consists of large irregular blocks, laid in horizontal courses without cement, agreeing in character with those of Chiusi and Todi. Above the *fascia* they blend almost imperceptibly with the masonry of the Roman period,

THE PORTA AUGUSTA

which, springing indistinguishable from the earlier courses, becomes characterized as it grows.[1]

Of the gateways which pierce these walls, six may still be seen, the huge blocks of travertine, which sustain their Roman or mediæval superstructures, testifying unmistakably to their Etruscan origin. To the northward is the PORTA AUGUSTA, the "Etruscan Arch" *par excellence*, which was called, at various times, "Porta Pulcra," "Porta Vecchia," "Porta della Penna," "Porta de' Vincioli," "Porta de' Pelloli," and "Porta Grimana." Originally, it seems to have stood upon the brink of a steep declivity (*il Fossato*), which included the neighbouring *Bulagaio*,[2] and to have been connected with the Borgo S. Angelo by a bridge.[3] Later on, when this chasm was filled up, the open space outside the gate was known as *il Pianello*.[4] It was not until 1536 that Cardinal Grimani constructed the Piazza which still bears his name.[5] The *Via Vecchia*, which leads up the hill to the Cathedral, is, perhaps, the oldest of Perugian streets, and is said to have been trodden by the foot of man for at least twenty-five centuries.[6] It, however, probably took its name from

[1] DENNIS, *The Cities and Cemeteries of Etruria* (edition cited), Vol. II. p. 401. See also E. H. and E. W. BLASHFIELD, *Italian Cities*. New York: Charles Scribner's Sons, 1900. I have not the book by me, but, if my memory serves me, I am indebted to their chapter on Perugia for the phraseology of the last three lines.

[2] According to Dott. R. Gigliarelli, the *Bulagaio* was the place where *se bujavano* or *bugliavano* the rubbish and sweepings of the city. We find the verb *bugliare* used in this sense in the Statute of 1342, as, for example, in Lib. iv. Rubric 33: "Nessuno ardisca overo presuma *bugliare* terra, paglia, emmondezza ne alcun altra cosa ne fare alcuna suzzura sopra el muro de la cita de Peroscia." Compare also, Lib. iii. Rubric 117 and Lib. iv. Rubric 43; while G. DI COSTANTINO (*ubi cit.*, p. 149) tells us that "Oratio Baglione fe levare el populo in arme, e *bugliaro* e' birra per le finestre del palazo."

[3] FABRETTI, *Cronache*, ii. 117: ". . . dove che era il pianello del Borgo era il fossato, che adesso è il Bolagaio et il fossato della Conca, e chi veniva dalla parte di S. Angelo per andare alla Porta della Penna passava per un ponte, e tutto il pianello è fatto per forza."

[4] "Ricordo come il dì sudetto [17 ottobre, 1532] entrarono per la Porta delle Volte cinque starne la mattina a ora di messa, e vennero nel Pianello di Porta S. Angelo, e due ne voltarono verso la Conca, e tre entrarono in S. Fortunato, e poi in certe botteghe, e furono prese. Dio ci dia grazia non sia di male augurio" (FABRETTI, *Cronache*, iii. 130).

[5] MARIOTTI, *Saggio*, etc., *op. cit.*, p. 364.

[6] SYMONDS and DUFF GORDON, *op. cit.*, p. 92 n.

22

the gate through which it passed, though that name, no doubt, acquired a fresh significance after the construction of the *Via Nuova* (now the *Via Bartolo*) in 1378.[1]

Next, to the eastward, in the *Via Bontempi*, we find the "Arco de' Montesperelli," or "de' Gigli"—so called because, in 1541, it was painted with the golden lilies of the Farnese to do honour to Pope Paul III.[2] This gate has been identified with the PORTA SOLE of Dante's *Paradiso*, though (*pace* the commentators) it is perfectly obvious that the poet referred not to the Gate but to the Ward of the city, the *Rione di Porta Sole*.[3] Moreover it is unquestionable that, at different periods, three different gates have been called by that name, and, in all probability, the original "Porta Sole" stood at the top of the *Piaggia de' Calderari*, the modern *Via Alessi*. It was destroyed in 1543, by the orders of the Cardinal of Rimini, that the stones might be used for the construction of the Papal Fortress.[4] According to Siepi, however, the true "Porta Sole" was identical with the so-called "Arco de' Tei," which "is still to be seen to the right of the Church of S. Maria Nuova, spanning the street which leads to the Borgo di S. Antonio and to the Pesa."[5]

On the south-east were PORTA CORNEA and PORTA MARZIA. The former, which was afterwards called the "Arco di S. Ercolano," from its proximity to the Church of that Saint, was also known as *Porta Berarda*,[6] as the "Arco de' Comitoli," and as "Porta Leonea"; the last-mentioned title being due to the Guelf Lion which was

---

[1] PELLINI, i. 1212.

[2] MARIOTTI, *Saggio*, etc., *op. cit.*, p. 634.

[3] *Paradiso*, xi. 47. See on the whole subject F. GUARDABASSI, *Dante in Perugia*, in *L' Umbria*, *op. cit.*, Anno iii. pp. 27-30.

[4] See A. ROSSI, *La Piazza del Sopramuro in Perugia, le Vie che mettono ad essa e gli Edifizi circostanti* (Perugia, Tip. G. Guerra e C., 1887), p. 14 ; GIGLIARELLI, *Perugia antica e Perugia moderna* (Perugia, Unione Tip. Coop., 1907-1908), pp. 37-38, and compare a letter of Prof. A. LUPATELLI in *L' Umbria* of June, 1899. That this gate still bore the name of "Porta Sole" in the fifteenth century is beyond question. See the *Cronaca perugina inedita*, in *Bollettino* cited, iv. 102, and FABRETTI, *Cronache*, ii. 120.

[5] SIEPI, *Descrizione topologico-storica della Città di Perugia*, Vol. I. p. 295.

[6] *Annali Decemv.*, an. 1451, c. 40.

THE PORTA CORNEA WITH THE CHURCH OF S. ERCOLANO

carved above the keystone in the thirteenth century, and which may still be seen there.[1]

The PORTA MARZIA, or " di Marzo," [2] or " di S. Pietro," [3] was bricked up in 1542, and its arch was built into the wall of the Papal Fortress, as near as possible to its former site. Its original appearance and position may, as I have said, be learned from Bonfigli's picture of the Siege of Perugia by Totila.[4]

In the south-western angle of the city is PORTA EBURNEA, though that name is now more usually applied to the corresponding gate in the mediæval circuit; the old Etruscan arch being always referred to as " Porta della Mandola "— a title which it has certainly borne ever since the sixteenth century.[5] Not only is it one of the most picturesque of Perugian gates, but here better than elsewhere may be studied the modifications which these ancient archways underwent during the Middle Ages, to the destruction of their inscriptions and the displacement of much of the original masonry.[6] Thus, for example, below the almost headless lion, on the left-hand side of the arch, we can still discern a large Roman S preceded by part of another letter, presumably the upstroke of a V; while lower down, near the steps of the *Via Paradiso*, are the letters VIB. The deduction is obvious. Like the " Porta Marzia," the " Porta Eburnea " once bore the inscription COLONIA VIBIA PERVSIA AVGVSTA, which was destroyed and scattered when the arch was narrowed and the mediæval battlement superimposed.

It may be remarked in passing that, according to Matarazzo, it was through this gate that the Magnificent

---

[1] PELLINI, i. 533 ; SIEPI, *op. cit.*, ii. 464.

[2] PELLINI, i. 14. Compare also FABRETTI, *Cronache*, iii. 3, 6, iv. 271, 273.

[3] Thus in the Statute of 1342 it is spoken of as " la porta sancto Pietro la quale se dice porta de Marzo " (Lib. iv. Rubric 33).

[4] As to the inscription of the " Porta Marzia " see *Arch. Stor. It.*, XVI. i. pp. lxxxix-cviii, and on the subject generally, GIGLIARELLI, *op. cit.*, pp. 47-53.

[5] See, for example, FABRETTI, *Cronache*, ii. 160, iii. 3, 199.

[6] The reader should consult the photographs published by GIGLIARELLI, *op. cit.*, pp. 54, 55. They will greatly facilitate his study of this gate.

House of Baglioni always passed when they went forth to do battle with their enemies ; "and," says he, "it is a common saying among us that it has ever been propitious and of good omen to issue thereby from the city in the suit and service of the war god Mars."[1]

From the "Porta Eburnea" the visitor should descend the steps of the *Via Paradiso*,[2] and, passing through the gate of the mediæval circuit, follow the extra-mural road to the right. He will thus obtain an excellent view of a long stretch of the ancient walls. Re-entering the city by the "Porta S. Andrea," and ascending the *Via della Sposa*, he will find the last of the Etruscan gates, the PORTA SANTA SUSANNA, at the bottom of the *Via de' Priori*. Like its fellows, the "Porta S. Susanna" has various names : "Porta Trasimena," "Porta Luzia," "Arco di S. Luca," and "Porta della Luna" (from the half moon surmounted by a cross, which is carved above the archway) ; while I find it referred to in the Statutes of 1528 as *Porta vetus que vocatur porta Senensis.*[3]

In dealing with the nomenclature of the various Etruscan gates, Felice Ciatti is as usual picturesque. " The heathen," says he, " believed that Dreams came from the Gates of the Sun ; and according to their division into true dreams or false, they assigned to them different gates—an Ivory Gate for the True Dreams, called *Eburnea*, and a Horn Gate for the False Dreams, called *Cornea*. Wherefore it is that Virgil, borrowing this conceit from Homer, says :

[1] MATARAZZO, *ubi cit.*, p. 208 ; MORGAN, *op. cit.*, p. 230. From this passage and from a sketch attributed to Antonio Sangallo, preserved in the Galleria degli Uffizi at Florence (No. 1207 of Index), which represents the "Porta Marzia" but is entitled "porta Bornia di Perugia," Ing. G. BACILE DI CASTIGLIONE, in his *Dal Corso a S. Giuliana* (article cited), argues that the "Porta Eburnea" was, in fact, identical with the "Porta Marzia" and that the former name was never applied to the "Porta della Mandola." This theory, however, seems to be quite untenable, and has been amply confuted by Dott. GIGLIARELLI, *op. cit.*, pp. 57-62.

[2] Almost opposite the lower end of the *Via Paradiso*, high up in the angle of the corner house, may be seen a roughly carved stone fish—probably the sign of the offices where, of old, the duties (*gabella*) were collected on the *lasche* which were brought into Perugia from the Lake. (See GIGLIARELLI, *op. cit.*, pp. 113-114.)

[3] Vol. III. Rubric 11 (Additio).

Sunt geminæ somni portæ quarum altera fertur
Cornea, qua veris facilis datur exitus umbris
Altera candenti perfecta nitens Elefanto,
Sed falsa ad Cœlum insomnia mittunt.

" In like manner, Lucian tells us that these Gates of
Dreams were called *Cornea* and *Eburnea*. Of these names
all three were given to three of the five gates of Perugia,
and have been borne by them wellnigh unto our own day ;
to wit, *Porta del Sole, Porta Cornea,* now called *di S. Pietro*
(from which the neighbouring hill takes its name of *Monte
Corneo*) and *Porta Eburnea*. Of the other two gates, one
is called *Augusta* . . . and the other *Trasimena*, because
it looketh toward Lake Trasimene. Thereafter was added
another gate of less importance, the which because it led
to the Temple of Mars was named *Marzia*." [1]

During the Middle Ages, long after the suburbs had
been enclosed within the newer circuit, that part of the
town alone which lay within the Etruscan walls was
recognized as " the City," and the distinction between the
Terra Vecchia and the *Terra Nuova*, or *Borghi*, was still
jealously maintained. Up to 1276 all the ancient gateways
were furnished with wooden doors which were locked after
dark, and although, in that year, it was resolved that from
thenceforward these doors should be left open both by day
and night,[2] the old practice seems to have been at least
partially revived some sixty years later.[3] In this matter,
however, Perugia was not peculiar. An analogous state of
things existed in many other cities. Thus, as we have seen,
Assisi, in the fourteenth century, was divided into *Città Vecchia*
and *Borghi*.[4] Agnolo di Tura, in a well-known passage of
his *Cronica Sanese*, speaks of the " *Borghi dentro alla
Città* " ;[5] while, in Lucca, the term *Città* was used exclusively to describe that part of the town which lay within
the walls as they existed in the Dugento ; and albeit, in
the following century, by an enlargement of the same

[1] CIATTI, *Perusia Augusta*, p. 345.   [2] PELLINI, i. 290.
[3] PELLINI, i. 544, ad ann. 1338.   [4] See p. 124 *supra*.
[5] *Cronica Sanese* in MURATORI, *R. I. S.*, xv. 124. Compare my *Palio
and Ponte, op. cit.*, p. 58 n. 1.

circuit, a great part of the suburbs, and in particular that of S. Frediano, became an integral portion of the walled city, they still continued to be spoken of as the *Borghi*.[1]

II.

The earliest notice which I have found regarding the mediæval circuit of walls belongs to the year 1327, when we learn that, Fabriano having rebelled against the Church and the *Parte Guelfa*, Perugia sent two hundred horse to the assistance of the Marquis of the March under Messer Oddo Degli Oddi ; and " then were the walls of the Conca built from S. Francesco to S. Matteo." [2] Moreover, the chroniclers inform us that, in the following year, on the approach of Lewis of Bavaria, " the Commune of Perugia caused the *Borghi* of the city, called the *Terra Nuova*, to be furnished with chains, having already surrounded them with walls." [3] Thus, we may, perhaps, take it that, up to the second quarter of the fourteenth century, the *Borghi* continued to be mere suburbs, wholly unprotected from attack except by the natural strength of their position, in those days, doubtless, greater than at present.   I apprehend, however, that the *Terra Nuova* possessed gates long before it was surrounded by walls, and how effectual a rampart may be formed by the back-walls of ordinary dwelling-houses, each family guarding its own and keeping watch from its lofty windows, may be realized by any one who will take the trouble to visit the little *castello* of Collestrada, on the road to Assisi.

[1] S. Bongi, *Bandi Lucchesi del Secolo decimoquarto* (Bologna, Romagnoli, 1863), p. 269.

[2] Fabretti, *Cronache*, i. 76-77.   Compare also *Arch. Stor. It.*, XVI. i. 64, 92.

[3] Fabretti, *Cronache*, i. 18, 79 ; Graziani, p. 98. Of the enormous number of these chains we may judge from the fact that Frolliere (*ubi cit.*, p. 473) tells us that, when they were finally removed, in 1540, " per esser molte si stimava che valessero sopra diecimila scudi d' oro," while G. di Costantino (p. 253) bewails their loss from an æsthetic standpoint, as a *superba cosa a vedere*.   The entire passage is worth quoting : " . . . e le catene, quale levaro per tutta la città, che ce n' erano gran quantità, commo se poie cognoscere per li segne ne li mura, dove erano, ed erano grose quanto un groso funichio, e ab anticho a tempo di guerra le strade s'encatenaveno, e chiudeveno con la chiave, ed era superba cosa a vedere."

The second circuit was supplemented by a third ; and in the old plans of the city a wall may be seen extending from the *Porta de' Ghezzi* to *S. Giuliana*, enclosing all the space now covered by the *Piazza d' Armi* and by the gardens in the valley beneath *S. Anna*.[1]

Campana tells us that each of the five *Borghi* had "its own gate, magnificently built ;"[2] but there were, of course, numerous other gates in addition to the five principal ones. Thus, starting from "Porta S. Angelo,"[3] at the northern end of the city, and following the walls to the eastward, we have "Porta dello Sperandio,"[4] "Porta delle Volte" or "delle Voltole,"[5] "Porta Bulagaio," "Porta S. Antonio," "Porta della Pesa," "Porta S. Simone" or "del Carmine,"[6] "Porta S. Margherita,"[7] "Porta S. Girolamo" or "Romana,"

---

[1] See, for example, *La Pianta Eusebiana di Perugia del* 1602, published by A. BELLUCCI in *Augusta Perusia, op. cit.*, Anno i. Fasc. 9.

[2] *Vita di Braccio Fortebraccio tradotta da P. Pellini, op. cit.*, p. 61.

[3] *Porta S. Angelo* was also known as *Porta di S. Matteo* and as *Porta S. Cristoforo*. The former title needs no explanation when we recall the fact that the little Church of *S. Matteo* may still be seen just outside the gate : while the latter seems to have been borrowed from an earlier gate of the same name which stood, about half way down the *Via Lungaro* (*Corso Garibaldi*) in the days when the *Borgo* had not yet completed its growth. In a diploma of the twelfth century we read of *Ecclesia sancti Angeli foris portam*. See BARTOLI, i. 239, and compare GIGLIARELLI, *op. cit.*, p. 74.

[4] The "Porta Sperandio" derived its name from the fact that it led to the Benedictine Monastery of Sperandio, suppressed in 1798 (see SIEPI, *op. cit.*, i. 207). Though long since walled up, this gate may still be seen with the following inscription upon a tablet above the keystone of its arch : A.D. M.CCC.XXIX. INDICT. XII. TEMP. D. IOHAN. PP. XXII. DIE. XXVI. MĒS JANVAR. PORTA. ISTA. RESTAVRATA. FVIT. PER. BONOS. HŌĒS LVDO-VICVM. CRESCIOL. ET. PELLOLVM. PAOLVTII.

[5] The "Porta delle Volte" has entirely disappeared. It was situated close to the Monastery of S. Agostino and appears in the *Pianta Eusebiana* (*ubi cit.*) at the bottom of a street leading into the *Piazza Grimana* (compare p. 337 *supra*, n. 4). It was through this gate that the *fuorusciti* entered the city on the 6th of June, 1491. See GRAZIANI, p. 742.

[6] As may be seen from the old maps, there was a fortified suburb outside the "Porta S. Simone," which was known as *Fontenuova* and possessed a gate of its own.

[7] The remains of the ancient "Porta S. Margherita" may still be seen at the bottom of the *Via Bonaccia*, where the *Via Bacciadonne* begins. It is also visible from the road outside the walls, a little to the northward of the modern gate of the same name.

with the adjacent "Due Porte,"[1] "Porta S. Costanzo,"
"Porta de' Ghezzi,"[2] "Porta di S. Maria degli Angeli,"[3]
"Porta delle Capuccinelle,"[4] "Porta de' Funari,"[5] "Porta
della Cerasa,"[6] "Porta di S. Carlo,"[7] "Porta del Rastello,"[8]
"Porta Crucia,"[9] "Porta di S. Giacomo" or "del Castellano,"[10]

[1] The " Due Porte " corresponded with the modern " Porta S. Pietro."
According to Adamo Rossi, it owed its name to the fact that there were
two gates there, one of which opened into the road leading through the
" Porta S. Girolamo " to *Ponte S. Giovanni*, and the other into that of the
Ponte Nuovo (FABRETTI, *Cronache*, iv. 150 n.).   He, however, cites no
authority for this statement, and it is, perhaps, more probable that, like
the present gate, the " Due Porte " consisted of two separate archways,
one inside the other.

[2] The " Porta de' Ghezzi " stood at the bottom of the street of the same
name.   It may still be seen from the *Viale di S. Anna*.

[3] The " Porta di S. Maria degli Angeli " was close to the " Porta de'
Ghezzi," and is clearly marked in the *Pianta Eusebiana* (*ubi cit.*).   It is
spoken of by MATARAZZO (p. 121) as " quella porticella che sta presso
Santa Maria de li Angioli."   *S. Maria degli Angeli* was a convent of Clarisses
dependent on that of *Monte Luce*, of which we have record as early as the
beginning of the fourteenth century.   The name of the gate was subsequently changed to *Porta di S. Maria de' Fossi*.   See GIGLIARELLI, *op.
cit.*, p. 100.

[4] The " Porta delle Cappuccinelle " stood about half-way between the
" Porta de' Ghezzi " and the " Porta de' Funari."   It appears in the map
which accompanies RAFFAELE GAMBINI'S *Guida di Perugia* (Perugia, 1826),
and, though walled up, it is still visible from the *Viale di S. Anna*.

[5] The " Porta de' Funari " (or " della Penna " or " di S. Croce ") stands
at the bottom of the *Via Vibi*, and has been converted into a *latrina
pubblica*.

[6] The " Porta della Cerasa " was situated close to the Convent of *S.
Giuliana* and may, I apprehend, be identified with the " Porta de Santa
Giuliana " mentioned by G. DI COSTANTINO, *ubi cit.*, pp. 262, 285.   It was
pulled down in 1802.   It appears in the *Pianta Eusebiana*, but without
any name.

[7] The " Porta di S. Carlo " was erected in 1612 in honour of S. Carlo
Borromeo, and was still standing when J. A. SYMONDS wrote his *Sketches
in Italy*.   See the Tauchnitz edition, p. 71.

[8] The " Porta del Rastello " stood close to the south-eastern extremity
of the Papal Fortress, apparently in the neighbourhood of the modern
prison.

[9] " Porta Crucia " is the gate in the mediæval circuit which corresponds
with " Porta Eburnea " or " della Mandola " in the Etruscan circuit.
It is also called *Porta Nuova di Borgne*, and existed as early as 1296.   As its
inscription shows, it became ruinous from age, and was restored in
1626.

[10] " Porta S. Giacomo "—*porta sancti Iacobi portæ Eburneæ*—may still
be seen at the bottom of the *Via delle Forze*.

"Porta S. Prospero,"[1] "Porta S. Andrea,"[2] "Porta del Piscinello,"[3] "Porta della Conca," "Porta dell' Elce di sotto" and "Porta dell' Elce di sopra"; not to speak of others which have entirely disappeared and of the very position of which we are completely ignorant.[4] After the *Guerra del Sale*, all but five of them are said to have been walled up by the orders of Cardinal della Barba,[5] and though many were afterwards reopened, Perugia, to-day, possesses scarcely a tithe of her ancient gates.

In the fourteenth century the walls of both the outer and inner circuits were defended by wide and deep moats, which the Statute provided should be kept "free and open."[6] In the name of the little church of *S. Giovanuccio del Fosso* we still possess a record of the moat which surrounded the Etruscan circuit.

III

As I have already stated, the City of Perugia, from a very early period, probably from the eleventh or twelfth centuries, was divided, for military and administrative purposes, into five quarters or wards, corresponding with its five principal gates,[7]

[1] The ruins of the towered arch of " Porta S. Prospero " may still be seen outside the present walls, in the gardens below the extra-mural road, a hundred yards or so from the " Porta di S. Giacomo."

[2] The " Porta S. Andrea " or " Porta S. Mustiola " stands at the top of the *Via Colomata*, whence we also find it spoken of as *Porta Colomata* (FABRETTI, *Cronache*, iv. 86). It was from this gate that the legal mile from the Ward of Porta S. Susanna was measured : " Anco en porta sancta susanna comenza el miglio da la porta la quale sta longo sancta mustiola e protende e va al turlo de sancto manno" (Statute of 1342, Lib. iii. Rubric 213). In the *Pianta Eusebiana* it is called " Porta S. Susanna."

[3] The " Porta del Piscinello " stood at the bottom of the street of the same name, almost opposite the " Porta S. Susanna " of the Etruscan circuit.

[4] On the whole subject see GIGLIARELLI, *op. cit.*, cap. ii. pp. 65-117.

[5] FROLLIERE, *ubi cit.*, p. 473.

[6] Statute of 1342, Lib. iv. Rubric 66 : " Anco che nullo ardisca chiudere overo per alcuno modo empedire glie fossa del comuno de peroscia ma deggano esser libere e spedite tucte e ciascune entorno entorno aglie mura de la cita e degle borghe."

[7] See p. 29 *supra*.

each of which possessed its own colours and its own device.[1] "These *Porte* or *Rioni*," says Mariotti, "diverge from the centre or highest point of the city, where are the two chief *piazze*; extending thence in five directions, like so many rays, across the mountain top, with as gentle a slope as the nature of the ground permits. They are, to the east, PORTA SOLE; to the west, PORTA S. SUSANNA; to the north, PORTA S. ANGELO; to the south-east, PORTA S. PIETRO, and to the south-west, PORTA EBURNEA." [2]

From the principal gate of each of these *Rioni* a main thoroughfare (*strada regale*) ran to the Piazza Grande, the

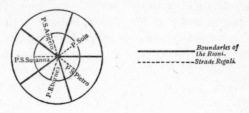

————————— Boundaries of the Rioni.
- - - - - - - - - - - -Strade Regali.

platea comunis.[3]   Thus, both the boundaries of the five *Rioni* and the five *strade regali* may be regarded as radii of a single circle, the centre of which was the *platea comunis*. Moreover, if we would understand the full meaning of the word "Porta," we must produce each of the five radii which form the boundaries of the *Rioni*, until they find a second and wider circumference in the frontiers of the State itself.

[1] Of the colours of the several *Porte* and of the *Compagnie per le porte* I have treated at some length in my *Palio and Ponte, op. cit.*, p. 141 *et seq.*

[2] MARIOTTI, *Saggio*, etc., *op. cit.*, pp. 14-15.

[3] Statute of 1342, Lib. iii. Rubric 74: "*La distintione de la piazza e de le strade regaglie.* A togliere ambiguita de le strade regale e de la piazza decemo e ordenamo che la strada regale sentenda en PORTA SANCTO PIETRO da la porta la quale e socta la chiesia de sancto pietro perfina a la piazza del comuno de peroscia venendo per la porta de la cita la quale se chiama porta de sancto pietro. En PORTA BORGNE sentenda strada regale da la porta de sancto prospero enfina la piazza del comuno de peroscia. En PORTA DE SANCTA SUSANNA sentenda la strada regale da la porta de sancto andrea enfina la piazza del comuno de peroscia. En PORTA SANCTO ANGNOLO sentenda strada regale da la porta la quale e oltra la croce de sancto angnolo enfina la piazza del comuno. En PORTA DE SOLE sentenda la strada regale da fonte nuova enfina la piazza del comuno venendo per la porta de sancto semone e la porta de la cita la quale se chiama porta soglie . . ."

For just as the *contadi* of Siena and Pistoia respectively were divided into three districts corresponding with the division of those cities into *Terzi*,[1] so was the Perugian *contado* divided into five districts corresponding with the division of Perugia into *Porte* ; and that these extramural districts were not only dependent on, but actually included in the *Porte*, seems clear from the words of Matarazzo when he tells us that " the enemy came *from Ponte Pattolo, through Porta S. Angelo, to the mills of the Rio.*"[2] The whole incursion obviously began and ended outside the city walls. Ponte Pattolo is a village on the Tiber, and the Rio is a small torrent to the north of Perugia.

Thus, in endeavouring to understand the topography of old Perugia, we start with two circuits of walls : the inner, or Etruscan circuit, being about two miles in circumference, the outer, or mediæval circuit, between four and five miles.[3] Next we have a great central Piazza, from which the five *strade regali* extend, like the spokes of a wheel, to the five principal gates of the city.[4] We know the position of some

---

[1] L. ZDEKAUER, *Il Constituto del C. di Siena, op. cit.*, p. lxviii. ; L. ZDEKAUER, *Breve populi pistoriensis* (Milano, Hoepli, 1891), p. lxx. Possibly however, Lucca affords an even better analogy, since, as MACHIAVELLI (*Vita di Castruccio Castracani*) tells us : " Perchè Lucca aveva cinque porte, divise in cinque parti il contado." Apparently, in 1370, this division by *Porte* was abolished and that of *Terzieri* substituted (see *Bandi Lucchesi, op. cit.*, p. 408). How this new arrangement affected the *contado* I do not know ; though the chronicle of SERCAMBI, ad ann., probably contains all the information required. The point which I desire to make is that the correspondence which I have described between the city and *contado* of Perugia was not an exceptional one.

[2] MATARAZZO, p. 31 ; MORGAN, p. 30. See also p. 29 n. 4 *supra*. The subject is so important for the proper understanding of the Perugian chronicles that I trust the reader will pardon this repetition.

[3] According to the article " Perugia " in the *Encyclopædia Britannica*, the actual measured distance is 8300 yards, while the length from S. Angelo to Porta S. Costanzo is 2500 yards.

[4] In the statutes the *Strade regali* are for many purposes classed with the *Piazza*. See, for example, the Statute of 1342, Lib. iii. Rubric 11 : " *De glie graffie da retenere*. Glie statute e ordenamenta en qua derieto facte de persequetare e prendere glie malfatore se oserveno e a executione se mandeno con quista gionta che da ciascheduno e ciascuna persona se possano prendere e ofenderse senza pena e oservense e ad executione se mandeno esse statute e ordenamente per la podesta e capetanio a pena de cinquecento libre de denare per ciascuno de loro. E che en ciascuna

half-dozen churches, such as *S. Agata*[1] in the Via de' Priori,
S. Martino del Verzaro,[2] *S. Maria degli Aratri*,[3] *S. Antonio
Abbate* in Porta Sole,[4] *S. Francesco delle donne*, said to have
been founded by Fra Filippo Lungo in 1212,[5] and, most
imposing of all, the Church of *S. Pietro*, built by Abbot
Pietro Vincioli in the tenth century on the ruins of the old
cathedral.[6] This, however, helps us but little; and although
we may be able to trace approximately the course of the
strade regali, we are forced to admit that every attempt to
reconstruct the greater proportion of the lesser thoroughfares, or *vie*,[7] with any approach to accuracy must necessarily
prove futile. To say nothing of the devastation wrought by
the Abbot of Mommaggiore, in the fourteenth century, and by
Paul III. in the sixteenth, the wholesale destruction of houses
and palaces which followed or accompanied each successive
outbreak of factional strife did much to transform the face
of the city, and to make way for that vast army of Renaissance buildings which have shamelessly thrust their
sacrilegious shoulders among the monuments of a nobler

casa e camora staente entorno a la piazza e longo le strade regale de la
cita e de glie borgara de peroscia sia tenuto uno graffio de ferro per gli
abitatore de le dicte case e camore a pena de vintecinque libre de denare
per ciascuno contrafacente . . ."

[1] See Symonds and Duff Gordon, *op. cit.*, p. 14.

[2] *Ibid.*, pp. 214-215.

[3] This church, which, as its name implies, formerly stood in the *Piazza
degli Aratri*, dates from the eleventh century. In 1488 it seems to have
been partially burned during the conflict between the Baglioni and the
Degli Oddi. (See the *Cronaca perugina inedita*, in *Bollettino* cited, ix.
308, and Pellini, ii. 850.) The façade, however, may still be seen in *Via
Alessandro Pascoli*, whither it was removed at the end of the last century.

[4] Said to have been founded in 1089, during a terrible outbreak of " St
Antony's Fire." (Compare Muratori, *Dissertazione*, xvi., at end.) Others
however, would have us believe that it was built as early as the third
century. Gigliarelli, *Perugia antica e Perugia moderna*, p. 356.

[5] Gigliarelli, *op. cit.*, p. 372. It is probably superfluous to remind the
reader that Fra Filippo Lungo is mentioned in the first chapter of the
Fioretti.

[6] See Symonds and Duff Gordon, *op. cit.*, pp. 167-176, and J. W. and
A. M. Cruickshank, *The Umbrian Towns* (Grant Richards, 1901), pp. 131-
135.

[7] As I have shown elsewhere, the *strade* were the great arteries which
connected the city with the country, while the *vie* were the lesser thoroughfares which opened into the *strade*. Compare L. Zdekauer, *La vita
pubblica nel Dugento, op. cit.*, pp. 31-32.

past. The old levels too are changed, and, as we wander about the town, we constantly descry ancient doorways high up in the walls of the houses, their stone sills some yards above the modern street, while others, yet again, are buried to their architraves.

Neither, as seen from a distance, is the aspect of Perugia less changed than within her walls. In the fourteenth and fifteenth centuries she, no doubt, deserved to be called, as John Addington Symonds calls her, the " empress of hill-set Italian cities," dark against the mystic Umbrian sky, austere and regnant, lifting to heaven her coronal of towers. *Perusia Turrita* they named her then—Perugia the towered.[1] But now, alas! the towers have vanished, all save one ; and instead, upon wellnigh the highest and certainly quite the most conspicuous point in all the city, the huge modern Prefettura and the unsightly rectangular block of the Grand Hotel Brufani stand forth blatant and aggressive, a perpetual, intolerable eyesore.[2]

[1] According to some writers Perugia possessed no fewer than seven hundred towers (see CRISPOLTI, *Perugia Augusta*, p. 15 ; SIEPI, *op. cit.*, ii. 828) : and, judging by analogy, the statement is by no means an improbable one. Thus Pisa boasted from 10,000 to 16,000 towers, " quibus in ædibus extructis orto dissidio ad mutua bella utuntur " (P. VIGO, *Una festa popolare a Pisa nel medio evo*, Pisa, Tip. Mariotti, 1888, p. 6, n.) ; Lucca had 700 towers, and, according to FAZIO DEGLI UBERTI (*Dittamondo*, iii. 6) they stood so close together that they made her look like a small wood :

> Andando noi vedemmo in piccol cerchio
> Torreggiar Lucca a guisa d' un boschetto—

a comparison which naturally recalls to mind the simile of UGURGIERI (*Le Pompe Sanesi*, ii. 306) when he tells us that " there were so many towers in Siena that the city seemed a canebrake." Bologna, in like manner, was so thickly studded with towers that the distance between them was often only a metre and a half (FRATI, *La vita privata di Bologna*, Bologna, Zanichelli, 1900, p. 3). Rome is said to have possessed 900 towers, while L. T. BELGRANO (*Della vita privata de' Genovesi*, Genoa, Tip. Sordo-muti, 1875, cap. vii. p. 27) maintains that Genoa had at least as good a right to be called *Turrita* as any of her rivals. As early as 1155, when Frederick Barbarossa sacked and burned Spoleto, there were already 100 towers in that city (SANSI, *Storia del C. di Spoleto, op. cit.*, p. 10). The list might, of course, be increased indefinitely, but enough has probably been said to prove that the assertion that Perugia possessed 700 towers is not necessarily an exaggeration.

[2] I have, of course, nothing to say against the *Grand Hotel Brufani* as an hotel. In my opinion it is without an equal in Central Italy ; and, owing

IV

If the *vie* and the *strade* were the veins and arteries of the mediæval city; the *Piazza* was its heart. Like the *Forum* of ancient Rome, it was the principal thoroughfare, the natural political, commercial, and religious centre, as well as the scene of most of the festivals arranged for the benefit of the populace. And, in this connection, it is well to repeat what I have already stated with regard to its extension. In the Middle Ages the *Piazza grande*, the *platea comunis*, was far larger than the modern *Piazza del Municipio*, being bounded at one extremity by the *Monte di Porta Sole* and at the other by *Colle Landone*. In other words, it extended from the spot now occupied by the *Teatro Turreno* to the *Piazza Umberto I.*, including the greater part of the present *Corso Vannucci*.[1] The ground, to the north of the *Via de' Priori*, now occupied by the *Palazzo Pubblico*, was covered by a huddle of houses, palaces, and shops, which went by the name of the *Isola della Piazza* (*insula platee comunis*),[2] including the towered dwelling of a certain Madonna Dialdana, and, on the north-west corner, the ancient church of *S. Severo*. To the westward stood the Bishop's Palace, the *Vescovado*,[3] while across the square to northward, adjoining the *Canonica*,[4] was the *Cathedral of S.*

to its conspicuous position, it commands one of the most magnificent views in all Umbria.

[1] Statute of 1528, Vol. III. Rubric 11 : " Platea magna incipiat ab Ecclesia S. Herrigii sive Isidori in pede platee existente et ducat usque ad palatium novum inceptum post Ecclesiam Sancti Laurentii." *Cf.* the Statute of 1342, Lib. iii. fo. 20, and GIGLIARELLI, *op. cit.*, pp. 442-444.

[2] PELLINI, i. 325. There was an *insula fori* in Spoleto. SANSI, *op. cit.*, i. 168.

[3] The Vescovado was probably built in the tenth century at about the same time as the cathedral of S. Lorenzo ; but, very possibly, all that remains to us of the original building is the ancient column in the courtyard. Compare GIGLIARELLI, *op. cit.*, p. 625.

[4] It was, as we have seen, burned to the ground in 1534, together with the *Vescovado*. See FABRETTI, *Cronache*, iii. 94 and iv. 205. " E abrus-ciosse netto " is the phrase used by Giulio di Costantino to express the completeness of the destruction of that portion of it which then formed the Palace of the Papal Governor (*Palazzo del Papa—Palazzo del Governatore*). The spot where that palace stood and the ruins which remained were granted by Pope Pius IV. to Cardinal Fulvio della Corgna for the

STAIRWAY LEADING FROM THE PIAZZA DEGLI ARATRI TO THE
CANONICA

Lorenzo, founded by Bishop Rogerius in the tenth century,[1] a building of very modest proportions, the entire length of which is said not to have exceeded the space between the choir and the second or third pillar of the modern church.[2] Thither was brought the body of S. Ercolano from the old cathedral of S. Pietro,[3] and thereafter the new cathedral was spoken of as *Ecclesia beatorum Laurentii et Herculani.* Nor did it lose its double title until another sanctuary had been erected to Perugia's patron saint on the spot to which tradition points as the scene of his martyrdom.[4] This fact is one of no little importance for a proper understanding of the ancient documents, since albeit the church which we now know as the *Church of S. Ercolano* was only begun in 1297, we find frequent references to *Ecclesia Sancti Herculani* at a much earlier date. In all such cases the *Duomo* is, of course, meant.[5]

Though, as we have seen, the thirteenth century Cathedral was small and insignificant, it possessed a noble *Campanile*, one of the loftiest towers in all Perugia, which is said to have long antedated the Church itself. Indeed, at the time of its destruction, in 1375, it was believed to have stood for three thousand six hundred years, and tradition declared construction of the *Seminario* (June, 1561). The present cloister also seems to be comparatively modern, but the open stairway leading into the *Piazza degli Aratri* remains one of the most picturesque architectural monuments of mediæval Perugia ; and it is interesting to note that by it the murderers of Messer Aurelio de Ubaldis entered the *Canonica* on the 14th of November, 1512 (*Arch. Stor. It.,* XVI. ii. 262). The *via delle Cantine* is said to derive its name from the fact that the cellars of the Canons were situated there. Compare PELLINI, i. 414 ; BONAZZI, i. 361, and SYMONDS and DUFF GORDON, *op. cit.,* p. 149.

[1] " Quod extra Civitatem sita esset (*i.e.* the old cathedral) Rogerius Episcopus novam in urbe Cathedralem excitavit ineunte Sæculo X." MABILLON, *Acta SS. Ordinis S. Benedicti,* Pars. i. pag. 63 ; ROTELLI, *Il Duomo di Perugia, op. cit.,* p. 7 ; GIGLIARELLI, *op. cit.,* p. 304 *et seq.*

[2] PELLINI, i. 565.

[3] PELLINI, i. 109; BARTOLI, i. 122.

[4] The work was begun in 1297, and, in February, 1298, an order was made for the payment of 200 *libbre* every three months " in opere ecclesie que fabricatur ad locum ubi fuit decapitatus sanctus Ercolanus . . . domno Angelo superstiti dicti operis." See on the whole subject A. BELLUCCI, *La Chiesa di S. Ercolano* in *Augusta Perusia, op. cit.,* Anno ii. (1907), pp. 11-19.

[5] See *Bollettino* cited, ix. 120-121 n., and compare page 21 *supra.*

that the Palladium of Troy lay buried beneath its foundations.[1] Cylindrical in form, it was embellished with three
tiers of porticoes and was surmounted by a bronze cock.[2]
On the wall of the tower, at a convenient height from the
ground, were marked the standard measures of the *canna*,
the *braccio*, and the *piede*, to the end that disputes between
merchants and their customers might be avoided.[3] At its
foot were stone steps, which seem to have been sheltered by
a *loggia* ;[4] and upon them the Magistrates sat or stood
when the *parlamentum* of the Perugian people assembled on
the Piazza.[5] Here, or in the Cathedral itself, they resolved
on peace or war, and deliberated concerning the most
important affairs of the Commune ; here they received submissions, and here, on the morning of the 1st of March, the
festival of S. Ercolano, the Priors sat in state to accept the

[1] FABRETTI, *Cronache*, i. 65.

[2] In one of the codices in the Pinacoteca there is a miniature representing
this tower. It is reproduced by R. A. GALLENGA STUART in his *Perugia*
(Bergamo, Istituto Italiano di Arti grafiche, 1905), p. 107. See also the
sketch in GIGLIARELLI, *op. cit.*, p. 406. Apparently, this cock must have
been transferred to the new Campanile, since we read that on the 5th
August, 1395 (twenty years after the old Campanile had been destroyed
by the Abbot of Mommaggiore, who drove the *ala* which connected his
fortress with the Palace of the Priors clear through the Cathedral. See
p. 255 *supra*), " venne una gran tempesta, e cascò una saetta nel campanile
dì S. Lorenzo e fracassò il gallo che fu ritrovato in piazza." FABRETTI,
Cronache, i. 52. Moreover, from the *Cronaca perugina inedita* (*Bollettino*
cited, ix. 39) we may, I presume, infer that even then it was not past
mending, since, under the year 1462, we read : " A dì 26 de luglio fo scoperto
il campanile de S. Lorenzo cioie levato el piombo e il Gallo quale era nella
cassa d' ariento."

[3] " Quando menutamente se vende el panno del lino vendase a la mesura
del braccio del campanile de sancto lorenzo li desegnato." . . . " El passo
sempre sentenda che sia de cinque pieie al pieie del comuno de peroscia
desegnato en lo campanile de sancto lorenzo."

[4] According to GIGLIARELLI (*op. cit.*, p. 319), " fin dal 1234 esisteva la
loggia rifatto poi a tempo di Braccio." He produces no satisfactory
evidence in support of his assertion, but that he is probably correct may
be inferred from the fact that, in 1286, the Chapter of S. Lorenzo granted
to the Commune of Perugia " omnia iura et actiones qua et quas habent
et habere possent ex quacunque causa in logia edifficata et scalis positis
iuxta ipsam logiam a scalis Palatii Comunis Perusii ad Palatium dicte
Canonice . . ." See BIBL. COM. DI PERUGIA, *Pergamene*, cassetta 30,
No. 513.

[5] " . . . sedentibus Dñis Prioribus in scalis lapideis quæ sunt ad portam
infimam ipsius campanilis."

palii of tributary towns and seigniors. Thus, in Perugia as elsewhere, " the Church was the first Palace of the People " ;[1] and we may perhaps infer that the frequent occupation of the Cathedral by the civic magistrates was one of the reasons why the chapter was wont to meet in the Campanile.[2] Moreover, the *Canonica* itself was invaded, the magistrates occupying that portion of it which was subsequently known as the *Palazzo del Papa* and eventually became the residence of the Papal Governor.[3] They, however, soon found their quarters too restricted, and, in 1281, according to Bonazzi, the *Canonica* was connected with the Bishop's Palace by massive arches, the remains of which may still be seen in the *Via delle Volte*. Upon these was constructed a great hall, capable of seating six hundred persons, entrance thereto being obtained by an external staircase, built against the wall of the *Canonica*.[4]

[1] TAMASSIA, *Vita di popolo nei Secoli XIII. e XIV.*, in *Arte, Scienza e Fede ai giorni di Dante* (Milano, Hoepli, 1902), p. 36 : " . . . la chiesa fu e rimane sempre la casa, la fortezza, il primo palazzo del popolo." Compare ZDEKAUER, *La vita pubblica nel Dugento, op. cit.*, pp. 72-73.

[2] Thus, in a document of 1303, cited by Dott. GIGLIARELLI (*Venere*, etc., *op. cit.*, p. 228 n.), we read : " Actum in Civitate Perusii in Campanile Cathedralis Ecclesie Perusine, ubi consuetum est Capitolum dicte Ecclesie congregari. . . ."

[3] See page 350 n. 4, *supra*. Thus the date of place in various public documents runs : " in Camera Canonice," " in Palatio S. Laurentij," etc. See *Bollettino* cited, iv. 163, viii. 137, x. 212-213 (Doc. l., lxxviii., clxiii., clxiv.) ; while in 1346, we find the " palazo de la Calonica " used by the Commune for a banqueting hall (GRAZIANI, p. 138).

[4] BONAZZI, i. 359-360. As we have already seen (p. 352 n. 4), in 1286, the Chapter of S. Lorenzo granted to the Commune certain rights which it possessed in a loggia and stairway contiguous to the Canonica, and, in 1289, we learn that the General Council assembled *in Palatio novo Comunis Perusii* (MARIOTTI, *Saggio*, etc., *op. cit.*, pp. 21-22). On the other hand, Professor A. ROSSI (*Il Palazzo del Popolo in Perugia*, p. 3) declares that the Palace of the Commune adjoining the *Canonica* was " di antichissima struttura," and that the consuls of the city resided there " ab immemorabili." Certain it is that the public documents abound in references to a *Palazzo del Comune* long before the year 1281. Thus, as early as 1210, we find that the oath of the Perugians to the Pope was taken " in the Palace of the Commune," while in 1212 we read of a *submissio bonorum* made " in camera superiori palatij Comunis " (see *Bollettino* cited, i. 149, viii. 148, and the *Libri delle Sommissioni, passim*). It is, no doubt, possible that the Magistrates had so completely monopolized *il Palazzo della Canonica* that they had learned to speak of it as *il Palazzo del Comune*, but upon no other hypothesis can the date given by BONAZZI be accepted as even approximately the correct one.

The *Via delle Volte*, being thus converted into a covered passage, began to be used as a convenient place for the storage of timber ;[1] while the citizens were accustomed to take advantage of its obscurity to satisfy certain necessary but quite unmentionable functions. The nuisance was the more intolerable owing to the immediate neighbourhood of the Cathedral and of the residence of the principal dignitaries of the Republic, both ecclesiastical and lay. Moreover, the street itself was an important one, if only as connecting the *Piazza* with the *Via del Verzaro*, which was then inhabited almost exclusively by the nobles.[2] Ere long the matter was brought before the General Council, and, as befitted the age, it was resolved to appeal to the superstition of the people. In mediæval Italy, as in mediæval England, " much law was dead letter. Statutes were often mere admonitions ; they expressed but an ideal, a pious intention." On the other hand, the continual intervention of the Celestial Powers in human affairs was never doubted ; the Saints were too useful as friends, too dangerous as enemies, to be wantonly provoked, and the magistrates resolved to enlist the Saints on the side of public decency. In January, 1297, it was decreed that *sub volta Palatii Comunis*, on the wall at the bottom of the street, close to the spot where the *Rimbocco de' Perinelli* (now the *Vicolo dell' Oratorio*) joins the *Via Ritorta*, should be painted figures of the Virgin, S. Lorenzo, S. Ercolano and S. Cristoforo, before which a lamp should be kept burning at the public expense. In 1335, this painting (said to be the most ancient in Perugia [3]) was enclosed in a church which was expressly constructed to protect it, and which is still known as the *Maestà delle Volte*.[4] The present build-

---

[1] Statute of 1342, Lib. iv. Rubric 5. It is printed by GIGLIARELLI, *Venere*, etc., *op. cit.*, p. 47 n.

[2] GIGLIARELLI, *Venere*, etc., p. 395 n. On the right-hand side of the *Via del Verzaro*, as one enters it from the *Piazza degli Aratri*, may be seen a typical mediæval palace, with its tower, and gateways furnished at the sides with stone sockets ; and here too, as I have said, is the very ancient church of *S. Martino del Verzaro*.

[3] See, however, CROWE and CAVALCASELLE, *A New History of Painting in Italy* (edition DOUGLAS), III. pp. 184-185; (edition HUTTON), II. p. 148.

[4] MARIOTTI, *Saggio*, etc., *op. cit.*, p. 22 ; SIEPI, i. 142 ; GIGLIARELLI,

ing only dates from 1590, but the arch of red and white marble to the left of the doorway formed part of the original structure, which was destroyed in 1534, together with the *volta* itself and a large part of the *Vescovado*, when Ridolfo Baglioni set fire to the Palace of the Vice-Legate.[1]

Below, in the *Via Ritorta*, on the left-hand side of the street, is an ancient doorway which probably once gave access to the Palace of the Potestà (*palatio comunis in quo Potestas conmoratur.*)[2] On the stones of its arch divers

Venere, etc., p. 46 n.   In the *Bollettino* cited, vii. 242, Professor A. BELLUCCI publishes an order for a payment to be made by the *Massarius Comunis* " Laurentio Caselle sutori, qui moratur ad exercendam artem suam in camera suptus voltam palatij Potestatis, pro lumine et honore faciendo ad reverentiam B. M. Virginis, que est picta in volta predicta et unde lumen fiat inde transeuntibus de nocte, duos mezolinos olei."   The date is 1319.

[1] See p. 350 n. 4, *supra*.

[2] According to BONAZZI (i. 359-360) the Potestà resided in the *Canonica* during the whole or almost the whole of the thirteenth century.   On the other hand, in the most ancient Perugian statute, that of 1279, we read (Rubric 215) : " Item Potestas et Capitaneus teneantur precise facere aptari per totum mensem maij et junij palatium comunis Perusij in quo Potestas comunis Perusij conmoratur, et ipsum faciant meliorari prout fuerit oportunum et terrenum quod fuerit necessarium pro ampliatione dicti palatij, emi facere teneantur ad iustam et convenientem extimationem per dictos v bonos homines faciendam. . . ."   The inference surely is that, at this period, the Potestà occupied a separate palace with ground around it which could be expropriated " pro ampliatione dicti palatij " ; while it seems that in the third decade of the Trecento the *Palatium Potestatis* stood behind the *Vescovado*, and so close to it that, in 1326, the two buildings were connected by a temporary scaffolding or " bridge," upon which apartments were constructed for the entertainment of the Duke of Calabria and his suite.   Of this we have conclusive evidence in the following entry : " [Die xxvij mensis Junii] . . . Vanni magistri Laurentij, magistro lignaminum, pretio lignaminum et pro acconcimine pontis facti a domibus domini episcopi usque ad palatium Potestatis pro adventu domini ducis Calabrie, cum ibidem stare debeat . . . triginta unum libras denariorum. . . ."   The document is published by A. BELLUCCI, in *Bollettino* cited, vii. 243.   That the Palace of the Potestà was situated behind the *Vescovado* I infer from the following passage from the Chronicle attributed to GRAZIANI (p. 103) : " Adì 25 luglio nel dicto millesimo [1329] se gettò fuoco de notte tempo nel palazzo del potestà, dove che se arsero tutte le camere del dicto palazzo, cioè de la volta, de sotto, e comenzosse a rapicciare et acendere lo vescovato dal lato de rieto. . . ."   Compare FABRETTI, *Cronache*, i. 20, 81, where, however, this fact is recounted with less particularity of detail.   PELLINI (i. 509) tells us that " si attaccò il fuoco di notte nel palazzo del Podestà

figures are carved, but so worn are they with age that it is by no means easy to determine what the majority of them were intended to represent. I am, however, disposed to believe that they are the ancient emblems of the five *Porte*, and are (on the Right) a Deer, a Bear, and a Horse, and (on the Left) a Sun and a Lion. The figure at the summit of the arch, occupying both the keystone and the stone to the right of it, is undoubtedly the Perugian Griffin. That these are not the modern emblems of the *Porte* is, of course, indisputable,[1] but according to the *Romanzo* of Prossimana and Oliver, to which I have already alluded,[2] the original devices were : *Porta Eburnea*, a Deer ; *Porta S. Susanna*, a Bear ; *Porta S. Angelo*, a Horse ; *Porta Sole*, a Sun, and *Porta S. Pietro*, a Lion. I readily admit that the Deer and the Bear might with equal propriety be described as an Ox and a Wild Boar, and that the wheel-like object next to the Lion only distantly resembles a Sun : but the order in which the various carvings are placed, their number, and the fact that they appear where they do, seems to me to lend considerable support to my hypothesis.

V

Even in low-lying Florence, the work of paving the city was only undertaken in 1236 ;[3] and it is reasonably certain that up to the latter half of the Dugento the majority of the smaller *piazze* of Perugia were mere open spaces, dusty in summer and muddy in winter, serving, perhaps, like the *pascuè* of Milan, as grazing places for swine and other domestic animals.[4] Nor is it impossible that the *platea*

dove si brusciarono tutte le stanze et botteghe del primo piano, et cominciò anco ad accendersi nel Vescovato dalla banda di dietro, e si arse più della metà di detto palazzo."

[1] See GIGLIARELLI, *Venere*, etc., p. 180 n.

[2] Chap. I. *supra*.

[3] MARCHIONE DI COPPO STEFANI, *Cronaca Fiorentina*, Rubric 81 : "Essendo in Firenze le vie assai brutte per la pianura in che era Firenze che riteneva l' acqua e il fango, perocchè era tutta terraccia, salvo le quattro vie de' cinque sesti, ch' erano ammattonate, provvidesi di lastricare tutta la città ; . . . e ciò fu negli anni di Cristo 1236."

[4] VERRI, *Storia di Milano* (Capologo, Cantone Ticino, Tip. Elvetica, 1837), Vol. I. p. 111.

comunis itself was in a similar condition. Certainly if it was paved at all it was paved with flagstones (*de lapidibus —de silice lapidum*) after the Roman fashion.[1] About the middle of the century, however, many of the Italian communes began to pave their *piazze* and afterwards their streets. Thus Todi paved her *Piazza* in 1261 and her streets in 1263;[2] between 1279 and 1300, the whole of the streets of Spoleto were paved;[3] and, in 1250, Perugia bethought herself to pave her *platea comunis*, compelling the inhabitants of Castel della Pieve to provide the bricks as a punishment for their recent rebellion.[4] The work seems to have been begun in 1253;[5] and, two years later, Martino Zorli of Siena was sent for by the Magistrates of Perugia *pro mattonando plateam civitatis eorum.*[6] The Sienese *maestri* were already famed for the excellence of their brick-on-edge paving.[7] In 1268 the principal streets of *Porta S. Pietro* and *Porta Eburnea* were paved;[8] while, in 1298, it was resolved that all the *strade* both in the *Città* and the *Borghi* should undergo the same treatment, beginning at the *Porta S. Angelo.*[9]

The next step towards the embellishment of the *Piazza* was the construction of the *Fonte Maggiore*, an enterprise which, according to Professor Mancini, may have been undertaken in emulation of the Cortonesi, who had already adorned the principal square of their town with a very beautiful fountain.[10] Be this as it may, we know that, in 1254, the Perugians resolved to build an aqueduct from *Monte Pacciano*,[11] though, owing to the difficulties to be surmounted,

---

[1] Brick-on-edge paving was an innovation of the thirteenth century. Compare ZDEKAUER, *La vita pubblica nel Dugento, op. cit.,* p. 32.

[2] CECI, *op. cit.,* Vol. I. p. 151.

[3] SANSI, *Storia del C. di Spoleto, op. cit.,* i. 168.

[4] PELLINI, i. 260.

[5] *Arch. Stor. It.,* XVI. i. 56.

[6] R. ARCH. DI STATO IN SIENA, *Consiglio della Campana,* iii. c. 45 1255, Sabbato, 25 Marzo.

[7] ZDEKAUER, *La vita privata,* etc., *op. cit.,* p. 36 n. 2.

[8] PELLINI, i. 279.

[9] MARIOTTI, *Saggio,* etc., *op. cit.,* p. 18.

[10] MANCINI, *Cortona nel Medio Evo, op. cit.,* p. 54. It was destroyed in 1550.

[11] For a beautiful description of Monte Pacciano and its reservoirs, see SYMONDS and DUFF GORDON, *op. cit.,* pp. 130-131.

the water did not reach the *Piazza* till 1280.[1]　The *Fonte Maggiore* is a fine example of Italian sculpture, but it has been described so often that it is unnecessary to treat of it in this place.　Suffice it to remind the reader that he will prove himself blind to one of its most important characteristics if he is content to regard it merely as a work of art. Not only is it invaluable as a record of the customs, habits, and appearance of all ranks of society at the end of the thirteenth century, but the whole monument was evidently designed "with the purpose of setting before us, by means of symbols, of personifications, of historical personages and scenes, of Bible stories and fables, *a complete philosophy of life and society*." [2]

Up to the last quarter of the century, the Captain of the People was still without any fixed residence.　The submission of the Seigniors of Rocca di Appennino, in 1258, was made "in domo domini capitanei que fuit olim Angelocti " ; [3] while, in 1263, he was lodged in a house with a cloister or peristyle, beneath which the public business seems to have been transacted.[4]　Fifteen years later, we find him "in domo et palatio nobilis mulieris domine Dialdane," on the south-west corner of the *Isola della Piazza*, behind the Church of *S. Severo*.　Madonna Dialdana was the widow of a noble feudatory, probably of German descent, and it is not likely that she bore much love for the guilds of merchants and artisans whose representative the Captain was.　We know that he occupied her palace against her will—"præter voluntatem ipsius domine," and he appears to have further asserted the rights of the sovereign People by refusing to pay her any rent.[5]

In 1279, it was resolved to put an end to this unseemly

[1] See BARTOLI, i. 438 *et seq.* ;　BONAZZI, i. 365 ;　PELLINI, i. 286, 294; and above all BELFORTI, *Memorie istoriche della Fonte di Piazza*, MS. N. 1348, in the Communal Library of Perugia.

[2] Beyond all comparison the best English account of the *Fonte Maggiore* with which I am acquainted is that of J. W. and A. M. CRUICKSHANK, *The Umbrian Towns, op. cit.*, pp. 62-81.

[3] *Bollettino* cited, iii. 195.

[4] *Bollettino* cited, x. 216: "In claustro domus ubi moratur d. Capitaneus."

[5] Statute of 1279, Rubric 424.　It is published by A. BELLUCCI, in *Bollettino* cited, v. 795.

state of things by the erection of a *Palazzo del Popolo*, wherein the Captain might reside with all the dignity befitting his high office ; and, with this object in view, it was determined to purchase a large part of the *Isola della Piazza*, five good and wise men—*quinque boni et sapientes viri*—being appointed to appraise the value of the property to be expropriated.[1]   This is the first notice which we possess concerning the construction of the *Palazzo Pubblico*.   The next, if I mistake not, is to be found in the *Historia di Perugia* of Pompeo Pellini, under the year 1296, where he tells us that " it was declared by certain men, thereto appointed by the Potestà and by the Consuls of the Arts of Perugia, that fifty *libbre di denari* should be paid to Messer Giacomo di Servadio and Giovannello di Benvenuto respectively, as their yearly salaries for superintending the construction of the new *Palazzo del Popolo* ; such payment being due for four years, beginning from the 12th of September, 1293, and ending in September, 1297."[2]

From this passage we infer that the new Palace was completed about 1297 ; while in August, 1298, the Council of the People decreed that a stairway should be built "ante palacium populi ad ingrediendum in dicto palacio."[3]   This is the earliest known record of that famous *Scala della Vaccara*,[4] whose original form is a question which still causes much heartburning among the *eruditi* of Perugia.[5]

The Palace of 1297 was, however, a mere nucleus of the

---

[1] Statute of 1279, Rubric 215.   [2] PELLINI, i. 317.

[3] *Reformationum Veterum Comunis Perusiæ. Liber fragmentorum* C. cta 138r ; A. BELLUCCI, *Sulla scala esterna del Palazzo del Popolo* (Perugia, Tip. Coop., 1899), p. 19.

[4] The origin of the name is doubtful; see GIGLIARELLI, *Perugia antica e Perugia moderna, op. cit.*, p. 572.

[5] See A. BELLUCCI, *Sulla scala esterna*, etc., *op. cit.*, and an article by the same author in *Bollettino* cited, vii. 223-246.   On the other side of the question the reader may consult LIBER (Professor L. TIBERI), *Per una Scala*, Perugia, Tip. Umbra, 1899.   Apparently Mr J. HEBB, when he wrote on " The Town-Hall of Perugia " in *The Journal of the Royal Institute of British Architects* (Vol. VI., Third Series, N. 17, pp. 524-527) was only acquainted with the arguments adduced by Professor Bellucci, or he would hardly have written so positively upon what remains a very open question. I confess that to my mind the weight of evidence is distinctly in favour of the theory that the original staircase possessed a double ramp.

modern *Palazzo Pubblico*.   On the side facing the *Corso*, it
terminated after the tenth window, where a distinct line
may still be seen in the masonry, and towards the Cathedral
it included only the first three windows of the present
edifice.   Thus the doorway to which the *Scala della Vaccara*
was built in 1298, and which gives access to the *Sala de'
Notari*, stood in the centre of the northern end of the building.[1]   Above it, on the outer wall of the Palace, were early
set the Perugian Griffin and the Guelf Lion, mute witnesses
of the civic patriotism and factional hate which divided Italy
into as many hostile nations as there were free cities.   At
their feet were hung, in 1321, the bars and keys of the
Gates of Assisi,[2] and, in 1358, the chains from the Gallows
of Pecorile outside Siena,[3] the pitiful trophies of fratricidal
strife.

The great hall (which is now known as the *Sala de'
Notari*) occupied the whole of the first floor ; and the upper
rooms were probably reached by an external stairway, which
must have occupied very much the same position as the
steps by which we now ascend to the *Pinacoteca*, though,
instead of leading into the *Piazza* (the modern *Corso*), it
apparently terminated in a narrow courtyard on the
southern end of the Palace.[4]

In the last years of the thirteenth century it was resolved
to purchase more land for the enlargement of the *Palazzo
del Popolo*, and, in 1298, a bull was obtained from Boniface
VIII. authorizing the sale to the Commune of the Church
of *S. Severo*, with the houses and other buildings thereunto
appertaining (*domibus et cameris ipsius*) ; [5] while, in 1300,
certain houses, shops, and cottages, which stood in that
portion of the *Isola della Piazza* not yet occupied by the
Palace, were expropriated.[6]   It was, however, provided in
the papal rescript that, before taking possession of *S. Severo*,
the magistrates should build another church in its stead ;

---

[1] A. Rossi, *Il Palazzo del Popolo in Perugia*.   Perugia : Stabilimento,
Tip. Lit., 1864.

[2] Page 124 *supra*.   [3] Page 233 *supra*.

[4] A. Rossi, *op. cit.*, pp. 5-6.

[5] The document is published by A. Bellucci, in *Bollettino* cited, vii. 233.

[6] Pellini, i. 325.

PORTICO BEFORE THE CHURCH OF S. SEVERO SHEWING PULPIT OF BANDITORE

and it was only in 1319 that the exchange was actually effected.[1] In that year the work of demolition began, although only the stairs, houses, and *camere* seem to have been pulled down ;[2] since, in 1326, we find the Consuls of the Merchants deliberating concerning the construction of a new *armarium* for the communal records as well as a chamber for the *Massarius,* "in the old church of *S. Severo* adjoining the *Palazzo del Popolo.*"[3] It was not until January, 1333, that the first stone of the new building was actually laid. "In the said year and month," says Graziani, "they began to build the Palace of the People where the church of *S. Severo* used to be."[4] This statement, however, must not be taken to imply that the church itself was destroyed ; the roof was removed and the new structure superimposed upon the old one. The ancient windows of *S. Severo* may still be seen in the *Via della Gabbia,*[5] while there too is the tower of Madonna Dialdana, which together with her palace was incorporated in the *Palazzo del Popolo.* In front of the Church of *S. Severo,* towards the Cathedral, a portico was erected,[6] with a pulpit for the *banditori* of the Commune.[7] The work seems to have been finished in

---

[1] *Bollettino,* cited, vii. 235-241.

[2] *Ibid.,* pp. 241-242.   [3] *Ibid.,* p. 244.

[4] *Arch. Stor. It.,* XVI. i. 108. Compare FABRETTI, *Cronache,* i. 22 ; PELLINI, i. 517.

[5] As to the *Via della Gabbia,* see SYMONDS and DUFF GORDON, *op. cit.,* pp. 120-121. The details which they there quote with regard to Angelo di Marino are to be found in the *Diario di Antonio de' Veghi* in FABRETTI, *Cronache,* ii. 25, 26, 27. GRAZIANI (p. 504) adds that "gridava el dì e la notte como uno matto." In the *Cronaca perugina inedita* (*Bollettino* cited, ix. 94) we read of another priest and a friar who suffered the same punishment for the same offence : "A dì 27 de maggio [1475] fo messo in gabbia un prete, chiamato Don Tomasso da Gobbio, e un frate, chiamato frate Antonio de Santa Maria de Servi, li quali aveon fatti moltissimi furti e molte altre ribaldarie. La gabbia fo messa appresso il palazzo del Podestà verso casa de Pier francesco de Gialomia." *Cf.* FABRETTI, *Cronache,* ii. 50.

[6] So GIGLIARELLI, *Venere,* etc., *op. cit.,* p. 225 n. According to A. BELLUCCI, *Sulla scala esterna,* etc., *op. cit.,* this portico already existed, and formed part of the Church of *S. Severo.*

[7] GIGLIARELLI, *Perugia antica e Perugia moderna, op. cit.,* p. 572. Only the lower part of this pulpit remains in its original position. When and by whom it was despoiled of its stone panels we do not know ; but those panels are still to be seen in the courtyard of a house at the bottom of the

1339 ;[1] and at this period we may, I suppose, take it that almost the whole of the *Isola della Piazza* was occupied by the Palace.   Of its subsequent enlargement over and beyond the *strada regale* (the *Via de' Priori*) it is unnecessary to speak at any length.   The great eastern gateway appears to have been completed about 1340.   In 1352 the house of the Priore del Fonte was demolished as a punishment for his rebellion against the Commune and the stones used for the building of the Palace,[2] which was only occupied by the Priors in the following year.   " On the 12th day of May [1353] the lord Priors of the Arts began to dwell in their new palace, the same being Whitsunday ; and this was at the time of the Priorate of Leggieri Andreotti and his companions."[3]   Up to that date, as we learn from a document of 1351, the Priors continued to reside *in palatio canonice S. Laurentii.*

Meanwhile, however, the construction of another important building had begun at the northern end of the *Piazza,* for hardly was the *Scala della Vaccara* finished than, in December, 1298, it was resolved to erect a public granary—" unam domum seu trasannam sub qua bladum vendi debeat et detineri."   This is, of course, the " casa del comuno de peroscia" of the Statute of 1342 ; and it probably stood on the spot now occupied by the *Teatro*

Via della Luna, built into the sides of a well.   Their identity is proved not only by their size and general characteristics, but also by the fact that one of them still bears the arms of Messer Manuello of the Marchesi di Massa (*nobilis et potens miles dominus Emanuel domini Andrea de Marchionibus Mussæ*), who was Potestà of Perugia in 1336.

[1] ROSSI, *op. cit.,* p. 7.

[2] " . . . e fulli guasto e scaricato il palazzo sino da fondamenti, e tutte le pietre vennero a Perugia e convertite nel palazzo de' Priori di Perugia, e 'l concime della muraglia d' esso palazzo dei Priori, il quale si murava a quel tempo. . . ."   FABRETTI, *Cronache,* i. 164.   See also p. 200 *supra.*

[3] GRAZIANI, *ubi cit.,* p. 169.   The enlargement of the Palazzo was resumed in the fifteenth century :   " A questi dì [luglio 1426] el Comuno, per crescere el palazo dei Priori, e fuor comparate le case fra el ditto palazzo e San Giovanne per fare el dormentorio dei priori " (*Ibid.,* 322).

" A dì 28 de aprile [1429] se comenzò a murare el fondamento della gionta del palazzo dei signori Priori fra el palazo e San Giovagne " (*Ibid.,* p. 333).

" A dì ditto [19 giugno, 1443] fo fornito de murare el palazzo nuovo dei Priori e mierlare, el quale fu comenzato nel 1429 " (*Ibid.,* p. 531).

Turreno. Neither is it, perhaps, too hazardous to assume that the carven hands holding ears of corn, which we still see upon the corners of the modern building—one towards the *Via Bartolo* and the other towards the *Via del Sole*—were set where they are to the end that they might bear mute record of this fact. The *Casa del Comune*, however, served for other uses besides that of a granary. It was furnished with a loggia where the *Maggior Sindaco* sat with his officials "both morning and evening to administer justice continually"; [1] while some idea of the size of the building may be gathered from the fact that it was large enough to hold the majority, if not the whole of the English prisoners of the White Company, who surrendered at S. Mariano in 1365.[2]

In the year of Jubilee, 1300, the citizens at last bethought them to enlarge their Cathedral ; and, on the 22nd of March, the General Council of the Artificers of all the Arts, both of the *Città* and the *Borghi*, assembled in the cloister of the

---

[1] Statute of 1342, Lib. i. Rubric 20 : " Ancora che ella casa del Comuno de Peroscia posta en capo de la piaza ella quale se uzò deponere e vendere el grano del Comuno lì dov' è el tecto d' essa casa se faccia uno terrato biene matonato e la trasanda el tecto se faccia puoje de sopre ; siche sia li una loia buona e acta ; e facciase alcuna scala conpetente per la ntrata de la dicta loja. E ella dicta loia continuamente da mane e da sera a l' ore devute tenuto sia e degga per legame de saramento el majure scendeco del Comune de Peroscia colle suoie offiziagle e ragioniere e fameglare besognevole sedere a ragione rendere e li rendere ragione continuamente essa loja fatta pena de 500 livre de denare e none altroie e che el Priore de l' arte che piu vaccio fare se poderà facciano fare e fornire el dicto lavoro ecc."

In the preceding rubric we read of " la volta de sancto Lorenzo la quale, e po' essa chiesia verso le case de coloro da Montemelino e la casa de Legiero de Nicoluccio." The word *po'* does not necessarily imply that the *volta* in question was actually attached to the Cathedral, and Dott. GIGLIARELLI (*Perugia antica e Perugia moderna, op. cit.*, p. 309) is disposed to believe that it may, in fact, be identified with the loggia of the *Casa del Comuno de Peroscia.* See also *Venere*, etc., *op. cit.*, p. 71.

[2] According to the chronicle attributed to GRAZIANI (p. 200) there were 1600 prisoners, part of whom " fuoro messe in pregione nel palazzo del podestà, et parte nelli magasini sotto al campione dove che se remetteva el grano del Comuno." In the *Memorie di Perugia*, however, we read that " si rendettero tutti per morti e prigioni ; e così furono menati a Perugia e messi prigioni nel Campione del grano " (FABRETTI, *Cronache*, i. 188).

del Sopramuro, can hardly, at their best and widest, have been less narrow and dark and crooked than the *Via della Luna* and the *Via Scura*, on the opposite side of the *Corso*.

Thus, the modern *Via del Commercio*, previous to its enlargement by Cardinal Domenico Pinelli, in 1591,[1] was a mere lane, named, from the calling of its inhabitants, the *Rimbocco degli Scudellari*, while the *Via Mazzini* seems to have been little better than a nameless alley—*vicus juxta Sanctam Mariam de Mercato*.[2] It was connected with the *Rimbocco de' Pollaioli*[3] by another narrow lane which bore

---

[1] FABRETTI, *Cronache*, v. 177. The work was performed by Valentino Martelli, an architect of high reputation, but unfortunately he was compelled to destroy a large part of the *Seggio de' Notari*, one of the most beautiful Quattrocento buildings in Perugia. Upon its walls may still be seen the remains of the iron supports which upheld the stone coats-of-arms of Pope Gregory XIV. and of Cardinal Pinelli himself. They were removed in March, 1798. A. ROSSI, *La Piazza del Sopramuro in Perugia, le vie che mettono ad essa e gli edifizi circostanti* (Perugia, Tip. G. Guerra, 1887), p. 15. The street was long known as *Via Pinella*.

[2] *S. Maria del Mercato* was one of the most ancient churches in Perugia, and even if it did not, as some writers affirm, date from the third century, it certainly existed as early as 1163. There the Priors were wont to take their oath of office (GIGLIARELLI, *Venere*, etc., *op. cit.*, p. 201. *Cf.* FABRETTI, *Cronache*, v. 33), and it is recorded that, in 1433, when the Emperor Sigismund visited the city, " li fu fatta una bella colazione di pinocchiati indorati e fratini imperiali, e si partirono li servitori con li detti confetti da S. Maria del Mercato con le trombe innanzi " (FABRETTI, *Cronache*, ii. 12). There too the students of the University assembled on the 20th November, 1486, as we read in the *Croncaca perugina inedita* (*Bollettino* cited, ix. 264) : " . . . la Sapienzza vecchia e la nova con altre scolare de la Università e alchuni de li sopredetti conseglieri se levaro su e fecero un tumulto, e tutti se adunaro in S. Maria del Mercato, e fecero un altro novo rechtore chiamato meser Gisberto de Sicilia. . . ." In 1547, the " vicus juxta Sanctam Mariam de Mercato " was enlarged by Cardinal Tiberio Crispo and took the name of *Via Nuova* or *Via del Popolo*. At the same time the old church was demolished and rebuilt " assai maggiore et magnifica " on the southern side of the new street. It was rechristened *S. Maria del Popolo*. ROSSI, *op. cit.*, pp. 17-18 ; SOZI, *Annali*, ad ann. 1547.

[3] The *Rimbocco de' Pollaioli* seems to have been flanked at the top (towards the *Piazza Grande*) by the houses of the Alfani and the Della Corgna (*cf.* GRAZIANI, p. 578 ; *Cronaca perugina inedita*, in *Bollettino* cited, iv. 105, ix. 69), and at the bottom by the sheep market, the *macello de le pecore*, adjoining which was the *macello grande*, famous throughout Italy, in the fourteenth century, for the abundance and excellence of its meat :—" Item ut domus Macelli Magni que p. totam Italiam famosa est . . . Macellum uberem et habundantem in omni carnium genere

the ill-sounding title of *Malacucina*, and of which traces are still to be seen to the left of the entrance to the *Albergo del Progresso*.[1]   Readers of Boccaccio will remember how Andreuccio of Perugia was conducted all unawares "in una contrada chiamata *Malpertugio*, la quale quanto sia onesta contrada il nome medesimo il dimostra,"[2] and *Malacucina* was a locality of equally evil reputation, for thence it was that the Commune drew its *gabella postribuli*.[3]   Probably, the largest of the streets which connected the two *piazze* was the modern *Via Danzetta*, originally known as the *Rimbocco della Salsa* and afterwards as the *Via de' Cappellari*.[4] Narrow and dark as it is, its history seems to prove that, even if it did not rise to the dignity of a *strada*, it was at any rate one of the *vie maggiori*.   On the 20th of June, 1484, a company of gentlemen who had spent a merry day in the country, feasting and dancing, returned to Perugia ; "and they took the road through *Sopramuro* and through the *Rimbocco della Salsa*.   And first went four or five

bonorum et splendidorum habetur et repetatur p. totam Italiam" (*Matric. Artis Macellatorum*, Rubrics 67, 72 ; Rossi, *op. cit.*, p. 6 ; Gigliarelli, *Venere*, etc., *op. cit.*, p. 209 n.).   The *Rimbocco de' Pollaioli* subsequently acquired the name of *Via della Chiavica* from the *chiavica* or sink which existed there.   To-day it is the *Via del Mercato*.

[1] See the plan facing p. 81 of Vol. I. of the *Documenti di Storia Perugina, editi da* A. Fabretti (Torino, 1887).

[2] *Decamerone*, ii. 5.

[3] See on the whole subject A. Fabretti, *La prostituzione in Perugia nei Secoli XIV., XV. e XVI.* (Torino, coi. tipi privati| dell' editore, 1890), and *Documenti di Storia Perugina, op. cit.*, Vol. I. Doc. xi.-xxiv.   It is not without interest to note that there was also a *Malacucina* in Florence inhabited by women of the same class.   Compare Degli Azzi, *Le Relazioni tra la Rep. di Firenze e l' Umbria*, etc., *op. cit.*, Vol. II. p. 145, § 569.

[4] The *Rimbocco della Salsa* was so called from the *olio di salsa* which the wool-carders (*battilani*), who inhabited the street, adopted in their business, the stench whereof is said to have pervaded all the neighbour-hood.   In the beginning of the sixteenth century the nuisance was felt to be intolerable, and the wool-carders were ordered to betake themselves elsewhere, their old quarters being occupied by the hatters (*cappellari*). Thereafter the *Rimbocco della Salsa* gradually came to be known as the *Via de' Cappellari* (Siepi, *op. cit.*, ii. 646-647 ; Rossi, *op. cit.*, p. 19). We infer, however, that the old name was not immediately forgotten, since we learn, from a document of 1554, that, on the 14th of August of that year, the members of the Arte degli Spadari assembled "in apotheca Iov. Herculani Spadarii sita in Rimbocco vulgariter dicto *de la Salsa*." Gigliarelli, *Venere*, etc., *op. cit.*, p. 193 n. 3.

horses all covered with beautiful housings, and after them followed the Signor Bernardino with his friends, four hundred persons, all in ordered array."[1] More than half a century later, Paul III. traversed the same street on his way to the new Citadel, and like the other streets through which he passed, it was decorated with flowers and triumphal arches.[2] Another and less fragrant memory of the place is to be found in the chronicle of Pietro Angelo di Giovanni; but, typical though it be of mediæval manners, it is perhaps more prudent to relegate it to the comparative obscurity of a footnote.[3]

According to Adamo Rossi, the *Sopramuro* was at first a street, only attaining to the dignity of a *piazza* in the fifteenth century. It originally extended from the Church of *S. Andrea* (where to-day is the doorway of the Court of Assizes) to *S. Donato* (now the *Maternità*) ; while, later on, its northern boundary was the *Portone di Porta Sole*, at the head of the *Piaggia de' Calderari*.[4] From the Church of *S. Andrea* a stairway descended to the *Campo di Battaglia* ;[5] and the *Sopramuro* obtained its name, not because it was situated above the wall of the ancient city, but because it was situated above the wall of the *Campo di Battaglia*.

[1] FABRETTI, *Cronache*, ii. 53-54. Compare also *Cronaca perugina inedita*, in *Bollettino* cited, ix. 191-192, 241.

[2] FABRETTI, *Cronache*, iv. 275 ; *Arch. Stor. It.*, XVI. ii. 389.

[3] *Bollettino* cited, ix. 58 : ". . . nel Rembocco del salsa la donna de mastro Semone medico passando Spirito de Ser Cipriano Gualtiere suo amatore glie bugliò un bacino pieno di merda in sul capo, de modo che tutto lo imbrattò, e puzzava, che non li se podea stare apresso, e questo lo fece per che tutto el dì la seguitava e non la podea lassare stare." The victim was Lorenzo Spirito, the poet.

[4] The reader who desires to illuminate the dull details of topography by the associations of the sites described may be glad of the following, from the *Cronaca perugina inedita* (*Bollettino* cited, iv. 102-103) : " Adì 2 de Genaio Piermateo de Agnielo de Pavolucio de Mal Sachetto avendo una schiava molto bella, la quale più e più volte li era fuggita, onde che retrovandola una mane la prese e m[esseli] li pagni cioè la camorra atorno ala centura e così la camicia, e così la andò frustando con uno staffilo infino in capo dela piazza deli calderari, cioiè li dal Portone de porta Soli, si che li fece le chiappe e le cosse e le gambe tutte sanguinose e rosse come un polmone, de modo che maj più fo veduta la più brutta cosa a vederla. . . ."

[5] See GIGLIARELLI, *Venere*, etc., *op. cit.*, p. 186 n.

Thus, in the Statute of 1342, we read of " la via la quale è supra muro del campo de la battaglia." [1]   As to the breadth of this *via* the authorities are at variance.   Professor Rossi, and I believe correctly, tells us that it occupied the entire width of the modern *piazza*, while Dott. Gigliarelli asserts that, in addition to the Churches of *S. Donato* and *S. Andrea*, there were other buildings, both public and private, which rendered the *via* itself extremely narrow.[2]   Be this as it may, we learn that, in 1276, "si pettoreggiò il muro del campo della battaglia, cioè il muro di S. Donato di sopra-muro." [3]   According to Polidori, *pettoreggiò* is equivalent to *afforzò, fortificò* ;[4] and it is unquestionable that about this time workmen were employed in strengthening the wall.[5] Professor Rossi, however, is of opinion that we must take the word *pettoreggiò* in this connection to mean that the *via* was furnished with a parapet, so that the citizens could more conveniently enjoy the panorama of " Umbria verde " and lean over to watch the *Battaglia de' Sassi* in the open space below.[6]

In the fourteenth century, as at the present day, the vendors of fruit and vegetables set up their stalls in *Sopra-muro*.[7]   There, too, in defiance of the statutes, they skinned and quartered the animals they had slaughtered, prepared wash (*brende*) for swine, stretched hides and fleeces, tanned leather, and made parchment.   From the windows they

---

[1] Lib. iv. Rubric 38.

[2] Rossi, *op. cit.*, p. 5 ; Gigliarelli, *Perugia antica e Perugia moderna*, pp. 530-531.

[3] *Brevi Annali*, ad ann.   [4] *Arch. Stor. It.*, XVI. i. 57 n. 1.

[5] Pellini, i. 286 : " Fu di quest' anno [1275] non tanto per ornamento, quanto per utilità pubblica alzato e fortificato il muro detto da loro del campo della battaglia, sopra il muro della Terra Vecchia volta a Levante dove sono hoggi lo Studio e il Palazzo del Popolo in Sopramuro." More-over, we learn from the *Ann. variorum annorum*, under the date of the 8th of August, 1269, that a Dominican friar was appointed " qui presit super laborerio muri et putei campi prelii " (*Bollettino* cited, iv. 166 n.) ; while a document of 1266 speaks of five citizens appointed to superintend the work (*Bollettino*, x. 218).

[6] Rossi, *ubi cit.*

[7] The Statute of 1342 (Lib. iv. Rubric 56) authorized any person to occupy such position as he pleased from the " mieta della dicta via verso le case de le spetial persone a tanto che nonempedementesca lentrate e luscite de le case a vendere glie pome e foglie e altre vituaglie."

hung out hides to dry, and flung horns, hoofs, and all kinds of offal over the wall into the *Campo di Battaglia*.[1] Yet here also, at the bottom of the modern *Via Mazzini*, stood one of the principal inns of the city, the *Osteria della Chiave*,[2] where Fra Moreale was entertained at the public expense, in August, 1354.[3] Most of the buildings, however, which now form the eastern boundary of the *piazza* date from the latter half of the Quattrocento;[4] and it appears that the *Sopramuro* remained unpaved until 1425. At any rate, we learn that in that year it was " matonato a spino," or paved with bricks set on edge and herring-boned;[5] while, in the months which followed, "sempre se attese a levar via profielli e trasande per magnificare la ditta piaza."[6] Henceforward it enjoyed the same privileges, immunities, exceptions, and advantages as did the *platea comunis* itself.[7]

Of the streets which lead out ot *Piazza del Sopramuro* two are worthy of special notice, if only for the evidence which they afford of the manifold changes which have taken place in the aspect of the city since the days of the free Commune. Thus the *Via delle Stalle*, to the northward, is now nothing but a covered passage-way—a mere tunnel

[1] ROSSI, *op. cit.*, p. 7 ; GIGLIARELLI, *Venere*, etc., *op. cit.*, pp. 186-187.

[2] GIGLIARELLI, *Perugia antica e Perugia moderna*, *op. cit.*, p. 451.

[3] GRAZIANI, p. 173 : "Adì 12 de agosto venne in Perugia fra Monreale. . . . Ditto fra Monreale arbergò allo arbergo da le Chiave et el nostro comuno pagò ogni spesa de lo arbergo. Adì 24 de agosto nel dicto millesimo fra Monreale se partì da Peroscia. . . ."

[4] ROSSI, *op. cit.*, p. 21 *et seq.* Compare also *Il Palazzo del Capitano del Popolo in Perugia* by the same author, in *Giornale di erudizione artistica*, Vol. III. fasc. ix. (settembre, 1874), pp. 257-277.

[5] GRAZIANI, p. 318 ; FABRETTI, *Cronache*, i. 220.

[6] GRAZIANI, p. 323. *Profiello* is defined as " una specie di ponte denanzi alle case, ad uno o più piani, appoggiato da una parte al muro, dall' altro sorretto da abetelli, in dialetto *ertoli*" (ROSSI, *op. cit.*, p. 6 n.). The *profielli* of Perugia seem to have corresponded with the *loggiati* of Siena (ZDEKAUER, *La vita pubblica*, *op. cit.*, p. 37), and with the *andavieni* of Cortona (MANCINI, *Cortona nel Medio Evo*, *op. cit.*, p. 157). In the former city the right of the citizens to build over the public streets was guaranteed by the *Constituto* of 1262 (Dist. iii. Rubric 32), while in Todi such structures were allowed to be erected " usque ad medietatem vie." Statute of 1275, Part I. Rubric 80 : *De plancis habendis supra vias. Trasande* were booths or awnings, corresponding to the modern *trabacche*.

[7] ROSSI, *op. cit.*, p. 6.

VIA DELLE STALLE

between the houses.   Originally it was known as the *Volte della Pace*,[1] and in the Middle Ages it was an open loggia with an extended view of the country towards Assisi.   It is said to have been furnished with marble benches,[2] whereon the good citizens could sit and gossip in the shade.   Traces of the ancient Gothic vaulting still remain to us, and it is easy to imagine how pleasant a spot it must have been before the modern buildings closed it in on the eastern side.   In the *Via dell' Ospedale*, which leads from the *piazza* to the *Porta Cornea*, we have ocular demonstration of the changed levels of the streets, for there we may see numerous mediæval doorways converted into first-floor windows—a transformation which probably occurred in the last quarter of the sixteenth century.[3]   The Hospital, from which the *Via dell' Ospedale* took its name, dates from the first decade of the Trecento ;[4] and although, when Cardinal Armellini constructed a new fish market (*pesceria*) there in 1525,[5] the street began to be known as the *Via della Pesceria*,[6] the old name seems never to have been wholly forgotten. At any rate, we read of *la piaggia dello Spedale* as late as 1581.[7]

[1] As to the derivation of the name nothing is very surely known, but the old writers speak of the healing of blood feuds and the consignment to oblivion of ancient enmities brought about in this place (see ROSSI, *op. cit.*, p. 15, and GIGLIARELLI, *Venere*, etc., *op. cit.*, pp. 78-79 n.).   The only references to the *Volte della Pace* which I remember to have found in the chronicles deal, however, with incidents of quite a different character. See, for example, GRAZIANI, p. 250, and *Cronaca perugina inedita*, in *Bollettino* cited, ix. 82.   *Cf.* also FABRETTI, *Documenti*, etc., i. 88.

[2] Possibly the *sedia* referred to in FABRETTI, *Cronache*, ii. 119, was one of these.

[3] FABRETTI, *Cronache*, v. 8 : " Ricordo che alli 17 detto dì [marzo, 1581] si è finita la piaggia dello Spedale, e l' hanno abbassata tanto che per andare alla chiesa dello Spedale bisognò una scala piena ; si dice che monsignor Governatore ne vuole fare un' altra per la Fortezza, e lì dallo Spedale lo vuole riempire, e per venire in piazza ci vuole fare le scale, cioè lì dal cantone dell' ospedale."

[4] BONAZZI, i. 606 ; GIGLIARELLI, *Venere*, etc., *op. cit.*, p. 185, and authorities there cited.

[5] FABRETTI, *Cronache*, iii. 76 : " Quest' anno 1525 circa il principio di marzo si cominciò a fabricare presso al Lione in Sopramuro dove il reverendissimo cardinale Armellini voleva fare il Campione e la Pescaria."

[6] ROSSI, *op. cit.*, p. 20.   [7] See note 3 *supra.*

It may not be without interest to note that the lions of the Commune were kept in this neighbourhood.[1]

Under the papal Government, the *Piazza del Sopramuro* became the scene of much sanguinary justice; the gallows were permanently erected not far from the door of the University, and the headsman's block usurped the place of the butcher's bench.   We have records of criminals *mazza-rellati, tanagliati,* and quartered in this piazza on market days, as an example to the public; of women ruthlessly scourged, of heads of outlaws exposed for recognition;[2] while here, on the 15th of September, 1586, Messer Raniero Franchi, Doctor of Law and Canon of S. Lorenzo, was handed over to the secular arm to be hanged and burned, after first suffering all the torture and ignominy of degrada-tion at the hands of the ecclesiastical authorities.[3]   The last burning which took place in this spot was not, however, the burning of a heretic or criminal, but of the original codex of the *Libro Rosso,* which, strange irony of fate, was given to the flames by the French Republicans, in 1799.[4]

[1] See p. 85 note 8 *supra.*
[2] ROSSI, *op. cit.,* p. 7.   Compare FABRETTI, *Cronache,* v. 65, 67, 75, 77, 85, 89.   The first execution in the *Piazza del Sopramuro* seems to have taken place in 1586: " Adl 19 detto [gennaio, 1586] sono stati apiccati due per ladri . . . sono stati appicati in piazza piccola a piedi la strada nova di S. Maria del Popolo davanti le scole : nè si ricorda più nessuno di aver veduto far giustizia in detta piazza."
[3] For full details of his crime and its punishment see the *Memorie di Romolo Allegrini,* in FABRETTI, *Cronache,* v. 83-86.   I speak advisedly when I use the word " torture " in this connection : " . . . e li fece radere la chierica, li labbri della bocca e li deti della mano fino che si vidde la carne viva. . . ."
[4] BONAZZI, i. 409 ; GIGLIARELLI, *Perugia antica e Perugia moderna,* p. 530.

CHAPTER XXV

LIFE IN OLD PERUGIA

IN an age when inaccessibility was deemed for the best of reasons a greater advantage than accessibility, Perugia would seem to have been even more inaccessible than many other cities. Engineering zigzags were not yet dreamed of, and the roads which led to her gates were mere stony tracks traced in a direct line up the mountain side.[1] Most of them have, of course, long since disappeared, but we still possess an excellent example of the old grades in the *Via Colomata*, outside the *Porta S. Andrea*. Though now closed to vehicular traffic, this road was once the principal route to Tuscany and to the rich corn-lands of Il Chiugi ; along its course the legal mile was measured to S. Manno ;[2] by it, on the 27th of August, 1433, the Emperor Sigismund entered the city,[3] and up its steep ascent the Degli Oddi rode to their ruin in 1495.

In the valleys the roads, even in the immediate neighbourhood of the city, were often practically impassable during the winter months ;[4] and men of all ranks and professions rode upon horses or mules.[5] In December, 1447, the mother of Pope Nicolas V., who was old and ailing, arrived

[1] Is it possible that we may here find the reason why Perugia never adopted the *Carroccio* ?

[2] Statute of 1342, Lib. iii. Rubric 213 : " Anco en porta sancta Susanna comenza el miglio da la porta la quale sta longo sancta Mustiola e protende e va al turlo de sancto Manno."

[3] FABRETTI, *Cronache*, ii. 12.

[4] Thus, for example, we learn from the Statute of 1342 (Lib. iv. Rubric 105) that the road " la qual comenza da la fonte de sancto Galgano . . . e va a la villa de sancta Lucia " was " sì sozza che a pena per essa passare se puo." Compare as to the condition of the country roads in general, GIGLIARELLI, *Perugia antica e Perugia moderna, op. cit.*, p. 128 *et seq.*

[5] Compare the letter of Jacques de Vitry published in *Bollettino* cited, i. 109-113. It contains " many picturesque details regarding the manner of travelling in the Middle Ages."

in Perugia "in un mulo con le bastriche." [1] Goods and merchandise were carried upon pack saddles. Such was the wellnigh universal mode of travel and transport during the Middle Ages ; [2] but Perugia seems to have lagged behind her neighbours. As late as the second half of the sixteenth century "everything" still entered the city on the backs of beasts of burden. [3]

The inaccessibility of Perugia no doubt reacted upon the condition of her streets, which here, perhaps longer than elsewhere, continued to be obstructed by *profielli* and *trasande*, [4] and often also by projecting stairways, some of which may still be seen in the minor thoroughfares ; while innumerable narrow bricked-up doorways, which must once have been approached by steps, are to be found in many parts of the town. [5] It was a violent age : too great accessibility was no more desirable for the private citizen than for the city itself ; and I am disposed to believe that an examination of these doorways and their corresponding steps will go far to dis-

---

[1] FABRETTI, *Cronache*, ii. 30 ; GRAZIANI, p. 597. PELLINI (ii. 566) paraphrases *bastriche* by the word *ceste* ; while POLIDORI, in a note to the chronicle of Graziani, tells us that the *Vocab. Aretino* of Redi defines *bastriga* as a rope or other appliance for tying a barrel on a pack-saddle (*basto*). In the passage under consideration it is obvious that the reference is to some appliance providing a comfortable seat for the old lady upon the back of the mule.

[2] Upon what authority I know not, Monsieur P. SABATIER, in his *Life of St Francis* (English edition, p. 3), speaks of the heavy waggons used by the Italian merchants who dealt in textile stuffs and journeyed to the Fairs of Champagne. Professor L. ZDEKAUER, a far greater authority, tells us that their bales were laden on the backs of mules, and he, be it noted, is speaking of a later period. See *Il Mercante Senese nel Dugento* (Siena, 1900), p. 13.

[3] *Giornale di erudizione artistica*, etc., *op. cit.*, i. 235 : " . . . essendo che ogni cosa bisognava condurre alla città per some et schiene d' animali." Even in 1582 many of the principal roads of the *contado* were still completely useless for wheeled traffic. See FABRETTI, *Cronache*, v. 20.

[4] See page 370 *supra*, and compare the *Cronaca perugina inedita*, ad ann. 1476, in *Bollettino* cited, ix. 99.

[5] According to one writer, " le scale delle case nelle strade principali di Perugia cominciaronsi a toglier via fin dal 1274 " (*Ricordi di cose notevole MS. Bibl. municipale*, p. 273, cited by GIGLIARELLI, *Venere*, etc., *op. cit.*, p. 190) ; but as late as September, 1542, many of them still remained, since we read that, when Paul III. came to the city for the fourth time, " fu levate tutte le trasande e scale dove che devia passare." FABRETTI, *Cronache*, iv. 275.

MAESTÀ DELLE VOLTE WITH PART OF THE VIA RITORTA, SHEWING
PROJECTING STAIRWAYS

pose of the tradition touching the existence of the so-called
porta del mortuccio.[1]   As far as Perugia is concerned, there
is, I believe, not a shred of direct evidence to support it.
The only argument in its favour is based upon analogy.[2]

In the twelfth century a large proportion of the houses
seem to have been built of wood, and in the *Borghi*, at any
rate, of hurdlework and straw plastered over with mud ;
while, even when made of less inflammable material, they
were probably frequently roofed with thatch or shingles.[3]
Perugia, we are told, was surrounded up to her very walls
by dense forests,[4] and timber would thus be easily obtain-
able.   Later on, in the thirteenth century, wood was largely
superseded by brick or stone in the construction of the
dwellings of the wealthier burghers, who early began to
decorate the walls of their rooms with gaudy geometrical
and polychromatic patterns painted in fresco.[5]   It has, how-

[1] SYMONDS and DUFF GORDON, *The Story of Perugia*, op. cit., p. 94.

[2] GIGLIARELLI, *Venere*, etc., op. cit., p. 217 n.   That such doors actually
existed in Cortona and in several of the cities of Umbria is, of course, indisputable (see MANCINI, op. cit., p. 171) ; but the argument from analogy
cuts both ways.   Very many mediæval houses were furnished with two
doorways—a smaller one which was often reached by steps or even by a
ladder (cf. FRATI, *La vita privata di Bologna*, op. cit., p. 5 and note),
and a larger one through which a man on horseback could pass (SANSI,
Storia del C. di Spoleto, op. cit., i. 157).   It is therefore quite clear that the
bare fact that a narrow pointed doorway is found at a certain height above
the ground is, in itself, no manner of proof that it was used as a *porta del
mortuccio*.   We require further evidence before any positive statement
can be made.

[3] BONAZZI, i. 353 ; GIGLIARELLI, *Venere*, etc., op. cit., p. 178 n. 1.   Compare for a similar state of things in other cities, MURATORI, *Diss*., xxi. ;
TOMMASI, *Historia di Siena*, op. cit., i. 110 ; VERRI, *Storia di Milano*,
op. cit., i. 111, and my *The " Ensamples " of Fra Filippo*, op. cit., p. 34.
Fra Salimbene of Parma speaks of wolves which crept into the city at night
and broke through the mud walls of the houses. (COULTON, op. cit., p. 60).

[4]   . . . nel monte e per valle e per costa
              Piccola primamente circondata
              M' ebber de mura tra silve nascosta.
                         LORENZO SPIRITO, *Altro Marte*.

[5] Compare L. DOUGLAS, *History of Siena*, p. 125.   An excellent example
of this kind of painting may be seen in the house of Professor Francesco
Moretti, where both the entrance-hall and a large vaulted chamber have
been decorated on the basis of the ancient pattern discovered beneath the
superimposed whitewash.   So skilfully has the work been done that it is
difficult for the untrained eye to perceive where the original ends and the
restoration begins.

ever, been justly remarked that a certain degree of elegance and taste often comes much earlier in the history of a people than solid comfort, and of solid comfort the Perugians as yet knew nothing. Their houses were built for shelter and defence, not for dwelling-places in the modern sense of the term. Chimneys they had none, and their fires were commonly lighted on the ground or in great chests filled with earth.[1] Glass was rarely used, and the windows were for the most part made of linen or of sheepskin, rendered semi-transparent by being soaked in oil extracted from flax-seed. In the place of Venetian blinds there were wooden shutters, made all in one piece ; and these, no doubt, served not only to exclude the sun of summer and the snows of winter, but also to protect the inmates against stones and other missiles as well as against unwelcome nocturnal visitors.[2] The poorer classes generally slept on the ground, or on mats or mattresses of straw ; and, in many cases, the floor consisted of a mixture of sand and rushes pounded hard, which absorbed the droppings of fowls and other domestic animals. As many as ten individuals sometimes occupied a single room.[3] Even in the houses of the well-to-do the furniture was of the scantiest, consisting of a large and low bed with a *predella* and very unhygienic curtains, a three-legged table, a strong-box, a bench, and a *cassone* or *goffano* for the housewife's finery. But of these things I have spoken elsewhere,[4] and it is sufficient in this place to point out that with such dwelling-places we can hardly wonder if the joys of domestic life had but little attraction for the Italian. In exile or absence he sighed not for his home but for his *patria*, his

[1] See my The " *Ensamples* " *of Fra Filippo*, etc., *op. cit.*, p. 51 *et seq.* In the centre of a room which now forms the terrace of his house, the same Professor Moretti who is referred to in the preceding note discovered a large stone which had evidently been used to light fires on in the Middle Ages. When it was taken up ashes were found between the cracks.

[2] See the Statute of 1342, Lib. iii. Rubric 79. " *Del bugliante la pietra en casa altruie.*" In Rubrics 71, 72, and 73 we find the penalties for entering or breaking into the house of a citizen or assaulting him therein.

[3] So GIGLIARELLI, *Venere*, etc., *op. cit.*, p. 178 n. Thus we perceive that the Minor Friars at the " Capitolo di Stuoie " (*Fioretti*, cap. xviii.) were subjected to no extraordinary hardship, but were simply living as common folk lived. Compare also MANCINI, *op. cit.*, p. 175.

[4] See my The " *Ensamples* " *of Fra Filippo*, etc., *op. cit.*, pp. 54-56.

VIA RITORTA

native city. Dante's affection and yearning for his *bel San Giovanni* was typical of the age.[1]

Yet, if the houses were comfortless, the streets can hardly have offered much inducement to loiter in them. Even the *strade regali* were far from spacious, and the vast majority of the *vie* were mere alleys, dark and crooked and sunless. A stroll through the *Via Ritorta* or the *Vicolo di S. Agata* will serve to give the reader an adequate idea of the average mediæval thoroughfare. Moreover, these *vie* were as filthy as they were narrow, soaked with excrement,[2] swine-haunted,[3] alive with fleas and other vermin, and swarming with flies in the hot weather.[4] Almost every house of any pretensions contained its quota of animals—mules in the houses of the

---

[1] Compare N. TAMASSIA, *Vita di popolo nei Secoli XIII. e XIV.*, *ubi cit.*, p. 47.

[2] Compare page 354 *supra*. In other cities of Italy the same conditions prevailed, and even the neighbourhood of the churches seems to have done nothing to restrain the beastly habits of the populace. Thus the Statute of Todi of 1275 (Rubric 103) provides " quod nemo audeat nec presumat facere aliquam turpitudinem sive çuçuram sive putridinem ante ecclesiam sanctorum Iohannis et Pauli, et infra ianuam dicte ecclesie et domibus ipsius." *Cf.* ZDEKAUER, *La vita privata*, etc., *op. cit.*, p. 23, and my *Palio and Ponte, op. cit.*, p. 65.

[3] BONAZZI, i. 353. It was the same all over Italy. Compare my *The " Ensamples " of Fra Filippo*, etc., *op. cit.*, pp. 39-41.

[4] The reader will remember how Matteo di Cantino, in SACCHETTI'S seventy-sixth *novella*, went into the piazza di Mercato Nuovo " sgambato per le pulci." Compare also COULTON, *op. cit.*, p. 71. JACOPONE DA TODI, in the laud beginning *O vita penosa*, writes :

Ecco la state che vien con gran calde,
Angustia grande con vita penosa ;
Di giorno le mosche d' entorno spavalde
Mordendone valde, che non ne don posa ;
Passa sta cosa, et entra la notte,
Le pulce son scorte a dar la beccata. . . .

We recall the fact that St Bernard excommunicated the flies, believing them to be devils, and that, in the *Gerusalemme Celeste* of Fra Giacomino da Verona, the cherub, who stood on guard with a flaming sword, kept out flies among other noxious things :

Lo qual no ge lassa de là nuja çent
Vegnir, tavan nè mosca nè bixa nè serpent. . . .

(See BARTOLI, *Storia della Letteratura Italiana*, Tom. II. p. 56.) Several of the tales told by FRANCO SACCHETTI are relevant in this connection. Thus the inn at Ferrara where Basso della Penna taught his " new game " to the archers must have swarmed with flies—*Nov.* xviii. Compare also *Nov.* xxi.

merchant, war-horses in the palaces of the nobles [1]—yet the streets seem to have been rarely swept, or how should we find it continually noted by the chroniclers that the coming of some illustrious guest was heralded by a proclamation that *se spazzassero le strade*, and, even then, not the *vie* but the *strade* ! [2]   Open cesspools polluted the air,[3] and every *tracasello* added its quota to the stench of the mediæval city,[4] while, as late as the middle of the fourteenth century, it was found necessary to pass special enactments to prevent the wells from being contaminated by the worst kind of filth.[5]   What marvel if the Italians of the Trecento acquired that exaggerated taste for perfumes and essences which marked them for so many centuries,[6] and that even the cells of the friars often resembled *botteghe di speziali o d' unguentari*.[7]

In Italy, however, the march of civilization was rapid, and to Dante the age of Bellincion Berti already seemed far off and rude.   The *Arti*, above all else, contributed, in the thirteenth century, to transform the cities from fortified *piazze* to great centres of commerce and wealth.[8]   Nor did Perugia lag behind her neighbours.   If her trade was not so great as that of Florence or Siena, she at least entered into commercial treaties with them on equal terms : [9] she cultivated friendly relations with Venice, and obtained special facilities for the importation of goods through the

[1] Even in the Palazzo del Popolo there was a stable (see GRAZIANI, p. 169) ; while Messer Oddo Degli Oddi was assassinated " entro la stalla del ser Gualfredo" (*ibid.*, p. 106).   Compare my *The " Ensamples" ot Fra Filippo*, p. 35.

[2] See, for example, *Bollettino* cited, iv. 356, ix. 48.

[3] Statute of 1342, Lib. iv. Rubric 44.

[4] In addition to the authorities cited on page 365 *supra*, and especially Boccaccio's story of *Andreuccio da Perugia*, see *Il Costituto del C. di Siena volgarizzato nel 1309-1310*, Dist. v. Rubric 397.

[5] Statute of 1342, Rubric 43.   Compare GIGLIARELLI, *Venere*, etc., *op. cit.*, p. 412.

[6] Compare LASSELS, *The Voyage of Italy* (edition of 1670), p. 3, and an article in the *Bullettino Senese di storia patria*, Vol. X. p. 491, entitled " The Orleans of Italy."

[7] *Decamerone*, vii. 3.

[8] See my *The " Ensamples" of Fra Filippo, op. cit.*, pp. 48-49, and ZDEKAUER, *La vita privata*, etc., *op. cit.*, pp. 54-55.

[9] See page 85 notes 1 and 2 *supra*.

custom-houses of that city ; [1] while, doubtless, her merchants also journeyed to the Fairs of Champagne, leaving their wives "for France in bed deserted." [2]   A notable indication of the increase of luxurious living is to be found in the law of 1266, *supra magnis et immoderatis expensis*, which was directed against the splendour and ostentation of marrige festivals, and especially the numbers of the retinue which accompanied the bride and bridegroom (*cortegii*), the exquisite and over-abundant viands (*provedalliæ*), and the giving of wedding presents (*manciæ*).[3]   As yet, however, no attempt seems to have been made to limit the citizens in the cost or fashion of their apparel ; and, probably, the earliest sumptuary legislation is referable to the year 1318.[4] Nevertheless, in spite of vast and rapid progress in the direction of greater refinement and luxury, the churches and the *piazze* long continued to be the real homes of the Italian people, and no one who could avoid it returned to his house except to eat or sleep.[5]

Throughout the Middle Ages, the churches were never regarded as places destined exclusively for religious worship, but rather as public buildings which had been erected at the expense of the Commune, and might be used by the citizens as such.[6]   "Quando (plebei) volunt facere aliquam seditionem vadunt in ecclesiam," says Odofredo,[7] and Giovanni Villani tells us that when, in 1250, "si fece il primo popolo" in Florence, the *buoni uomini* of the city

---

[1] BELFORTI, *Bolle e Diplomi*, Sec. XIV. No. 48 ; *Arch. Stor. It.*, XVI. ii. 495.

[2] *Paradiso*, xv. 120.   As to the lives of the merchants in France, compare *Decamerone*, ii. 9, and as to those of their wives at home, the *Prediche inedite del B. Giordano da Rivalto* (Bologna, Romagnoli, 1867), p. 70.

[3] A. FABRETTI, *Statuti e ordinamenti suntuarie intorno al vestire degli uomini e delle donne in Perugia dall' anno 1266 al 1536, raccolti ed annotati* (Estratto dalle *Memorie della R. Accademia delle Scienze di Torino*, Serie ii. Tom. XXXVIII., 1888), cap i. pp. 21-25.   PELLINI (i. 290) states that this law was enacted in 1276, but I have consulted the *Annales divers. ann.*, sign. †, fol. 71-72, and find that the true date is 1266.

[4] A. FABRETTI, *ubi cit.*, p. 30 ; *Ann. Decemv.*, an. 1318, fol. 40.

[5] TAMMASIA, *Vita di popolo*, etc., *ubi cit.*, pp. 43-44.

[6] See page 353 *supra*.

[7] TAMMASIA, *Odofredo, Studio storico-giuridico* (Bologna, Tip. Fava e Garagnani, 1894), p. 167 n. 2.

assembled in the Church of S. Firenze.[1] In Rimini, before the erection of a Communal Palace, the councils were ordinarily held in S. Colomba;[2] while a similar state of things existed in Siena.[3] The custom was, in fact, universal; and in Perugia, not only did the magistrates hold their sessions in the Cathedral or on the stone steps at the foot of its Campanile, but in every ward of the city the inhabitants gathered in their respective churches to elect their representatives or to criticize the actions of their rulers. Neither were these the only secular purposes for which the churches were used by the people. Fra Salimbene of Parma relates, without the slightest hint of disapproval, how a maid-servant went tripping through the Cathedral of Pisa, singing in the vulgar tongue:

> If thou carest not for me
> I will care no more for thee.[4]

Bishop Buonfiglio of Siena found it necessary to insert in his constitutions for the good government of the clergy a provision *quod nullus Clericus patiatur Joculatores tempore Officii in Ecclesia joculari*,[5] while many, like the little Musgrave in the old ballad,[6] frequented the sacred precincts simply to ogle the ladies or to make assignations, until, at last, Fra Bernardino of Siena counselled his female hearers

---

[1] G. VILLANI, vi. 39.

[2] L. TONINI, *Rimini nel Secolo XIII., ossia volume terzo della Storia civile e sacra Riminese* (Rimini, Tip. Malavolti e Ercolani, 1862), Doc. xiii.

[3] See my *The " Ensamples " of Fra Filippo, op. cit.,* p. 33.

[4] COULTON, *From St Francis to Dante, op. cit.,* p. 99.

[5] PECCI, *Storia del Vescovado della Città di Siena* (Lucca, 1748), p. 210.

[6]
> Little Musgràve came to the church door,
> The priest was at the mass;
> But he had more mind of the fine womèn
> Than he had of our Ladyes grace.
>
> And some of them were clad in greene,
> And others were clad in pall;
> And then came in my Lord Barnardes wife,
> The fairest among them all.
>
> She cast an eye on little Musgràve
> As bright as the summer sunne:
> O then bethought him little Musgràve
> This ladyes heart I have wonne.

to go thither but little and never to go alone.[1] It was in a
church that Cavalcanti first saw his Mandetta and Boccaccio
his Fiammetta ; the first glimpse which Petrarch caught of
his Laura was *in ecclesia sanctæ Claræ Avenoniensis*, and we
all remember how the Nencia di Barberino of Lorenzo il
Magnifico's poem, when she goes to church in her best
clothes,

> . . . si pone in terra alla distesa
> Per esser lei veduta.

In January, 1460, all the fine ladies of Perugia assembled
in the Cathedral before going to a dance,[2] and, in 1482, we
read of a *bella collatione* given there, to which many
gentlemen and citizens were invited.[3] At the end of the
century the Baglioni turned it into a fortress ; yet it does
not appear that their action at all interfered with its use
as a place of worship. " E offiziavase benissimo," writes
Matarazzo.[4]

It was, however, in the Piazza that the life of the
mediæval city was seen at its fullest. There the *parlamentum* of the Perugian people assembled from the earliest
days of the free commune ; there the subject towns and
seigniors made their yearly offerings of tribute and of *palii* ;
there the *banditori* proclaimed the decrees of the magistrates ; there the merchants bought and sold ; there great

---

[1] *Prediche volgari, op. cit.*, ii. 196 : " Alla chiesa vâvi poco e non v' andare
sola, e non v' andare segreta." Compare my *The " Ensamples " of Fra
Filippo, op. cit.*, pp. 86 n., 163 n., where I have cited numerous passages
from the sermons of Fra Bernardino illustrative of the secularization of
the churches. That women who frequented the churches of Perugia
incurred the same dangers as elsewhere may be inferred not only from the
provisions of the Statute of 1342 (Lib. iii., Rubric 100, *De lo engiuriante
le femmene a le perdonanze*), but also from the following passage in the
Cronaca perugina inedita (Bollettino cited, ix. 88) : " A dì 8 de aprile el
venerdì santo [1474] certi nostri cettadini . . . se vestirono da vedove,
e andaro a S. Lorenzo, e poi se miseno in fra le donne, facendo molte dis-
onestà, in fine foro conosciuti, e sì li fo levato el romore adosso con gran
sgridate." In the sixteenth century the churches seem to have become
the favourite rendezvous of prostitutes. See GRAF, *Attraverso il Cinquecento, op. cit.*, pp. 247-249, and notes.

[2] *Cronaca perugina inedita*, in *Bollettino* cited, iv. 387.

[3] *Ibid.*, ix. 216. Compare F. SACCHETTI, *Nov.* 200.

[4] MATARAZZO, p. 7 ; MORGAN, *op. cit.*, p. 7.

preachers urged men to repentance;[1] there the citizens gossiped together and played at chess or tables;[2] there the companies of the city danced on holidays; there the nobles jousted[3] and feasted,[4] and fought out their blood-feuds; there they executed their enemies or hurled them ruining from the windows of the Palazzo del Popolo, until at last it became necessary to re-bless a spot which had been polluted by so great slaughter of Christian men;[5] there, too, was celebrated the *Battaglia de' Sassi* on each recurrent 1st of March, until, somewhere in the first half of the Trecento, it was transferred to the Campo di Battaglia;[6] and there, if I am not mistaken, the children played their games of ball and spun their tops,[7] and worried their elders with their mischievous pranks.[8]   Indeed, long after the primitive

[1] In addition to Fra Bernardino of Siena, we recall Fra Michele in 1462, and Fra Bernardino da Montefeltro in 1486. See *Bollettino* cited, ix. 38, 247.

[2] And for choice apparently " en la volta de sancto Lorenzo," until the law compelled them to move elsewhere. See GIGLIARELLI, *Venere*, etc., *op. cit.*, p. 228.

[3] See, for example, *Cronica perugina inedita*, in *Bollettino* cited, iv. 360.

[4] *Arch. Stor. It.*, XVI. ii. 256 : " A dì 24 detto, messer Ranaldo predetto fe a piedi la Piazza la collazione, dove era uno steccato amplo con li seggi : e vi furono gli signori Priori, molti gentiluomini, tutti li dottori, e molta altre gente : fu cosa assai bella."   I quote this particular passage because of the mention of the *steccato*. Compare G. CONTI, *Fatti e Aneddoti di Storia Fiorentina* (Firenze, Bemporad, 1902), p. 7. This mediæval custom of closing up the streets or piazze and using them for feasting still survives in Siena. See my *Palio and Ponte*, *op. cit.*, p. 255.

[5] *Cronaca perugina inedita*, in *Bollettino* cited, ix. 365 : " A dì 27 detto [giugno, 1491] for dette molte messe in piazza per rebenedirla ; e for fatte 3 dì ala fila le processione. Se fecero in piazza 35 altare, e dette molte messe solenemente, e durò 3 dì el dire dele messe e il gire le processione. La piazza fo rebendetta dali frate de S. Domenico." *Cf.* GRAZIANI, p. 749 ; FABRETTI, *Cronache*, ii. 66.

[6] See the Statute of 1342, Lib. iii. Rubric 117.

[7] See F. SACCHETTI, *Nov.* 68.   From the *Fioretti* (chap. ix. of " The Life of Friar Juniper ") we learn that the children of St Francis' day played at see-saw : while Fra Salimbene of Parma speaks of a game played by laying hand upon hand, which seems to correspond with the " Pat a cake, pat a cake, baker's man " game (see COULTON, *op. cit.*, p. 217). Apparently also they made mud pies (see G. SANSEDONI, *Vita del Beato Ambrosio Sansedoni da Siena*, Roma, 1611, p. 8).

[8] F. SACCHETTI, *Nov.* 76.   As to the upbringing of boys, see COULTON, *op. cit.*, p. 18, and authorities there cited, particularly the *Vita* of Thomas of Celano (pp. 2-3 of Mr FERRERS HOWELL'S translation) ; as to that of

discomfort of the thirteenth-century houses had given place
to comparative luxury, the Piazza continued to be crowded ;
and almost to our own day, "a house in the city-square"
was considered the ideal residence for a person of quality.
The modern Perugian's conception of perfect happiness is
said to be "a house in the Piazza, a villa at Prepo, and a
fifteen-year-old wife." [1]

For the rest, it would be a pleasant and a profitable thing
were we able to call up before the mind's eye a picture of
the ever-shifting crowd which thronged the "piazza del
comuno de Peroscia" in the fourteenth century ; and,
mutatis mutandis, there can be but little doubt that Antonio
Pucci's description of the scene in the Mercato Vecchio of
Florence should prove invaluable for this purpose. [2] Some
of his verses I have quoted elsewhere, [3] and if what I have
written in the earlier pages of the present work has enabled
the reader to form a tolerably accurate idea of the topography of the place, the rest should follow as he studies
the chronicles of the city.   A word as to the colouring of
our mental picture may, however, prove useful.   In the
many-hued garments of the populace red and green will, of
course, predominate : [4] but, if it be a gala day, the windows

girls, my *The " Ensamples " of Fra Filippo, op. cit.*, pp. 118-119 and notes.
In mediæval society, however, the girls were of very little importance.
We all remember how indignant Fra Salimbene was with his mother
because she saved his sisters first in a time of earthquakes, " seeing that
she should have cared more for me, her son, than for her daughters"
(COULTON, *op. cit.*, p. 13) ; while, three centuries later, we find Teseo
Alfani writing as if it were a strange thing that he should grieve at the
death of his infant daughter : ". . . e benchè fosse femina ne dolse la sua
morte assai" (FABRETTI, *Cronache*, iii. 74).   At twelve years old a girl
was supposed to have reached a marriageable age ; while we find boys
of sixteen grown men and ruffling it with the best (*cf.*, for example,
G. DI COSTANTINO, *ubi cit.*, p. 182).

[1] I do not, of course, suggest that this ideal is altogether a serious one,
though I have heard it proclaimed again and again.   The saying seems to
have originated, in a slightly different form, with a certain Bovarini early
in the last century.   See GIGLIARELLI, *Perugia antica e Perugia moderna*,
p. 484.

[2] PUCCI'S *Centiloquio* is published in the *Delizie degli eruditi toscani*,
Vol. VI.

[3] *The " Ensamples " of Fra Filippo, op. cit.*, pp. 174-175.

[4] See my *Palio and Ponte, op. cit.*, p. 11.

will probably be hung with cloths and arras, woven in blue with figures of men and animals, with trees and letters and magic symbols. In the *tessuti* of Perugia, blue has been the prevailing colour ever since the thirteenth century.[1] One other detail must also be added, since, as far as I am aware, it was peculiar to Perugia. By the rubric "*De glie graffie da retenere*" it was provided that "in every house or shop situated in the Piazza or in any of the *strade regali*, an iron gaff should be kept by the inhabitants of the said houses or shops" for the capture of evil doers.[2] Can we not see the merchants and artisans rushing forth from their booths and workshops to intercept the flying criminal, for all the world like the demons of the fifth Bolgia?

Poi l' addentar con più di cento raffi.[3]

Later on, in the fifteenth century, we find that the merchants were ordered to keep "*forcelle*," with which to interpose to prevent breaches of the peace and to separate the combatants.[4] Not without good reason did the Sienese poet, Bindo Bonichi, exhort his readers not to linger in the Piazza.[5]

Of the sports of mediæval Perugia and their intimate connection with the Companies of the Gates, I have treated elsewhere.[6] Suffice it then to recall the fact that, in addition to their Battles of Stones, their bull-fights, and their *palii*,

---

[1] Professor Mariano Rocchi (243 Via Nazionale, Roma) possesses a fine collection of such fabrics, sixty-eight specimens of which were exhibited in 1907, at the *Mostra di Antica Arte Umbra* in Perugia. The industry is still carried on, and towels and table-cloths decorated with the old patterns may be purchased by the modern tourist. Did space permit, a lengthy chapter might be written on the subject. I must, however, content myself with referring the reader to the following articles, all of which are illustrated : A. BELLUCCI, *Un antica industria tessile perugina*, in *L' Arte*, 1905, fasc. ii. p. 113 ; I. ERRERA, *Tessuti perugini*, in the *Emporium*, aprile, 1906 ; A. MELANI, *Biancheria d' arte nella vita perugina*, in *Natura ed Arte*, 1906, 1 settembre, p. 466 ; A. J. RUSCONI, *Antichi tessuti perugini*, in *Vita femminile italiana*, aprile, 1907, p. 411 ; P. PERALI, *Tovaglie e mantili di Perugia* (Sec. XIII.-XIV.) *con segni e simboli magici*, in *Augusta Perusia*, Vol. II. fasc. v. p. 65.

[2] See page 347 note 4 *supra*.   [3] *Inferno*, xxi. 52.

[4] *Cronaca perugina inedita*, in *Bollettino* cited, ix. 234.

[5] *Rime di* BINDO BONICHI DA SIENA (Bologna, Romagnoli, 1867), p. 83.

[6] See my *Palio and Ponte, op. cit.*, Book II. chap. ii.

which were run on the festivals of various saints,[1] the Perugians had their *corsa all' anello* and tilted at the quintain;[2]
while later on, as we have seen, the nobles constantly
organized tournaments for the diversion of the proletariat.
The frequent religious processions formed so many splendid
pageants, filling the streets and *piazze* with movement and
with colour ; and, albeit the life of the mediæval Italian
may have been comfortless and even squalid, it certainly was
not dull. A higher civilization has, doubtless, brought us
many blessings, but it can hardly be denied that something
has been lost. The world was younger then ; for those that
lived in it, were

> Struggle and turmoil, revel and brawl, . . .
> Bells that clash in a gaudy chime,
> Swords that clatter in onsets tall ;

for us, what is left but

> The scene of a faded festival ?

In the old vivid, violent days, beauty and ugliness, comedy
and tragedy, good and evil walked hand in hand ; and the
very punishments meted out to criminals were often spec-
tacular and dramatic. Thus a witch was carried to her
burning, "mounted upon an ass, with her face towards the
tail ; with a mitre on her head, and with two demons, one
upon the right hand and the other upon the left, who held
the said mitre."[3] In like manner, a certain Giovan Battista

---

[1] PELLINI, i. 1244, 1281, 1341.

[2] *Ibid.*, i. 1163 ; *cf. Bollettino* cited, iv. 136.

[3] GRAZIANI, p. 563. Compare the Statute of 1342, Lib. iii. Rubric 102 :
De le facente le fature. And here it may be remarked that witches and
warlocks still haunt the cross-roads at night-time in the neighbourhood of
Perugia, and especially on the Vigils of Christmas and of St John, when he
who will pay the price may obtain all that his heart desires. Great is
their power over hailstorms, which they direct whithersoever they will ;
and not only are the same stones and shells and teeth and tusks which
are found in prehistoric tombs still believed to possess occult virtues and
used as amulets against witchcraft and the evil eye, but the Christian
symbols themselves are all too often converted to superstitious uses.
See on the whole subject G. BELLUCCI, *La grandine in Umbria* (1903) ;
Il feticismo primitivo in Italia e le sue forme di adattamento (1907), and
Un capitolo di psicologia popolare : gli Amuleti (1908), all of which are
published by the Unione Tip. Cooperativa Editrice in Perugia. The
learned author promises to complete the series with a monograph on

25

di Nicolò, who had connived at and profited by his wife's dishonour, was scourged through the city, wearing " the head of an ox with the horns thereof." [1]   The symbolism is subtle and was doubtless appreciated by the populace.

In most Italian cities much may be learned concerning the manners and customs of the people from a study of their literature and their art ; and, in the case of the Tuscan communes at any rate, the works of the great painters may be used as documents, the neglect of which would stamp the historian as wholly ignorant of his trade.   Unfortunately,

Il fulmine nelle tradizioni popolari antiche e moderne.   As recently as June, 1908, a veritable witches' kitchen was discovered in the *Vicolo Faustino*, stored with all the paraphernalia of the craft.   Many of the incantations which were confiscated by the authorities have all the flavour of the Trecento, and as of old the principal clients of the *strega* seem to have been despairing lovers.   The following will serve as an example :—

Cinque dita appoggio al muro :
Cinque diavoli vi scongiuro :
Cinque preti, cinque frati,
Cinque anime dannate,
Tutti insieme uniteve
Dentro al corpo di Amedeo . . . (cognome) entrerete.
Che non potesse nè mangiare, nè bere, nè dormire nè riposare.
Che potesse sopra me pensare.
Che potesse soffrire e smaniare tormenti e tormenti
Quanti ne soffre una parturiente.
Diavoli, diavoli della libertà, pigliatelo per . . . e portatelo da me.
E se non vuole venire, che possa nè campare nè morire.

Very curious too is the following invocation, with its conversion of mediæval machinery to modern uses.   The three numbers mentioned in the last line are obviously required for the government lottery :

Elena, madre di Costantino, imperatore di Roma,
Che pel mare andaste, e pel mare ritornaste,
Tre chiodi di Cristo ritrovaste ;
Uno nel mare lo gettaste ;
L' altro al passeggero lo donaste ;
E il terzo datelo a me.
Per provvidenza.
In nome della santa Trinità
Dateme tre numeri, per carità.

The arrest of the *strega* was reported in *L' Unione Liberale* of 15th June, 1908.

[1] *Cronaca perugina inedita*, in *Bollettino* cited, ix. 36.   The wife was punished with him, but " a lei no li fu dato quasi mai con le granate e a lui si. . . ."

however, the Umbrian School is a product of the Quattro-cento.[1] The free commune had practically ceased to exist when Bonfigli painted his affreschi in the Palazzo Pubblico ; Fiorenzo di Lorenzo, Perugino, and Pintoricchio were later yet, and though the study of their works is, no doubt, most important for the times of the Baglioni,[2] they can throw but little light upon the period with which, in these pages, we are most concerned. Perugino has taught us to see Umbria, with its splendour of space and its light that never was in any other sky ; Fiorenzo beheld " the very spirit of the fifteenth century objectively."[3] But what of that ? We cannot use their paintings as documents for the illustration of an earlier age.

Nor are we much more fortunate in the matter of Perugian literature. Even the full-throated outburst of song, amid which the thirteenth century passed swan-like away, found and left Perugia wellnigh mute ;[4] during the *bel secolo della lingua* she produced neither poet nor *novelliere*, hardly even a chronicler ; while Dante Alighieri, in his treatise *De Vulgari Eloquentia*, ranks her dialect as among the worst in all Italy.[5] His judgment in this respect has been impugned by later writers ;[6] but the fact remains that in Perugia longer than

---

[1] See CROWE and CAVALCASELLE, *A New History of Painting in Italy*, edited by E. HUTTON (Dent & Co., 1909), Vol. II. chap. vi., and especially pp. 147-149.

[2] Miss Symonds and Miss Duff Gordon have said some wise things in this regard (*op. cit.*, pp. 232-233). Especially do I applaud their strictures on the outrage embodied in the Pinacoteca, and it is difficult to understand how any lover of Italy can willingly enter it a second time. On the other hand, the view that " the art of Umbria was only another form of that spirit which produced the teaching of St Francis " is certainly open to serious question, and we may well doubt whether the " escape or reaction " of which they speak was not, in fact, rather intellectual than spiritual. It has been well said that the indirect argument from art to morals is utterly fallacious, and we cannot help remembering that, according to Vasari, Pietro Perugino, perhaps the greatest master of the school, was little better than a materialist. Compare COULTON, *op. cit.*, pp. 350-351.

[3] E. HUTTON, *The Cities of Umbria* (London : Methuen & Co., 1905), chap. xiii.

[4] We have a few names of versifiers anterior to or contemporary with Dante—Cione de' Baglioni, Ceccolino, Fabbruzzo, Arcolano, Stramazzo, but we know little if anything of their works. See BONAZZI, i. 349.

[5] *De vulg. eloquentia*, Lib. i. cap. xi., xii.

[6] See, for example, DEGLI AZZI, *Il Dialetto Perugino nel Secolo XI* Perugia, Tip. Umbra, 1899.

elsewhere, Latin continued to be the language of educated men. This is attributed by Bonazzi to the intimate relations which existed between the Commune and the Roman Curia, as well as to the influence of the University, whose professors, of course, lectured exclusively in " the tongue consecrated to the majesty of the law." In the fourteenth century such of the Perugians as were not warriors were jurisconsults, and the very few who cultivated literary pursuits devoted themselves to the study of the classics.[1] Thus, with the exception of the Statute, almost all that remains to us of Italian in the Perugian dialect of the Trecento are the litanies of the Flagellants, chanted, not to the slow and stately measures of the ancient Latin hymns, but to the rhythm of leather thongs, mercilessly beating time upon quivering flesh.

The first apostle of the flagellant madness was Fra Rainerio Fasani, a Perugian ; and hardly had he proclaimed his gospel of self-torture than " much folk began to strip themselves naked and to discipline themselves ; and on the second day thereafter, by the working of Divine Grace, no man was left in all the city who went not naked, disciplining himself."[2] A few months later, the infection had spread to half the towns of Italy ;[3] and, when the Pope, fearing lest so much enthusiasm should give birth to some new heresy, prohibited their public processions,[4] the Flagellants formed themselves into lay brotherhoods and continued their exercises in private. The statutes of the various confraternities imposed upon their members the double obligation of scourging themselves and of singing lauds, and it was from this circumstance that they acquired the title of *Laudesi*. In Perugia a company of *Laudesi* was formed as early as 1260, and assumed the name of *Disciplinants of Jesus Christ*.

[1] BONAZZI, i. 349.

[2] See the *Lezenda de Fra Rainero Faxano*, published by MAZZATINTI, in *Bollettino*, ii. (1896), 561-563.

[3] See, on the whole subject, G. GALLI, *Disciplinati dell' Umbria e le loro laudi*, in Supplemento ix. of the *Giornale storico della letteratura italiana*. Torino, Loescher, 1906.

[4] The processions of the Flagellants seem to have ceased, in Italy at any rate, in January, 1261. GREGOROVIUS, *op. cit.*, Vol. II. Lib. ix. cap. vii. p. 868 n. 75.

Citizens of every rank joined the new brotherhood, and, for many years, their enthusiasm seems to have continued unabated, until, finally, Cardinal Albornoz, "seeing the multitude of the Disciplinants of Jesus Christ and liking well the institution but fearing the assembling together of so many lay folk, ordered that they should divide themselves into three parts." The result was the formation of the confraternities of S. Agostino, S. Domenico, and S. Francesco.[1] Apparently, however, these were not the only Companies which flourished in Perugia. Vermiglioli tells us that, all together, the confraternities of the city numbered no fewer than forty.[2] Many of their lauds still remain to us, and enough of them have been printed to enable us to acquire an adequate notion of their character and scope.[3]

What, however, we are most concerned with in this place is the enormous influence which these confraternities must have exercised on the daily life of Perugia during the years which witnessed her greatest triumphs. Even a little leaven leaveneth the whole lump, and the *Laudesi* included among their members no small proportion of the citizens. A cult which manifests the sincerity of its beliefs by consistent self-abnegation must always command respect ; and we are not surprised to find that, for all her determination not to be priest-ridden, the Perugia of the Trecento was an eminently religious city.[4] Neither is it well to forget that not only the stately ceremonial dances of the Magistrates of the Commune, which were, I suppose, not without religious significance,[5] but also the purely secular dances of the Companies of the Gates in the fifteenth century, owed their origin to the same source.[6] After the Dramatic Laud had developed into the

---

[1] *Constituzioni e capitoli generali delle Confraternite di S. Agostino, S. Domenico and S. Francesco di Perugia.* Perugia, Zecchini, M.DCLI.

[2] VERMIGLIOLI, *Storia e costituzioni della Conf. de' Nobili della Giustizia* (Perugia, 1826), p. 1.

[3] ERNESTO MONACI, *Uffizi drammatici dei Disciplinati dell' Umbria.* Estratto dalla *Rivista di filologia romanza* (Imola, Galeati, 1874), Vol. I. fasc. iv.

[4] See SCALVANTI, *Considerazioni*, etc., *op. cit.*, cap. ii. pp. 30-45.

[5] See pp. 203, 251, 266 *supra*.

[6] D'ANCONA, *Origini del Teatro Italiano* (Torino, Loescher, 1891), i. 279.

PRINTED BY
TURNBULL AND SPEARS,
EDINBURGH